Corporate Level Strategy

The challenges faced by diversified corporations—firms that operate in more than one industry or market—have changed over the years. In this new edition, Olivier Furrer helps students of corporate strategy to consider the impact of critical changes in resources, businesses, and headquarters roles on the firm's ability for establishing and sustaining corporate advantage.

New to this edition are stimulating pedagogical features and additional material such as a new chapter on the theoretical foundations of multibusiness firms, along with a host of new examples from across the world.

A companion website supplements the book, providing PowerPoint slides, a test bank of questions, and lists of suggested case studies.

Olivier Furrer is Chaired Professor of Marketing at the University of Fribourg in Switzerland.

A range of further resources are available on the companion website: www.routledge.com/cw/furrer/

This highly readable book is a valuable guide to assess ways in which a corporate parent can add or destroy value to its portfolio of businesses. With a keen eye for the history of the field, Furrer provides a welcome overview of what constitutes strategy at the corporate level in a way that is accessible to both students of management and practitioners alike.

Rick (H.L). Aalbers, *Assistant Professor Strategy & Innovation, Radboud University, the Netherlands*

This book blends theory and practice and gives voice to the adage that the best theory is the best practice and vice versa. The book is written to stress learning and thus each chapter begins with learning objectives and each chapter ensures that it covers material that should provide the reader with knowledge to accomplish those objectives. In closing, it is a very valuable book on a very important subject.

Devanathan Sudharshan, *Professor, University of Kentucky, USA*

This book provides an excellent roadmap and a set of essential tools for every step in the ongoing struggle between diversifying and restructuring around the blurred boundaries of corporate and competitive levels of strategy. A bedside handbook for students and C-level managers of any firm.

Miguel González-Loureiro, *Associate Professor, University of Vigo, Spain and CIICESI, Portugal*

There are many textbooks in Strategic Management but very few in Corporate Strategy. Furrer not only fills this gap but also offers a comprehensive presentation of the main issues on this important area of strategy. He covers the traditional topics such as diversification strategies, vertical integration and mergers and acquisitions as well as, most importantly, including some less well researched areas, such as defining the business, restructuring strategies and managing and organizing the multibusiness firm. This is an essential book for Corporate Strategy.

Luis Ángel Guerras-Martín, *Professor, Universidad Rey Juan Carlos, Spain*

Olivier Furrer provides an all-encompassing, eloquent, and imperative insight in corporate strategy. Building on a solid theoretical foundation, he details on multiple contemporary topics, including firm growth, multi-market competition, restructuring, and corporate social responsibility. The book is rich with mind-expanding examples, which reinforces the book's freshness and enables an easy comprehension of the content. If one seeks to obtain an understanding about what corporate strategy is, and why it matters, this book is a must have!

Brian Tjemkes, *Associate Professor, VU University Amsterdam, the Netherlands*

Corporate Level Strategy
Theory and applications
Second edition

Olivier Furrer

LONDON AND NEW YORK

First published 2016
by Routledge
2 Park Square, Milton Park, Abingdon, Oxon OX14 4RN

and by Routledge
711 Third Avenue, New York, NY 10017

Routledge is an imprint of the Taylor & Francis Group, an informa business

© 2016 Olivier Furrer

The right of Olivier Furrer to be identified as author of this work has been asserted by him
in accordance with sections 77 and 78 of the Copyright, Designs and Patents Act 1988.

All rights reserved. No part of this book may be reprinted or reproduced or utilised in any
form or by any electronic, mechanical, or other means, now known or hereafter invented,
including photocopying and recording, or in any information storage or retrieval system,
without permission in writing from the publishers.

Trademark notice: Product or corporate names may be trademarks or registered trademarks,
and are used only for identification and explanation without intent to infringe.

British Library Cataloguing in Publication Data
A catalogue record for this book is available from the British Library

Library of Congress Cataloging-in-Publication Data
Names: Furrer, Olivier, author.
Title: Corporate level strategy : theory and applications / Olivier Furrer.
Description: Second edition. | Abingdon, Oxon ; New York, NY : Routledge,
2016. | Includes bibliographical references and index.
Identifiers: LCCN 2015041040| ISBN 9780415727211 (hardback) | ISBN
9780415727228 (pbk.) | ISBN 9781315855578 (ebook)
Subjects: LCSH: Diversification in industry—Management. | Strategic
planning. | Industrial management.
Classification: LCC HD2756 .F87 2016 | DDC 658.4/012—dc23
LC record available at http://lccn.loc.gov/2015041040

ISBN: 978-0-415-72721-1 (hbk)
ISBN: 978-0-415-72722-8 (pbk)
ISBN: 978-1-315-85557-8 (ebk)

Typeset in Amasis
by FiSH Books Ltd, Enfield

To Arthur

CONTENTS

Illustrations	ix
Preface	xii
Acknowledgements	xiv

1 What is corporate level strategy? · 1

2 Why do multibusiness firms exist? Theoretical approaches to diversification · 17

3 Managing the multibusiness firm: theoretical approaches to corporate level strategy · 35

4 Defining the business · 45

5 Diversification strategies: creating corporate value · 60

6 The issue of relatedness: creating synergies · 78

7 Diversification and performance: limits to the scope of the firm · 95

8 The role of the parent: managing the multibusiness firm · 106

9 Organizing and structuring the multibusiness firm · 125

10 Vertical integration: coordinating the value chain · 141

11 The growth of the firm: internal development, mergers and acquisitions, and strategic alliances · 154

12 Restructuring strategies: reducing the scope of the firm · 170

13 Multipoint competition: managing market power · 184

14 International diversification: global integration and local
   responsiveness   198

15 Corporate governance: controlling top managers and meeting
   corporate responsibilities   212

   Glossary   224
   Bibliography   234
   Index   269

ILLUSTRATIONS

FIGURES

1.1	Level and types of diversification	3
1.2	Rumelt's scheme	4
1.3	Walt Disney's business portfolio	5
1.4	The corporate strategy triangle	7
2.1	Antecedents and consequences of diversification	18
2.2	Level of risk and diversification	26
3.1	Core competencies as the roots of competitiveness	40
3.2	The dominant logic	43
4.1	Ansoff's growth matrix	48
4.2	Abell's three-dimensional framework	52
4.3	Ten types of differentiation	56
5.1	The corporate headquarters as an intermediary	61
5.2	Sharing value chain activities	65
7.1	Curvilinear relationship between diversification and performance	98
8.1	Parenting styles	111
8.2	Managing linkages	114
8.3	The BCG matrix	117
8.4	The GE/McKinsey matrix	119
8.5	Parenting as fit	123
9.1	Types of organizational structures	126
9.2	Strategy and structure growth pattern	132
9.3	Cooperative *M*-form	136
9.4	Competitive *M*-form	137
9.5	SBU *M*-form	139
10.1	Stages in the industry value chain	141
10.2	Full and taper integration	149
10.3	Integrating theoretical approaches to vertical integration decisions	152
11.1	Types of acquisition integration approaches	165
11.2	Classification of strategic alliances	167
12.1	Structure and elements of corporate restructuring	171
13.1	Multipoint competition between two hypothetical firms	184
13.2	Multipoint competition and intensity of rivalry	188
13.3	The relationship between the number of multipoint contacts and the intensity of rivalry	188

13.4	Multipoint contact and intensity of rivalry	189
14.1	Internationalization framework	199
14.2	The integration responsiveness framework	206
15.1	Owner–manager prisoner's dilemma	218
15.2	A firm's stakeholder groups	219
15.3	A pyramid of corporate social responsibilities	221

TABLES

3.1	Six types of real options	41
5.1	Corporate value creating mechanisms	63
5.2	Value creating mechanisms and types of diversification	76
6.1	Typology of relatedness measurement methods	85
6.2	Rumelt's classification of diversification strategies	86
6.3	Determinants of strategic relatedness between businesses	93
7.1	Theoretical rationales and empirical evidence of the diversification–performance link	99
8.1	Characteristics of the three parenting styles	113
9.1	The characteristics of the different *M*-forms	139
10.1	Some advantages and disadvantages of vertical integration	144
11.1	Summary of the benefits and drawbacks of the different entry modes	168
12.1	Divestitures	173
12.2	Causes of corporate restructuring	173
13.1	Overview of responses in Karnani and Wernerfelt's model	195
14.1	Relationships between internationalization and diversification strategies	210
15.1	Differences between agency and stewardship theories	217
15.2	Comparison of the different approaches	223

BOXES

1.1	An early definition of corporate level strategy	1
1.2	The interrelationship between business and corporate level strategies	2
1.3	Rumelt's diversification typology	4
1.4	Managing the corporate strategy triangle	10
1.5	Textron: An example of conglomerates	13
1.6	Diversification in emerging countries	16
2.1	European Union competition law	19
2.2	Wanadoo fined € 10.35 millon for stifling competition	21
2.3	Pixar's acquisition by Disney	23
2.4	Managers, shareholder risk, and diversification	26
2.5	A note on property rights theory	27
2.6	Strategic renewal at IBM	31
3.1	The AOL-Time Warner merger	43
4.1	Example definitions of businesses	46
4.2	Ansoff's growth matrix	48
4.3	Standard industrial classifications	50
4.4	Bayer's 2010 mission statement and business definition	53
4.5	Novartis' business definition	57
5.1	Spreading risk from a stakeholder perspective	61

5.2	Demand side synergies	63
5.3	Nestlé's new product technology center, water	66
5.4	Globalizing and localizing manufacturing at Toyota: The role of the global production center	69
5.5	Portfolio management at Bayer and Haniel	70
5.6	Extending the capital market argument	72
5.7	Novartis announces agreement to acquire Chiron	73
5.8	Veto for the merger of D&S and Falabella	75
6.1	The search for synergies: Skype acquisition by eBay	79
6.2	Relatedness the P&G way: Leveraging global scale and scope	82
6.3	Relatedness the Virgin way	83
6.4	Resource based measures of relatedness	92
7.1	Different types of diversification strategies	96
7.2	Competing subsidiaries: The enemy within	102
7.3	The institutional context of diversification	104
8.1	Diversification strategy and the tasks of the corporate headquarters	108
8.2	The tasks of Philips' headquarters	108
8.3	Headquarters' role and value creation	115
8.4	Managing P&G's portfolio	118
8.5	Limitations of the BCG matrix	120
8.6	The role of headquarters: Centralization and decentralization	122
9.1	The spread of the multidivisional form	128
9.2	The rise and fall of Dow Chemical's matrix structure	129
9.3	Mitsubishi: A network organization	131
9.4	Organizational structure and the growth of the firm	132
10.1	Vertical integration works for Apple: But it won't for everyone	142
10.2	Measuring vertical integration	143
10.3	Delta Air Lines' vertical integration into the refinery of oil	148
10.4	Vertical integration and technological change	149
10.5	Korea's *chaebols*	150
11.1	Bain's typology of entry conditions	157
11.2	Reducing exit barriers	159
11.3	The hubris hypothesis of takeovers	160
11.4	The winner's curse	166
12.1	Primary reasons for divestitures	173
12.2	Nestlé's acquisition of Perrier	177
12.3	Primary reasons for divestitures	180
12.4	Divesture: The lesson from the apple farmer	182
12.5	Research on divestures	183
13.1	Choosing where to compete: The 'Marlboro Friday'	185
13.2	Multipoint contact's asymmetry	193
13.3	Microsoft's entry into the home video game industry	194
13.4	Total war between Walt Disney and AOL-Time Warner	196
13.5	Three rivals multipoint competition	197
14.1	Pfizer's new global strategy	202
14.2	Toyota taps Japan for exports to small markets	208
14.3	Globalizing and localizing manufacturing at Toyota	209
15.1	Sarbanes-Oxley Act of 2002	216

PREFACE

Corporate level strategy is "concerned primarily with answering the question what set of businesses should we be in?" (Hofer & Schendel, 1978, p. 27). More specifically, Collis & Montgomery (2005, p. 8) define corporate level strategy as: "the way a company creates value through the configuration and coordination of its multimarket activities."

This definition has three important components that are emphasized throughout the chapters of this book: first, this definition emphasizes that the ultimate purpose of corporate level strategy is value creation; second, it focuses on the multimarket scope of the firm (i.e., *configuration*), including its product, geographic, and vertical boundaries; and third, it takes into account how the firm can manage the activities and businesses that lie within the corporate hierarchy (i.e., *coordination*).

In their analysis of the structure and evolution of the strategic management field, Furrer, Thomas, & Goussevskaia (2007b) found that between 1980 and 2005, scholars' interest in diversification and corporate level strategy issues has been continuously growing. As noticed by Collis, Young, & Goold (2007), if it was almost unknown in 1900, the diversified firm is today the dominant organizational form for the conduct of industrial activities (Fligstein, 2001). In the United States, about 60 percent of output is undertaken by such multibusiness entities (Villalonga, 2004b). The percentage is similar in Europe (Pedersen & Thomsen, 1997), while 'groups' are also ubiquitous in developing countries (Khanna & Palepu, 1997a).

Research into corporate level strategy emphasizes three sets of issues. First, the determinant of firm scope: why is it that some firms are highly specialized in what they do while others embrace a wide range of products, markets, and activities? Second, what is the relationship between scope and performance? Clearly, specialized firms tend to be smaller than diversified firms, but what about profitability and shareholder returns on investments? Third, what can we say about the management of multibusiness firms in terms of structure, management systems, and leadership? This book seeks to answer these three sets of issues. To answer these questions, the book presents and uses various theories and analytical frameworks that help managers (and students) to identify the sources of corporate advantage. By focusing on what makes some corporate level strategies strong and sustainable, while others remain weak and vulnerable, we seek to develop managers' (and students') ability to consider the impact of change and other important environmental forces on the opportunities for establishing and sustaining corporate advantage.

A considerable body of theory has evolved within the disciplines of strategy, economics, finance, marketing, organization theory, and international business that have salient implications for the management of corporate level strategies. Thus, the book starts with presenting these relevant concepts and theoretical framework, before applying them to specific issues related to the development and implementation of corporate level strategies.

The book is organized as follows: we start by introducing what is corporate level strategy and by presenting the evolution of the concept over time with an historical perspective. In relation to this general introduction, the starting point of the book is the following question: why do multi-business firms exist? The question is relevant because the neoclassical theory of the firm generally assumes single-business firms operating in perfect markets and competitive equilibrium. Because the existence of profitable multibusiness firms in the real world challenges these assumptions, the reason for their existence must be understood before further theory development can occur. Furthermore, from an application point of view, understanding why multibusiness firms exist may help us to recognize the rationales for firms' diversification strategies, understand how multibusiness firms create corporate value that single-business firms or shareholders investing in single-business firms cannot, and comprehend the roles of headquarters in managing multiple businesses, as well as the importance of corporate governance in controlling the work of managers.

The question is a theoretical one, thus, we present the different theoretical frameworks, which have been developed to answer this question: industrial organization theory, transaction cost theory, agency theory, dominant logic, the resource-based view, strategic contingency and institutional theories, and, finally, real option theory. Then, once we know why multibusiness firms do exist, we try to understand how they should be managed. To do so, we review the recommendations implied by the different theories we already presented. The logic is as follows: if multibusiness firms exist for a specific purpose, then the must be managed accordingly in order to achieve this purpose. The objective of this theoretical presentation is to help managers (and students) to understand the coherence and the logic of the different theories. However, whereas the presented theories are sometimes complementary, to some extent, they also provide contradicting recommendations.

Therefore, to understand how theses theories can be combined in a comprehensive way, we apply them to pressing corporate strategy questions. The first of these questions is how to define a business, the main unit of analysis of corporate level strategy. We pursue with explaining how multibusiness firms create value through diversification, which leads us to the thorny issue of relatedness and the limits of the scope of the firm. Then, we turn our attention to the implementation of diversification and the role of the parent in managing the multibusiness firm, raising the question of the organizational structure of the diversified firm: the multidivisional structure. It is then important to better understand how different types of diversification strategies are implemented with different organizational structures, which use different styles of coordination and control. The multidivisional structure is well adapted to deal with horizontal diversification, but multibusinesses also diversify their activities vertically, leading our discussion toward vertical integration and the coordination of the value chain.

After understanding how diversification creates value and the multibusiness firm is organized to create and capture this value, the next question is how does a firm become diversified? This question deals with the growth of the firm and its different alternatives: internal growth, strategic alliances, and mergers and acquisitions. As multibusiness firms sometimes become overdiversified, the next question deals with the reduction of the scope of the firm and restructuring strategies.

The last three chapters of the book deal with three contemporary issues in corporate level strategy, which transcend the different questions answered in the book. These issues are: how do multibusiness firms compete against each other (i.e., multipoint competition)? Is international diversification something different from business diversification? And, what are the social responsibilities of the multibusiness firm?

ACKNOWLEDGEMENTS

Many thanks to my students for their feedbacks on the first edition of this book; their comments helped me to improve the readability of the text.

Chapter

1

WHAT IS CORPORATE LEVEL STRATEGY?

THE DEFINITION OF CORPORATE LEVEL STRATEGY

Of the many definitions of corporate level strategy in the literature, perhaps the earliest, and still very helpful, conceptualization described it as the pattern of decisions that determine a firm's goals and objectives, produces the principal policies for achieving these goals and objectives, and defines the range of businesses that the firm is to pursue (Andrews, 1971). Subsequent definitions identified several levels of strategy, distinguishing between business level (i.e., competitive) strategy, which pertains to how to build and maintain a competitive advantage in each of its discrete and identifiable markets or businesses, and corporate level strategy, which pertains to the overall plan for a diversified firm (Hofer & Schendel, 1978; Porter, 1987) (see Box 1.1).

BOX 1.1 AN EARLY DEFINITION OF CORPORATE LEVEL STRATEGY

To differentiate corporate level strategy from business level strategy, Hofer and Schendel (1978, p. 27) specify that:

> Corporate level strategy is concerned primarily with answering the question what set of businesses should we be in? Consequently, scope and resource deployments among businesses are the primary components of corporate strategy. Competitive advantage and synergy are also important for related product, multi-industry firms, but much less so for conglomerates. Synergy, to the degree it exists at all at the corporate level, is concerned with how the firm's different businesses reinforce each other, as they might in sharing corporate staff, financial resources, or top management skills. The two major types of functional area policy decisions that are universally important at the corporate level involve financial structure and basic design of organizational structure and processes.

Despite the potential benefits of distinguishing between business and corporate level strategies, this hierarchical categorization appears to be somewhat problematic because it neglects the interdependencies between the two levels (Bowman & Ambrosini, 2007; Collis & Montgomery, 2005). The hierarchical distinction between business and corporate levels of strategy implicitly restricts corporate level strategic activities to corporate headquarters. However, a firm's corporate level strategy acts as both a catalyst for and a constraint on the strategies of its business units; and therefore also involves business level managers. Furthermore, if the business level strategies do not support the firm's corporate level strategy, synergies become impossible. For example, we explain in Chapter 5 that a firm can create value at the corporate level by allocating additional resources to its business units to help them implement their business level strategies, but it also can create value at the corporate level by aligning the competitive strategies of its business units to create synergies (see Box 1.2 and Chapter 13 on multipoint competition).

BOX 1.2 THE INTERRELATIONSHIP BETWEEN BUSINESS AND CORPORATE LEVEL STRATEGIES

Business and corporate level strategies are interrelated and should be mutually reinforcing each other to create value for the firm as a whole. For example, value can be created by coordinating business level strategies across business units. Such coordination can both improve the business units' bargaining positions *vis-à-vis* suppliers and buyers, as well as improve their individual competitive position *vis-à-vis* rival firms (De Wit & Meyer, 2010). Business units can improve their bargaining position *vis-à-vis* suppliers by ordering larger quantities for lower prices from the same suppliers and *vis-à-vis* buyers by offering a broad assortment of related products and services to their common customers. Coordination of business strategies within the firm can also prevent business units from fighting fiercely against each other (De Wit & Meyer, 2004). Furthermore, it is also possible for business units to support each other in attacking together the same rival, for example by setting a common standard or aggressively pricing selected products on selected markets.

To overcome the limitations of a hierarchical definition of corporate level strategy, Collis and Montgomery (2005, p. 8) developed a more general definition: "Corporate strategy is the way a company creates value through the configuration and coordination of its multimarket activities." This definition has three important components: first, the emphasis is on *value creation* as the ultimate purpose of corporate (level) strategy; second, it focuses on the multimarket scope of the firm (i.e., *configuration*), including its product, geographic, and vertical boundaries; and third, it also put an emphasis on how the firm can manage the activities and businesses that lie within the corporate hierarchy (i.e., *coordination*).

As it includes these three components (value creation, configuration, and coordination), this definition is more inclusive than previous conceptualizations of corporate level strategies. In particular, it does not restrict the relevance of corporate level strategy to large, diversified firms (Collis & Montgomery, 2005), because it implicitly takes into account that smaller, and most likely, less diversified firms also need to make configuration and coordination decisions, such that they also require a corporate level strategy. Moreover, the definition recognizes that corporate level strategy involves more than strategic activities by corporate headquarters. To create value, corporate headquarters must contribute to the competitive advantage of its businesses, so this definition includes the relationships between the corporate whole and the business units of the firm. Another important characteristic of this definition is its recognition of the importance of both the implementation and the formulation of corporate level strategy. Through the configuration and coordination of its multimarket activities, a firm must create value at the corporate level.

CORPORATE LEVEL STRATEGY AND DIVERSIFICATION

A firm with multimarket activities is said to be diversified. However, diversification is not a yes or no situation, but rather a matter of degree or level. A firm's level of diversification is one of the main concepts of corporate level strategy. Diversification refers to the scope of the firm in terms of the markets and industries (i.e., businesses) in which it competes, and how managers buy, create, merge, split, or sell businesses to match strengths and resources with opportunities presented to the firm (Bergh, 2001). The scope of any firm and its diversification strategy can be represented according to three dimensions: customer groups (including geographical diversification), customer needs (including product market diversification), and technology (including vertical integration) (see Chapter 4 for more details about the ways firms define their business activities). The overall diversification level of a firm therefore comprises the extent of its diversification in these three dimensions.

Levels of diversification

Diversified firms vary in their level of diversification and the connections between and across their businesses (Rumelt, 1974). Figure 1.1 lists five types of diversification, according to increasing levels of diversification (Hitt et al., 2004; Rumelt, 1974) (see also Box 1.3). Single and dominant business firms pursue relatively low levels of diversification, as shown on panel (a) of Figure 1.1, whereas more diversified firms consist of related—shown on panel (b)—and unrelated types—shown on panel (c). Single business firms are not diversified and focus their activities in only one

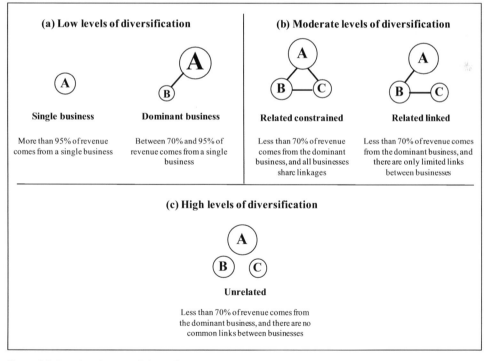

Figure 1.1 Level and types of diversification

Source: Adapted from Rumelt (1974) and Hitt et al. (2005)

BOX 1.3 RUMELT'S DIVERSIFICATION TYPOLOGY

In his seminal text, Rumelt (1974) provides some quantifiable measures of a firm's level of diversification, which we discuss in more detail in Chapter 6. A firm that pursues a low level of diversification (i.e., focused strategy) uses either a single or a dominant diversification strategy. In a single business diversification strategy, the firm generates 95 percent or more of its sales revenue from its core business area. With the dominant business and dominant unrelated diversification strategies, the firm generates between 70 percent and 95 percent of its total revenue within a single business area. A firm generating more than 30 percent of its sales revenue outside its dominant business and whose businesses are related to each other in some manner uses a related diversification strategy. When there are direct links between all (or most) of the firm's businesses, a related constrained diversification strategy is at play. The firm with a portfolio of businesses with only a few links between them is using a related linked diversification strategy. Finally, a highly diversified firm, which has no relationships between its businesses, follows an unrelated diversification strategy. Figure 1.2 graphically represents the different diversification strategies.

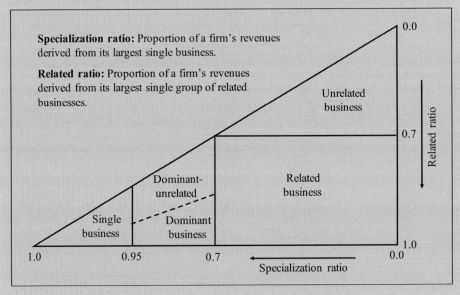

Figure 1.2 Rumelt's scheme

business market and dominant business firms are mostly active in one core business, but have one or a limited number of peripheral businesses that only represent a small percentage of activity. The peripheral businesses might or might not be related to the core business. A firm's businesses are related when there are several links between them. The more links among businesses, the more 'constrained' is the relatedness of the diversification. A firm with a related constrained diversification strategy seek to link all of its business together to achieve maximum synergy; a firm with a related linked diversification create a chain of businesses by relating one business to one other (such a strategy is also called vertical integration and is discussed in Chapter 10). Unrelatedness refers to the absence of direct links between businesses. Firms with an unrelated diversification strategy are often called conglomerates and is discussed in more detail below in this chapter. The links between business units are critical as they represent potential sources of economies of scope and synergies. The concept of relatedness is discussed more extensively in Chapter 6.

A firm's diversification strategy entails a dynamic process. As a firm grows, its portfolio of businesses becomes more complex, and its level of diversification is more difficult to evaluate. Highly diversified firms may be active in several hundred businesses (Haspeslagh, 1982), whose interrelationships cannot really be represented in the formal depiction of its organizational structure. Firm growth often starts within its core industry. Over time, the diversifying firm then moves outside its initial industry, first in closely related businesses, then in increasingly unrelated activities—as in Figure 1.1, which graphically depicts the typical firm's portfolio with just a few businesses. It could be useful to represent more complex business portfolios in the same way. To do so, core businesses are represented close to the center and more distant businesses to the periphery of the figure. The extensive business portfolio of the Walt Disney Company is represented in this way in Figure 1.3.

Figure 1.3 illustrates such a representation with the example of the portfolio of businesses owned by the Walt Disney Company. It competes in a range of businesses, including film and television production, theme parks, and consumer products (Montgomery, 1992; Collis, 1995), which are all related in a way to its animated feature film core business. Around this core business, located in the center of the figure, lie several businesses closely related to Disney's animated films and their characters. They represent the first level of Disney's diversification. Theme parks (in the

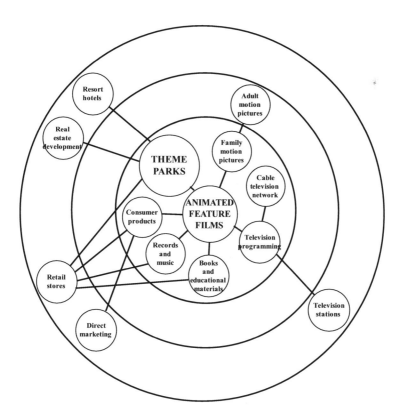

Figure 1.3 Walt Disney's business portfolio

Source: Adapted from Montgomery (1992) and Collis (1995)

United States, Tokyo, Europe, and Hong Kong), consumer products, records and music, and books and educational materials, all use Disney's animated movie characters. The movies themselves are distributed through the cable television networks and television programming. Disney also produces family motion pictures under the Touchstone and Walt Disney labels, which target the same public as its animated feature films. At a second level of diversification, we find adult motion pictures, which are not directly related to the animated feature films—they do not use the same technology and do not target the same public—but which share some of the same resources than the family motion pictures. At more distant location and somewhat less related to Disney's core business, some more businesses represent a third level of diversification. Resort hotels and real estate development do not have much in common with Disney's animated movies, but have the same customers than the theme parks. The direct marketing and retail store businesses, of which some are located in the theme parks, are there to distribute the consumer products, records, and books with Disney characters. And the television stations are broadcasting Disney's TV programs.

The web of relationships between Disney's businesses represented in Figure 1.3 graphically portrays Disney's portfolio and its interrelationships and provides a picture of Disney's diversification strategy. Such a molecular representation of a firm's business portfolio developed by Montgomery (1992) and Collis (1995) can be quite useful for visualizing the level of diversification of a firm and the interrelationships between its businesses.

DOES CORPORATE LEVEL STRATEGY MATTER?

A skeptical view, arguing that corporate strategy does not matter, has gained considerable influence in the 1990s among strategy scholars. As Bowman and Helfat (2001) summarize, this view largely stems from empirical results derived from variance decomposition studies that reveal negligible corporate effects associated with the profitability differences between businesses. Researchers have sought to assess the relative importance of industry, business, and corporate factors in determining profitability differences between firms. In perhaps the best known of these studies, Rumelt (1991) finds that effects specific to individual businesses explain the greatest portion of variance in business level profitability, followed by much smaller industry effects. Rumelt also finds that corporate level effects explain almost none of the variance in profitability. Based on Rumelt's work, many scholars have then suggested that industry effects on profitability actually are small and that corporate effects do not exist (e.g., Carroll, 1993; Ghemawat & Ricart i Costa, 1993; Hoskisson et al., 1993a). By implication, they argue that the vast research, teaching, and consulting efforts related to corporate level strategy may be a waste of time (Bowman & Helfat, 2001).

However, until recently, these variance decomposition studies only placed limited focus on the issue of corporate effects on profitability (with the notable exception of the work by Wernerfelt & Montgomery, 1988). Some more recent studies have directly focused attention on the corporate effect though (Brush & Bromiley, 1997; Chang & Singh, 1999). These and some other studies (McGahan & Porter, 1997; Roquebert et al., 1996) found considerably greater estimates of corporate effects than did prior studies (Rumelt, 1991; Schmalensee, 1985). In many of these studies, the corporate effects are far from nil—sometimes on the order of 18 percent or more.

Reanalyzing data from previous studies, Bowman and Helfat (2001) found that when the analysis of large manufacturing companies includes only firms in which corporate effects would be expected—that is, multibusiness firms—the estimated corporate effects are substantial. For large multibusiness firms only, Roquebert et al. (1996) estimate an average corporate effect of 18 percent, and McGahan and Porter (1997) suggest an effect of 23.7 percent—compared with an estimated corporate effect of 13.7 percent when the analysis also includes single business firms. Furthermore, Chang and Singh (1997) estimate a corporate effect of 11 percent for the largest firms in their sample of U.S. manufacturing firms. And using the same data source as Schmalensee (1985) and Rumelt (1991), Fox et al. (1997) define industries more narrowly and thus find a corporate effect of 8.2 percent. As Bowman and Helfat (2001) have rightly concluded, these results demonstrate that corporate level strategy does indeed matter.

CORPORATE LEVEL STRATEGY: AN ORGANIZING FRAMEWORK

Collis and Montgomery (1998, 2005) have proposed a conceptual framework that seeks to encompass the different elements and activities that fall under the scope of corporate level strategy. The *corporate strategy triangle* of Figure 1.4 is an adaptation of Collis and Montgomery's framework and serves as an organizing guide for this book.

In this framework, the three sides of the triangle—resources, businesses, and the roles corporate headquarters—represent the foundations of corporate level strategy. Collis and Montgomery (1998, 2005) argue that only when they align with managers' dominant logic, can resources, businesses, and the roles of the headquarters produce a corporate advantage. Therefore, there cannot be one single best corporate level strategy, or even a limited set of generic, corporate level strategies, that leads to success (Collis & Montgomery, 1998, 2005). Instead, there can be as many effective strategies as there are possible coherent combinations of the four constitutive elements. A corporate level strategy creates value when, and only when, these elements fit together as a system.

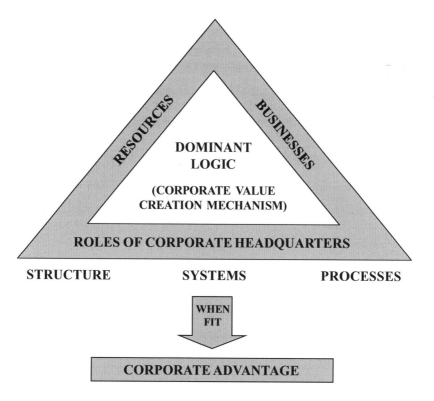

Figure 1.4 The corporate strategy triangle

Source: Adapted from Collis & Montgomery (2005)

In the next paragraphs, we therefore present and describe the four elements of the framework in turn: (1) vision, goals, and objectives; (2) resources; (3) businesses; (4) the role of the corporate office, including its structure, systems, and processes; and the outcome of their combination: (5) corporate advantage.

Dominant logic: The corporate value creation mechanism

The idea of "dominant logic," proposed by Prahalad and Bettis (1986), offers a way to align the three sides of the corporate strategy triangle. The dominant logic is "the lens through which managers see all emerging opportunities" (options) for the firm (Prahalad, 2004, p. 172). In this view, managers' dominant logic is central to the firm's corporate level strategy, as it sets how the different part of the triangle should be combined. When managers' dominant logic does not match the needs of the businesses, tensions and problems arise, such as the wrong managers might be appointed to the businesses, inappropriate plans and investments might be sanctioned, and the wrong targets might be selected (Goold & Luchs, 1993). Wiersema and Bantel (1992) found that managers' dominant logic is associated with the propensity to change in diversification level, and Calori et al. (1994) showed that the chief executive officer's (CEO) cognitive map affects the breadth of the business portfolio.

The dominant logic pertains to the corporate mission, goals, and objectives. Corporate mission refers to the definition of the domain of the firm's activities, such that it is primarily concerned with establishing the boundaries of the firm (i.e., "what set of businesses should we be in?"). We discuss corporate mission in greater detail in Chapter 4. If the vision describes what a firm wants to be, the firm also needs a set of shorter-term goals and objectives. Whereas goals refer to qualitative intentions, objectives indicate specific, short- and medium-term, quantitative targets. Both goals and objectives should be in line with managers' dominant logic and the firm's mission and act as steppingstones toward achieving that mission. At the corporate level, managers' dominant logic often pertain to the choice of the firm's main corporate value-creation mechanism (such as sharing resources, transferring skills, creating an internal capital market or restructuring, discussed in Chapter 5).

Resources

Resources constitute the critical building blocks of a strategy (Wernerfelt, 1984), because they determine not what a firm wants to do but what it can do. At the business level, these stocks of assets can be a source of competitive advantage and can distinguish one firm from another. If all firms had identical resources, all would pursue the same strategy, and the basis for competitive advantage would disappear (Barney, 1991). It is only when resource differences arise among firms that they can develop distinctive strategies. At the corporate level, resources determine the range of market opportunities that are appropriate for the firm to pursue (Collis & Montgomery, 2005). Therefore, they have a major impact on a firm's corporate level strategy. With valuable resources combined in unique ways, a firm can compete successfully in more than one market (Prahalad & Hamel, 1990). Resources thus are the ultimate source of value creation, both within and across businesses. Identifying, building, and deploying these valuable resources are critical aspects of both corporate and business level strategy.

Businesses

As defined here, corporate level strategy refers to the multimarket or multibusiness activities of a firm. Businesses refer to the industries or markets in which a firm operates, as well as to the business level strategy it adopts in each. Industry choice is critical to the long-term success of a corporate level strategy, and the best predictor of firm performance is the profitability of the industries in which it competes (Rumelt, 1991; Montgomery & Wernerfelt, 1988; Schmalensee, 1985). This set of industries in which it operates also influences the extent to which the firm can share resources across its various businesses or transfer skills and competencies from one business to the other. The particular competitive strategy a firm pursues within each industry finally affects its overall corporate performance (Collis & Montgomery, 2005).

The role of the corporate headquarters: Structure, systems, and processes

The corporate headquarters is critical for providing goals, directions, guidelines, structure, and control systems to business unit managers (Burgelman, 1983). Collis, Young, and Goold (2007, p. 385) define the corporate headquarters as "the staff functions and executive management with responsibility for, or providing services to, the whole of (or most of) the company, excluding staff employed in divisional headquarters." In a diversified firm, corporate managers rarely can, or should, make all critical business-unit decisions. Instead, they should influence delegated decision making through the careful design of the organizational structure, systems, and processes in which business-unit managers operate (Collis & Montgomery, 2005). Another important issue is the extent of involvement of the corporate headquarters in the operational activities of its business units. The corporate office could decide to minimize its involvement and delegate most operational decisions to business units, making them as independent as possible; alternatively, it can play an important role in the business units' decision-making process to increase coordination across business units. The corporate office influences business units' decisions through the firm's organizational structure, systems, and processes. (We discuss the role of headquarters in more detail in Chapter 8.) Organizational structure refers to the way the firm is divided into discrete units and describes the formal organization chart that delineates the allocation of authority within the corporate hierarchy. Systems are formal policies and routines that govern organizational behavior, as well as the set of rules that define how tasks, from strategic planning to personnel evaluations, should be fulfilled (Collis & Montgomery, 2005). Processes describe the informal elements of an organization's activities. (We discuss the different aspects of the firm's organizational structure, systems, and processes in Chapter 9.)

Corporate advantage

An effective corporate level strategy results from a harmonious combination of the previously discussed elements. The elements work together as a system to create value through multimarket activity, that is, to yield a corporate advantage (Collis & Montgomery, 1998, 2005). Although some value may be created at the corporate level itself—through a lower cost of capital, for example—most corporate advantages are realized at the business unit level, where individual businesses use the benefits of corporate affiliation to outperform their rivals in a particular industry (Goold et al., 1994; Porter, 1987). Consequently, a corporate advantage can be established and corporate value created when, and only when, a firm's business units are able to create more value within the firm than outside the firm as independent entities or as part of the portfolio of another firm (Goold et al., 1994). Corporate advantage is the *raison d'être* of a multibusiness firm, as we discuss in the next chapter.

An important question is corporate level strategy is then how can we achieve fit between the different elements of the triangle. Box 1.4 present some examples of strategic actions that can be undertaken to achieve fit in the triangle; they are further discussed in later chapters.

BOX 1.4 MANAGING THE CORPORATE STRATEGY TRIANGLE

The idea behind the corporate strategy triangle is that the three sides of the triangle (resources, businesses, and the roles of the headquarters) should be aligned with each other and aligned with managers' dominant logic (which is the main mechanism for creating corporate values—portfolio management, restructuring strategy, share resources, transferring skills and competences) to achieve a corporate advantage. In order to align these elements, a firm can undertake several strategic actions related to the configuration and coordination of its businesses and resources:

1   It could acquire new resources through internal development, merger and acquisition (M&A), or strategic alliances (i.e., a growth strategy) in order to create a better fit between its resources and businesses. For example, the firm could acquire another firm with complementary resources to develop synergies, such as sharing resources to gain economies of scale.

2   It could divest some unrelated businesses in order to reduce its scope so as to have a better fit with its related diversification strategy, which in turn fits with a dominant logic based on sharing resources or transferring skills.

3   It could restructure its business portfolio (by combining or splitting businesses) to make a better use of its resources, for example, to increase resource sharing or better spread the risks across its portfolio of businesses.

4   It could restructure its incentive systems at the headquarters (by establishing bonuses based on firm's performance or business units' performance) in order to motivate business units' managers to better collaborate with each other or alternatively to compete with each other.

5   It could restructure its financial structure (e.g., by going private through a leveraged buyout) in order to align the goals and interests of the managers with the goals and interests of the owners to make a better used of the financial resources of the firms (i.e., the use of free cash flow).

6   It could restructure its organizational structure to have a better control over the activities of its businesses and improve decision-making at the corporate level.

These different ways to tilt the corporate strategy triangle to achieve fit is discussed in more detail in the remaining chapters of this book.

A HISTORICAL PERSPECTIVE IN CORPORATE STRATEGY

Before digging further into the theories and applications of corporate level strategy, it is important to realize that corporate strategy, as an academic field, has dramatically changed over the last 60 year to adapt itself to the evolution of corporate strategy practices. The corporate level strategy of multibusiness firms has undergone enormous change over time, affecting their scope, management, and organizational structure. The merger and acquisition (M&A) booms in the 1960s and 1980s extended the scope of multibusiness firms. In the 1990s, capital market pressures forced many diversified firms to reassess their business portfolios, the size of their headquarters, and the way they coordinated and controlled their multimarket activities. At that time, new forms of corporate hierarchies, such as the leveraged buyout (LBO) partnerships, challenged traditional hierarchical structures and forced highly diversified conglomerates to refocus on their core businesses or die. More recently, new collaborative structures, such as joint ventures, strategic alliances, and franchising, have become increasingly popular to benefit from the advantages of diversification without bearing the costs (Harrison et al., 2001).

Mirroring these changes, scholars and leading consulting agencies have adapted their analytical tools and normative prescriptions for corporate level strategy. From an emphasis on financial performance in the 1960s, through managing the corporation as a portfolio of strategic business units and searching for synergy between them in the 1970s, to the emphasis on free cash flow and shareholder value in the 1980s, then to the refocusing on core competencies in the 1990s, and finally the industry restructuring in the first decade of the twenty-first century, corporate level strategy has continued to change and to become more sophisticated. By the end of 2010 there were only 22 conglomerates left in the U.S. of which three had announced their intention to split up (Cyriac et al., 2012). The refocusing trend is marked in the U.S. but is also evident in Canada and Europe and, to a lesser extent, in Japan (Franko, 2004, Grant, 2013).

To manage the multibusiness firm today and tomorrow, it is critical to understand this evolution. The historical evolution of corporate level strategy presented in this section draws on, synthesizes, and update prior accounts by Montgomery and Porter (1991), Goold and Luchs (1993), Grant (2002, 2008), Collis and Montgomery (2005), and Campbell et al. (2014).

Origin of the modern corporation

Although the entrepreneurial firm has long been recognized as the fundamental unit of business and an institution for organizing productive activity, the "company" is a relatively recent phenomenon (Chandler, 1962). People have engaged in production and trade since prehistoric times, but most of these business activities were undertaken within clans. Even during the early phases of the Industrial Revolution, companies were rare, and most production and trade were conducted by individuals and families. The companies that did exist were relatively small, and by the early nineteenth century, the only large firms were colonial trading companies, such as the Dutch East India Company (in Dutch, Vereenigde Oost-Indische Compagnie or VOC) (De Vries & van der Woude, 1997) and Hudson's Bay Company (Galbraith, 1957). As late as the 1840s, the largest enterprises in the U.S., in terms of both capital employed and numbers of workers (i.e., slave workers), were agricultural plantations (Chandler, 1977).

Even when economies of scale encouraged larger production units, the limited size of local markets constrained the growth of those individual firms, and multiplant firms were not possible without an effective means of communication. The advent of railroads and the telegraph changed all that (Chandler, 1977). Very quickly, regional and national markets could be supplied from a single location in a timely manner, and the activities of multiple subsidiaries could be coordinated from a single office. With the increasing size of firms, management developed as a specialized activity. The railroad companies themselves were the first to realize the potential of the new transportation and communications technologies and thus established the "first administrative hierarchies in American business" (Chandler, 1977, p. 87).

These modern corporations applied administrative hierarchies and standardized decision-making, financial control, and information management systems. Their structures enabled the companies to expand the size and scope of their activities even further (Chandler, 1990). Consolidations through M&A resulted next in the appearance of the first "holding companies" during the late nineteenth century, as firms acquired controlling interests in a number of subsidiaries. Beyond the appointment of the subsidiary boards of directors though, corporate headquarters exercised little strategic or operational influence over their subsidiary firms.

The multidivisional corporation

The multidivisional firm emerged as a response to the problems posed by the increasing size and diversification path taken by traditional industrial enterprises and the new holding companies. For example, when DuPont, a functionally organized producer of explosives and chemicals, expanded its product line, "the operations of the enterprise became too complex and the problems of coordination, appraisal and policy formulation were too intricate for the small number of top officers to handle both long-run, entrepreneurial and short-run, operational administrative activities" (Chandler, 1962, pp. 382–383).

DuPont's solution, in the 1920s, was to create separate product divisions, each independently responsible for operations, sales, and financial performance, leaving corporate headquarters the responsibility for tasks such as coordination, strategic leadership, and control. A few years later, General Motors (GM), a holding company created from M&A among many automobile and component producers, adopted a similar multidivisional structure (also called *M-form*). The divisional managers of Cadillac, Oldsmobile, Buick, Pontiac, and Chevrolet were responsible for the operations and performance of their own divisions, while the corporate president monitored performance, established the terms for interdivisional transactions, and formulated company wide product and technology policies (Sloan, 1963). During the next 30 years, the multidivisional structure allowed the product and national divisions to pursue their operational strategies, while the corporate headquarters managed corporate level strategy. In the meantime, financial planning became increasingly prevalent in the U.S. (Chandler, 1962; Fligstein, 1985) and Europe (Hannah, 1991).

Patterns of diversification in the 1960s and 1970s

Not only were firms becoming more diversified, but their diversification strategies progressed from closely to more loosely related businesses, and then toward unrelated businesses (Rumelt, 1974). The postwar diversification trend was a consequence of several factors. First, the multidivisional structure (or *M-form*) allowed corporations to control an extensive array of different businesses. This innovation, just one of several organizational and managerial developments, facilitated the establishment of large firms with unprecedented business and geographical scopes (Chandler, 1990). Second, the rapidly advancing "science of management" promoted the view that the essence of management was not the entrepreneurial deployment of industry specific experiential knowledge but rather the application of general tools and principles. The universality of the principles of management implied that professional managers trained in business schools and armed with the appropriate tools could successfully manage any type of business.

The development of these concepts and techniques pertaining to corporate strategy, such as the growth matrix and SWOT (i.e., strength, weakness, opportunity, threat) analysis, during the late 1960s and early 1970s (Ansoff, 1965; Learned et al., 1971), reinforced the view that professional managers were not constrained by industry boundaries. In addition, the tools of strategic analysis, as developed in the 1970s and 1980s, permitted standardized yet sophisticated approaches to diversification and resource allocation decisions (Goold & Luchs, 1993). These tools included, for example, business portfolio analysis (Boston Consulting Group, 1972; Haspeslagh, 1982, 1983; Pidun et al., 2011), industry analysis (Porter, 1980), and quantitative approaches to the performance implications of market structure and competitive positioning (Buzzell & Gale, 1987). During the 1970s, an increasing number of firms adopted portfolio management, with the largest diversified firms being among the earliest adherents (Campbell et al., 2014). A large scale study involving 345 senior executives showed that by 1979, 45 percent of the Fortune 500 firms were using some form of portfolio management, mainly to allocate resources efficiently or respond more effectively to performance problems (Haspeslagh, 1982).

The growing scale and scope of firms presented a fundamental change to the capitalist system. Managerial or corporate capitalism, operated by professional managers using new scientific tools of management, was inherently superior to the old form of market capitalism in terms of allocating resources, organizing production, and managing innovation (Chandler, 1962). Yet the rise of professional managers had other, negative implications too. The separation of control from ownership encouraged top managers to pursue diversification to grow, often at the expense of profitability (Jensen, 1988; Marris, 1964). The increasing scope of many firms also was stimulated by research into the performance implications of diversification (e.g., Wrigley, 1970; Rumelt, 1974), which attempted to discover the optimal types and extent of diversification. Its main contribution therefore was the introduction of archetypes of diversification patterns and their links to particular organization structures.

The conglomerates

By the early 1970s, the emergence of a new type of firm—the conglomerate—with no core business and no direct linkages between its many businesses represented the pinnacle of the diversification trend (Davis et al., 1994). Conglomerates, such as Textron and ITT, not only grew rapidly, but also profitably (see Box 1.5). These conglomerates, created by multiple acquisitions, exemplified the belief in the generality of management principles and the irrelevance of industry specific knowledge for the top management tasks of leadership, control, and strategic direction (Campbell et al., 2014; Grant, 2002).

BOX 1.5 TEXTRON: AN EXAMPLE OF CONGLOMERATES

Textron is an American industrial conglomerate, whose business divisions include Bell Helicopter, Cessna Aircraft, E-Z-GO, AAI Corporation, Lycoming Engines, and Greenlee, among others. Textron started as a small textile company in 1923, when 27-year-old Royal Little founded the Special Yarns Corporation in Boston to manufacture synthetic yarns, a niche product at the time. By the start of World War II the company was known as Atlantic Rayon Corporation, and manufactured parachutes. As war production wound down, the company started making civilian products as well, and renamed the company Textron: "Tex" for "textiles," and "tron" from synthetics such as "Lustron." In 1953, Textron purchased its first non-textile business, Burkart Manufacturing Co. This company supplied cushioning materials to the automotive market. The pace of acquisitions was great and among the more important businesses added in the early 1950s were Homelite, which was retained until 1994; Camcar, which was retained until 2006; and CWC, which still remains part of Textron today. In 1960, Textron purchased Bell Aerospace—which included Bell Helicopter—to balance Textron's earnings base by increasing its government business. At the same time, it added another company: golf car manufacturer E-Z-GO. Consumer product businesses were the focus of Textron in the 1960s and 1970s. Notable acquisitions during this period included Speidel, maker of watchbands; Sheaffer Pen; staple and nail gun maker Bostich; and Rhode Island silver company Gorham. In February 1985, Textron acquired Avco Corporation of Connecticut, a conglomerate of almost equal size with pre-acquisition revenue of US$2.9 billion. Overnight, with the addition of its Avco subsidiary, Textron nearly doubled in size. In 1992, Textron acquired Cessna Aircraft Company, a leader in light and medium sized commercial business jets. Cessna balanced Bell's significant defense related business activity. In 1994, following the acquisition of the plastics operations of Chrysler's Acustar Division, Textron's six automotive businesses were combined into one company,

Textron Automotive Company. Similarly, in 1995, Textron Fastening Systems Inc. (TFS) was formed by merging five Textron fastening companies to form a global fastener group, making TFS the largest producer of engineered fastening products and solutions in the world. At the start of the new century, Textron needed to take difficult—yet critical—steps toward restructuring and reconfiguring the firm. These strategic steps led to initial restructuring savings of approximately $154 million in 2001 and the divestiture of several businesses, which contributed $1.6 billion in revenues. Most significantly divested was the Textron Automotive Trim business. By the end of 2005, Textron had achieved significant shareholder returns and, for the first time since undertaking the company's transformation, exceeded the targeted rate of return on invested capital. At that time, a new vision for the corporation was developed to become the premier multi-industry firm, recognized for its network of powerful brands, world class enterprise processes and talented people. This shared vision, established in 2002, became both a mantra and a driving force for Textron employees worldwide. This vision would not have been possible without elevating the concept of synergy—leveraging and combining where it makes strategic sense, while enabling businesses and brands to do what they do best as they serve their unique customers and markets. This approach established the "networked enterprise" and led to the implementation of common processes and powerful tools, while allowing businesses the freedom to manage their business on a day to day basis, develop talent, encourage innovation, and better address customer needs. Textron continued to make strategic divestitures and complementary acquisitions to strengthen its strategic portfolio, including the divestitures of its Fastening Systems business in August 2006, the sale of its Fluid & Power business in November 2008 and the sale of HR Textron in 2009. Meanwhile, Textron has continued to make acquisitions to complement its core businesses, including Overwatch Systems in 2006 and United Industrial Corporation (which owns AAI Corporation) in 2007. On December 26, 2013, Textron agreed to purchase Beechcraft, including the discontinued Hawker jet line, for $1.4 billion. The sale was concluded in March 2014 after government approval.

Source: www.textron.com/about/company/history.php

These conglomerates prompted heavy criticism from finance scholars (Lintner, 1965; Sharpe, 1964), who argued that if individual investors could spread risk by diversifying their portfolios of stocks, the conglomerate firm could offer no real benefits. Empirical evidence from a series of finance studies showed that overall conglomerates did not outperform mutual funds in terms of risks and returns (e.g., Lubatkin & Chatterjee, 1994). Citing their overhead costs, such as those required to pay for corporate headquarters, finance scholars even came to argue that conglomerates were destroying rather than creating value (Jensen, 1989).

The stock market in 1969 fell by 10 percent and the prices of conglomerates by as much as 50 percent (Attiyeh, 1969). The financial crisis of the mid-1970s caused many conglomerates to run out of cash. Some conglomerates, such as Ling-Temco-Vaught in the U.S. and Slater Walker in the U.K. went bankrupt; others, like ITT Corporations and Textron, just survived (Campbell et al., 2014). In response to these pressures, diversified firm's managers were recommended to more effectively use the vast assets under their control and consider the use of divesture to channel asset deployment (Attiyeh, 1969). Most conglomerates had to slim down and restructure the portfolios to raise cash. In the 1960s only 1 percent of U.S. firms refocused, while 25 percent diversified their portfolio. In contrast, in the 1980s, 20 percent refocused while only 8 percent diversified (Markides, 1993).

Downsizing, outsourcing, and refocusing

A new emphasis on profitability and the creation of shareholder value became prevalent in response to the economic downturns and interest rate spikes of 1974–76, 1980–82, and 1989–91, which exposed the inadequate profitability of many large conglomerates and diversified firms. Increased pressure from shareholders and financial markets, including a new breed of institutional investors, led to the rise of shareholder activism. For example, a swath of CEO firings in the early 1990s highlighted the increasing independence of corporate board members (Fligstein & Shin, 2007). An even bigger threat to incumbent management was the use of debt financing by corporate raiders and LBO associations in their effort to acquire and then restructure underperforming firms. The LBOs' activities highlighted the vulnerability of many large diversified corporations. The lesson to other poorly performing conglomerates was clear: restructure voluntarily or have it done to you through a hostile takeover. As a result of this pressure, corporate managers increasingly focused their attention on the stock market valuation of their firm.

The dominant trends of the last two decades of the twentieth century were downsizing and refocusing. Large industrial firms reduced both their product scope, by refocusing on their core businesses, and their vertical scope, through outsourcing. Reductions in vertical integration through outsourcing involved not just greater vertical specialization but also a redefinition of vertical relationships. The new supplier–buyer partnerships typically involve long term relational alliances that avoid most of the bureaucracy and administrative inflexibility associated with vertical integration. The extent of outsourcing and vertical deintegration in turn has given rise to a new organizational form: the virtual corporation, whose primary function is to coordinate the activities of a network of suppliers (Davidow & Malone, 1992).

The narrowed corporate scope also has been apparent in firms' retreat from product diversification. In Britain, the most highly diversified companies of the late 1960s became less diversified during the late 1970s and early 1980s (Jammine, 1984). In the U.S., the average index of diversification by the Fortune 500 declined from 1.00 to 0.67 between 1980 and 1990 (Davis et al., 1994). The surge of U.S. M&A activity in the late 1980s and early 1990s also was driven by divestitures of unprofitable diversified businesses (Hoskisson & Hitt, 1994).

This trend toward refocusing, currently dominant in most Western countries, has not spread to less developed countries, where highly diversified firms still dominate the corporate landscape. Several studies propose that diversification is more likely to be profitable in emerging economies (Chakrabarti et al., 2007; Khanna & Palepu, 1997a; Kock & Guillén, 2001). The underlying argument is that in emerging economies, intermediate institutions, such as financial and market intermediaries, are inefficient or absent. In such environments, diversified firms can gain scope and scale advantages from internalizing functions typically provided by institutions and markets in advanced economies (Chakrabarti et al., 2007). See Box 1.6 for some examples.

New ideas about strategic management have influenced corporate level strategies. In the 1970s and 1980s, strategy scholars were confident about the universality of management principles; in the first decade of the twenty-first century, the development and exploitation of organizational capability has become a central theme in strategy research (Collis & Montgomery, 2005). The recognition has dawned that a strategy of exploiting linkages (i.e., relatedness) across different business sectors does not necessarily require diversification and that a wide variety of strategic alliances and other synergistic relationships might exploit economies of scope across independent firms (Grant, 2008).

BOX 1.6 DIVERSIFICATION IN EMERGING COUNTRIES

The refocusing trend is less evident in Asia, Eastern Europe, and other emerging market economies than in the advanced market economies of North America and Western Europe. A handful of *chaebols*—Samsung, Daewoo, Hyundai, and Goldstar—continue to dominate the South Korean business sector, and in Southeast Asia, sprawling conglomerates such as Charoen Pokphand of Thailand, Lippo of Indonesia, and Keppel Group of Singapore have even become more prominent. These geographical differences may be partly explained by the lack of efficient, well developed capital markets outside the US and Western Europe, which offer internalization advantages to diversified companies (Khanna & Palepu, 1997a).

The cross country differences in the relative costs of organization due to market transactions and internal management may create international differences in firm boundaries too (Hill, 1995). Thus, Lee and Sirh's (1999, p. 14) research on Korean *chaebols* concludes that "the optimal diversification level … is higher in Korea than in advanced countries such as the US." More generally, despite the common trends toward diversification and divisionalization across countries, substantial international differences remain across the corporate strategies of large companies. Not only does the "stakeholder capitalism" associated with continental Europe and Asia tend to promote higher levels of diversification than the "Anglo-Saxon shareholder capitalism" associated with the English speaking world, but country specific organizational forms (Japan's *keiretsu*, Korea's *chaebols*, the holding firms of continental Europe) also tend to persist. The global diffusion of market capitalism, accompanied by privatization and deregulation, has created only limited convergence in corporate strategy. In Chile and India, deregulation and internationalization during the 1990s did little to undermine the role of diversified business groups; on the contrary, these large conglomerates appear to have thrived and increased their internal linkages over the period (Khanna & Palepu, 2000a).

CONCLUDING REMARKS

In this chapter, we started by defining the concept of corporate level strategy and its key components. Using Collis and Montgomery's (2005) definition, we establish that corporate level strategy encompasses decisions, guided by a vision and more specific goals and objectives, about the scope of the firms in terms of their businesses, resources, and the leveraging of those resources across businesses, as well as the role of corporate headquarters for the organizational structure, systems, and processes. There is no single best corporate level strategy; rather, many value creating corporate level strategies can be developed based on different configurations of the various components of corporate level strategy. We further argued that diversification is one of the main elements of corporate level strategy, such that a firm's level of diversification influences its performance and that its corporate level strategy matters. We concluded this chapter by describing how the level of diversification of firms has evolved over time in response to the pressures of the firm's external as well as internal environments.

In the rest of the book, we present and discuss in more detail the relationships among corporate level strategy, diversification, and firm performance. We start with a theoretical perspective to explain why multibusiness firms exist and how they create value (Chapter 2) and how they can be strategically managed (Chapter 3). Then, using an application based perspective, we discuss how multibusiness firms can implement their corporate level strategy and align its different components to create value. Chapter 2 thus starts by explaining why multibusiness firms exist.

Chapter

2

WHY DO MULTIBUSINESS FIRMS EXIST?

THEORETICAL APPROACHES TO DIVERSIFICATION

As defined in Chapter 1, corporate strategy is the way a company creates value through the configuration and coordination of its multimarket activities. However, before we present and discuss the theories and applications of corporate level strategies any further, we need to answer a fundamental question first: why do multibusiness firms exist? The question is fundamental because the neoclassical theory of the firm generally assumes single business firms operating in near perfect markets and competitive equilibrium (Teece, 1980, 1982). Thus, because the existence of profitable multibusiness firms in the real world challenges this assumption, it is critical to understand the reason for this existence before further theory development about the management of multibusiness firms can occur (Hill, 1994; Markides, 2002). We discuss these developments in Chapter 3. Furthermore, from an application point of view, understanding why multibusiness firms exist may help us recognize the various rationales for firms' diversification strategies. This is important to further understand how multibusiness firms create corporate value that single business firms or shareholders investing in single business firms cannot (Barney, 2007; Porter, 1987), and comprehend the roles of headquarters in managing multiple businesses (Chandler, 1991; Goold et al., 1994). It has also some implications for corporate governance and the control of the work of managers (Jensen & Meckling, 1976).

From a theoretical point of view, multibusiness firms exist for several reasons, which is why single business firms seek to diversify their activities into related and unrelated businesses. Diversification helps increase the firm's value by improving its overall performance, through economies of scope or increase revenues. In turn, some firms might diversify to gain market power relative to competitors, often through vertical integration or mutual forbearance. However, other reasons for a firm to diversify its activities may have nothing to do with increasing a firm's value. Diversification could have neutral effects on a firm corporate advantage, increase coordination and control costs, or even reduce a firm's revenues and its financial value. These negative reasons pertain to diversification undertaken to match and thereby neutralize a competitor's market power, as well as diversification to expand the firm's portfolio of businesses to increase managerial compensation or reduce managerial employment risk. Incentives to diversify come from both the external environment and a firm's internal environment. External incentives include antitrust regulations and tax laws, whereas internal incentives include poor performance, uncertain future cash flows, and the pursuit of synergy and reduced risk for the firm. Although a firm may have incentives to diversify, it also must possess the resources and capabilities to create value through diversification. Figure 2.1, adapted from Hoskisson and Hitt (1990), summarizes and graphically represents these different arguments.

The different arguments represented in Figure 2.1 derive from theories that we review in this chapter: industrial organization theory, transaction cost theory, agency theory, the resource based view, strategic contingency and institutional theories, and, finally, real option theory. It is important

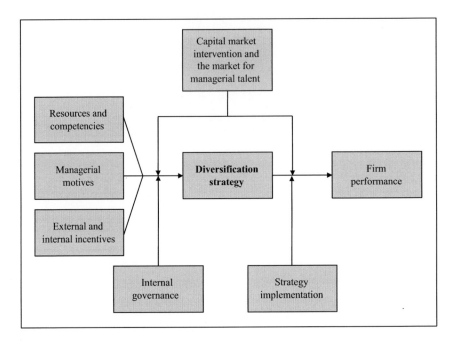

Figure 2.1 Antecedents and consequences of diversification

Source: Adapted from Hoskisson & Hitt (1990)

to have a clear understanding of these different theories and how they relate to diversification and the existence of the multibusiness firm, because in the rest of this book we apply them to different areas of corporate level strategy. They thus can help us understand how multibusiness firms create value, as well as recognize the relationship between diversification and performance. They further help us comprehend the role of the firm's headquarters and how a diversified firm should be controlled and coordinated. Finally, these theories assist in the choice among various growth strategies, such as internal development, alliance, and M&A.

INDUSTRIAL ORGANIZATION THEORY

According to the structure–conduct–performance (S–C–P) paradigm from industrial organization (I/O) economics, the structure of an industry determines the behavior of the firms active in that industry, which drives their performance (Bain, 1956, 1968; Porter, 1980, 1985). Firms' behavior is strongly influenced by their relative market power within the industry, and their strategies aim to increase this power or compensate for their lack of power. For example, if the industry structure is not favorable (e.g., customer and supplier bargaining power is high), firms may engage in fierce competition to increase their power relative to their competitors. However, such fierce competition reduces their profitability. According to the I/O perspective, firms diversify their activities because doing so increases their market power by reducing their dependence on a single business, which improves their performance (Montgomery, 1994). According to Shepherd (1970, p. 3), "[m]arket power is the ability of a market participant or group of participants (persons, firms, partnerships, or others) to influence price, quality, and the nature of the product in the marketplace." In order to avoid firms gaining market dominant positions, governments have develop regulations to prevent abuses of market power (see Box 2.1)

BOX 2.1 EUROPEAN UNION COMPETITION LAW

European Union (EU) competition law concerns regulation of competitive markets in the EU, particularly to ensure that firms do not abuse of market power. It is largely similar to the U.S. antitrust law. EU competition law derives from articles 101 to 109 of the Treaty on the Functioning of the European Union, as well as a series of regulations and directives. The four main policy areas of EU competition law include: (1) cartels (i.e., control of collusion and other anticompetitive practices); (2) market dominance (i.e., preventing the abuse of firms' dominant market positions); (3) M&A (i.e., control of proposed mergers, acquisitions, and joint ventures involving firms that have a certain amount of turnover in the EU; and (4) state aid (i.e., control of direct and indirect aid given by member states of to individual firms. Points 2 and 3 about market dominance and M&A are the ones that are relevant to corporate level strategy within industrial organization theory.

Article 102 of the Treaty on the Functioning of the European Union is aimed at preventing firms who hold a dominant position in a market from abusing that position to the detriment of consumers. Abusing a dominant position means actions such as: (a) directly or indirectly imposing unfair purchase or selling prices or other unfair trading conditions; (b) limiting production, markets, or technical development to the prejudice of consumers; (c) applying dissimilar conditions to equivalent transactions with other trading parties, thereby placing them at a competitive disadvantage; (d) making the conclusion of contracts subject to acceptance by the other parties of supplementary obligations that, by their nature or according to commercial usage, have no connection with the subject of such contracts. EU law defines a dominant market position based on market share. If a firm has beyond a 39.7 percent market share then there is "a special responsibility not to allow its conduct to impair competition on the common market."

Multibusiness firms bundling one product into the sale of another can be considered abuse too, because it is restrictive of consumer choice and depriving competitors of outlets. This was the alleged case in Microsoft Corp that lead to a fine of EU€ 497 million for including its Windows Media Player with the Microsoft Windows platform. In addition in March 2004, the European Commission further forced Microsoft to offer a Microsoft Windows version without the Windows Media Player preinstalled within the EU (*The Economist*, 2006).

Another issue prohibited under EU competition law is predatory pricing. This is the practice of dropping a product's price so low that smaller competitors cannot cover their costs and fail. France Telecom SA, a broadband Internet firm, was forced to pay € 10.35 million for dropping its prices below its own production costs. It had no interest in applying such prices except that of eliminating competitors and was being cross-subsidized to capture a dominant market share of the market (see Box 2.2).

Under Article 102 of the Treaty on the Functioning of the European Union, the European Commission can not only to regulate the behavior of large multibusiness firms abusing their dominant positions or market power, but also regulate firms trying to gain such a position. The European Community Merger Law requires that all mergers, acquisitions, takeovers, and joint ventures that have a European Community dimension and that would results industry concentration to be subject to the approval by the European Commission. This is merger or acquisition and is likely to involve the concentration of market power in the hands of fewer firms than before. The central issue under EU law is whether the planned merger would lead to a concentration that would significantly impede effective competition, in particular as a result of the creation or strengthening of a dominant position. The market shares of the merging firms is assessed and added to determine the extent of concentration. If the merger is likely to result in a dominant market position, then the European Commission can prohibit the merger.

In January 2013, the European Commission prohibited under the EU Merger Regulation the proposed acquisition of TNT Express by UPS. The Commission found that the takeover would have restricted competition in 15 member states when it comes to the express delivery of small packages to another European country. In these member states, the acquisition would have reduced the number of significant players to only two or three, leaving sometimes DHL as the only alternative to UPS. The concentration would therefore have likely harmed customers by causing price increases (http://europa.eu/rapid/press-release_IP-13-68_en.htm).

Similarly in February 2013, the European Commission prohibited, on the basis of the EU Merger Regulation, the proposed takeover of the Irish flag carrier Aer Lingus by the low cost airline Ryanair. The acquisition would have combined the two leading airlines operating from Ireland. The Commission concluded that the merger would have harmed consumers by creating a monopoly or a dominant position on 46 routes where, currently, Aer Lingus and Ryanair compete vigorously against each other. This would have reduced choice and, most likely, would have led to price increases for consumers travelling on these routes (http://europa.eu/rapid/press-release_IP-13-167_en.htm).

Source: Van den Bossche et al. (2015)

Diversified firms can reduce competition through several mechanisms that are largely unavailable to their more focused counterparts (Caves, 1981; Grant, 2008; McCutcheon, 1991; Montgomery, 1985, 1994; Palepu, 1985; Palich et al., 2000; Scherer & Ross, 1990; Sobel, 1984; Williamson, 1975).

- **Cross-subsidization** involves the use of cash flow gained in one industry to support activities in another. For example, diversification may allow a firm to blunt the efforts of competitors through *predatory pricing* (Grant, 2008; Montgomery, 1994; Rhoades, 1973; Scherer & Ross, 1990; Shepherd, 1970), generally defined as sustained price cutting with the goal of driving existing rivals from the market or discouraging potential rivals from entering. Short term losses are offset with gains from future higher prices (Saloner, 1987), and sustained losses can be funded through cross-subsidization, because the firm taps excess revenues from one product line to support another (Berger & Ofek, 1995; Palich et al., 2000; Scherer & Ross 1990).

  A single business firm has no access to investments from cross-subsidization, so its basic sources of capital are external, through debt and equity, which generally are more costly than internally generated funds (Froot et al., 1994; Lang et al., 1995). The diversified firm has much greater flexibility in capital formation because it can access both external sources and internally generated resources (Lang & Stulz, 1994; Stulz, 1990). That is, the diversified firm can attract external funding for expansion, but it can also shift its capital (and other critical resources) between businesses within its portfolio (Meyer et al., 1992). Thus, diversification can generate efficiencies that are unavailable to the single business firm (Gertner et al., 1994).

  However, cross-subsidization could be considered as an abuse of a dominant market position that is forbidden by competition laws in most countries. For example, in 2003, following complaints by AOL, the European Commission fined France Telecom € 10.35 million. for predatory pricing of ISP services by its subsidiary Wanadoo (see Box 2.2). A single business competitor, which presumably lacks the *deep pockets* required to sustain low price levels, eventually may be forced out of the industry. Short term losses then can be offset against gains from future higher prices (Saloner, 1987).

- **Reciprocal buying and selling** can be applied if a firm's potential customer is also the firm's potential supplier. The firm thus gives preference in purchasing decisions or contracting requirements to suppliers that are, or are willing to become, good customers (Scherer & Ross, 1990; Sobel, 1984). The two firms then can come to a favorable agreement, like "I buy from you if you buy from me" (Williamson, 1975, p. 163). The chances that a firm can be both supplier and buyer simultaneously are higher when it diversifies into several businesses (Palich et al., 2000). In a recent case, Intel refused to supply microprocessors to Intergraph Corporation unless Intergraph licensed certain technology to Intel free of charge (Cavanagh, 2001). The result of such agreements is that markets are closed to undiversified competitors (Montgomery, 1994).
- **Bundling**. A diversified firm can extend its power in one market into a related market by bundling two products together (Grant, 2013). In some extreme case, bundling, like cross-subsidization, might be considered as an abuse of a dominant market position. For example, the U.S. Justice Department claimed Microsoft abused its monopoly power in PC operating systems by bundling its Explorer Web browser with Windows, thereby squeezing Netscape out of the browser market. The EU made a similar case against Microsoft regarding the bundling of its media player with Windows (*Economist*, 2006) (see Box 2.1).
- **Mutual forbearance**. Diversified firms that meet each other in multiple businesses recognize their mutual dependence. For example, if a firm competes too fiercely in one industry, a diversified competitor can retaliate in either the focal industry or in all other industries they share. Therefore, they might decide to compete a little less vigorously. For a fuller development of the mutual forbearance explanation, see Chapter 13.

BOX 2.2 WANADOO FINED € 10.35 MILLION FOR STIFLING COMPETITION

The European Commission levied a € 10.35 million fine on French Internet service provider Wanadoo after finding it guilty of stifling competition in the market for high speed Internet access. "The commission found that up until October 2002, the retail prices charged by Wanadoo were below-cost," the Commission stated. This practice, it said, "restricted market entry and development potential for competitors." Wanadoo, which is 72 percent owned by the government controlled France Télécom, saw its market share of high speed Internet access service provision jump from 46 to 72 percent between January 2001 and September 2002 in a market that grew fivefold during that time. By October, no competitor held a market share of more than 10 percent, and one ADSL service provider, Mangoosta, went out of business in August 2001. The Commission added that the impact of Wanadoo's below cost strategy was also felt by cable operators offering high speed Internet access. Furthermore, while Wanadoo was suffering substantial losses during this period, its parent was making healthy profits on its provision of wholesale ADSL connections to competitors of Wanadoo. "The commission considers that practices designed to capture strategic markets such as the high-speed Internet access market call for particular vigilance," the EU executive said, adding that it may open similar investigations in other member states. Earlier this year, the Commission fined Deutsche Telekom € 12.6 million for failing to unbundle the local telecommunication loop in Germany.

Source: Financial Times, 2003; www.computerweekly.com, 17 July 2003

Product diversification as a means to wield market power thus can benefit the financial performance of the firm. As seen in the above example, the verdict from a policy-maker's perspective, however, is that any strategy that has anticompetitive effects is potentially harmful to society as a whole. Such practices also likely contravene both the World Trade Organization's (WTO) antidumping rules and national antitrust laws (Grant, 2013). But despite the conceptual rationale, empirical work offers little evidence of an association between diversification and anticompetitive behaviors, as hypothesized in market power arguments (Grant, 2013; McCutcheon, 1991). Furthermore, the use of cross-subsidization within diversified firms could also represent a potential source of value destruction because it reduces revenues (e.g., Berger & Ofek, 1995; Lamont & Polk, 2002). Therefore, predatory pricing appears less frequently and, when it is used, achieves only limited success (Geroski, 1995). Empirical research on reciprocal buying similarly has produced mixed evidence at best, shifting the focus of recent research away from market power as a justification for diversification activity (McCutcheon, 1991).

TRANSACTION COST THEORY

Transaction cost theory proposes an alternative explanation for the existence of multibusiness firms. In neoclassical economic theory, activities in two different businesses should be assigned to two independent firms, because any necessary coordination between the two firms could take place through the market at a lower cost. However, Williamson (1975) identified factors that would lead to high transaction costs that cause *market failure*. When these factors are present, activities are more efficiently coordinated within firms, instead of through market relationships. For example, if one firm produces jet engines and the other produces aircrafts, the two could write a contract for the supply of jet engines. But because, for several reasons discussed below, markets can fail (Williamson, 1975), these activities might need to be coordinated within one firm, which then becomes diversified. Diversification thus is a potential response to market failure.

A classic example of how high transaction costs lead to market failure comes from General Motors' (GM) relationship with Fisher Body in the 1920s for the supply of car bodies (Klein et al., 1978). GM wanted Fisher Body to build a new plant adjacent to GM's car assembly plant. Fisher Body refused, fearing than once the plant was built, GM could threaten to pay little more than the variable cost of stamping car bodies. At that point, Fisher Body would have no real choice other than to supply GM, because of the costs involved in finding and switching to a new customer. Thus, the threat that GM would exploit Fisher Body once it had made the investment led to a market failure. To avoid this situation, and to move the stamping plant next to its own plant to reduce transport costs, GM just bought Fisher Body and *internalized* the transaction costs (for a complete account, see Casadesus-Masanell & Spulber, 2000; Coase, 1988a, 1988b, 1988c, 2000; Freeland, 2000; Klein, 1988, 2000; Klein et al., 1978). The vertical merger of Fisher Body and GM has also been analyzed in the light of property rights theory (Mahoney, 2005). A similar example, which however involved intellectual assets, is the takeover of Pixar by Disney in 2006 (see Box 2.3).

Market relationships fail when they are subject to opportunism, asset specificity, uncertainty, and/or high transaction frequency.

Opportunism

A premise of transaction cost theory is that people are self-interested and if they can, they behave opportunistically. That is, they seek benefits for themselves at the expense of others (e.g., Williamson, 1975). It is the possibility of firms acting in this way that causes market failure, because firms seek to protect themselves against such opportunism, which has a cost. The other three conditions create the potential for a firm to act opportunistically.

BOX 2.3 PIXAR'S ACQUISITION BY DISNEY

On January 24, 2006, Robert A. Iger, president and CEO of The Walt Disney Company, announced that Disney has agreed to acquire computer animation leader Pixar in an all stock transaction for $7.4 billion. According to Iger, the acquisition would combine Pixar's preeminent creative and technological resources with Disney's unparalleled portfolio of world class family entertainment, characters, theme parks, and other franchises, resulting in vast potential for new landmark creative output and technological innovation that could fuel future growth across Disney's businesses. Garnering an impressive 20 Academy Awards, Pixar's creative team and global box office success have made it a leader in quality family entertainment, known for its incomparable storytelling abilities, creative vision, and innovative technical artistry. However, the acquisition actually may have resulted from the threat of a holdup of Disney by Pixar.

In 1991, Pixar made a $26 million deal with Disney to produce three computer animated feature films, the first of which was *Toy Story*. However, Pixar and Disney had disagreements after the production of *Toy Story 2*. Originally intended as a straight to video release (and thus not part of Pixar's three picture deal), the film was upgraded to a theatrical release during production. Pixar demanded that the film then be counted toward the three picture agreement, but Disney refused. Pixar's first five feature films collectively grossed more than $2.5 billion, equivalent to the highest per film average gross in the industry. Although profitable for both studios, Pixar complained that the arrangement was not equitable: Pixar was responsible for creation and production, and Disney handled marketing and distribution. Profits and production costs were split 50–50, but Disney exclusively owned all story and sequel rights and also collected a distribution fee. The lack of story and sequel rights was perhaps the most onerous element to Pixar and set the stage for a contentious relationship. The two firms attempted to reach a new agreement in early 2004, focused only on distribution, as Pixar intended to control production and own the resulting film properties itself. The firm also wanted to finance its films on its own and collect 100 percent of the profits, paying Disney only the 10–15 per cent distribution fee. More important, as part of any distribution agreement with Disney, Pixar demanded control over films already in production under their old agreement, including *The Incredibles* and *Cars*. These conditions were unacceptable to Disney, but Pixar would not concede.

Disagreements between Pixar CEO Steve Jobs and then Disney CEO Michael Eisner made the negotiations even more difficult than they otherwise might have been. They broke down completely in mid-2004, with Jobs declaring that Pixar was actively seeking partners other than Disney. Pixar did not enter negotiations with other distributors though, and after a lengthy hiatus, negotiations between the two companies resumed, following the departure of Eisner from Disney in September 2005. In preparation for potential fallout between Pixar and Disney, Jobs announced in late 2004 that Pixar would release movies not during the Disney dictated November timeframe but rather during the more lucrative early summer months. As an added benefit, it delayed the release of *Cars*, which extended the timeframe remaining on the Pixar–Disney contract to enable both sides to see how things would play out. Being held up by Pixar, Disney announced on January 24, 2006 that it decided to acquire Pixar.

Source: Adapted from Grover (2006), Wikipedia, and http://corporate.disney.go.com

Asset specificity

Market failure requires asset specificity, that is, an asset that is dedicated (i.e., specific) to a particular application. In such cases, the party that has made the investment is vulnerable to exploitation, because the asset would be worthless in another application. Types of asset specificity include location and physical and human capital (Williamson, 1985). *Location specificity* occurs when unique locational advantages exit and when therefore buyers and sellers locate fixed assets in close proximity to minimize their transport and inventory costs (Joskow, 1985). This is the situation presented in the above GE-Fisher Body example. *Physical asset specificity* includes requirements for specialized machine tools and equipment (Caves & Bradburd, 1988). Physical asset specificity occurs when one or both parties to a transaction invest in equipment dedicated to a particular, limited use. *Human capital specificity* involves uniquely related learning processes and often involves teamwork as well (Masten et al., 1989). Human capital specificity also occurs when employees develop skills that are specialized to a particular relationship or a given organization.

As Williamson (1985) argues, investments specific to a transaction create a *small number* bargaining problem. The fewer the partners in the market, the stronger is their individual power and therefore their capability to increase transaction costs. After making such an investment, the investing firm is unable to negotiate freely and equally with other potential partners (only one partner remains), as it might have before the investment. Instead, the firm is locked into its relationship with its partner. Therefore, the partner gains bargaining power that enables it to act opportunistically, which leads to market failure. To avoid such a problem, firms diversify their activities and *internalize* those for which markets fail. Internalization refers to the firm deciding to do the activities subject to market failure by itself rather than relying on an external supplier. Internalization can occur either through acquisition or internal development (see Chapter 10).

Uncertainty

A solution to the problem of a party acting opportunistically would be to write a contract that prevents opportunistic behavior; this point is where the condition of uncertainty comes into play. It is impossible to write a comprehensive long term contract when the nature of the transaction is such that all possible future eventualities cannot be identified, as it is most often the case. If the contract had to cover an enormous number of clauses, it becomes prohibitively expensive to write and enforce (Williamson, 1979). The more uncertainties there are, the more difficult it is to write a long term contract that covers all possible contingencies, and the more likely it is that the market will fail and firms will diversify.

High transaction frequency

Finally, high transaction frequency increases the likelihood of market failure. Frequent transactions expose a firm to *holdup*, in which situation haggling and negotiation occur more often, creating costs. As illustrated by the Disney-Pixar example described in Box 2.3, to eliminate these search and negotiation costs, and remedy market failure, internalization is often necessary (Williamson, 1985).

AGENCY THEORY

In modern corporations, which are characterized by the separation of ownership and managerial control, managers are decision-making specialists who act on behalf of the firm's owners (Berle & Means, 1932; Chandler, 1977; Demsetz, 1983; Fama & Jensen, 1983). As such, they have some latitude (i.e., discretionary power) to make strategic choices that should be in the best interest of the firm's owners (Jensen & Meckling, 1976). They also are primarily responsible for the performance and sustainability of the firm (Barnard, 1938). However, self-interested managers may make strategic decisions that maximize their own personal power and welfare and minimize their personal risk rather than maximize shareholder value (e.g., Amihud & Lev, 1981; Berger et al., 1997; Jensen & Meckling, 1976; Jensen & Murphy, 1990). Diversification is one such strategic decision (Denis et al., 1997, 1999). Therefore, according to agency theory, multibusiness firms exist not because they create more value than single business firms, but because managers act opportunistically.

Agency theory is concerned the conflict of interest between shareholders and top managers (Berle & Means, 1932). Diversification can enhance a firm's value, which would serve the interests of both shareholders and top managers. But diversification also might result in three benefits to managers that shareholders do not share, such that top managers may prefer more diversification than do shareholders (Hoskisson & Hitt, 1990; Montgomery, 1994). First, diversification usually increases the size of the firm, and size relates positively to *top managers' compensation* (Cordeiro & Veliyath, 2003; Gray & Cannella, 1997; Wright et al., 2002). Moreover, beside size diversification also increases the complexity of managing a firm and its portfolio of businesses, and therefore may require an additional increase in managerial pay to deal with this complexity (e.g., Geletkanycz et al., 2003). As increased diversification provides an opportunity for top managers to increase their compensation, it may serve as a motive for managers to engage in diversification (Finkelstein & Hambrick, 1989; Wright et al., 2002). Empirical studies provide support this managerial compensation motive of diversification (Brenner & Schwalbach, 2003; Denis et al., 1997, 1999).

Second, *managerial entrenchment* occurs when managers make investments that are more valuable under their management than under the management of others. For example, managers may might specific diversification strategies that increase demand for their particular skills, even if those investments do not maximize shareholder value. In this case, shareholders suffer from a *moral hazard* in contracting with managers. In other words, "managerial entrenchment occurs when managers gain so much power that they are able to use the firm to further their own interests rather than the interests of shareholders" (Weisbach, 1988, p. 435). Entrenchment is particularly problematic from a shareholder's point of view because "by making manager-specific investments, managers can reduce the probability of being replaced, extract higher wages and larger perquisites from shareholders, and obtain more latitude in determining corporate strategy" (Schlefer & Vishny, 1989, p. 123).

Third, to reduce their risks, shareholders can pursue a portfolio that contains stock from several firms. One firm's bad financial performance, or even bankruptcy, then can be compensated for by the good results of another firm. A top manager cannot diversify away her or his employment risk by taking charge of various independent firms, but the diversification of the firm into several businesses might serve as a substitute. That is, to *reduce employment risk*, such as job losses, loss of compensation, or loss of managerial reputation (Gomez-Mejia et al., 2001), managers might increase diversification of the firm, because doing so makes the firm and its upper level managers less vulnerable to reduced demand associated with fewer businesses.

Another potential agency problem pertains to the firm's free cash flows, over which top managers have control. Firms, especially those that are active in mature industries, often have what Jensen (1986) calls *free cash flow*, or cash flow in excess of that needed to fund all projects with a positive net present value. Free cash flow should be returned to shareholders, because reinvestment in the firm would harm its value, but top managers may be reluctant to surrender it, which would reduce the resources they control and the power they wield. Instead, they prefer to spend free cash flow on non-profitable projects. In contrast to managers, shareholders likely prefer that free cash flows be distributed to them as dividends, which would enable them to control how the cash gets invested (Brush et al., 2000; DeAngelo & DeAngelo, 2000).

In general, shareholders prefer riskier strategies and more focused diversification. They reduce risks by holding a diversified portfolio of equity investments. In contrast, because managers cannot balance their employment risk by working for a diverse portfolio of firms (Fama, 1980), they tend to prefer a level of diversification that maximizes firm size and their compensation while reducing employment risk. Diversification thus represents a potential agency problem that could require principals to incur costs to control their agents' behaviors (Denis et al., 1997, 1999).

> **BOX 2.4** MANAGERS, SHAREHOLDER RISK, AND DIVERSIFICATION
>
> Curve S in Figure 2.2 depicts the shareholders' optimal level of diversification. Owners seek a level of diversification that reduces the risk of the firm's total failure while simultaneously increasing the company's value through economies of scale and scope. Shareholders likely prefer the diversification strategy noted by point A on curve S. Of course, the optimum level of diversification that owners seek varies from firm to firm. Factors that affect shareholders' preferences include the firm's primary industry, the intensity of rivalry among competitors in that industry, and the top management team's experience with implementing diversification strategies (Hoskisson & Turk, 1990; Hitt et al., 2004).
>
>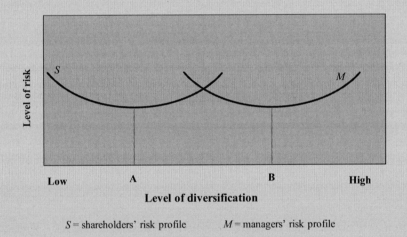
>
> S = shareholders' risk profile M = managers' risk profile
>
> *Figure 2.2* Level of risk and diversification
>
> Source: adapted from Hoskisson & Turk (1990) and Hitte et al. (2005)
>
> As do shareholders, top managers seek an optimal level of diversification. Declining performance resulting from too much diversification increases the probability that the firm will be acquired in the stock market. After a firm is acquired, the employment risk for the firm's top managers increases substantially. Furthermore, a manager's employment opportunities in the external managerial labor market are affected negatively by a firm's poor performance. Therefore, top managers prefer diversification, but not to the point that it increases their employment risk and reduces their employment opportunities (Amihud & Lev, 1981; Berger et al., 1997; Jensen & Meckling, 1976; Jensen & Murphy, 1990). Curve M in Figure 2.2 shows that executives prefer higher levels of diversification than do shareholders. For example, top managers might prefer the level of diversification represented by point B on curve M (Hoskisson & Turk, 1990; Hoskisson et al., 2005).

Governance mechanisms, such as a board of directors, monitoring by owners, executive compensation ceilings, or markets for corporate control, can limit managerial tendencies to over-diversify. However, such governance mechanisms may not be strong enough; in some instances, managers diversify the firm to the point that it fails to earn even average returns (Hoskisson & Turk, 1990; Janney, 2002; Lorsch et al., 2001). The loss of adequate internal governance also may result in poor relative performance, which would trigger the threat of takeover. Although takeovers may improve efficiency by replacing ineffective managerial teams, managers likely try to avoid them through defensive tactics, such as *poison pills*, or reduce their own exposure with *golden parachute* agreements (Gaughan, 2002; Kahan & Rock, 2002). Therefore, an external governance threat, though it restrains managers, does not perfectly control managerial motives for diversification (Anderson et al., 2000; Seward & Walsh, 1996; Walsh & Seward, 1990; Wesphal, 1998).

Most large, publicly held firms are profitable because managers are responsible stewards of firm resources, and their strategic actions (including diversification strategies) generally contribute to the firm's success (Wiersema, 2002; see also Chapter 14). Thus, it is overly pessimistic to assume that managers usually act in their own self-interest rather than their firm's interest (Ghoshal, 2006). Managers also may be held in check by concerns about their reputation. If a positive reputation facilitates power, a poor reputation likely reduces it. Likewise, a strong external market for managerial talent may deter managers from pursuing inappropriate diversification, because they could be replaced more easily (Fama, 1980). In addition, a diversified firm may serve to police other firms by acquiring those that are poorly managed to restructure its own asset base. Knowing that their firms could be acquired if they fail to manage them successfully should encourage managers to use value creating strategies. Accordingly, the assumption that managers need disciplining may not be entirely correct, and sometimes governance may create consequences that are worse than those resulting from over-diversification. For example, excessive governance may cause a firm's managers to be overly cautious and risk averse (Berger et al., 1997).

BOX 2.5 A NOTE ON PROPERTY RIGHTS THEORY

Some of the arguments discussed above within transaction costs theory and agency theory common with arguments from property rights theory. Indeed, property rights theory has common intellectual antecedents with transaction costs theory and agency theory (Barney & Ouchi, 1986), and is yet distinct from these theories (Kim & Mahoney, 2005; Mahoney, 2005). Property rights theory emphasizes value appropriation through ownership via residual claimancy and residual control rights (Alchian & Demsetz, 1972; Grossman & Hart, 1986), as well as the implications of property rights partitioning for the economic value creation of resources (Kim & Mahoney, 2005; Jensen & Meckling, 1976). An important insight of property right theory is that different specifications of property rights arise in response to the problem of allocating scarce resources, and the specification of property rights affects firm behavior and performance outcomes (Kim & Mahoney, 2005). In combination with transaction costs theory and agency theory, property rights theory is valuable in explaining various corporate level strategy phenomena, such as vertical integration (Mahoney, 1992a) and corporate diversification (Teece, 1982). However, because of the overlaps between property rights theory and transaction costs theory, agency theory, and to some extent resource based theory, we do not provide a separate section on property rights theory. For a systematic comparison of these theories and their respective merits, see Kim and Mahoney (2005) and Mahoney (2005).

THE RESOURCE BASED VIEW

The resource based view (RBV) of the firm is concerned with the rate, direction and performance implications of diversification strategy (Mahoney & Pandian, 1992; Wan et al., 2011). It can be seen as a response to the dominant influence on firm behavior and performance that industrial economics assigns to industry. That is, the RBV emphasizes a firm's resources. Resources include assets—plants, patents, cash flows—and competencies, which represent the know-how associated with creating a new asset or expanding existing assets (Markides & Williamson, 1996). If these resources possess certain characteristics, such as non-tradability, non-substitutability, and non-imitability, they can serve as a driver of corporate level strategy and a key source of corporate advantage for a firm (Barney, 1991; Peteraf, 1993; Schmidt & Keil, 2013).

RBV has contributed to a large stream of research on diversification strategy (Ramanujam & Varadarajan, 1989). Wan et al. (2011) identified 65 research articles in top management journals incorporating RBV and diversification. RBV at the corporate level encompasses four areas (Mahoney & Pandian, 1992): first, RBV considers the limitations of diversified growth (via internal development, strategic alliances, and M&As). Second, RBV considers important motivations for diversification and the existence of the multibusiness firm. Third, RBV provides a theoretical perspective for predicting the direction of diversification. Finally, RBV provides a theoretical rationale for predicting superior performance for certain types of related diversification. In this chapter, we focus on the second area (the rationales for diversification); the other areas are discussed in subsequent chapters.

RBV is based on two fundamental assumptions (Peteraf, 1993; Wan et al., 2011). First, different firms possess different indivisible bundles of resources and capabilities, and some firms within the same industry may perform certain activities better than others based on these resources (Barney, 1991; Dierickx & Cool, 1989). Second, resources differences among firms can be persistent (less mobile) due to rarity and difficulties in acquiring or imitating those resources and capabilities (Barney, 1986, 1991; Luffman & Reed, 1982). Based on these two assumptions, a significant portion of recent management literature on diversification follows a RBV logic to explain the rationale for the existence of the multibusiness firm (Barney, 1986; Montgomery, 1994; Peteraf, 1993; Rumelt, 1982; Wernerfelt, 1984) (see Wan et al., 2011 for a systematic review). According to the RBV, resources or capabilities such as specialized human capital (Farjoun, 1998), managerial know-how (Prahalad & Bettis, 1986), and technological know-how (Miller, 2006; Robins & Wiersema, 1995; Tanriverdi & Venkatraman, 2005) can create value when they are shared across businesses (Markides & Williamson, 1994; Miller, 2006), and are costly to transfer across firm boundaries (Teece, 1980). The proponents of the RBV argue that multibusiness firms exist because some resources are sources of economies of scope (Panzar & Willig, 1981; Teece, 1982), though subject to transaction costs (Williamson, 1975). Thus, a firm has an incentive to diversify if it possesses the necessary (excess) resources to make diversification economically feasible (Teece, 1982; Wernerfeldt, 1984).

Penrose (1955, 1959) was one of the first scholars to identify the role of resources in firms' diversification. In addition to analyzing the limits of the rate of a firm's growth, she also examined the motives for diversified expansion. She argued that it is rare for all functional units within a firm to be operating at the same speed and capacity, and that this phenomenon creates an internal incentive for firms' growth. Unused productive services from existing resources present a "jig-saw puzzle" for balancing processes (Penrose, 1959, p. 70). Excess capacity of certain resources due to indivisibility, and cyclical demand, to a large extent drives the diversification process (Chandler, 1962; Teece, 1980). Indeed, many resources cannot be built or acquired in small increments. Firms cannot build half of a factory, especially when there are economies of scale in production, or hire half of a marketing manager. In addition, although resource immobility prevents other firms from easily acquiring or imitating a firm's resources, it also implies that a firm may find difficult to sell some of its excess resources in the market (Lippman & Rumelt, 1982; Nelson & Winter, 1982). In contrast, transferring such resources to related businesses within the firm represents an optimal strategy because the marginal costs of using these resources within a related industry are often minimal and the benefits of using them in another business can be substantial (Wan et al., 2011). Thus, the resources that are unused, human expertise in particular, may drive diversification (Farjoun, 1994). Resources and capabilities lay upstream from the end product and may find variety of end uses (Caves, 1981; Teece, 1982). Excess capacity leads to related diversification when it is end product specific and to unrelated diversification or it is not (Chatterjee & Wernerfelt, 1991).

In summary, according to RBV, firms diversify to take advantage of excess resources and to capture value that would not be realized in a single-business firm (Furrer et al., 2001). As such, RBV suggests that a firm's level of diversification and its performance are significantly influenced by its resources and capabilities (Wan et al., 2011).

STRATEGIC CONTINGENCY AND INSTITUTIONAL THEORIES

Another explanation for corporate level strategy and diversification derives from strategic contingency theory (Venkatraman, 1989) and institutional theory (Kogut et al., 2002), in which the underlying idea is that a fit between a firm's strategy, on the one hand, and external and internal conditions or contingencies, on the other, increases performance. Thus, a firm depends on its environment (Pfeffer & Salancik, 1978), and its strategy is a response to various external and internal contingencies (Andrews, 1971; Hofer & Schendel, 1978; Hoskisson & Hitt, 1990). In turn, diversification (i.e., investing in different types of businesses, manufacturing different types of products, vertical integration, geographic expansion) helps the firm reduce its dependence on a single product, service, market, or technology (Kotter, 1979; Pfeffer & Salancik, 1978; Zeithaml & Zeithaml, 1984). Relevant external contingencies include government policy and market failure (Hoskisson & Hitt, 1990). For example, through antitrust law (Gaughan, 2011), policy-makers try to prevent large concentrations of power in an industry. If the government's antitrust policy is stringent and firms still want to grow, they must expand into different industries—that is, diversify. The theory of market failure as an incentive for diversification is similar to that we discussed with regard to transaction cost economics and the RBV. If markets fail, the coordination of activities across different industries within a firm is more efficient (Williamson, 1975), so the firm becomes diversified. Johnson and Thomas (1987) identify an optimal level of diversification within an industry that balances economies of scope and diseconomies of organizational scale.

Examples of some pertinent internal contingencies are low performance, uncertainty, and risk reduction. If a firm performs poorly in an industry, it may flee to a different industry in an attempt to improve its results (Anand & Singh, 1997). Similarly, uncertainty about future cash flows in the current industry may drive a firm into a new industry. Finally, firms may diversify into several industries to spread their risks. As explained in terms of agency theory though, risk reduction is a suspicious reason for diversification in the eyes of the shareholders, even if it might offer a valid incentive.

Antitrust policies and tax laws

Government antitrust policies and tax laws provided strong incentives for U.S. firms to diversify in the 1960s and 1970s (Lubatkin et al., 1997). Antitrust laws prohibiting mergers that created increased market power (through vertical or horizontal integration) were stringently enforced during that period (Champlin & Knoedler, 1999), which meant that many of the mergers during the 1960s and 1970s were "conglomerations," involving firms pursuing different lines of business. Merger activity that produced conglomerate diversification was encouraged primarily by the

Celler-Kefauver Antimerger Act (1950), which discouraged horizontal and vertical mergers. For example, between 1973 and 1977, 79.1 percent of all mergers involved conglomerates (Scherer & Ross, 1990).

During the 1980s though, antitrust enforcement declined, resulting in more and larger horizontal mergers (i.e., acquisitions of target firms in the same line of business, such as a merger between two oil companies) (Shleifer & Vishny, 1991). In addition, investment bankers became more willing to support the various kinds of mergers facilitated by the change in the government regulations; as a consequence, takeovers increased to unprecedented levels (Chatterjee et al., 2003; Lubatkin et al., 1997; Ravenscraft & Scherer, 1987). The conglomerates, or highly diversified firms, of the 1960s and 1970s became more focused in the 1980s and early 1990s, as merger constraints continued to be relaxed and restructuring was implemented (Williams et al., 1988; Zalewski, 2001). By the late 1990s and early 2000s, antitrust concerns emerged again due to the vast volume of M&A (see Chapter 10). Thus, mergers are now receiving more scrutiny than they did in the 1980s and early 1990s (Croyle & Kager, 2002).

The tax effects of diversification stem from not only individual tax rates but also corporate tax changes. Some companies (especially mature ones) generate more cash from their operations than they can reinvest profitably. Some argue that these free cash flows should be redistributed to shareholders as dividends (Jensen, 1986), but in the 1960s and 1970s, dividends were taxed more heavily than ordinary personal income. As a result, before 1980, shareholders preferred firms to use free cash flows to buy and build companies in high performance industries. If the firm's stock value appreciated over the long term, shareholders might receive a better return on those funds than if the funds had been redistributed as dividends, because their returns from stock sales would be taxed less under capital gains rules than would their dividends.

In the U.S., the 1986 Tax Reform Act reduced the top individual ordinary income tax rate from 50 to 28 percent, and the special capital gains tax changed around the same time, such that the government now treats capital gains as ordinary income. These changes created an incentive for shareholders to stop encouraging firms to retain funds for the purposes of diversification. These tax law changes also prompted an increase in the divestitures of unrelated business units after 1984. Thus, whereas individual tax rates for capital gains and dividends created a shareholder incentive to increase diversification before 1986, they encouraged less diversification after 1986, unless it was funded by tax deductible debt. The elimination of personal interest deductions, as well as the lower attractiveness of retained earnings to shareholders, might have prompted the use of more leverage (debt) by firms, for which the interest expense is tax deductible.

Corporate tax laws similarly affect diversification. Acquisitions typically increase a firm's depreciable asset allowances. Because increased depreciation (a non-cash flow expense) produces lower taxable income, they have an additional incentive to acquire. Before 1986, acquisitions appeared to be the most attractive means for securing tax benefits, but the 1986 Tax Reform Act diminished some of the corporate tax advantages of diversification. Recent changes recommended by the Financial Accounting Standards Board (FASB)—such as the elimination of the "pooling of interests" method for accounting for an acquired firm's assets and prohibiting write-offs for research and development—reduce some of these incentives to gain acquisitions, especially in high technology industries (Hitt et al., 2001b).

Despite the loosening of federal regulations in the 1980s and their retightening in the late 1990s, many industries, including banking, telecommunications, oil and gas, and electric utilities, have experienced increased merger activity as a result of industry specific deregulation. Changes to the relevant regulations also have affected the convergence between media and telecommunications industries and permitted many mergers, such as the successive Time Warner and then AOL Time Warner mergers (Hoskisson & Hitt, 1990).

Low performance

Some studies show that low returns relate to greater levels of diversification (e.g., Park, 2002). If "high performance eliminates the need for greater diversification" (Rumelt, 1974, p. 125), then low performance may provide an incentive for diversification. Indeed, firms with a mature or declining core business and no prospect for improved performance might be motivated to diversify they activities to move away from the low performing business and invest in new and more attractive business. Matsusaka (2001) shows that some firms repeatedly enter new businesses and exits old ones in the search for a good match with their resources. During this process of strategic renewal (Agarwal & Helfat, 2009), firms need to be ambidextrous and simultaneously build new businesses and manage mature ones (O'Reilly & Tushman, 2004, 2005). However, poor performance leads to increased diversification only if the resources exist to do so (Matsusaka, 2001). This is because strategic renewal is often implemented through acquisitions (Graebner et al., 2010; Karim & Mitchell, 2000), which requires financial strengths. For firms operating a strategic renewal, diversification might only be a temporary status before the divestment of the failing original core business (see Chapter 11). An example of a firm that successfully operated a series of strategic renewals is IBM, as described by Agarwal and Helfat (2009) and summarized in Box 2.6.

BOX 2.6 STRATEGIC RENEWAL AT IBM

IBM's history is characterized by multiple efforts at major strategic transformations along with continued strategic renewal. IBM first successfully transformed itself from an electro-mechanical accounting equipment firm into an electronic computing firm during the period 1940 to 1965. IBM undertook this first transformation in response to a technological advance in electronic computing that occurred in the external environment as a result of university research. In the face of this technological change, many of the leading electromechanical business machine firms failed. Of the companies that survived, IBM is was one that made the more efforts to use its resources to move towards electronic computing. The firm had strong sales relationships with customers, and a reputation for manufacturing reliable machines and servicing them effectively in the field, which helped the firm to convince customers to purchase the new electronic machines from IBM rather than from competitors. Thus, IBM was able to leverage these complementary assets.

More recently, IBM has transformed itself from a hardware based computing company with a substantial personal computer business into a business computing services company. Initially labeled "e-business on demand," IBM combines software, hardware, and consulting expertise to provide business computing services to corporate customers. IBM has once again leveraged some of its historical strengths, including its reputation for superior customer service, relationships with customers, and research and development (R&D) expertise to develop significant competitive strength against rivals and reduce its reliance on more commoditized businesses such as software or hardware alone.

Both strategic renewals involved replacement of the company's main business during the process of which the firm had to be diversified and ambidextrously manage the old and new business. These replacements occurred because either a new technology or a changing competitive landscape threatened to make IBM's current business outdated.

Source: Summarized from Agarwal & Helfat (2009, pp. 285–288)

Uncertain future cash flow

As a firm's product line matures or becomes threatened, diversification may represent an important defensive strategy (Bergh & Lawless, 1998; Bernardo & Chowdhry, 2002; Simerly & Li, 1999). Small firms and companies in mature or maturing industries sometimes find it necessary to diversify to support their long term survival (Harper & Viguerie, 2002; Sandvig & Coakley, 1998; Smith & Cooper, 1988). Uncertainty was one of the predominant reasons for the diversification among railroad firms during the 1960s and 1970s (Hoskisson & Hitt, 1990). That is, the railroads diversified primarily because they perceived that the trucking industry would have significant negative effects on rail transportation, which created demand uncertainty. Uncertainty also can come from supply and distribution sources as well as from demand sources though. Therefore, firms may diversify their suppliers and distribution channels to reduce their supply risks.

Synergy and firm risk reduction

Diversified firms pursuing economies of scope often make investments that are too specialized to enable them to realize synergy among business units, leading to several problems. In particular, synergy exists when the value created by business units working together exceeds the value that those same units create working independently. But as a firm increases the relatedness among its business units, it also increases its risk of corporate failure, because synergy produces joint interdependence, which constrains the firm's flexibility to respond. This threat may require two basic decisions.

First, the firm could reduce its level of technological change by operating in more certain environments. This behavior likely makes the firm risk averse, uninterested in pursuing new product lines that have potential but that are not proven. Second, the firm could constrain its level of activity sharing and forgo the benefits of synergy. Either or both decisions may lead to further diversification. The former should prompt related diversification into industries in which more certainty exists, whereas the latter likely produces additional but unrelated diversification (Kay & Diamantopoulos, 1987). Research further suggests that a firm using a related diversification strategy is more careful in bidding for new businesses, whereas a firm pursuing an unrelated diversification strategy may be more likely to overprice its bid, because it lacks full information about the unrelated firm it is acquiring (Coff, 1999; Raynor, 2002).

REAL OPTION THEORY

Because any strategy, at either the business or the corporate level, is pursued under uncertain conditions, flexibility, or the ability to change direction quickly and at low cost in response to unanticipated changes in the environment, is critical (Kogut, 1991). Real option theory addresses the concept of flexibility by taking into account uncertainty in strategic decisions (Luehrman, 1998). It builds on option theory, which was developed in financial fields (see Black & Scholes, 1973) and has gained increasing influence in strategic thinking since the seminal works of Kester (1984) and Myers (1977, 1984). Real option theory has made unique contribution to strategic thinking by providing theoretical explanation for why firms make investment decisions that differ from what the net present value (NPV) approach would prescribe (Li et al., 2007). Traditional investment theory holds that investment should be made when the NPV of an investment opportunity equals or exceeds zero and assumes that the investment must be made now or never. Such an approach, however, fails to consider that managers can adapt or revise their strategies in response to unexpected environmental changes that cause cash flows to deviate from their original expectations (Li et al., 2007). The traditional NPV approach moreover ignores the possibility that investment can be started or stopped at a later time.

An option is the right, but not the obligation, to buy or sell a specified asset at a pre-specified price on or before a pre-specified date (Amram & Kulatilaka, 1999). Options traditionally were written on financial assets, but they also can be written on real assets, such as physical, human, and organizational assets that a firm may use to implement its corporate level strategy. The ability to delay the decision to buy or sell an asset at any point up until the pre-specified date introduces flexibility into the option approach. Without an option, the decision to buy or sell the asset must occur immediately, regardless of any uncertainty about the future value of that asset. With an option though, the decision can be delayed as uncertainty about the future value of the asset resolves itself over time. When this uncertainty becomes at least partly resolved, the owner of the option can decide whether to exercise it and purchase or sell the asset, or not. Thus, an option increases its owner's flexibility.

The cost of this flexibility is the cost of the option. Indeed, actions that firms take to create flexibility are not costless. For example, the creation of flexibility may reduce the firm's ability to engage in other alternatives (Leonard-Barton, 1992). Many strategic investments create subsequent opportunities, and so the investment opportunity can be viewed as a cash flow stream, plus a set of options (Amram & Kulatilaka, 1999; Luehrman, 1998; Myers, 1977). Because strategic decisions typically involve making investments in real strategic assets, these options are called "real options."

The significant costs associated with implementing a strategy of flexibility through options means that flexibility is valuable only in highly uncertain conditions (Amram & Kulatilaka, 1999), such as those that often surround corporate level strategic decisions (Raynor & Bower, 2001). Scholars applying a real options framework emphasize its advantages compared with traditional NPV approaches under conditions of uncertainty (Amram & Kulatilaka, 1999; Dixit & Pindyck, 1994; Li et al., 2007; Luehrman, 1998; Trigeorgis, 1993). Furthermore, options offer the greatest value for decisions for which the traditional NPV is close to zero. In these situations, managers must respond flexibly to new information, and the real option theory is a useful approach for doing so.

Real options theory provides a theoretical basis for considering why firms may or may not diversify their business activities, and accordingly provides a rationale for the existence of the multibusiness firm. For example, in regard of international diversification, Kogut and Kulatilaka (1994) investigate the option value of a multinational network, arguing that the coordination of a network of subsidiaries throughout the world provides "operational flexibility" that adds value to the firm. This operating flexibility entails an advantage gained by being a multinational corporation (MNC). They explain that being an MNC can be conceived of as owning the option to respond effectively to uncertain events, such as government policies, competitors' decisions, or the arrival of new technologies in some parts of the world (Kogut & Kulatilaka, 1994).

Similarly, Raynor (2002) argues that in turbulent businesses, diversification can add value not only by increasing performance but also by reducing risk in ways that investors cannot replicate by themselves. In such businesses, diversification provides a way for firms to hedge the competitive risk that is attendant to convergence phenomena. In businesses in which a firm's optimal scope might be in question because the promise of convergence cannot be exploited using market mechanisms, the firm might over-diversify to hedge against uncertain future reconfigurations of its industry's boundaries. In other words, the firm diversifies to create real options on future integration. A telecommunication firm, such as KPN in the Netherlands, might have diversify its activities into Internet businesses, because these businesses appear to be converging.

In the next chapter, we discuss how different types of options, such as options to wait, to exit, or switch, might be used to explain different corporate level strategies.

CONCLUDING REMARKS

In this chapter, we have reviewed the main theories pertaining to diversification and the existence of multibusiness firms. We focused on the theories seeking to answer the question "Why do multibusiness firms exist?" It is a fundamental question because the neoclassical theory of the firm generally assumes single business firms operating in near perfect markets and competitive equilibrium (Teece, 1980, 1982).

Some of the reviewed theories provide conflicting arguments about the existence of multibusiness firms, however, Mahoney and Qian (2013) stress that they all share a common element that position them against neoclassical economics: market friction. They explain that market frictions are fundamental building blocks for the existence of multibusiness firms and that various theories, such as transaction costs, property rights, real options, and RBV, emphasize different combinations of market frictions, leading to market imperfection, market inefficiency, or market failure. Across these different theories, Mahoney and Qian (2013) identify seven types of market frictions that provide justifications for the multibusiness firm: (1) asymmetric and imperfect information; (2) uncertainty and opportunism; (3) sunk costs and asset specificity; (4) economies of scale and indivisibilities; (5) demand synergies and economies of scope; (6) externalities (inter-temporal and inter-project spillovers) and positive transaction costs; and (7) poorly defined or undefined property rights. These market frictions are the buildings blocks on which firms should base the corporate level strategy to create corporate value.

In the next chapter, we examine theories (sometimes the same ones) providing recommendations about the management of multibusiness firms. If multibusiness firms exist to create corporate value, then how can they align the different elements of the corporate strategy triangle to create such value?

Chapter

3

MANAGING THE MULTIBUSINESS FIRM

THEORETICAL APPROACHES TO CORPORATE LEVEL STRATEGY

Whereas in the previous chapter we focused on the 'why' question (why do multibusiness firms exist?), in this chapter we focus on the 'how' question (how do multibusiness firms create value?). As discussed in Chapter 1, managing the multibusiness firm to create corporate value consists of aligning the different part of the corporate strategy triangle. The theories we reviewed in Chapter 2 not only provide rationales for the existence of the multibusiness firm, but also offer recommendations about how to manage it and to align the corporate strategy triangle. However, whereas most of these theories argue that multibusiness firms exit to create value at the corporate level, they tend to disagree about how to create such value.

Focusing on business responsiveness and market power and risk, I/O economics recommends firms to diversify in unrelated businesses to spread risk and to generate uncorrelated cash flows that can be used to increase market power through cross-subsidization. I/O theory also recommends firms to minimize coordination between businesses to increase their responsiveness to adapt to the specificities of each business. Transaction cost theory, which pertains to the choice of governance structures, argues that firms should internalize business activities whenever transaction costs are higher than management and coordination costs. Different types of market failures causing transaction require different diversification strategies, which in turn require different types of governance structures. Next, agency theory provides recommendations related to the alignment between the types of business portfolios and the role of the headquarters. Agency theory argues that in order to control managerial opportunism, incentive systems should be adapted to the type—related or unrelated—of diversification strategy. Focusing on the resource side of the corporate strategy triangle, the RBV seeks to explain how its resources constrain which businesses a firm can or should diversify in and also how these resources influence the mode of entry into new businesses and the mode of exit from current businesses. The dominant logic suggests that the perceptions of the managers at the headquarters influence the direction of the firm's diversification strategy depending on the way they conceptualize relatedness between businesses. Finally, real option theory provides recommendations about how and when should firms diversify to minimize the risk of such a strategy by taking into account the option value of resources and businesses.

In the next sections, we detail the arguments of these different theories about how to manage the multibusiness firm to create corporate level value.

INDUSTRIAL ORGANIZATION THEORY

As explained in the previous chapter, the I/O economics' S–C–P paradigm stipulates that every industry is different with a different power structure among its participants. Therefore, in order to improve their performance, firms should adapt their strategy to the structure of the industry (Bain, 1956, 1968; Porter, 1980, 1985). For multibusiness firms, this implies that each business might require a different business level strategy, different resources, and different managerial practices to be more responsive to the specific needs of their business environment (De Wit & Meyer, 2010). Thus, each business should be managed as autonomously as possible to insure its responsiveness.

In addition, I/O economics argues that, in a given industry, a business's performance depends on its relative power compare to the other industry participants (i.e., rival incumbents, new entrants, suppliers, and customers). Therefore, in order to create corporate value, multibusiness firms should use competencies located at the headquarters and draw resources from other businesses to help each individual business to increase its market power and competiveness.

Business responsiveness

Responsiveness is defined as "the ability to respond to the competitive demands of a specific business area in a timely and adequate manner" (De Wit & Meyer, 2010, p. 313). A business unit is responsive when it is able to tightly match its business strategy to the demand of its industry competitive environment. If a business unit is not responsive it will be at a competitive disadvantage compared to more responsive competitors. Therefore, according to I/O economics, corporate headquarters should grant business units as much autonomy and flexibility as possible to adapt to their particular environment.

Indeed, in a multibusiness firm, besides increasing governance costs, the coordination of the activities of the different business units is likely to have a negative impact of the their responsiveness. Coordination at the corporate level is likely to slow down decision-making and action. Coordination might also lead to suboptimal strategies as 'one fits all' business level strategy is unlikely to be optimal given the differences across industry environments. More over, coordination might also result in maladapted control mechanisms and incentive systems, which are likely to impede business units' responsiveness.

Therefore, given the need for business responsiveness and the costs and problems inherent to coordination, I/O economics recommends firms to diversify into unrelated businesses that do not require costly coordination and to provide them with the needed independence and autonomy in strategy-making.

Market power

However, a multibusiness firm with independent and autonomous business units might not be able to create additional value at the corporate level compared to single business firms. Then, to create corporate value, corporate headquarters should also help business units to increase their market power through direct contribution in terms of competencies and bargaining power and through resource allocation across business units (Caves, 1981; Grant, 2013; Montgomery, 1994; Scherer & Ross, 1990).

For example, as discussed in the previous chapter, multibusiness firms can draw resources, in particular financial resources, from a business with excess cash flows to subsidize another business needing cash. By doing so, the multibusiness is able to provide additional power to the receiving business, which can reduce prices to gain a competitive advantage.

Being present in multiple businesses provides diversified firms with increased bargaining power against their suppliers and customers, through reciprocal buying and selling and bundling (see Chapter 2). Corporate headquarters should use this increased bargaining power to improve the competitiveness of its different business units. Mutual forbearance can also be used against multipoint competitors to reduce the intensity of competition in different businesses (see Chapter 13).

According to I/O economics, managing a multibusiness firm to create corporate value consists in minimizing coordination between businesses to allow them to be as responsive as possible and to provide them with market power to gain competitive advantages in each business. This implies that a multibusiness firm diversifies its activities in unrelated businesses that can be managed autonomously and that the main role of the corporate headquarters should be to transfer financial resources across businesses depending on their needs to achieve a competitive advantage.

TRANSACTION COST THEORY

Transaction cost theory pertains to the choice of a governance structure (Williamson, 1975) and argues that a firm should internalize activities when transaction costs are higher than management and coordination costs, and externalize them otherwise. According to transaction cost theory, two different types of markets influence a firm's diversification strategy: the capital market and the market for excess resources (Koen, 2005). Failures in any of these markets push firms to internalize activities and diversify into related or unrelated businesses.

Market for excess resources failure

According to transaction cost theory, a firm should diversify its activities when it possesses excess resources (Penrose, 1959; Teece, 1982), such as physical equipment or know-how that it does not need for its current activities but that could be put to use in a new business. This is because the costs of developing the resources have already been incurred, the firm can then realize economies of scope if it redeploys them into new activities. Economies of scope arise when the cost of the combined production of several products or services is lower than the cost of producing each product or service separately (Panzar & Willig, 1981). However, economies of scope might not provide a sufficient reason for a firm to diversify, because excess resources also could be traded to another firm active in a different business. However, transaction theory argues that in many cases markets for excess resources fail (Teece, 1982). For example, know-how often cannot be described in the form of a blueprint or formula because it has a tacit and 'learning by doing' character. Therefore, the transfer of know-how to the buying firm necessitates ongoing support by a team from the selling firm, which may be costly to organize across firms. To economize on these transaction costs, managers may decide to use excess resources they have to start activities in the other business on their own and to diversify.

As the excess resources have been developed internally, they are likely to be related in some ways to the core resources of the firms and therefore the diversification move is likely to be in a related business. As old and new businesses are related the coordination costs are likely to be lower than if businesses were unrelated, and also lower than the transaction costs that would occur if the firm would have sold the resources to another firm.

Capital market failure

Consistent with I/O economics, transaction cost theory also explains how and why multibusiness firms that diversified into unrelated business should create an internal capital market to create corporate value. Transaction cost theory argues that, at a point of time, a firm might need to attract outside capital to fund a new investment proposal—such as, entering into a new attractive business, which might be unrelated to the core business of the firm. To obtain such capital from the financial market, the firm is likely to need to provide external investors with the necessary information for them to assess the potentials and the risks of the project. However the firm will be likely to be reluctant to disseminate all relevant information to potential outside investors, as they could use the information opportunistically and copy the investment proposal to start their own activities or pass the information on to competitors.

This danger is reduced when the firm uses an internal capital market rather than external one. Every business of a multibusiness firm can present its investment proposals to corporate head-quarters for funding (Bower, 1970). The headquarters owning the businesses has no incentive to use the information opportunistically. Subsequently, corporate headquarters reallocates the free cash flows that it has withdrawn from its businesses to fund the most attractive investment pro-posals. As the risks of opportunism are lower, the internal capital market is more efficient than the external one. In addition, corporate headquarters has also at its disposal a wide range of mechanisms to motivate business managers (as discussed in the next section on agency theory). The external capital market only has crude mechanisms, such as the market for corporate control and managerial talents, to discipline managers (Williamson, 1975).

The headquarters of the diversified firm is better positioned to optimize the allocation of these resources because it has superior access to information (Servaes, 1996; Shleifer & Vishny, 1991; Williamson, 1986). For example, corporate headquarters can allocate investment cheaply and effi-ciently (compared with external sources), directing capital away from slow growing, cash generating operations to businesses in the portfolio that are expanding rapidly and have great commercial potential but need investments (Scherer & Ross, 1990; Shleifer & Vishny, 1990). This scenario is especially pertinent for relatively new ventures that lack a track record and are unknown to external sources of capital, even if these sources would otherwise show great interest in invest-ing (Grant, 2013). Chapter 5 provides a further discussion of how portfolio management and the creation of an efficient internal capital market can create corporate value.

Thus, according to transaction cost theory, firms should diversify into related businesses when there are failures in the market for excess resources and can diversify into unrelated businesses when they have financial excess resources and when the external financial market is less efficient than the internal capital market. In such situations, the role of the corporate headquarters is to ensure that the management and coordination costs within the diversified firms stay lower than the potential transaction costs.

AGENCY THEORY

Agency theory provides recommendations related to the alignment between a firm's business portfolio and the role of the corporate headquarters. It argues that in order to control for mana-gerial opportunism, when a firm is diversified into unrelated businesses, the role of the corporate headquarters should be limited to the allocation of cash flows and managerial incentive systems should seek to foster internal competition between business units for these cash flows. On the contrary, when a firm is diversified into related businesses and coordination is important to achieve economies of scope and synergies, then the role of the corporate headquarters is to insure col-laboration between business units through an adapted incentive system.

Lack of managerial control and monitoring provides incentives for business unit managers to opportunistically over-diversify to increase their unit's size and scope and improve their personal revenues (Hoskisson & Hitt, 1994). When monitoring is costly and likely to be inefficient, per-formance based incentive systems might be preferable.

According to agency theory, to reduce business unit managers' opportunism and limit moni-toring costs, corporate management should design an incentive system that aligns business unit managers' goals with those of corporate managers (Hill, 1994). To motivate business unit managers to improve the performance of their business unit, corporate management may provide incentives based on business level performance, such as a share of the profit generated by their unit in the form of bonuses. Business unit managers also receive an implicit promise of promotion if they increase their unit performance. However, because business unit managers' tenure in their job is likely to be limited—the incentive system pushes them into new promotions and increased income categories—they may underinvest in assets and upgrades, which increases the current and short term profits of their unit at the cost of long term efficiency and profits (Hoskisson & Hitt, 1988; Hill, 1994).

In addition to the short term profit maximization problem, performance based incentive systems for business unit managers may encourage another form of opportunism. That is, by gearing bonus pay to business unit performance and allocating capital among the business units on the basis of relative yields, the firm reinforces the business unit managers' incentive to maximize their unit performance. The system therefore likely produces competition among business units for more investment capital (Williamson, 1975). This type of rivalry can impair the transfer of skills and knowledge across business units and reduce cooperation, which eliminates economies of scope. In contrast, the firm could encourage cooperation by implementing incentive systems that emphasize interunit cooperation rather than each business unit's performance as an independent business (Gupta & Govindarajan, 1986; Kerr, 1985; Lorsch & Allen, 1973; Pitts, 1974; Salter, 1973). When corporate level profitability depends on interunit cooperation, these reward systems provide business unit managers with a good incentive to cooperate. However, a corporate level performance based incentive system also may induce opportunism in the form of free riding. When a business unit manager's rewards depend on the efforts of other units' managers, opportunistic managers might be inclined to reduce their efforts without strongly affecting their individual bonuses.

Overall, agency theory recommends multibusiness firms implement an incentive system based on corporate level performance when it is diversified into related businesses in order to ensure cooperation and synergies, and an incentive system based on business units' performance when it is diversified into unrelated businesses to foster healthy competition between business units.

THE RESOURCE BASED VIEW

Besides explaining why multibusiness firms do exist and the motivation for and performance consequences of diversification, RBV also provides explanation for the direction of diversification (Kochhar, 1996; Mahoney & Pandian, 1992; Montgomery & Hariharan, 1991). RBV argues that a firm might use its excess resource capacity in a different, but to some extent related, business, which would lead to diversification (Montgomery, 1994; Penrose, 1959; Teece, 1980). In general though, tangible resources (e.g., machines) and intangible resources (e.g., brand names) can be used for only a relatively narrow range of products or services. A firm with excess capacity in these areas thus should choose related diversification (Chatterjee & Wernerfelt, 1991), because it is only in such businesses that the resources can be efficiently leveraged (Lemelin, 1982; Teece, 1982). For example, excess capacity in a sales force is more effective with related diversification, because the firm can use it to sell similar products. The sales force would be more knowledgeable about related product characteristics, customers, and distribution channels (Capron & Hulland, 1999). In contrast, more fungible (i.e., flexible) resources—and financial resources in particular—can be used for more unrelated diversification (Chatterjee & Wernerfelt, 1991; Montgomery & Wernerfelt, 1988; Wernerfelt & Montgomery, 1988).

Only if the resources used for diversification have the characteristics required for competitive advantage will diversification increase firm performance (Mahoney & Pandian, 1992). For example, free cash flows are a financial resource that the firm can use to diversify, but because they tend to be more flexible and common, they are less likely to create value and less likely to be a source of competitive advantage than are other types of resources (Kochhar & Hitt, 1998). However, as a financial resource, cash also can enable investments in other resources that provide more valuable and less imitable advantages. Excess financial resources, for example, could easily be returned to the capital market and made available to other companies. In contrast, other excess tangible and intangible resources likely are difficult to trade across markets, so they provide a more solid foundation for profitable diversification (as discussed above with transaction cost theory).

Prahalad and Hamel (1990, p. 82) argue that a firm's core competencies, which they define as "the collective learning in the organization, especially how to coordinate diverse production skills and integrate multiple streams of technologies," are complex sets of intangible resources and capabilities that link the different businesses in a diversified firm through managerial and technical know-how, experience, and wisdom (Chatterjee & Wernerfelt, 1991). For example, Honda manufactures and sells a wide range of products: luxury cars, motorcycles, lawn mowers, portable electric generators. These various products all draw on a single core competence though: manufacturing small engines and power trains (Prahalad & Hamel, 1990). Most of the products share few, if any, activities, but they nevertheless are linked by Honda's core competence (Figure 3.1).

When a diversified firm exploits a core competence, the operations of each of its different business are significantly affected by the accumulated knowledge, experience, and wisdom gained from the firm's previous business activities (Markides & Williamson, 1994). These different businesses may all exploit similar technologies, address similar kinds of customers, or adopt similar management principles. Although they differ in important ways, managers moving from one of these businesses to another likely experience many common elements, despite the firm's

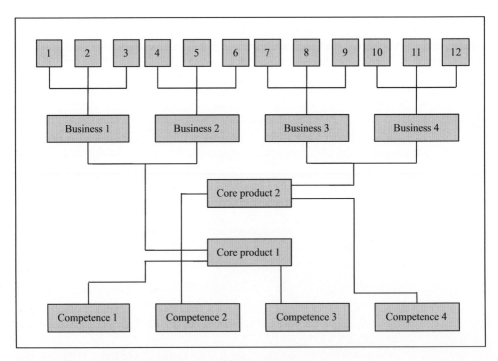

Figure 3.1 Core competencies as the roots of competitiveness
Source: Adapted from Hamel & Prahalad (1990)

diversification. Over time, the firm develops additional products and technologies and manufactures and sells these products and services, so it further develops its core competences (Hamel & Prahalad, 1990). Thus, a core competence is usually a strength that provides the direction for the firm's diversification. However, if the firm continues to emphasize it even after this competence is no longer relevant, it can become a *core rigidity* (Leonard-Barton, 1992). Events in the firm's external environment often create other conditions in which core competencies become core rigidities, generate inertia, and eventually stifle innovation.

In sum, according to RBV, a firm's resources act both as motivations for diversification and constraints in the direction of this diversification. This is, the possession of excess resources motivates firms to diversify and the nature of these resources constrains firms in diversifying their activities into businesses in which these resources can efficiently be put to use and synergy achieved (Kochhar, 1996).

REAL OPTION THEORY

As discussed in the previous chapter, real option theory argues that any strategy is pursued under uncertain conditions, and therefore, flexibility, or the ability to change direction quickly and at low cost in response to unanticipated changes in the environment, is critical (Kogut, 1991). Studies have used a real option lens to study different diversification decisions (Raynor, 2002). Research identifies six real options, based on the associated type of flexibility required by firms (Fichman, 2004; Fichman et al., 2005; Trigeorgis, 1993): stage, abandonment (or exit), defer, growth, scale, and switch (see Table 3.1).

Kogut (1991) argues that a fundamental problem facing the firm is the decision to invest and expand into new product markets (i.e., diversify) that are characterized by uncertain demand; this problem is exacerbated when the new business is unrelated to the firm's current activities. Using a real option perspective, he proposes considering a firm's initial investments in new markets, such as those in a joint venture, as the rights to expand investment in the future. Following Kogut's analysis, several authors similarly have looked at joint ventures as real options (Folta, 1998; Nöldeke & Schmidt, 1998; Seth & Kim, 2001). In these studies, joint ventures represent the options to grow,

Table 3.1 Six types of real options

Option	Definition
Stage	A project can be divided into distinct stages, such that the pursuit of each stage depends on a reassessment of the costs and benefits at the time the previous stage is completed.
Abandon	A project can be terminated midstream, and the remaining project resources can be redeployed relatively easily.
Defer	A decision to invest can be deferred for some period of time without imperiling the potential benefits.
Growth	An initial baseline investment opens the door to a variety of potential follow-up opportunities.
Scale	Resources allocated to a project can be contracted or expanded, or the operational system enabled by a project can be scaled up or down easily.
Switch	An asset developed or acquired for one purpose can be redeployed to serve another purpose.

Source: Adapted from Fichman et al. (2005)

defer, or abandon. Depending on the evolution of the new markets, the firm may decide later to acquire its joint venture partner or dissolve the alliance. In addition to assessments of joint ventures, real option perspectives have been used to analyze the timing of entry into new markets, which represents an option to defer (Folta et al., 2006; Miller & Folta, 2002). Philippe (2005) even studies corporate governance choices as options for growth and to abandon.

Real option theory provides a means to study the value of other corporate level decisions too. Bernardo and Chowdhry (2002) also use a real option approach to investigate a firm's diversification strategy. A firm may diversify its activities by leveraging the capabilities, skills, and assets that provide the source of its corporate advantage (Penrose, 1959; Wernerfelt, 1984). However, the firm might be uncertain about the degree to which its resources generate economic rents in new businesses. Bernardo and Chowdhry (2002) explain that one way the firm can learn about the value of its resources is by undertaking investments and observing their outcomes. The realizations of performance outcomes, such as cash flows, revenues, and growth in market share, provide valuable signals to guide future investment decisions. Therefore, diversifying investments should be valued not only according to their stand alone expected cash flows but also on the basis of the information that might be learned (Bernardo & Chowdhry, 2002).

Real option theory has been used by both scholars and corporate managers, according to a survey of 4,000 Chief Financial Officers (quoted by Copland & Tufano, 2004), which reports that 27 percent of these respondents claimed they "always or almost always" used some sort of options approach to evaluate and determine growth opportunities.

DOMINANT LOGIC

Similar to agency theory, the dominant logic perspective assumes that the top management of a firm should not be viewed as a "faceless abstraction" but rather as a "collection of key individuals" who have significant influence on the way the firm is managed (Prahalad & Bettis, 1986). Top managers largely influence the style and process of management and, as a result, key resource allocation choices (Donaldson & Lorsch, 1983). The dominant logic of top management refers to "the way in which managers conceptualize the business and make critical resource allocation decisions" (Prahalad & Bettis, 1986, p. 490). Grant (1988) and Goold and Campbell (1987) make this concept more tangible by translating it into administrative mechanisms, such as formulating and coordinating business strategies, allocating resources to businesses, and setting and monitoring performance targets for businesses. Ginsberg (1990) also shows that a dominant logic is essentially a social construction, influenced by top managers' sociocognitive processes. However, Bettis and Prahalad (1995, p. 7) view the dominant logic (see Figure 3.2) as an information filter that focuses the organization's attention

> on data deemed relevant by the dominant logic. Other data are largely ignored. 'Relevant' data are filtered by the dominant logic and by the analytic procedures managers use to ad strategy development. These 'filtered' data are then incorporated into the strategy, systems, values, expectations, and reinforced behavior of the organization.

The dominant logic should match the strategic characteristics of the businesses; otherwise, hidden costs ensue. Hidden costs encompass inappropriate and tardy responses that result from a lack of understanding of the businesses.

In terms of corporate level strategy, the implication is that the dominant logic of a firm's top management team drives diversification strategy and the portfolio of businesses that can be managed successfully. If the top management team has a single dominant logic, the firm should either stick to one business or diversify into businesses with similar strategic characteristics (Prahalad &

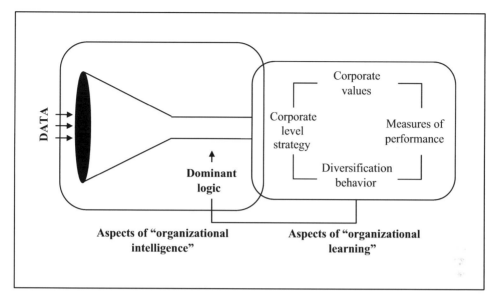

Figure 3.2 The dominant logic
Source: Adapted from Bettis & Prahalad (1995)

Bettis, 1986). Diversification into businesses with different strategic characteristics can succeed only if the top management team adopts multiple dominant logics, which requires altering at least the composition of the top management team (Prahalad & Bettis, 1986).

The dominant logic also represents a break with the more traditional notions of relatedness, which emphasize similarities in end products or services, or else the resources used to produce them. Instead, the dominant logic focuses on similarities in strategic characteristics, such as the maturity and high tech nature of the businesses. This conceptualization might help explain the success of some conglomerates with small corporate offices and limited management capacity. Their businesses may appear unrelated but strategically could be very similar. For example, Goold and Campbell (1987) show that the outstanding performance of two British conglomerates, Hanson Trust and BTR, reflected their application of uniform corporate systems of tight financial controls and high business unit autonomy, which were characterized by maturity, high market share, low levels of international competition, and low levels of technological change. Moreover, the dominant logic approach may help to explain the failure of some takeovers that seemed to offer great potential for synergies. After the takeover, the different businesses might have turned out to require different dominant logics, which the top management team cannot provide. Examples might include the failure of the merger between AOL and Time Warner (see Box 3.1) and that between Daimler and Chrysler.

BOX 3.1 THE AOL-TIME WARNER MERGER

It was touted as the largest corporate merger in history, the most significant coming together of mass media and the Internet. The $165 billion AOL-Time Warner deal was announced in January of 2000 by Steve Case, chairperson of America Online, and Gerald Levin, Time

> Warner's chair and CEO. While Time Warner had more properties and higher profits, AOL was at the peak of its Internet boom, its total stock valued at $200 billion, more than double Time Warner's. But not long after the new company's signs went up, the stock went down, as did investor confidence. Less than three years later, the company was valued at $100 billion, and its stock had fallen more than 70 percent. Analysts were left wondering whether the "synergy" of the two companies ever really existed.
>
> *Source*: www.pbs.org/newshour

Empirical support for the dominant logic perspective comes from studies of managers' perceptions of relatedness. Stimpert and Duhaime (1997) find that managers have different perceptions about relatedness. Some managers think about relatedness in terms of similarities in products, markets, or technologies, which is consistent with traditional economic theories about diversification. Yet managers also hold alternative conceptualizations of relatedness, including that characterized by an emphasis on shared differentiation and marketing skills. Pehrsson (2006a) argues that even if managers hold different conceptualizations about relatedness, their conceptualizations may be shared among managers of different firms in the same industry. Furthermore, Pehrsson shows that relatedness conceptualizations consist of five broad classes: product technology, general management skills, end customers, brand recognition, and supply channel types.

CONCLUDING REMARKS

In this chapter, we have reviewed the main theories pertaining to corporate level strategy and the management of the multibusiness firm. However, the usefulness of a theory is limited to the domain of its application. Therefore, the rest of this book is organized around different themes related to corporate level strategies. By contrasting and combining these different theories, we provide a better understanding of how multibusiness firms create value, how they should be managed and controlled, how they compete in a global environment, and how they can meet their social responsibilities.

However, before developing these applications, we need to define one more concept—probably one of the most important: what is a business?

Chapter

4

DEFINING THE BUSINESS

■ ■ ■ ■ ■ ■

Now that we know why multibusiness firms exist and how they should be managed, it becomes important to investigate what a business is and how it might be practically defined. Defining its businesses and their scope is critical for a multibusiness firm, because the definition directly influences its corporate level strategy. As discussed in Chapter 1, corporate level strategy is primarily concerned with answering a seemingly simple question: what sets of businesses should we be in? (Hofer & Schendel, 1978, p. 27). Learned et al. (1971) explicitly define corporate level strategy as the definition of the businesses in which a company competes. As stated by Campbell et al. (2014, p. 94), "[t]his raises the question of what is a business. Is a single product a business? Is a single location a business? Is the whole company just one business?" Defining what a business is represents a prerequisite for the development and implementation of any corporate level strategy (Abell, 1980), even though there is no objective way of doing it. That is, according to the dominant logic (Prahalad & Bettis, 1986), the subjective perceptions and strategic goals of the firm's managers matter most.

As a start, we might define a business as a set of goods or services that serves similar functions, is created by the use of similar technology, and/or is used by similar consumers (Abell, 1980; Abell & Hammond, 1979). Multibusiness firms employ different criteria to define the boundaries of their business units (also called divisions, strategic business units or SBUs, business groups, or companies), as Box 4.1 details.

In 1980, Abell argued in a seminal book that defining the business provides the starting point for strategic planning. Defining the business entails a creative act, which demands an approach that leads to competitive superiority. This chapter follows the same logic and argues that defining the business represents the starting point for corporate level strategy.

WHY WE NEED TO DEFINE THE BUSINESS

Defining the business is critical in several respects, namely: (1) defining the corporate mission, (2) formulating business unit strategies and setting performance goals, (3) crafting the organizational structure and resource allocation system, (4) conceptualizing relatedness and developing synergies, (5) developing the firm's growth strategy, and (6) resolving agency problems.

Defining the corporate mission

For some firms, any business is good business, as long as they can make a reasonable return on investment (ROI). Yet if any business seems fine, the firm lacks a sense of direction (De Witt & Meyer, 2004). Most firms should adopt a clear identity that they derive from their active

BOX 4.1 EXAMPLE DEFINITIONS OF BUSINESSES

Procter & Gamble: P&G business is defined around four industry based sectors that are focused on common consumer benefits, share common technologies, and face common competitors: (1) Baby, Feminine and Family Care; (2) Beauty, Hair and Personal Care, (3) Fabric and Home Care, and (4) Health and Grooming (www.pg.com/en_US/company/global_structure_operations/corporate_structure.shtml).

CEMEX: CEMEX's corporate level strategy is to create value by building and managing a global portfolio of integrated cement, ready-mix concrete, aggregates, and related businesses (www.cemex.com/InvestorCenter/BusinessStrategy.aspx#sthash.WOJ9Kee9.dpuf).

Nestlé Group: Managed by geographies (i.e., zones denoting Europe/Middle East/North Africa, Americas, and Asia/Oceania/Africa) for most of its food businesses, with the exceptions of Nestlé Waters, Nestlé Nutrition, and Nestlé Professionals, which are managed on a global basis (www.nestle.com/aboutus/management).

General Motors (GM): Defined in terms of brand names. In 2014, GM sold approximately 9.9 million cars and trucks globally under the following brands: Chevrolet, Buick, GMC, Cadillac, Baojun, Holden, Isuzu, Jiefang, Opel, Vauxhall, and Wuling. From electric and mini-cars to heavy duty full size trucks, monocabs and convertibles, GM's dynamic brands offer a comprehensive range of vehicles in more than 120 countries around the world (www.gm.com/company/aboutGM/our_company.html).

Philips: Main focus on health and well-being. Philips serves professional and consumer markets through three overlapping sectors: healthcare, lighting, and consumer lifestyle. Throughout our portfolio, we demonstrate our innovation capacity by translating customer insights into meaningful technology and applications that improve the quality of people's lives (www.philips.com/about/company/businesses/index.page).

Tata: Seven different business sectors: information systems and communications, engineering, materials, services, energy, consumer products, and chemicals. Tata companies deliver a wide variety of products and services, aligned under two headings: consumer products and services or business products and services (www.tata.com/htm/Group_Investor_pieChart.htm).

involvement in a particular line of business. Based on the dominant logic of their top managers, these firms need to define a clear corporate mission. For such firms, a delimiting definition of the business they wish to be in helps them define their core competences (Prahalad & Hamel, 1990) and strongly focuses the direction in which they want to develop (Ansoff, 1965). That is, a business definition functions as a guiding principle that helps managers distinguish opportunities from diversions (e.g., Abell, 1980; Pearce, 1982). Of course, if a clear business definition can focus manager's attention and effort, it also can lead to shortsightedness and the loss of business opportunities (e.g., Ackoff, 1974; Levitt, 1960).

Formulating business unit strategies and setting performance goals

A business is the unit of analysis of any competitive strategy, so the way a firm defines its businesses influences the way it identifies its customers and competitors (Abell, 1980; Porac & Thomas, 1990). A good business definition enables the formulation of business strategies and establishment of performance targets. For example, a broad definition might result in a smaller market share, whereas a narrow definition implies a larger market share. In whatever way the business is defined, each business unit should be large enough to represent independent business activities (afford and maintain critical resources and to operate on an efficient scale) but not so large that its market scope is too broad or that it is inflexible and does not respond quickly to customer needs, to the tactics of competition, and to market opportunities (Walker & Ruekert, 1987) and small enough that a business new manager can manage it effectively (Haspeslagh, 1982).

Crafting organizational structures and resource allocation systems

Businesses may not be strategically autonomous units directly rooted in an industry's structure, but they should be integrated into the corporate whole (Haspeslagh, 1982). A firm can determine the size, shape, and number of its business units only in light of its prior organizational constraints and history, the limits of its managers' intelligence and imagination (i.e., dominant logic), and the multiple interdependencies among its businesses (i.e., their relatedness).

Therefore, the definition of business units and their boundaries should reflect the organizational structure of the firm, which governs the interrelationships between those businesses in regard to coordination and control. Firms may design relatively small, narrowly focused business units, but then have two or more units sharing functional programs or facilities such as common manufacturing plants, R&D programs, or a single sales force. Thus, managers of such narrowly defined business units can stay in close contact with their customers and competitors while the shared programs increase economies of scope and synergy across units (Walker & Ruekert, 1987).

The boundaries of a business unit also should help minimize coordination costs, even as the business units maintain as much independence as possible. Such independence helps create a competitive internal capital market, in which capital and other resources should get allocated according to established financial and strategic criteria (Bower, 1986; Williamson, 1975). In turn, an internal capital market for resources provides a powerful incentive system for business units that may prevent them from free-riding and force them to focus on their business targets (Porter, 1987).

Conceptualizing relatedness and developing synergies

The boundaries of a business unit should be drawn not only to minimize coordination costs but also to maximize economies of scope and synergy. Business unit boundaries and groupings of businesses can powerfully exploit relatedness opportunities. Stimpert and Duhaime (1997) find that some managers think of relatedness in terms of similarities in products, markets, and technologies, consistent with traditional economic theories about diversification. Yet managers also appear to hold other conceptualizations of relatedness, based on a specific dominant logic, including that characterized by an emphasis on shared differentiation and marketing skills (Prahalad & Bettis, 1986). These different conceptualizations represent potential ways to define business units and their boundaries.

Developing the firm's growth strategy

A delimiting definition of the business they wish to be in strongly focuses the direction in which firms develop (Ansoff, 1965). Ansoff's (1957, 1965) growth matrix model derives from the premise that within a firm's businesses, there must be a core capability. To establish links between past and future corporate activities, Ansoff identifies four key strategy components: (1) the product to market scope, to identify what business a firm should be in; (2) a growth vector that explores how growth may be attempted; (3) a competitive advantage that should enable the firm to compete

Defining the business

effectively; and (4) synergy, for ensuring that the overall business is greater than the mere sum of its parts. This is consistent with Penrose's (1959) resource based account of the limit to growth and direction for growth discussed in Chapter 3.

Ansoff's matrix also allows managers to consider ways to grow their business through existing and/or new products and in existing and/or new markets. The four possible product/market combinations—market penetration, product development, market development, and diversification (see Box 4.2)—in the matrix can suggest the growth strategy a firm should take, based on its current performance.

BOX 4.2 ANSOFF'S GROWTH MATRIX

Ansoff's growth matrix consists of two dimensions and four strategies:

1   Market penetration (existing markets, existing products): the company enters or penetrates a market with its current products.
2   Product development (existing markets, new products): a firm with an existing market for its current products embarks on the development of new products to cater to the same market (though the new products need not be new to the market; rather, the product is new to the company).
3   Market development (new markets, existing products): an established product in the marketplace gets targeted toward a different customer segment.
4   Diversification (new markets, new products): in this inherently risky strategy, the firm moves into businesses in which it has little or no experience.

	Existing products	**New products**
Existing markets	**Market penetration**	**Product development**
New markets	**Market development**	**Diversification**

Figure 4.1 Ansoff's growth matrix

Resolving agency problems

As discussed in Chapter 2, a shortcoming of the modern corporation is that shareholders wish to maximize the value of the firm, while their top managers are more interested in salaries, security, and power. With limited power of shareholders to discipline and replace managers, and the tendencies for top management to dominate the board of directors, a clear definition of the business units and their boundaries may act as a partial remedy to the ongoing agency problem. By acting as an interface between the stockholders and the business unit managers, corporate headquarters can enforce adherence to corporate profit goals. When business units get designated as profit centers, headquarters can readily monitor financial performance, and divisional managers can be held responsible for their performance failures. As long as corporate headquarters focuses on shareholder goals, the definition of the business units' boundaries should support a system that enforces profit maximization at the business unit level. However, if the boundaries of the business units are clearly delimited and enforced by corporate headquarters, business unit managers may not be able to diversify their business unit's activities outside these boundaries.

There is no single best way to define the boundaries of a business (Abell, 1980); however, Williamson (1975) identifies four key efficiency criteria for defining both business units and their boundaries:

1   **Adaptation to bounded rationality**. If managers are limited in their cognitive, information processing, and decision-making capabilities, they cannot be responsible for all coordination and decision-making within a complex organization. The business boundaries must permit dispersed decision-making.
2   **Allocation of decision-making**. Decision-making responsibilities should be separated according to the frequency with which different types of decisions are necessary. The business boundaries should send high frequency decisions (e.g., operating decisions, such as launching an advertising campaign) to the divisional level but leave infrequent decisions (e.g., strategic decisions, such as whether to enter a new market) to the corporate level. Similarly, businesses that require different types of decisions should be separated.
3   **Minimizing coordination costs**. As long as close coordination between different business units is not necessary, most decisions about a particular business can occur at the divisional level. This assignment eases the information and decision-making burden on top management.
4   **Avoiding goal conflict**. The boundaries of the business should permit business heads, acting as the business units' general managers, to pursue profit goals that are consistent with the goals of the firm as a whole.

LIMITATIONS OF TRADITIONAL BUSINESS DEFINITIONS

Historically, economists have addressed the issue of defining the business by specifying several *a priori* criteria to classify firms. Two sets of criteria receive most of the attention (Scherer & Ross, 1990): industry and market. According to industry criteria, firms compete with one another (i.e., are in the same business) when they share similar technological attributes and can produce similar outputs. For example, two firms that manufacture steel might be defined as members of the steel industry and therefore be considered competitors. Alternatively, market criteria suggest that firms compete when their output attributes fulfill similar client functions, which makes them substitutable. For example, a firm that manufactures electronic automobile components might be considered in the same business with a firm that produces metal automobile parts, because both types of outputs satisfy a demand for automotive products. These two criteria also provide the basis for the Standard Industrial Classification (SIC) approach to industries (see Box 4.3), a widely used coding scheme to measure a firm's diversification and relatedness level (see Chapter 6).

BOX 4.3 STANDARD INDUSTRIAL CLASSIFICATIONS

The Standard Industrial Classification (SIC) code was developed to classify establishments according to the type of activity in which they engage, as well as to promote uniformity and comparability in the presentation of statistical data collected by various agencies of the U.S. government, state agencies, trade associations, and private research organizations.

The SIC code, a four-digit number assigned to various, distinct business industries, attempts to address the entire field of economic activities, including agriculture, forestry, fishing, hunting, and trapping; mining; construction; manufacturing; transportation, communications, electric, gas, and sanitary services; wholesale trade; retail trade; finance, insurance, and real estate; personal, business, professional, repair, recreation, and other services; and public administration. For instance, SIC Code 5021 represents furniture, 7372 refers to prepackaged software, and 8721 indicates accounting services.

The SIC combines two general approaches: the supply side and the demand side. A supply side, or production oriented, approach aggregates entities according to the similarity of the production processes used to make them. In the technical language of economists, a group of establishments exists if each establishment has the same or a closely similar production function. A demand side, or commodity oriented, classification approach, in contrast, relies on the use of the commodity or service, such that those commodities or services that serve similar purposes, are used together, or are functionally related in use enter into the same grouping.

However, in 1992, the U.S. Office of Management and Budget established an Economic Classification Policy Committee to conduct a complete examination of SIC and design an improved conceptual framework for industrial classification. A series of concerns and issues provoked this reexamination, such as the lack of internal consistency in SIC; its overemphasis on manufacturing and underemphasis on services, as well as its inability to cope with high technology and other emerging industries; and the need, imposed by the North American Free Trade Agreement, to achieve consistency in data collections across the participating countries. The resulting scheme, developed jointly by Canada, Mexico, and the U.S., is a production oriented conceptual framework called the North American Industry Classification System (NAICS). Across North America, producing units that use the same or similar production processes are grouped together according to the NAICS.

In Europe, the EU developed a similar classification in 1970, known as the Statistical Classification of Economic Activities in the European Community, or NACE. In this system, each industry sector takes a unique five or six digit code; for example, DA.15.83 pertains to the manufacture of sugar. In the last decade of the twentieth century, an in depth revision of international statistical nomenclature resulted in an integrated classification system of economic activities and products. In turn, the system of different nomenclatures has been harmonized and related to the world, EU, and national scales. Other countries employ similar classifications, such as the ANZSIC in Australia and New Zealand, the JSIS in Japan, and so forth.

The United Nations (UN) developed its International Standard of Industrial Classification of All Economic Activities (ISIC) code to suggest a standard way to classify economic activities. The ISIC code groups enterprises that produce the same type of goods or services or use similar processes (i.e., same raw materials, processes of production, skills, or technology). The ISIC system has been widely adopted by governments and international bodies; a key purpose of this code is to standardize data collection and promote international comparability.

Source: www.census.gov/eos/www/naics/; http://ec.europa.eu/competition/mergers/cases/#by_nace; www.unece.org/stats/

Defining businesses in this fashion simplifies the inter-organizational comparison process considerably, though for several reasons, such classifications also are unsatisfactory as tools to create cognitive accounts of how decision-makers actually solve comparative dilemmas (Porac & Thomas, 1990). First, there is no reason to believe that managers use the same criteria as policy-makers when defining competitors and businesses. For example, Stimpert and Duhaime (1997) found that managers express different perceptions about relatedness between businesses, in what some managers think of relatedness in terms of similarities in products, markets, and technologies (consistent with traditional economic theories about business definitions), whereas others use business definitions characterized by their emphasis on shared differentiation and marketing skills. Second, both industry and market criteria can be ambiguous. Nightengale (1978) thus argues that industry classifications often lead to somewhat arbitrary groupings, and Robinson (1956, p. 361) asserts that "a precise and meaningful definition of an industry is a vain objective." Similar arguments protest the economic market criterion (e.g., Day et al., 1979; Rao & Stekel, 1998). Third, and perhaps most important, both criteria beg the question of limiting inter-organizational comparisons, because information about technological similarities and product substitutions often is incomplete (Day et al., 1979). Imperfect information means that industry and market business definitions are as much inference as fact, and neither criterion truly explains how managers define their businesses.

However, despite the numerous critics about their managerial applicability for strategic decision-making, SIC are still relevant and useful for research purposes. The fact that there are standardized, systematic, and relatively simple makes them particularly suitable for comparing firms' level of diversification across a wide range of industries. In particular, we explain in Chapter 6 that SIC are often used by scholars to measure firms' diversification strategies.

ABELL'S THREE DIMENSIONAL DEFINITION OF BUSINESS

To palliate SIC deficiencies and provide a managerially useful way to define businesses for decision-making, Abell (1980; Abell & Hammond, 1979) proposes to define a business along three dimensions: *customer groups* describe the categories of customers, or whom the business satisfies; *customer functions* describe customer needs, or what is being satisfied; and *technologies* describe the way the firm satisfies customer needs (see Figure 4.2). In an updated version of his seminal book, Ansoff (1988) extends his two dimensional matrix with a third dimension to match Abell's dimensions. He also argues that the use of three dimensions is a "more realistic" way to describe the complex nature of a business (pp. 83–84). Therefore, a business can be characterized by the application of a particular technology to satisfy a particular function required by a specific customer group.

Customer groups

Defining customer groups requires understanding customers' identities. Some common dimensions for describing identity include geography, demography, socioeconomic class, life style, personality characteristics (in a consumer goods situation), or user industry and size (in an industrial goods situation). Thus, for example and in order of these dimensions, a firm might identify its customer groups as those living in urban settings, people between the ages of 50 and 75 years, those who earn more than $50,000 per year, active exercisers, people who aim to achieve near celebrity status through their purchases, or entities that need massive industrial sorting capabilities.

Defining the business

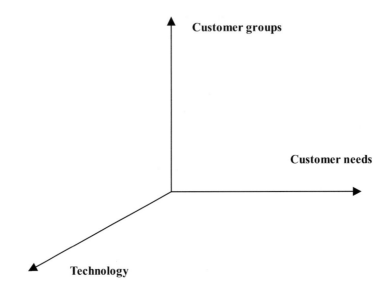

Figure 4.2 Abell's three dimensional framework
Source: Adapted from Abell (1980)

Customer functions

Products and services perform certain functions for customers. However, functions must be separated conceptually from the way the function is performed (i.e., technology), as well as the attributes or benefits that a customer may perceive as important criteria for choice. In this sense, transportation is a function; a taxi is a way of performing the function; and price, comfort, speed, and safety are the attributes or benefits associated with the choices. Likewise, teeth cleaning is a function; fluoride toothpaste and regular toothpaste are two different ways of performing this function; and flavor, brightness, decay prevention, and price are attributes or benefits associated with a particular purchase.

Alternative technologies

Technologies describe the alternative ways in which a particular function could be performed for a customer. Therefore, in this context, a technology represents the form of the solution to the customer's problem. If the function is transportation, the technologies might include road, rail, and/or sea travel. Further subdivisions into private car, rented car, bicycle, or mass transportation also are possible.

Business scope and differentiation

Along all three dimensions, *scope* and *differentiation* also define the business.

Business scope. Any business unit's scope can be defined along the three generic dimensions of customer groups, customer functions, and technologies. That is, scope refers to the number of customer groups, customer functions, and technology combinations achieved or served by the business unit. A business unit with a broad scope thus could serve many customer groups achieve multiple functions through the use of various technologies, and a business unit that only used one form of technology to serve its many customers still might be representative of a broad scope business unit. Alternatively, a firm may operate a portfolio of many different business units, each of which with a narrow scope (i.e., one customer group, one customer function, and one technology combination). As discussed below, the choice between defining a business broadly or narrowly depends to some extent to the degree of differentiation a firm wants to achieve.

Differentiation. Across market segments, differentiation provides a measure of the degree to which firms treat market segments differently. So similar to scope, differentiation can apply to customer groups, customer functions, or technologies. Differentiation occurs in two main ways: by variation in the physical product itself or by variation in some element of the firm's marketing strategy (e.g., advertising, promotion, sales approach, channels, services). Customer groups may perceive physical product differentiation and/or marketing differentiation. That is, a firm might offer different products to different customer groups, or it could provide the same product but market it differently (e.g., a mobile phone is a business tool for corporate customer groups but a safety device for older consumers). Across customer functions, some physical product variation usually exists, perhaps with or without marketing differentiation. However, in the consumer market for baking soda, for example, the same physical product performs a variety of functions (cooking, cleaning, odor removal). Finally, across technologies, by definition the product must be differentiated; the marketing program may or may not be differentiated. In many cases, a company that markets products that rely on substitute technologies will market them in an identical fashion.

BOX 4.4 BAYER'S 2010 MISSION STATEMENT AND BUSINESS DEFINITION

We have set out to create an enterprise that is keenly focused on its customers, its strengths, its potential and the markets of the future: a top international company renowned for product quality, employee skills, economic performance and innovative strength, and committed to increasing corporate value and achieving sustained growth. The Bayer brand symbolizes these goals throughout the world. To sharpen our focus on innovation and growth, we have carried out a strategic realignment, placing our businesses into three subgroups that operate virtually independently and are fully aligned to their respective markets. They are supported by competent service companies. With our distinctive knowledge of people, animals, plants and materials, we intend to focus in future on the areas of: (1) health care, (2) nutrition, and (3) high-tech materials. By applying our skills in these areas we aim to prevent, diagnose, alleviate and cure diseases, contribute to ensuring a sufficient supply of high-quality food for an ever-increasing global population, help people to lead fulfilling, active lives through the contributions made by our products in the fields of communications, mobility, sports and home living. These activities offer access to major growth markets. This mission statement underscores our willingness as an inventor company to help shape the future and our determination to come up with innovations that benefit humankind. Of special importance in this respect are: new products emerging from our active substance research, the consumer health business, the growth markets of Asia, new areas such as biotechnology, and nanotechnology.

Bayer HealthCare. In HealthCare we are among the industry's innovative, global players. We have positioned our *Pharmaceuticals Division* as a medium-sized supplier with global activities. Its research and development are directed toward therapeutic areas where there is particular scope for innovation and where we already have to our credit successful products and/or promising product developments. We plan to continue strengthening our core indications through *inlicensing*. An extensive network of external partners and long-term alliances, such as those with biotechnology companies, strengthens our research platform and gives us attractive business opportunities in the markets of the future. We believe biotechnologically derived active ingredients have considerable growth potential. We plan to further expand our successful business in products for the *companion animals* market.

The *Consumer Care* and *Self-Testing divisions* each hold leading positions in their respective consumer health markets with such famous brands as Aspirin, Alka-Seltzer, Aleve, Bepanthen, Rennie, and Ascensia. In the future we will focus more strongly on our skills and experience in these near-patient markets. We plan to systematically exploit opportunities for both internal and external growth. Our goal is for Bayer HealthCare to become the world's leading consumer health company.

Bayer CropScience. Our *CropScience subgroup* is strongly positioned in the insecticides, fungicides, herbicides, and seed treatment segments. In addition, our *Environmental Science business* has a leading position in nonagricultural markets, for example in pest control. In the *BioScience business group*, we are active in the seed segment and in the rapidly expanding field of plant biotechnology. We focus on crops for which we already have cutting-edge technologies and solid market positions—particularly cotton, canola, rice, and vegetables.

Through the use of plant biotechnology and modern breeding, we are enhancing plants to increase the quantity and quality of food, feed, and fiber. Plant biotechnology also affords us innovative opportunities for partnering within the Bayer Group, including plant-based production of pharmaceutical active ingredients and high-tech materials such as specialty plastics. With our best-in-class portfolio and promising product pipeline, we aim to achieve growth rates well above the market average. Our goal is to be the global leader in the crop science industry.

Bayer MaterialScience. Our *MaterialScience* business units are among the global leaders in their respective markets. We hold particularly strong positions in raw materials for polyurethanes, isocyanates for coatings, and in high-performance polycarbonate plastics. We possess acknowledged leading-edge technologies which, in light of the complex manufacturing processes and sophisticated products involved, should give us competitive advantages in the medium to long term. We will concentrate on promising growth areas and markets and expand our activities, particularly in engineering plastics. The major focus of our investment in the coming years will be on the growth markets of Asia, especially China.

In MaterialScience, also, major opportunities are presented by new technologies which in many cases we are developing together with partners in the respective user industries. Here, new compounds with creative functional properties and novel biotechnologically produced raw materials provide access to numerous fields of innovation. We plan to use nanotechnology to develop intelligent materials for products such as self-healing coatings or scratch-resistant, self-cleaning surfaces for plastics. Our electrically conductive polymers have led to completely new applications in luminescent films, electronic displays and high performance capacitors, for example. Our goal is to build a highly profitable business based on our leading market positions.

Bayer support companies. *Bayer Business Services* is an established international supplier of IT-based administrative, commercial, and scientific services. Forming the technological backbone of the Bayer Group, *Bayer Technology Services* offers innovative and comprehensive solutions in all areas of technology. The extensive range of services provided by *Bayer Industry Services* supports efficient manufacturing operations at Bayer's chemical parks in Germany.

Innovation and growth. Bayer is an inventor company infused with a pioneering spirit. We invest extensively in technology because innovation is the foundation for competitiveness and growth, and thus for our future success. By focusing our resources on the expanding areas of our innovative HealthCare, Crop-Science and MaterialScience businesses, we lay the foundations for sustained, long-term growth in future markets. We believe synergistic potential exists in the use of our technologies by more than one of our subgroups. Here we draw on the expertise that our scientists have acquired over decades of interdisciplinary research. Innovative applications for biotechnology and nanotechnology also hold promise for us in the future. Supplementing the subgroups' targeted R&D activities is our subsidiary *Bayer Innovation GmbH*, set up specifically to turn innovative project ideas into new business concepts. This company not only looks at individual products but also seeks to open up new business opportunities, such as those offered by the combination of materials and active substances in medical applications, or the continuing development of optical data storage media for security systems.

Source: www.bayerandina.com/descargas/bayer-mission-statement-2010-10-01.pdf

Scope and differentiation relate in complex ways. One way to conceptualize these interrelationships is in terms of a typology of business definitions (Kotler, 1975). According to the typology, there are three alternative strategies for defining a business: (1) focused strategy, (2) differentiated strategy, and (3) undifferentiated strategy.

Focused strategy. A business may choose to focus on a particular customer group, customer function, or technology segment. Focus therefore implies a basis for segmentation along one or more of these dimensions, a narrow scope that centers on only one or a few chosen segments, and differentiation from competitors through the careful tailoring of the offering to the specific needs of the specific segment(s) targeted.

Differentiated strategy. When a business combines its broad scope with differentiation across any or all of the three dimensions, it follows a differentiated strategy. By tailoring the offering to the specific needs of each segment, the company automatically increases its chances for competitive superiority.

Undifferentiated strategy. Finally, when a firm combines its broad scope across any or all of the three dimensions with an undifferentiated approach to the customer group, customer function, or technology segments, it follows an undifferentiated strategy.

The choice among focused, differentiated, and undifferentiated strategies exists at the customer group, customer function, and technology levels. A firm therefore could participate broadly by pursuing a range of customer groups and differentiate its offerings for these customers, while still narrowly defining the customer functions that it serves and the technologies it encompasses. One of its competitors instead could concentrate on a narrowly defined group of customers but offer a broad range of products that serve complementary functions by exploiting several alternative technologies.

The adoption of such a three dimensional framework to define a business implies a similar three dimensional framework for conceptualizing changes in the business definition. Yet this framework needs to be reconciled with conventional product-market two dimensional schemes. As Ansoff (1988) notes, adopting Abell's three dimensional framework is more realistic to describe a firm's growth vector and manage the future scope of the firm. Similarly, Porter (1996) identifies three generic ways to position a firm's business according to the three dimensional framework: (1) *variety based positioning*, which consists of producing a subset of an industry's products or services to satisfy a specific customer need expressed by any customer group through the use of any technologies necessary; (2) *need based positioning*, or serving most or all the needs of a particular group of customers, using the necessary technologies; and (3) *access based positioning*, which consists of segmenting customers according to their unique forms of accessibility. Although their needs may be similar to those of other customers, the best way to reach such customers is through different technologies (e.g., shop, phone, Internet).

As suggested by Abell (1980), there may be even more complex combinations of businesses, as well as more complex positioning strategies.

A firm could define its business according to a focused definition of its target customer group, focused definition of the served customer function, or focused definition of the technology it uses (type 1). Or it could decide to serve a specific customer function with a specific technology but address a broadly defined, undifferentiated customer group (type 2). Alternatively, the firm might focus on a specific customer group with a specific technology and provide a large number of undifferentiated functions (type 3). It can also use a single technology (core competence) to serve various undifferentiated customer groups and functions (type 4). When the firm adopts a focused business definition and then decides to diversify its activities, it can expand in several undifferentiated directions, increasing the scope of either the customer group or the customer function (type 5). The firm also might diversify its product portfolio and add technologies that will serve the same customer group(s) and customer function(s) (types 6–9). Finally, a firm may diversify in an unrelated manner to service several customer functions of multiple customer groups using different technologies (type 10). Consider, for example, the business definition that Novartis adopts (see Box 4.5). It exemplifies the combination of several of the types outlined in the previous paragraph.

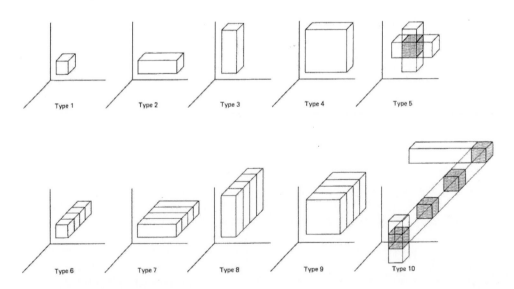

Figure 4.3 Ten types of differentiation

Source: Abell (1980)

BOX 4.5 NOVARTIS' BUSINESS DEFINITION

Novartis' complementary healthcare businesses address the changing needs of patients and societies worldwide. With innovative pharmaceuticals at the core, Novartis is also a global leader in generics, vaccines, and consumer health products. Novartis believes this targeted portfolio best meets the challenges and opportunities in a dynamically changing healthcare environment.

Novartis pharmaceuticals. The Pharmaceuticals Division of Novartis is recognized worldwide for the innovative medicines we provide to patients, physicians and healthcare organizations. This business develops and markets patent-protected prescription drugs for important health needs. Our products are concentrated in major therapeutic areas: (1) Cardiovascular and Metabolism, (2) Oncology and Hematology, (3) Neuroscience and Ophthalmics (NSO), (4) Respiratory, and (5) Immunology and Infectious Diseases (IID). Novartis Pharmaceuticals' current product portfolio includes more than 45 key marketed products, many of which are leaders in their respective therapeutic areas. The product development pipeline involves about 140 projects in various stages of clinical development—including potential new products as well as potential new indications or formulations for existing products.

Vaccines and diagnostics. The Novartis Vaccines and Diagnostics Division provides more than 20 products to fight vaccine-preventable viral and bacterial diseases, and makes sophisticated equipment to test blood donations for infections. Novartis formed this division when it acquired Chiron Corporation in 2006. The division consists of two businesses: Novartis Vaccines and Chiron, the blood testing business.

Novartis Vaccines. Novartis Vaccines is dedicated to delivering on the promise of prevention through the research, development, and production of innovative, safe, and effective vaccines. At the heart of everything we do is our commitment to preventing the spread of life-threatening diseases, protecting vulnerable populations, and keeping healthy people healthy. By focusing on disease prevention, Novartis Vaccines plays a key role in the company's core mission: keeping people healthy, alleviating suffering and enhancing quality of life. The current vaccine portfolio includes vaccines to prevent: Influenza, Meningitis, Rabies, Japanese encephalitis, Tick-borne encephalitis, Haemophilus Influenzae type B (Hib), Polio, Diphtheria, Tetanus, and Pertussis (whooping cough).

Chiron: the blood testing business. As the world leader in blood safety for the transfusion industry, Chiron develops novel tools, products, and services to protect the global blood supply. Screening blood is critical to patient health. A single unit of infected blood may infect up to four transfusion recipients or more than 1,000 other units of blood used to manufacture blood-derived products. Chiron products are used to test more than 25 million blood donations annually around the world, preventing thousands of transfusion-transmitted diseases. Chiron now provides products to test blood donations for HIV (the AIDS virus), HCV, hepatitis B and West Nile Virus.

Sandoz. Novartis is the only pharmaceutical company with a global leadership position in both patented prescription and generic pharmaceuticals. Sandoz plays a critical role in the Novartis strategy of offering a range of treatment options to patients, physicians and healthcare providers worldwide. This broad portfolio helps to make affordable, high-quality medicines available to patients around the world and stabilize healthcare systems. There are two main elements to the Sandoz business strategy: Global reach and reputation. In addition to its unique position within Novartis, Sandoz benefits from a strong global presence and powerful brand recognition worldwide. Sandoz differentiates itself through its ability to develop and produce difficult-to-make medicines. Sandoz is the pioneer of biosimilars—follow-on versions of biopharmaceuticals following patent expiry—with the first two marketed products (human growth hormone Omnitrope and anemia medicine Binocrit). A third product, oncology medicine Zarzio, was approved in 2009.

Consumer health. The Consumer Health Division creates, develops, and manufactures a wide range of products designed to restore, maintain or improve the health and well-being of our customers. The division focuses on three business units: *Over-the-Counter.* Novartis Consumer Health, Inc. is a world leader in consumer healthcare, providing self-medication products for the treatment and prevention of common illness and conditions, and the enhancement of overall health and well-being. *Animal Health.* Novartis Animal Health focused on the well-being of companion animals and on the health and productivity of farm animals. *CIBA Vision.* CIBA Vision is a global leader in the research, development, and manufacturing of contact lenses and lens care products.

Source: www.novartis.com/about-novartis/our-businesses/index.shtml

CONCLUDING REMARKS

It should be clear by now that just as with industries and markets, there is no best way to define the boundaries of a business (Abell, 1980). However, defining a firm's business (and businesses) may be the most important strategic question that corporate managers face; it provides the context for considering all other strategic questions in the firm. For example, the question of vertical integration discussed in Chapter 10 and the question of international diversification discussed in Chapter 14 require clear definition of the firm's business.

A business should be defined explicitly, just as the objectives for a business should be explicitly stated. When a business definition is not explicit, various undesirable consequences may result. First, acquisitions and new products emerge independently of one another, with each evaluated solely on its own merits. The consequence may be growth in customer groups, customer functions, and technologies, even as the company fails to consider or appreciate the long run benefits and the critical pitfalls that may be involved. The likely final outcome therefore involves a business unit defined in such a way to prevent both efficiency and effectiveness. Second, the failure to be explicit often means that significant changes in external elements, such as customer behavior or other environmental factors, never appear in the ongoing redefinition of the business. Third, without a clear, firm wide understanding of how the business is and shall be defined, there may be no clear sense of corporate mission. Thus, the myriad of strategic and tactical decisions that occur up and down the organizational ladder likely lack coherence and internal consistency.

Being explicit about a business's definition means, at a minimum, establishing screening procedures that channel the firm's growth into areas of maximum opportunity and competitive advantage, from both incremental and overall points of view. Screening procedures must incorporate efficiency and effectiveness criteria into examinations of any new opportunity. This step forces clear recognition of the impact of new business additions on the overall business definition. In most cases, and perhaps despite the fears of some members of the firm, screening procedures do not promote growth in one dimension to the exclusion of others. Rather, balanced growth may create a predominance of one dimension over others, but the key purpose of screening is to channel that growth into directions that concentrate rather than fragment the firm's key resources.

Furthermore, explicitness about business definition needs to proceed another step, beyond simply screening. That is, the business definition should become a central element within the overall corporate strategic plan. Thus, customer behavior, resource requirements, cost behavior, and company competences require regular analyses, with a view to defining the business in a competitively superior manner. Therefore, an explicit definition of the business becomes a guide for new product development and acquisition policies, rather than simply a passive screen against which to evaluate incremental options.

There is, of course, no single right way to define a business. Two competitors may coexist and succeed, even if they define their businesses in two quite different ways. However, certain trade-offs are evident. A broad definition along the customer group dimension usually results in efficiencies in manufacturing and R&D, but it also may induce fragmentation in sales, distribution, and service activities. Entrants into new and unfamiliar markets often find that they may have products and technologies to satisfy a customer need, but they have no established channels, sales personnel, or service force to reach these targets. In a panicked response, they may establish small, inefficient sales and service organizations to deal with each emerging end user customer group.

In contrast, a broad definition along the customer function dimension runs the corollary risk of potential fragmentation in the firm's technological and manufacturing resources. Strategic alliances might compensate partially for this risk, but firms still could find themselves having to embrace a wide range of technical and manufacturing capabilities. Such diverse capabilities could be offset by efficiencies in other areas though, such as sales, distribution, and service, because the same marketing organization handles all products that serve the several customer functions.

Finally, a broad definition along the technological dimension, as with breadth in customer functions, runs the risk of fragmented manufacturing and R&D. In this case though, there may not be any offsetting gains in marketing efficiency, especially if the products that result from the different technologies each require specialized channels, sales, or services.

Abell's (1980) three dimensional framework provides a means to consider, weight, and balance all these factors explicitly and for any particular situation. Yet this approach cannot be of assistance if the business definition is conceptualized only in conventional product/market terms. The relative desirability of selling an overall system rather than a narrow line of products to many different customers, or else a broad line of products based on competing technologies, simply cannot be compared in just two dimensions. Managers concerned with corporate level strategy formulation therefore should think about their businesses in terms of their customer groups, customer functions served, and technologies utilized. This vital first step leads toward an explicit business definition.

As argued in this chapter, defining the business is critical. Ultimately though, this definition requires choosing which business to enter and which business not to enter, and that choice determines the long term success of a corporate level strategy (Collis & Montgomery, 2005). An important predictor of firm performance involves the profitability of the industries in which it competes (Montgomery & Wernerfelt, 1988; Rumelt, 1991; Schmalensee, 1985)—a finding that appears true not only for single business firms but also for firms that operate in multiple businesses (Collis & Montgomery, 2005). The underlying economics of the industries in which a firm competes therefore play instrumental roles in determining its performance (Porter, 1980). The *attractiveness test* (Porter, 1987), which we discuss in the next chapter, therefore provides an early step a firm must take to assess the corporate value creating potential of a diversification strategy.

Chapter

5

DIVERSIFICATION STRATEGIES

CREATING CORPORATE VALUE

■ ■ ■ ■ ■ ■

Diversification into new business areas can be economically justified only if it leads to value creation. Therefore, the mere existence of economies of scope is a necessary but not a sufficient condition for diversification to be economically valuable (Barney, 2007). Rather, economic value derives from economies of scope that both exist and are less costly to realize within the boundaries of the firm than they would be through alternative forms of governance, such as market transactions or strategic alliances (Teece, 1980; Williamson, 1975, 1985; Ye et al., 2012).

For example, a diversified firm might create value by spreading its risk across multiple businesses. Most of the time, cash flows from different businesses do not correlate perfectly, so the riskiness of the cash flows of diversified firms should be lower than that of single business firms (for a demonstration, see Barney, 2007). Yet even if a firm reduces its overall risk by engaging in a portfolio of businesses, these risk reducing strategies are not necessarily valuable to the firm's outside investors or shareholders, who tend to have their own, lower cost ways to reduce their risk (Chang & Thomas, 1989; Williamson, 1975). For example, they could invest directly through the stock market in their own diversified portfolio; doing so usually is much less costly than conceiving and implementing a corporate diversification strategy. Moreover, most investors modify their portfolios easily and cheaply by buying or selling stocks. In contrast, modifying a firm's portfolio of businesses, through M&A, internal development, or other means (see Chapters 10 and 11), tends to be far more costly. For these reasons, outside investors generally prefer to diversify their own portfolios to reduce risk by themselves rather than have managers diversify for them (Jensen, 1968; Jensen & Meckling, 1976). Empirical research in several industries also suggests that when firms pursue diversification strategies solely to reduce shareholders' risk, the strategies actually harm the economic performance of these firms on average (e.g., Amit & Livnat, 1988a; Hill & Hansen, 1991). However, as shown in Box 5.1, diversifying in order to spread risk may be rational from a stakeholder perspective in specific cases.

For a diversified firm to create value for its shareholders, Goold and colleagues (Campbell et al., 1995; Goold et al., 1994) propose that the corporate headquarters—which they refer to as corporate parents—should serve merely as an intermediary between shareholders and the business (see Figure 5.1). As would any intermediary, the corporate parent must justify its existence by creating additional value, beyond simple risk reduction. Goold et al. (1994) further argue that business units create value (i.e., business value) through their direct contacts with customers, whereas the corporate parent, which lacks any external customers, only generates costs, not revenues. An important test for the corporate parent, as an intermediary, therefore becomes whether it can create value (i.e., corporate value) for its businesses in any other forms. If they were stand-alone firms, would the company's business units perform better or worse, in aggregate?

BOX 5.1 SPREADING RISK FROM A STAKEHOLDER PERSPECTIVE

Whereas diversifying to spreading risk is not economically rationale from a shareholder perspective, it may be rationale from a stakeholder point of view. From a shareholder point of view diversification is a costly way of spreading risk as the can invest in multiple firms at almost zero cost. However, several stakeholders, such as managers, employees, or customers, cannot spread risk at low cost by themselves, therefore in such cases diversification may create value for these stakeholders by reducing the risk of the firm's bankruptcy.

From an agency theory point of view, diversification for risk reduction is the negative outcome of conflicts between shareholders and managers, since it reduces managers' employment risk, but at the expense of the shareholders of the firm (Amihud & Lev, 1981). However, from an RBV perspective, diversification for risk reduction may be potentially valuable for both shareholders and employees (including managers), because it encourages employees to invest in firm specific knowledge and skills (Wang & Barney, 2006). Indeed, according to RBV, firm specific assets, especially intangible ones, are a source of sustainable competitive advantage (Furrer et al., 2001; Wang et al., 2009). However, employees might be reluctant to invest in firm specific knowledge and skills because the represent sunk costs that are not valuable outside the firm (Dierickx & Cool, 1989), and would place them in a weak bargaining position, which might result in a hold-up situation (Wang et al., 2009). Therefore, without effective safeguard or substantial trust between them and the firm, employees will not invest in firm specific knowledge and skills. Diversification in related businesses (less perfectly correlated with the firm's core business) might reduce the risk of bankruptcy, which is valuable for the employees, but it will also ensure that employees with firm specific knowledge and skill can be transferred from one business to the other, rather than being fired if their current business is failing (Wang & Barney, 2006).

However, Goold et al. (1994) also recognize that the creation of net value is only one side of the coin, so the value that the corporate parent creates also should be benchmarked against the value derived from alternative ownership structures (e.g., joint ventures) or alternative parents (e.g., a competitor). That is, does the corporate parent create more value for its businesses than they could attain with any alternative owner, such as outside investors, or any other corporate parent? If so, in relative terms, the corporate parent destroys rather than creates corporate value.

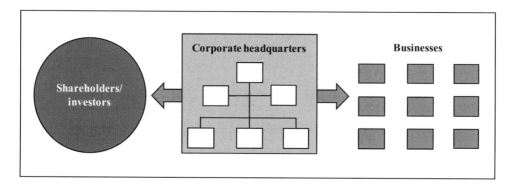

Figure 5.1 The corporate headquarters as an intermediary

Source: Adapted from Goold et al. (1994)

To assess the corporate value-creating potential of a multibusiness firm formally, Porter (1987) developed three tests to ensure a diversification strategy creates economic value:

- **The attractiveness test**. To be a potential target for the diversification efforts of a firm, a business "must be structurally attractive, or capable of being made attractive" (Porter, 1987, p. 47). In other words, firms should enter businesses only when the chances are good that they can build a profitable competitive position. Each new business must be judged in terms of its competitive forces and the opportunities available to it to sustain a competitive advantage.

  The attractiveness test consists of a rigorous examination of the business' external environment as a means to establish its long-term average profitability (Collis & Montgomery, 2005). The most often used tool to conduct such an analysis is Porter's 'five forces' framework, which assesses the degree of rivalry, the threat of new entrants, the threat of substitutes, the bargaining power of suppliers, and the bargaining power of buyers (Porter, 1980).

  Campbell et al. (2014) suggest that the attractiveness of a business can also be assessed by calculating the average profitability of the competitors in the market. If the average profitability is significantly above the cost of entry, the business is attractive. If the average profitability is significantly below the cost of entry, then the business in unattractive. This leads to the second of Porter's test, the cost of entry test.

- **The cost of entry test**. Simply, "The cost of entry must not capitalize all the future profits" (Porter, 1987, p. 47). Firms should enter a new business only if it is possible to recoup the investments required to do so. Although important for internally generated new business ventures, this requirement is absolutely critical for external acquisitions. Diversification can create economic value only if the firm purchases or develops businesses for less than the value of their marginal productivity, in combination with its current businesses (Makadok, 2001).

  Empirical research shows that on average, firms significantly overpay for acquisitions, which makes it virtually impossible to compensate for the value they give away during the purchase process (e.g., Cornett et al., 2003; Jensen, 1988; Sirower, 1997). Barney (1986) even argues that if the market for corporate control is reasonably competitive and efficient, systematically increasing a firm's *ex ante* expected profit through diversification is possible only if the firm has superior information about how valuable the new business is, in the combination with its existing portfolio of businesses.

- **The better off test**. Either the new unit must gain a competitive advantage from its link with the corporation, or the corporation must benefit from linking with the new unit (Porter, 1987). In other words, firms should enter new businesses when it is possible to create significant synergies. If it is not the case, the new unit would be better off as an independent firm or with a different parent company, cut loose from the focal corporation.

  This third test is consistent with Goold and colleagues' (Campbell et al., 1995; Goold et al., 1994) view of the corporate parent as an intermediary—that is, can the firm create value (i.e., corporate value) for the business, or would the business perform better as a stand-alone firm or with another parent? This test should be conduced when the firm wants to diversify its activity, but it also should be part of any periodic review of the firm's portfolio. Are our businesses worth more inside our portfolio or outside the firm?

In the next step, the firm needs to investigate several challenging questions: if business value derives from the revenues generated by the relationship between the business units and their customers, how is corporate value created? What are the mechanisms through which a corporate parent creates value for its business and shareholders? What is the dominant logic behind the firm's corporate level strategy? How can a business pass Porter's three tests?

Within a multibusiness firms, corporate value emerges through three broad mechanisms: (1) operating economies of scope; (2) financial economies of scope; and (3) anticompetitive economies

Diversification strategies | **63**

of scope (e.g., Barney, 2007; Collis & Montgomery, 2005; Dess et al., 2008; Goold & Campbell, 1998; Goold et al., 1994; Hitt et al., 2004; Markides, 2002; Porter, 1985, 1987) (see Table 5.1).

This chapter reviews all three mechanisms in turn.

BOX 5.2 DEMAND SIDE SYNERGIES

Most of strategy research has emphasized producer side synergies obtainable from corporate diversification, as those summarized in Table 5.1. However, synergies can also be created from the consumer side or demand side. For example, Priem (2007) and Tanriverdi and Lee (2008) show that consumer benefits occurs when knowledge developed while using one product can be transferred to reduce the learning time required to use a related product (e.g., an iPhone and an iPad). Consumer benefits that translate into higher willingness to pay and increased revenues for the diversified firm. Thus, consumer based synergies can create value independently from producer side synergies.

Consumer synergies can be defined as a means to create increased value for consumers by offering product and/or service combinations that together expand the consumer utilities offered by the individual products or services (Ye et al., 2012). Servitization, this is offering services complementarily to tangible product, is an example of such a combination providing value for consumers (Furrer, 2010). Consumer synergies can be obtained even through diversification strategies that would be viewed as unrelated from the producer side (Ye et al., 2012).

Ye et al. (2012) provide two examples of diversification strategies to create demand side synergies: (1) the concept of one stop shopping, wherein a collocated assortment of products or services is offered to consumers, as in the case of combining a gasoline station and a convenience store or locating side by side a bookstore and a coffee shop; and (2) two side markets, wherein cross group externalities result in complementary increases in consumer utility, as in speed dating services offering platforms to link the male and female sides of the dating market.

Amazon.com is a recent web based example of a one stop shopping diversification strategy that provides value to customers by providing them the opportunity to purchase a variety of items at the same place. eBay is an example of a two side market in which an increase in buyers makes listings on the site more attractive to sellers, and an increase in sellers makes the site more attractive to buyers.

Table 5.1 Corporate value creating mechanisms

Operational economies of scope

- Sharing resources and activities
- Transferring skills and leveraging core competencies

Financial economies of scope

- Portfolio management or efficient internal capital market
- Business restructuring
- Tax advantages

Anticompetitive economies of scope

- Using bargaining power
- Vertical integration
- Multipoint competition

OPERATIONAL ECONOMIES OF SCOPE

To achieve operational economies of scope, firms should build on or extend their resources, capabilities, and core competencies and thereby create additional corporate value (Capron, 1999; Doukas & Lang, 2003). These operational economies of scope are available to firms that operate in multiple businesses, and they entail the cost savings that arise when the cost of the combined production of several products or services is lower than the cost of producing each product or service separately (Panzar & Willig, 1981).

Firms can create corporate value from operational economies of scope through two basic mechanisms: **sharing activities** (Ansoff, 1965; Goold & Campbell, 1998; Porter, 1985; Rumelt, 1974; Teece, 1980) and **transferring or leveraging corporate core competencies** (Grant, 1988; Nelson & Winter, 1982; Prahalad & Bettis, 1986; Winter, 1987). The difference between the two mechanisms reflects the use of separate resources to create economies of scope. Tangible resources, such as plants and equipment, must be shared to create economies of scope (Porter, 1985). Although less tangible resources, such as manufacturing know-how, can be shared (Schroeder et al., 2002), such joint activities suggest a transfer of know-how between separate businesses, such that the core competence has been transferred rather than shared.

Sharing resources and activities

Firms can create operational economies of scope by sharing resources or activities. A business unit might potentially share any value based activity with another business unit in the firm, including both primary (e.g., inventory delivery systems) and supporting (e.g., purchasing practices) activities (Porter, 1985), as Figure 5.2 shows.

Traditionally, operational economies of scope through resource sharing originated from the firm's production processes (e.g., sharing a production site to manufacture both cars and trucks). Today, firms rely more on economies of scope that do not relate directly to their production process (Collis & Montgomery, 2005). Instead, they share R&D, sales and marketing, distribution, transportation, and overhead capabilities, which offer greater potential for economies of scope. For example, Nestlé Waters invested in a R&D center dedicated to water that its various bottled water brands all can access (see Box 5.3).

Intangible assets such as corporate reputations and brand names also might be shared across businesses. As Montgomery and Wernerfelt (1992) show that using the same brand name, through a practice called umbrella branding, enables firms to reduce their risk and create more corporate value. Virgin, with its music, airlines, and mobile phones (to name just a few), offers a good example of a diversified firm that benefits from the same brand name across a variety of businesses. Indeed, part of Virgin success is attributable to its strong brand image (i.e., edgy, risk taking, exciting) (see Box 6.2 in the next chapter). The study by Hitt et al. (2001a) illustrates how synergies can be obtained at diversified law firms through knowledge sharing across multiple legal service areas.

Sharing resources and activities creates corporate value only if it lowers the cost or enhances differentiation levels enough to exceed the costs of sharing, provided that sharing is difficult for competitors to match (Porter, 1985). Porter (1985) argues that sharing an activity provides a significant cost advantage when it involves an activity that represents a significant fraction of the operating costs or assets, though the sharing also must lower the cost of performing the activity. If the cost of an activity is driven by economies of scale, learning, or the pattern of capacity utilization, sharing has a stronger potential to reduce costs. Because it increases scale of an activity and the rate of learning (if learning is a function of cumulative volume, that is, the learning curve effect), sharing also may improve the pattern of capacity utilization, assuming involved business units employ the focal activity at different times. If scale, learning, and patterns of utilization are not important cost drivers, sharing probably will raise costs.

Diversification strategies

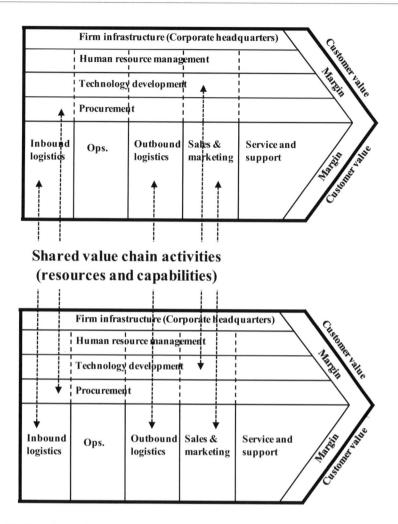

Figure 5.2 Sharing value chain activities
Source: Adapted from Porter (1985)

Furthermore, sharing might enhance differentiation if it increases the uniqueness of an activity or reduces the cost of being unique (Porter, 1985). In this sense, sharing is most important to differentiation if it affects those activities that are most important for creating or signaling value. In the Nestlé Waters example in Box 5.1, sharing the R&D center enhances differentiation because differentiation in this market depends heavily on innovation. Thus, sharing can make an activity more unique directly, or it might do so through other drivers of uniqueness (Porter, 1985). In the former case, for example, a shared activity, such as selling different products through the same channel, becomes is more valuable to buyers when it involves more than one business unit, which makes their purchase more convenient. The indirect effect likely flows through the impact of the cost of differentiation on the cost drivers of differentiating activities. For example, by relying on shared procurement, two small bakeries in the same town might lower the cost of purchasing premium grains and heritage quality fruits. However, additional complexity represents a cost of sharing, which must be weighted against the benefits.

BOX 5.3 NESTLÉ'S NEW PRODUCT TECHNOLOGY CENTER, WATER

Paris, September 8, 2004—Nestlé Waters officially inaugurated Nestlé's first R&D center entirely dedicated to water, on September 7 in Vittel, France. Frits van Dijk, Nestlé Waters CEO, and Werner Bauer, Nestlé's executive vice president, technical, attended the inauguration. The Product Technology Center, Water (PTC, Water) is intended to gather all knowledge necessary to rapidly and sustainably develop Nestlé Waters' business activities. It brings together a wide range of expertise from the environment to science, technology and basic research, thanks to a multidisciplinary team of 80 specialists. The creation of the center required an investment of €8 million.

The main missions of this R&D center are focused on: (1) experimenting with new industrial processes to improve plant performances; (2) defining and implementing new analysis techniques to guarantee high quality products; (3) compiling data and developing models to provide and share water related information and practices among all Nestlé Group units in a timely fashion; and (4) quickly developing new products and packaging (innovation and renovation) to satisfy ever evolving consumer expectations.

In a highly competitive market, innovation and renovation play a major role in a brand's life. They help energize the brand's image while enhancing consumer loyalty and attracting new consumers. Recent Nestlé Waters' innovations include a new 2 liter Vittel bottle with integrated handle; Perrier Fluo and its surprising array of flavors; and the Contrex flavored range.

Source: www.press.nestle-waters.com

Sharing activities always involve a cost. Businesses must modify their behavior in some way, and doing so can induce three types of costs (Porter, 1985): the cost of coordination, the cost of compromise, and the cost of inflexibility.

Coordination costs. Businesses must coordinate their scheduling and priorities, as well as resolve any conflicts, before they can share activities. Such coordination demands costs in the form of time, personnel, and money (Porter, 1985). Moreover, the costs of coordination reflect added complexity associated with a shared activity. Activity sharing in particular may demand shared strategic control over business units and thereby create additional overhead (or corporate) costs. For example, if a business manager believes another unit receives a disproportionate share of the joint gains created, conflicts between unit managers likely arise, which then reduces their collaboration and thus the amount of synergy created. To ensure collaboration, costly control mechanisms and incentive systems probably must be installed (Hoskisson & Hitt, 1988; Nayyar, 1992).

Compromise costs. Sharing an activity requires that the activity be performed in a consistent way, which may not be optimal for either business involved (Porter, 1985). For example, sharing a brand name could dilute the brand value. Furthermore, sharing almost inevitably involves a trade-off between generalists and specialists, so a shared marketing department may be able to handle different types of product, but it cannot specialize in any one of them.

Inflexibility costs. Finally, inflexibility takes two forms: potential difficulties in responding to competitive moves and exit barriers. If two businesses share a production facility, difficulties would clearly emerge if one of them decided to switch its production technology to improve its competitiveness. Exit barriers also arise when the ties between the business units create links between their outcomes. If demand for one business's product falls, there may not be sufficient revenues to cover the fixed costs needed to operate the shared facilities. Such inflexibilities reduce the likely success of shared activity and resource sharing as sources of corporate value (Marks & Mirvis, 2000); they also create rigidities (Leonard-Barton, 1992).

Yet despite the costs and risk associated with activity sharing, research shows that it generally creates value. For example, studies examining the acquisitions of firms in the same industry (i.e. related businesses) show that sharing resources and activities, and thereby creating operational economies of scope, leads to post acquisition increases in performance and higher returns to shareholders (Brush, 1996; Delong, 2001; Park, 2003; Zhang, 1995). Firms that sell off related units that helped produce economies of scope through resource sharing instead produced lower returns, especially compared with companies that sold off businesses unrelated to their core business (Bergh, 1995). Moreover, firms with more related units enjoy lower risk (Lubatkin & Chatterjee, 1994). Thus, creating economies of scope by sharing activities across businesses may be an important means to create corporate value. Even more appealing results emerge from activity sharing when a strong corporate headquarters facilitates it (Kono, 1999; Van Oijen & Douma, 2000).

The issues related to the limits of the scope of firms receive a further, more detailed treatment in Chapter 7. Chapter 8 outlines the role of corporate headquarters in efforts to achieve economies of scope, and the control and coordination mechanisms appear in Chapter 9.

Transferring skills and leveraging core competencies

The second mechanism associated with operational economies of scope is the leverage of core competencies, which generally means transferring skills from one business to another (Porter, 1985, 1987; Prahalad & Hamel, 1990) or from the parent to the lower level businesses (Campbell et al., 1995; Goold et al., 1994). As it operates a single business unit, a firm can gain know-how that it then might apply to other businesses and thereby improve their operations. Transferring such know-how can potentially create corporate value. For example, Tsai (2001) shows how the transfer of human and economic resources can contribute to business unit innovativeness and performance. The transfer of skill and competencies can move in either direction—from existing to new business units or from new business units back to existing units—and can occur anywhere in the value chain (Porter, 1985). Moreover, when the corporate parent transfers skills and competencies to its businesses, it should create corporate value through a parenting advantage (Campbell et al., 1995; Goold et al., 1994). For example, General Electric's 'Six Sigma' quality program offers a valuable, rare, and costly to imitate corporate resource that the firm exploits across each of its lines of business (Armstrong & Shimizu, 2007). Corporate headquarters also should improve its own businesses' plans and budgets and provide especially competent central functions, such as legal, financial, human resource management, and procurement functions. These resources represent core competencies that can be leveraged widely across many products and markets (Hamel & Prahalad, 1990).

According to Porter (1985), the transfer of skills and competencies leads to corporate value when the improvement in the cost of differentiation in the business unit receiving the know-how exceeds the costs of transferring it (Capron & Pistre, 2002). Therefore, the know-how residing in one business must have been paid for already, and transferring it must involve little cost compared with the cost of developing it anew.

The intangibility of the skills and competencies transferred offers a second source of corporate value creation (Furrer et al., 2001). That is, intangible assets are difficult for competitors to understand and imitate (Prahalad & Hamel, 1990), so the unit receiving a transferred competence should gain an immediate competitive advantage over its rivals (Spencer, 2003). However, transferring skills and competencies also always involves some cost, such as the time of skilled personnel involved with the transfer or the need to protect against the leakage of proprietary information outside the firm during the transfer.

For the transfer of skill and competencies to create corporate value, the business units involved should display some similarities. Porter (1985) identifies four key similarities: (1) generic competitive strategy (e.g., low cost, differentiation), (2) types of buyers, (3) configuration of value, or (4) important value activities. Even if activities are not shared, similarities among businesses imply that the know-how gained by one business could be valuable and transferable to another (Furrer et al., 2001).

Just as is the case for sharing activities and resources, the transfer of skills does not guarantee operational economies of scope. In particular, transferring expertise in manufacturing based businesses often fails to improve performance (St John & Harrison, 1999). Moreover, corporate parents often facilitate competency transfers by moving key personnel into new management positions in a different business unit (Bartlett et al., 2008). But a business manager of a division may be reluctant to transfer those personnel with the most accumulated knowledge and experience, because they are critical to the division's success. In turn, managers with the ability to facilitate the transfer of a core competence come at a premium, and the key personnel may not want to transfer. Top level managers from the transferring division similarly may not want their strong competencies moved over to a new division, just to fulfill the firm's diversification objectives. However, for businesses that enjoy improved performance, the result is often a corporate passion for the pursuit of skill transfers and appropriate coordination mechanisms for realizing operational economies of scope, as Box 5.4 describes.

The transfer of skills and competencies also might move from the corporate parent to businesses through the use of corporate core competencies, that is, the complex sets of resources and capabilities that link different businesses together, primarily through managerial and technological knowledge, experience, and expertise (Capron et al., 1998; Chatterjee & Wernerfelt, 1991; Kotabe et al., 2003; Mehra, 1996). These corporate competencies act as central functions that help businesses achieve budgets, plans, and other strategic decisions, including acquisitions, divestures, and new internal developments. Such corporate capabilities also help businesses increase their revenues and profits (as Chapter 8, regarding the role of the parent, makes clear).

FINANCIAL ECONOMIES OF SCOPE

A second category of corporate value creation mechanisms relates to the financial advantages associated with diversification. For example, effective portfolio management and efficient internal capital allocations can enhance value through the development of an internal capital market, which is more efficient than the external market and reduces the firm's cost of capital (Porter, 1987). Another type of financial economy involves the purchase other firms. By restructuring of their assets, this second approach diversifies the company's assets and enables it to operate more profitably; it also can sell the acquired company for a profit in the external market later (Porter, 1987). Finally, financial economies of scope may come from the tax advantages for diversified firms compared with a single business firm. For example, a diversified firm can use losses in some of its businesses to offset profits in others, which reduces its overall tax liability. Diversification also can increase a firm's debt capacity, creating corporate value in tax environments in which interest payments on debt are tax deductible.

Portfolio management or efficient internal capital markets

Porter (1987) identifies portfolio management as one of two value creating strategies that firms with unrelated businesses can use, though this strategy adds little real value to the firm's various businesses, which run autonomously with minimal corporate involvement. An unrelated portfolio of businesses instead achieves corporate value through two main mechanisms: (1) the ability to identify and acquire businesses that are undervalued, along with a willingness to sell any business for an opportunistically high price, and (2) the ability to create an internal capital market that is more efficient than the external capital market in terms of allocating resources to business units.

BOX 5.4 GLOBALIZING AND LOCALIZING MANUFACTURING AT TOYOTA: THE ROLE OF THE GLOBAL PRODUCTION CENTER

There are a number of hurdles that the globalization of production has to overcome. Among these the most important is "quality assurance," which requires that "no matter where Toyota vehicles are made, they have the same quality." To put it another way, we don't put a label on our vehicles which says "Made in such and such a country;" we put the same label on all vehicles which reads "Made by TOYOTA." Toyota believes that the way to achieve "quality assurance" and to "spread the Toyota Way" is by educating people: "Making things is about developing people." So, in 2003, we established the Global Production Center (GPC) within the Motomachi Plant in Toyota City.

Before 2003, when Toyota had a "mother plant system," the personnel development for overseas production bases took place primarily at mother plants in Japan. However, as overseas facilities have expanded in line with the increase in overseas production, the instructional content provided to personnel has become different and varied. This phenomenon was responsible for the realization that something needed to be done to more strongly reinforce the "Made by TOYOTA" thinking. In order to ensure quality, Toyota needed to establish "best practices" for itself and then spread these to all of its affiliates; and the organization created to carry out this mission is the Global Production Center (GPC).

The GPC was established within the Motomachi Plant in July 2003. Outstanding personnel from the various Toyota plants within Japan were assembled to determine what Toyota's "best practices" should be, and then company-wide initiatives were begun with the aim of achieving global quality assurance. The two main activities and achievements of the GPC are: "Human Resources Development" and "Localization of Model Switchovers."

Toyota's human resources development training program is geared towards developing supervisors and trainers at overseas bases as well as employees, assistants and supervisors from Toyota's headquarters who are going overseas. As of November 2006, approximately 5,000 people have been through Toyota's human resources development training program.

Another activity the GPC is involved with is helping plant personnel learn how to prepare for the production of redesigned and/or different vehicle models, so that, when new models of global vehicle series such as the Corolla come out, plants can efficiently switch over to making them. Traditionally, when it came time to switch production to a new model, a number of employees from Japan would be dispatched to overseas bases to support the switchover. Now, during an early stage of the switchover preparations, members from all of the overseas affiliates gather at the GPC to refine the design drawings and confirm feasibility of implementation. The overall effect this has had on preparations for production of redesigned and/or different models has been to reduce by half the number of support man-hours required.

In order to make the globalization of the GPC training system even faster, in 2006 GPC offices were opened in the United States, the United Kingdom and Thailand and have begun skills training and human resource development within the North American, European and Asia-Pacific regions respectively. This expansion has further solidified the "Made by TOYOTA" philosophy.

Source: www.toyota.co.jp/en/vision/globalization/gpc.html

Therefore, the logic of portfolio management concepts requires several vital assumptions (Bettis & Hall, 1981; Pidun et al., 2011; Porter, 1987). If a firm's diversification plan involves meeting the attractiveness and cost of entry tests, it must find good but undervalued firms or businesses. The acquired firms must be truly undervalued, because the corporate parent does little for the new unit once it is acquired. To meet the better off test, the benefits that the corporate parent provides then must yield a significant corporate advantage to the acquired units. Finally, the operating style across the highly autonomous business units must both lead to sound business strategies and motivate managers, as Bayer's and Haniel's statement in Box 5.5 suggests.

BOX 5.5 PORTFOLIO MANAGEMENT AT BAYER AND HANIEL

Bayer's 2010 mission statement. [Bayer is a German multinational chemical and pharmaceutical company founded in Barmen, Germany in 1863 and headquartered in Leverkusen, Germany.] A core element of our corporate strategy is rigorous value management. Our performance-related compensation systems reward and incentivize the achievement of our value-creation targets. Portfolio management will continue to play a crucial role in the Bayer Group. We aim to continue improving our market positions through strategic acquisitions and alliances. We will divest activities that in the long term are unlikely to yield a return exceeding their capital costs.

Source: www.bayerandina.com/descargas/bayer-mission-statement-2010-10-01.pdf

Haniel's portfolio strategy in 2013. Haniel [German family-owned group of companies with the holding company headquartered in Duisburg, Germany] manages a diversified portfolio, pursuing a sustainable long-term investment strategy as a value developer. With the expertise of the employees at the holding company, Haniel offers its shareholdings crucial added value in development and professionalization, a clear value orientation as a framework for activities, and a high level of reliability in terms of the holding period for its shareholdings. Haniel has set itself the goal of expanding the portfolio to comprise up to 10 shareholdings. Investments come into question only if they are a good fit for the company and the values it puts into practice. This ensures a close-meshed investment filter that examines the potential business models with regard to criteria including how much of a contribution they make to the diversification of Haniel's portfolio, how sustainable they are, and whether they can generate an appropriate value contribution for further growth.

Source: www.haniel.com/en/company/strategy/

In large diversified firms, corporate headquarters distributes capital to business units to create value for the overall firm, which could provide gains from the internal capital market allocation relative to the external capital market (Williamson, 1975). While managing the firm's portfolio of businesses, the corporate office should gain access to detailed and accurate information regarding the businesses' actual and prospective performance. During the 1970s and early 1980s, several leading consulting firms developed portfolio matrices to depict the competitive position of a firm's overall portfolio of businesses, suggest alternatives for each of the businesses, and identify priorities for capital and resource allocations (the matrices and their usages appear in Chapter 8, together with the role of the parent).

However, the potential for corporate value creation through portfolio management is often limited, because in a market economy, capital markets should allocate capital efficiently. If this assumption holds true, an internal capital market likely cannot be more efficient. But in certain situations, external capital markets clearly fail. In particular, compared with corporate office personnel, investors have relatively limited access to internal information and can only estimate divisional performance and future business prospects. Businesses seeking capital must provide information to potential suppliers (e.g., banks, insurance companies), but firms with internal capital markets enjoy at least two informational advantages. First, the information provided to capital markets, through such sources as annual reports, rarely include negative information and instead emphasize positive prospects and outcomes. The external sources of capital in turn have only limited ability to understand the operational dynamics of the large organizations; even those external shareholders with access to information have no guarantee of full and complete disclosure. Second, a firm must disseminate information, so the information becomes simultaneously available to current and potential competitors. With insights gained from studying such information, competitors might duplicate a firm's competitive advantage. In contrast, an ability to allocate capital efficiently through an internal market may help the firm protect its competitive advantages.

If, to make corrections to capital allocations, the firm requires intervention from outside, significant changes are likely, such as forcing the firm into bankruptcy or changing the top management team. Alternatively, in an internal capital market, the corporate office can fine-tune corrections, such as adjusting managerial incentives or suggesting strategic changes in a division. Thus, capital might be allocated according to more specific criteria than would be possible with external market allocations. Furthermore, with its lack of accurate information, the external capital market could fail to allocate resources adequately to high potential investments rather than corporate office investments. The corporate office of a diversified company can perform such tasks more effectively, including disciplining underperforming management teams through resource allocations (Miller, D. et al., 2002; Raynor & Bower, 2001; Taylor & Lowe, 1995).

Yet in efficient capital markets, the unrelated diversification strategy instead may be discounted (Campa & Kedia, 2002; Kwak, 2001; Lamont & Polk, 2001; Rajan et al., 2000). For example:

> stock markets have applied a 'conglomerate discount': they value diversified manufacturing conglomerates at 20 per cent less, on average, than the value of the sum of their parts. The discount still applies, in good economic times and bad. Extraordinary manufacturers (like GE) can defy it for a while, but more ordinary ones (like Philips and Siemens) cannot.
>
> (*Economist*, 2001)

Although diversified firms may gain significant financial benefits from using internal markets for capital and other resources (Grant, 2008; Ravenscraft & Scherer, 1987; Rumelt, 1982; Taylor & Lowe, 1995; Williamson, 1986), empirical support for this argument is not universal (Palich et al., 2000). Bhide (1990; see also Comment & Jarrell, 1995; Markides, 1992; Matsusaka, 1993) argues that internal market advantages from diversification were prevalent in the 1960s, but the information asymmetries that produced this edge diminished during the 1970s and 1980s due to economic, technological, and regulatory changes.

The main weakness of portfolio management in developed economies is that the corporate value created through this strategy has a fairly short life cycle because financial economies are more easily duplicated by competitors than are the gains derived from operational relatedness and corporate relatedness. However, this is less of a problem in emerging economies, where the absence of a soft infrastructure (including effective financial intermediaries, sound regulations, and contract laws) supports and encourages the use of portfolio management (Khanna & Rivkin, 2001). In fact, in emerging economies, diversification increases the performance of firms affiliated with large diversified business groups (Khanna & Palepu, 2000a, 2000b). Consequently, many firms are still using portfolio management strategies (Amit & Livnat, 1988b; Denis et al., 1999); these firms are found in several Eastern European countries and throughout emerging economies, where the external capital market is less efficient (Whittington et al., 1999).

Portfolio management primarily has been a concern for the management of an efficient internal capital market, but as Box 5.6 describes, the argument also can extend to other types of resource markets, such as human resources and knowledge assets.

BOX 5.6 EXTENDING THE CAPITAL MARKET ARGUMENT

Markides (2002, p. 110) argues that the efficient internal capital market argument extends beyond the capital market and proposes that the diversified firm can act as an alternative to, for example, inefficient labor, legislative, and educational markets and institutions. Thus, the more inefficient the outside institutions, the greater the benefits that diversification could confer. Markides (1990, 1995) also uses this argument to explain why firms might refocus. Because outside institutions such as capital and labor markets have increased efficiency, diversification has lost some of its benefit; in turn, firms reduce their scope.

Business restructuring

Financial economies might emerge when firms learn how to create value by buying and selling other companies' assets in the external market (Chang & Singh, 1999; Hitt et al., 2001c; Porter, 1987). As in the real estate business, buying assets at low prices, restructuring them, and selling them at a price that exceeds their cost generates a positive return on the firm's invested capital (Ng & de Cock, 2002).

To create corporate value, business restructuring requires the firm to find either poorly performing firms with unrealized potential or firms in industries on the threshold of significant, positive change (Dess et al., 2008). The corporate parent intervenes, perhaps by selling parts of the business; infusing the business with new technologies, processes, and reward systems; changing the top management; reducing payroll or unnecessary sources of expenses; and changing strategies (Bowman & Singh, 1993). For example, Microsoft announced in July 2014 a restructuring plan to simplify its organization and align the recently acquired Nokia Devices and Services business with the company's corporate level strategy. The restructuring is expected to result in the elimination of up to 18,000 positions over time. At the completion of the restructuring process, the firm can either sell the business at a higher price and capture the added value or retain the business in its corporate portfolio and benefit from its financial and competitive advantages.

For the restructuring strategy to work, corporate headquarters must have the insight to detect undervalued firms (i.e., cost of entry test) or firms competing in high potential industries (i.e., the attractiveness test). It also must have the required skills and resources to improve the acquired businesses, as Box 5.7 implies. Creating financial economies by acquiring and restructuring other companies' assets requires in particular a good understanding of significant trade-offs. For example, success usually calls for a focus on mature, low technology businesses, which do not face the uncertainty of demand that marks high technology products. Otherwise, resource allocation decisions become too complex, creating information processing overload for the small corporate staffs of the unrelated diversified firms. High technology businesses often depend on human resources; these employees can leave or demand higher pay and appropriate or deplete the value of an acquired firm (Cascio, 2005; Coff, 2003). Thus, restructuring a service business can be a risky strategy.

Restructuring might involve changes in assets, capital structure, or management. Asset restructuring means the sale of unproductive assets or those that are peripheral; it also may involve

BOX 5.7 NOVARTIS ANNOUNCES AGREEMENT TO ACQUIRE CHIRON

Basel, October 31, 2005—Novartis announced today that it has entered into a definitive merger agreement with Chiron Corporation to acquire all of the remaining publicly held shares of Chiron it does not currently own. This transaction will strengthen Chiron's capabilities to better meet the needs of patients with high-quality vaccines and provide Novartis entry into this dynamic growth market. "Our plan is to turn around the Chiron vaccines business, which will require investments in R&D and manufacturing to increase quality and capacity, so that we can better meet customer demand and address public health needs. Together with the dynamically growing diagnostics business, vaccines will form a new division, while biopharmaceuticals will be integrated into the existing pharmaceuticals business of Novartis," said Daniel Vasella, Chairman and CEO of Novartis.

Source: www.uk.sandoz.com/site/en/company/news/news/detail/chiron2005.shtml

acquisitions that strengthen the core business. Capital restructuring suggests changing the debt–equity mix; management restructuring involves changes in the composition of the top management team, organization structure, or reporting relationships of the business. The strategies used to restructure a business or a portfolio of businesses, whether to turn them around or sell them off, are subject to more in depth discussion in Chapter 12.

Tax advantages

Finally, a financial economy of scope from diversification may stem from possible tax advantages, which reflect one or a combination of two effects (Barney, 2007). For example, a diversified firm can use losses in some of its businesses to offset profits in others, which would reduce its overall tax liability. As long as the business losses are not too large, the diversified firm's tax liability should decline. Empirical research suggests that diversified firms sometimes offset profits in some businesses with losses in others, though the tax savings tend to be small (Scott, 1977).

For example, multinational firms can manipulate transfer prices (i.e., prices of goods and services transferred between businesses of the firm) to reduce their tax liabilities and benefit from the differences in taxation across countries. If the corporate tax rate is higher in the parent firm's country than in one of its businesses' country, the parent could set a low transfer price on the products or services it sells to the business, which then keeps the taxable profits low in its own country but higher in the business country. The parent also might set a high transfer price on products sold to it by the business. Although the firm seemingly should be able to manipulate transfer prices to avoid tax liabilities, this ability does not mean the firm should perform this manipulation. Because this practice often violates at least the spirit of the law, the ethics of engaging in transfer pricing are dubious at best.

Diversification also can increase a firm's debt capacity, especially when the cash flows of the diversified firm's businesses are perfectly and negatively correlated. However, even if cash flows were perfectly and positively correlated, there may be a (more modest) increase in debt capacity. Debt capacity is particularly important in tax environments in which the interest payments on debt are tax deductible. In this context, diversified firms can increase their leverage up to debt capacity and reduce their tax liability accordingly. Empirical studies also suggest diversified firms enjoy greater debt capacity than undiversified firms (Berger & Ofek, 1995; Lewellen, 1971), though low marginal corporate tax rates, at least in the U.S., make the average accompanying tax savings relatively small (Stapleton, 1982).

ANTICOMPETITIVE ECONOMIES OF SCOPE

A third category of corporate value creating economies of scope derives from the reduction of competition. Because intense rivalry pushes prices downward, diversified firms can increase their benefits in ways that are not possible for single business firms by reducing the level of rivalry. Diversified firms use three mechanisms to reduce this level: market power, vertical integration, and multipoint competition.

Market power

Market power exists when a firm can sell its products at above the existing competitive level or reduce the costs of its primary and support activities below a competitive level, or both (Chatterjee & Singh, 1999; Porter, 1985). As discussed in Chapter 4, market power offers the main argument behind industrial organization (I/O) theory (Arnould, 1969; Berry, 1975; Gort, 1962; Utton, 1979). Diversification provides additional market power, which creates corporate value through cross-subsidization and pooled bargaining power.

Cross-subsidization

Internal allocations of capital may enable the firm to exploit, in some of its businesses, market power advantages it enjoys in other businesses. Suppose a firm earns monopoly profits in its business A. This firm can use some of the monopoly profits from A to subsidize the operations of another of its businesses—say, B. This cross-subsidization might take several forms, including predatory pricing, or setting prices lower than the subsidized business' costs (see Chapter 2). The effect of this cross-subsidy may be to drive competitors out of the subsidized business, in which case the firm can obtain monopoly profits. In a sense, diversification enables the firm to apply its monopoly power in several different businesses (e.g., B, C, and D). The objective market power economies of scope then enable the business to sustain losses caused by extremely low prices, long enough to force competitors out of business.

Managers experience limits on their ability to use market power to create corporate value through diversification, because government regulations often restrict owned shares of particular markets (Dess et al., 2006). Famously, in 2001, the European Union Commission blocked General Electric's (GE) attempt to acquire Honeywell, noting that GE's market power would have expanded significantly with the deal. In particular, GE would have supplied more than half of the parts needed to build several aircraft engines; therefore, according to the Commission, GE could have used its increased market power to dominate the aircraft engine parts market and push its rivals out of the market altogether (http://ec.europa.eu/competition/mergers/cases/decisions/m2220_en.pdf). A more recent case appears in Box 5.8.

Pooled bargaining power

Diversification also strengthens a firm's bargaining power relative to suppliers and customers and enhances its position with regard to its competitors. For example, compared with a small, single business food manufacturer, a multinational giant such as Nestlé can exercise much more bargaining power in negotiations with its suppliers and distributors, because in total, it makes far more and larger purchases from suppliers and provides a wide variety of products to distributors.

Vertical integration

Market power might also be achieved through vertical integration (Dess et al., 2006; Porter, 1980),

BOX 5.8 VETO FOR THE MERGER OF D&S AND FALABELLA

In May 2007, D&S, Chile's largest supermarket chain, which also has a sizable share of the country's financial and real estate sectors, and Falabella, a Chilean department store chain also active in finance, supermarkets, real estate, and home improvement stores, announced with great fanfare that they were planning to merge into a single conglomerate. When the news of the merger was announced, share prices for the two companies immediately shot up because the strategic hook-up would create the second largest retailing group in the Latin American region, second only to Wal-Mart's operations in Mexico. The new firm would have a market capitalization of more than $ 15 billion.

In June 2007, the two retailers presented their case for a merger before Chile's TDLC, the Court for the Defense of Free Competition, the institution responsible for safeguarding free competition in the marketplace. The TDLC did not approve or reject the corporate merger proposal, but the two firms had to present documents to the TDLC, in which they explained the objectives of their merger and outlined its positive impact on the market. As the companies saw it, the efficiency of Falabella, which provides consumer credit cards, married with D&S' skill in the supermarket sector, would trigger cost synergies and new economies of scale. All these gains in efficiency would generate additional savings by individuals, which would also benefit society, argued a report by independent economists. The study also showed that the merger would provide the newly expanded company with greater opportunities to globalize their operations. A greater capacity for globalization would lead to higher profits, and to benefits not only for foreign consumers and the owners of the merged firm, but also for some Chilean suppliers that would see their sales grow as a result of greater demand for their products as a result of this globalization process.

However, on January 31, 2008, the TDLC categorically rejected their merger application. Shares of both companies collapsed on the Chilean stock market, while local consumers rose up to applaud the court's decision. The key argument of the TDLC was that the Chilean retail sector is already very concentrated. The more concentrated it becomes, the greater the tendency for monopolistic practices that have a negative impact on consumers. The integration of D&S and Falabella would have created a new company with a market share of about 22 percent. Its closest competitor would have been Cencosud, which has a 12 percent share. Carrying out this merger would lead to enormous change in the structure of the market, creating an enterprise that would be the dominant player in integrated retailing as well as in practically all of its segments (department stores, home improvement, supermarkets, real estate and associated financial businesses.) The regulatory body also established that high barriers to entry would make it very unlikely that a newcomer could enter the market and compete within a reasonable period of time. The TDLC added that the merger would affect the purchasing decisions of Chileans and it would have harmful effects, in terms of well-being, on prices and on both the quantity and quality of products traded.

Source: Knowledge@Wharton, April 16, 2008, www.wharton.universia.net/index.cfm?fa= viewfeature&id=1505&language=english

---

which exists when a company produces its own inputs (backward integration) or owns its own source of output distribution (forward integration) (see Chapter 10). In some instances, firms may partially integrate their operations, producing and selling their products by using both firm businesses and outside sources. Market power increases as the firm develops its ability to minimize the costs of its operations, avoid market costs, improve product quality, and, possibly, protect its

Diversification strategies

technology from imitation by rivals (Chatterjee, 1991). Market power also blossoms when firms tie their assets strongly together, especially when no market prices exist. Establishing a market price results in high search and transaction costs, so firms seek to integrate vertically rather than remain separate businesses (Williamson, 1996).

Yet the limits to vertical integration become acute when an outside supplier produces the product at a lower cost. In this case, internal transactions through vertical integration may be more expensive and reduce the profitability of the firm relative to its competitors. Bureaucratic costs also often accompany vertical integration. Because vertical integration can require substantial investments in specific technologies, it may reduce the firm's flexibility, especially when technology changes quickly. Finally, changes in demand create capacity balance and coordination problems. If one division builds a part for another internal division, but achieving economies of scale requires the first division to manufacture quantities beyond the capacity of the internal buyer to absorb, it must sell the leftover parts outside the firm. In this sense, though vertical integration can create value in the form of market power over competitors, it is not without risks and costs. Chapter 10 includes a more detailed discussion of the coordination of vertical integration as a source of corporate value creation.

Multipoint competition

Multipoint competition exists when two or more diversified firms compete in multiple markets simultaneously. Multipoint competition can facilitate a particular type of tacit collusion, called mutual forbearance (Edwards, 1955). Because in a multipoint situations, firms have more opportunities and are better able to hurt each other in the course of their competition, multipoint competitors avoid damaging competition, which tends to result in higher prices and larger margins than would exist if the firms were not diversified. This argument appears more fully developed in Chapter 13.

CONCLUDING REMARKS

The different corporate value creation mechanisms discussed in this chapter have several implications for the type of diversification strategy that a firm pursues. In terms of the corporate

Table 5.2 Value creating mechanisms and types of diversification

Value creating mechanism	Diversification	
	related	unrelated
Operational economies of scope		
• Sharing resources and activities	X	(X)
• Transferring skills and core competences	X	(X)
Financial economies of scope		
• Efficient internal capital market	X	(X)
• Business restructuring	(X)	X
• Tax advantages	X	X
Anticompetitive economies of scope		
• Market power	X	X
• Vertical integration	X	
• Multipoint competition	X	

Source: Adapted from Barney (2007); Dess et al. (2006); Hitt et al. (2005)

strategy triangle presented in Chapter 1, there are some systematic relationship between the dominant logic in the center of the triangle and the business side of the triangle. Table 5.2 summarizes the relationships between value creation mechanisms and types of diversification.

Operational economies of scope, including shared resources and activities and transfers of skills and core competencies, can be realized mainly in conditions of related diversification (Hitt et al., 2005). Operational links among a related but diversified firm's businesses represent the main sources of these economies of scope. However, sharing an intangible resource, such as a brand name, also becomes possible when a firm diversifies in unrelated businesses, as in the case of Virgin and its many offerings. The creation of operational economies of scope through the transfer of skills and competencies usually requires businesses to relate in some way, because when the businesses are unrelated, the transferred skills and competences rarely are relevant to the receiving business or are too costly to adapt. However, the transfer of generic skills, such as planning and budgeting, from the parent to a subsidiary business may be beneficial even in unrelated diversified firms.

Portfolio management, as a financial economy of scope, appears in both related and unrelated diversification situations. As long as the firm's businesses' cash flows are not perfectly and positively correlated, any form of diversification enables the diversified firm to transfer cash flows from one business to another. However, an efficient internal capital market, which provides a financial economy of scope, usually can be realized only when the firm implements a related diversification strategy (Barney, 2007). For internal capital markets to achieve a capital allocation advantage over external capital markets, firm managers must have access to better information than do the external sources of capital. Moreover, managers need to evaluate and interpret this information in a subtle, complex way to understand the business' performance and prospects more completely than external sources of capital can do. Meeting these information processing requirements seems most likely when the firm's multiple businesses relate along important dimensions. Therefore, the evaluation experience developed in one business helps evaluate other businesses. Moreover, business restructuring can be accomplished by both related and unrelated diversified firms; a business purchased just to be turned around and sold does not need to relate to any of the firm's other businesses. If the restructuring process requires the firms to pool several businesses together to achieve economies of scope or increased bargaining power though, relatedness is key. Tax savings also can be accomplished by both related and unrelated diversified firms. For both types, the chance that losses in some businesses will offset profits in other businesses holds promise as long as the businesses' cash flows are not perfectly and positively correlated over time. Debt capacity and the ability to deduct interest payments also might be enhanced in the related and unrelated cases, though unrelated diversification may provide the more efficient context, because cash flows are less likely to correlate in this situation.

Exploiting market power similarly might operate in either related or unrelated diversification strategies. Alternatively, firms exploiting their market power advantages could simply allocate monopoly profits from one business to support the ongoing price competition in another, unrelated business. Alternatively, the use of pooled bargaining power requires that businesses share suppliers or customers, a form of relatedness. Similarly, when a firm integrates vertically, it diversifies across related businesses by taking over the activities of its customers and suppliers Finally, multipoint competition is most likely to operate in conditions of related diversification. Mutual forbearance requires firm managers to set price and output levels across all diversified businesses simultaneously. This joint price/output determination process is a form of related diversification.

This distinction between relatedness and unrelatedness is crucial because it implies different corporate value creating mechanisms and requires different roles and tasks for the corporate parent. Moreover, it is a particularly delicate issue, because relatedness may be conceptualized in very different ways. Therefore, in the next chapter, we turn to the very question of relatedness.

| Chapter

6

THE ISSUE OF RELATEDNESS

CREATING SYNERGIES

In the previous chapter, we discussed how related and unrelated diversification strategies create corporate value. During the 1980s and 1990s, many large, diversified conglomerates refocused their activities, seeking to improve their performance (Fan & Lang, 2000; Franko, 2004; Grant, 2002; Markides, 1992). But in refocusing their activities around their core competences to achieve synergies, these firms also increased the level of relatedness between their remaining businesses. As a rationale for this refocusing, most diversified firms likely would argue that the exploitation of relatedness produces higher corporate performance. Fan and Lang (2000) found that between 1979 and 1997, firms' average relatedness level increased by approximately 10 percent, and Markides (1992) empirically demonstrates that during 1980–1988, reduced diversification levels was associated with greater shareholder value creation.

In this chapter, we dig deeper into the concept of relatedness in an effort to understand better how relatedness can be achieved and measured. A thorough understanding of the concept of relatedness is critical, because relatedness between business units represents a condition *sine qua non* for the realization of synergies. If potential synergies are abundant, achieving actual synergies may be far more difficult (see Box 6.1). Furthermore, the issue of relatedness might be exacerbated, as the nature of relatedness often only resides in the mind of the managers (Stimpert & Duhaim, 1997).

In this chapter, we discuss the different conceptualizations of relatedness in prior literature that account for the existing types of synergies (see Chapter 5). We also pay careful attention to the way relatedness can be and has been measured, because without precise measures of relatedness, it is impossible to assess the relationship between level of relatedness and firm performance, which means it would be impossible to evaluate the true value creation potential of a diversification strategy.

To create corporate value, the benefits that result from the development of synergies should outweigh the costs of achieving them. For example, achieving synergies by sharing key resources across business units requires coordination, which has costs that could outweigh the benefits derived from sharing. The pursuit of synergies often entails major opportunity costs, because it distracts managers' attention away from their core competitive strategies and slows down other initiatives that might generate other benefits. If they are too demanding in terms of time and efforts, synergy programs may backfire, eroding customer relationships, damaging brands, and undermining employee morale, which means they destroy rather than create corporate value (Goold & Campbell, 1998).

Many announced synergy programs never get implemented because of their potential costs, especially in mergers or acquisitions (M&A) settings (see Chapter 11). In addition, the difficulties associated with implementing these synergy programs, potential synergies do not always translate

BOX 6.1 THE SEARCH FOR SYNERGIES: SKYPE ACQUISITION BY EBAY

On September 12, 2005, eBay Inc. announced it had agreed to acquire the Luxemburg based Skype Technologies SA, a global Internet communications company, for approximately $2.6 billion. Since its founding in 1995, according to its own claims, eBay has connected hundreds of millions of people around the world every day, empowering them to explore new opportunities and innovate together, by providing the Internet platform of choice for global commerce, payments, and communications. In the past decade, eBay has expanded to include some of the strongest brands in the world, including eBay, PayPal, Skype, StubHub, Shopping.com, and others. eBay is headquartered in San Jose, California.

The acquisition was designed to strengthen eBay's global marketplace and payments platform, while also opening several new lines of business and creating significant new monetization opportunities for the company. The deal represented a major opportunity for Skype to advance its leadership in Internet voice communications and offer international consumers new ways to communicate in a global, online era. Skype, eBay, and PayPal would create an unparalleled e-commerce and communications engine for buyers and sellers, all around the world. Thus, synergies were the primary drivers of the acquisition.

"Communications is at the heart of ecommerce and community," said Meg Whitman, then-president and CEO of eBay. "By combining the two leading ecommerce franchises, eBay and PayPal, with the leader in Internet voice communications, we will create an extraordinarily powerful environment for business on the Net."

Founded in 2002 by Niklas Zennström and Janus Friis, Skype offers high quality voice communications to anyone with an Internet connection, anywhere in the world. The Skype software is easy to download and install and enables free calls between Skype users online. Skype's premium services also provide low cost connectivity to traditional fixed and mobile telephones. The software offers a robust set of features, including voicemail, instant messaging, call forwarding, and conference calling. One of the fastest growing companies on the Internet, at the time of the acquisition, Skype already had 54 million members in 225 countries and territories and was adding approximately 150,000 users a day. Skype also had attained market leadership in virtually every country in which it functioned. In North America alone, Skype had more users and served more voice minutes than any other Internet voice communications provider.

"Our vision for Skype has always been to build the world's largest communications business and revolutionize the ease with which people can communicate through the Internet," said Niklas Zennström, Skype CEO and co-founder. "We can't think of any better platform to fulfill this vision to become the voice of the Internet than with eBay and PayPal."

"We're great admirers of how eBay and PayPal have simplified global ecommerce and payments," said Janus Friis, Skype co-founder and senior vice president strategy. "Together we feel we can really change the way that people communicate, shop, and do business online."

According to eBay, online shopping depends on multiple factors to function well. Communications, including those related to payments and shipping, are critical. Skype could streamline and improve communications between buyers and sellers if it were integrated into the eBay marketplace. That is, buyers would gain an easy way to talk to sellers quickly and get the information they needed before purchasing, and sellers could build relationships more easily with customers and close more sales. As a result, Skype could increase the velocity of trade on eBay, especially in categories that required more involved communications, such as used cars, business and industrial equipment, and high end collectibles.

The acquisition also would enable eBay and Skype to pursue entirely new lines of business. For example, in addition to eBay's current transaction based fees, e-commerce communications could be monetized on a pay per call basis through Skype. Pay per call communications in turn introduce new categories of e-commerce, especially in sectors that depend on a lead generation model, such as personal and business services, travel, new cars, and real estate. eBay's other shopping Web sites—Shopping.com, Rent.com, Marktplaats.nl, and Kijiji—further would benefit from the integration of Skype within the eBay portfolio. Finally, PayPal and Skype make a powerful combination; a PayPal wallet associated with each Skype account could make it much easier for users to pay for Skype fee based services, add to the number of PayPal accounts, and increase payment volume.

Skype could help expand eBay's and PayPal's global footprint by providing buyers and sellers in emerging e-commerce markets, such as China, India, and Russia, with a more personal way to communicate online. Consumers in markets where eBay currently has a limited presence, such as Japan and Scandinavia, could learn about eBay and PayPal through Skype. Skype also might help streamline cross-border trading and communications. With its rapidly expanding network of users, the Skype business complements the eBay and PayPal platforms. Each business is self-reinforcing, such that it organically produces greater returns with each new user or transaction. The three services therefore would reinforce and accelerate the others' growth, thereby increasing the value of their combined businesses. Working together, they could create an unparalleled engine for e-commerce and communications around the world.

However, the synergies proved more difficult to achieve than these promising avenues suggested. Less than four years later, on April 14, 2009, eBay announced its plans to separate Skype from the company, beginning with an initial public offering (IPO), intended to be completed in the first half of 2010. The specific timing of the IPO will depend on the market conditions.

"Skype is a great stand-alone business with strong fundamentals and accelerating momentum," said eBay's new president and CEO, John Donahoe. "But it's clear that Skype has limited synergies with eBay and PayPal. We believe operating Skype as a stand-alone publicly traded company is the best path for maximizing its potential. This will give Skype the focus and resources required to continue its growth and effectively compete in online voice and video communications. In addition, separating Skype will allow eBay to focus entirely on our two core growth engine–e-commerce and online payments–and deliver long-term value to our stockholders."

The decision to separate Skype reflects a timeline that John Donahoe outlined when he became eBay's CEO in April 2008. At the time, the company said it would spend a year evaluating Skype and its potential synergies within the eBay portfolio before making any decisions. Donahoe installed a new management team at Skype, led by Josh Silverman, that has driven stronger momentum and improved performance. In 2008, Skype generated revenues of $551 million, up 44 percent from 2007, and segment margins of approximately 21 percent. Registered users increased to 405 million persons by the end of 2008, up 47 percent from 2007, and user metrics improved significantly throughout the year. The company also recently announced that it expects Skype to top $1 billion in revenue in 2011, which will represent nearly double the level of its 2008 revenues.

Thus, Donahoe has been able to issue the following positive spin: "Under the leadership of Josh Silverman and his management team, Skype has become a stronger business in the past year, and I expect it will be even stronger a year from now ... Skype has accelerated global user growth and strong fundamentals, diversified revenue streams and is competitively positioned in a large market. We expect Josh and his team to continue delivering results as we prepare Skype for an IPO."

Source: http://about.skype.com/2005/09/ebay_to_acquire_skype.html;
http://about.skype.com/2009/04/ebay_inc:announces_plan_for_20.html

into actual economies of scope. However, this is the actual, not the potential synergies, which provide corporate value to diversified firms (Nayyar, 1992).

The key factor for the successful implementation of synergies appears to be the amount of relatedness that exists between business units. When two or more business units relate in some way, it becomes less costly to implement a synergy program and achieve economies of scope. If two business units sell different products to the same customers, for example, which means they are related in terms of customers served, it should be relatively less expensive for them to share the same distribution channel.

As discussed in the previous chapter, the different types of corporate value creation mechanisms are based on different ways to achieve economies of scope. These different means to create synergies in turn derive from the various ways business units are related. Operational economies of scope occur when business units are related through common or similar resources, activities, skills, competences, or knowledge (see Box 6.2).

As seen in the previous chapter (Table 5.2), the implementation of financial and anticompetitive economies of scope might also require some degree of relatedness between business units. For example, to achieve an efficient capital market, corporate managers need better information about the value of the units in their business portfolio than the external financial market possess, which requires some communality across the different businesses of the firm. Similarly, to achieve anticompetitive economies of scope through multipoint competition, the coordination, or relatedness, of the competitive strategies used by the firm's business units is necessary (Gimeno & Woo, 1999).

A key issue is that there are different ways to conceptualize relatedness between business units. The relatedness between two business units may be thought of in terms of similarities in their resources (e.g., serving the same customers, using the same technology), activities (e.g., same competitive strategies), skills (e.g., financial management), competence (e.g., sharing managerial leadership), or knowledge (product knowledge, customer knowledge, managerial knowledge). Furthermore, following the dominant logic (Prahalad & Bettis, 1986) and the parenting advantage (Goold et al., 1994) perspectives, relatedness is not necessarily objective but rather should be assessed from the perspective of top managers to implement economies of scope (Stimpert & Duhaim, 1997). According to these perspectives, two businesses are not related to each other because they objectively have something in common, but rather because managers perceive some communality between them; and they act upon it (see Box 6.3). If managers do not perceive relatedness, synergies cannot be achieved.

According to Farjoun and Lai (1997), similarity judgments by top managers (i.e., perceived relatedness) provide the basis for identifying and managing relatedness and synergies between business units. Accordingly, managerial judgments of relatedness between business units should be central to diversification decisions and have major corporate performance implications (Nayyar, 1992; Prahalad & Bettis, 1986; Stimpert & Duhaime, 1997; Pehrsson, 2006a). We discuss the relationship between diversification and performance in detail in Chapter 7. Such decisions pertain to, for example, investments in products and markets (Rumelt, 1974, 1982; Sharma, 1998; St John & Harrison, 1999; Tsai, 2000), M&As (Brush, 1996; Lubatkin et al., 1997; Ramaswamy, 1997; Seth, 1990), the formation of joint ventures (Merchant & Schendel, 2000), and divestures (Markides, 1992).

However, the subjectivity of the concept of relatedness is problematic because it makes it very difficult for managers, as well as external observers, such as investors and financial analysts, to assess the potential value of synergy programs (Grant, 2002). These difficulties appear in detail in the rest of the chapter, in which we also review the different approaches to conceptualize relatedness and the different methods used to measure it.

BOX 6.2 RELATEDNESS THE P&G WAY: LEVERAGING GLOBAL SCALE AND SCOPE

The most differentiating aspect of P&G's approach to corporate level strategy is the scale and scope of our business and brand portfolio, science and technology platforms, and geographic reach.

The diversity of our business portfolio creates highly valuable scope benefits. Our Health & Beauty businesses take advantage of purchasing pools created by Household businesses such as laundry, diapers and paper products. This enables them to purchase packing materials and basic commodities at lower prices than their direct competitors. Similarly, Household Care enjoys economies of scale created by the large advertising budgets supporting our Health & Beauty Care businesses.

The diversity of P&G's brand portfolio gives us the opportunity to innovate in many aspects of consumers' lives. P&G brands are in every room of the house, at virtually every hour of the day. As a result, we get to see more of consumers' needs. This helps us spot more problems P&G innovation can help solve and more aspirations P&G brands can help achieve.

Our science and technology portfolio is another huge scale advantage. Bleach technology from Laundry has been used in Health & Beauty Care products such as Crest White Strips and Nice 'n Easy Perfect 10 Hair Colorant. Non-woven top sheet technology started in Diapers, traveled to Feminine Care then moved to Swiffer and Olay Daily Facials. Proprietary perfume technology has been used to enhance the performance of Bounce, Febreze, Fine Fragrances, Camay and most recently Secret and Gillette Clinical Strength deodorant. We are now combining Gillette's expertise in mechanical engineering with our expertise in chemical engineering. This is a very significant source of corporate advantage.

Another area in which we can leverage P&G scope is our geographic reach. In developed markets like the U.S., where P&G brands can be found in virtually every household, we leverage household penetration as a scope advantage. In developing markets, we are using our portfolio of leading brands to attract and build a network of best-in-class, often exclusive distributors in countries such as China, India and Russia. Today our distributor network in China reaches about 800 million people. In India, our distributor network covers 4.5 million stores, an increase of two million stores in just five years. In Russia, we now have access to 80% of the population.

P&G's global scale allows us to quickly flow innovation across developing countries. We create innovation to meet consumer needs in a particular region and then quickly flow that technology across multiple countries. For example, consumers who wash clothing by hand need improved rinsing with less water. This is a common need in many developing countries. We launched Downy Single Rinse in Mexico, and have since expanded it into twelve countries, including China, the Philippines, and Peru. We did the same with Naturella, an innovative feminine protection product created specifically for low-income consumers in Latin America; we are now expanding Naturella throughout Eastern Europe. We have created highly cost-effective laundry detergent formulations that we have expanded rapidly across developing markets. We have created a "better and cheaper" dentifrice formulation for Crest that was first introduced in China and has now been expanded into Eastern European markets.

Source: Adapted from P&G's 2008 Annual Report (www.pg.com/annualreport2008/letter/leveraging.shtml)

BOX 6.3 RELATEDNESS THE VIRGIN WAY

The Virgin Group covers a huge array of businesses, from airlines to bridal stores. However, all Virgin businesses share certain similarities: they tend to be start up companies that have benefited from Sir Richard Branson's entrepreneurial spirit and expertise; they sell to final consumers; they function in sectors that offer opportunities for innovative approaches to differentiation; and they all benefit from the Virgin brand and its rebel image. As a venture capital firm, Virgin is still one of the world's most recognized and respected brands. Conceived of in 1970 by Richard Branson, the group has gone on to grow successful businesses in a broad spectrum of sectors, ranging from mobile telephony to transportation, travel, financial services, media, music, and fitness. Virgin also has created more than 200 branded companies worldwide, employing approximately 50,000 people around the world, operating in over 50 countries. Global branded revenues of GB£15 billion (approximately $24 billion) in 2012. With such a variety of businesses working in so many different industries, Virgin may appear to have an extremely unrelated portfolio. But in the eyes of its founder, relatedness marks all of Virgin's businesses.

When Virgin starts a new venture, it seeks to draw on talented people throughout the group, such that new ventures often receive close guidance from members of other parts of the Virgin Group, who bring with them the Virgin management style, skills, and experience. Virgin's growth strategy is neither random nor reckless. Each successive, carefully chosen venture demonstrates potential fit with Virgin's values. Once a company has been integrated into the Virgin portfolio, several factors contribute to its continued performance, including the Virgin name; Branson's own personal reputation; Virgin's network of friends, contacts, and partners; the Virgin management style; and Virgin's efforts to empower talented persons to flourish. These elements then come to constitute the relatedness across Virgin's portfolio of businesses. Virgin's companies also are part of a family, rather than a hierarchy. They are empowered to run their own affairs, yet they simultaneously help one another, and solutions to problems often come from other areas in the group. In a sense, Virgin is a commonwealth, with shared ideas, values, interests, and goals, along with its own concept of relatedness.

Source: www.virgin.com/about-us/

BUSINESS ATTRIBUTES AND RELATEDNESS

Early research on diversification made a key distinction between *related* and *unrelated* diversification (Berry, 1975; Rumelt, 1974; Wrigley, 1970), though the existence of the various types of economies of scope discussed in the previous chapter raise some important issues pertaining to the nature of relatedness between businesses. Relatedness generally has been conceptualized with respect to similarities in certain types of business attributes (Pehrsson, 2006a, 2006b). The most often used attributes are variants of product market, resource, or value chain attributes.

Product market attributes provide the most common means to conceptualize relatedness, starting with seminal work by Rumelt (1974). Product market attributes offer a basis for operational synergies and can be identified according to the three dimensions outlined by Abell (1980) to define a business: technology, customer functions (or needs), and customer groups (see Chapter 4). Using product market attributes, early diversification studies, including those by Wrigley (1970) and Rumelt (1974), defined relatedness in terms of technological linkages (e.g., common core technology) and market linkages (e.g., common customer need). Similarly, industrial economics literature relies on the notion of 'adjacent sectors,' or those within the same Standard Industrial Classification (SIC) two digit industry code, such that unrelated diversification only occurs across the two digit codes (Berry, 1975) (for a discussion of the SIC system, see Chapter 4, Box 4.4).

The RBV offers an alternative approach to the analysis of business relatedness (Collis & Montgomery, 1998, 2005). In particular, Lemelin (1982) was among the first to identify the importance of resource attributes as sources of relatedness. He argues that the most important sources of economies of scope and synergies are not similarities between product markets but rather those between key resources that could be shared between business units. The resources that provide the basis for business relatedness in turn can be organized along a continuum, ranging from unique and specialized assets to skills, and capabilities that denote a competitive advantage for the individual businesses to general management skills (Pehrsson, 2006a). If economies of scope in resources and capabilities represent important sources of corporate value creation, then the ability to deploy common resources and capabilities can be a basis for relatedness between business units (Prahalad & Hamel, 1990). Empirical RBV studies suggest different methods to measure relatedness, mainly focused on the identification of common resources and capabilities (e.g., Coff, 2002; Farjoun, 1994; Markides & Williamson, 1994; Robins & Wiersema, 1995), as we discuss in the next section.

Value chain attributes also can help conceptualize relatedness (Pehrsson, 2006a, 2006b; Porter, 1985; Rumelt, 1974). St John and Harrison (1999) show that business units can develop interrelationships between any sequences of the firm value chain. For example, interrelationships between procurement and production or between production and marketing indicate relatedness between these functional activities. Using an extended value chain approach, Tsai (2000) argues that relatedness based on input flows (i.e., interrelationships with suppliers) differs from relatedness based on output flows (i.e., interrelationships with distributors and customers). Similarities in sales and supply channel types, suppliers, and even after-sales services can constitute aspects of relatedness and therefore sources of potential synergies (Pehrsson, 2006a).

Some authors argue in favor of the combination of different types of attributes, as a means to capture the multidimensionality of relatedness (e.g., Farjoun, 1998; Pehrsson, 2006a; Stimpert & Duhaime, 1997; St John & Harrison, 1999). According to this argument, the value of a related diversification strategy and the potential for economies of scope and synergies depend not on any attribute of relatedness separately but on the combination of the various different sources of relatedness. The value creation potential for economies of scope thus depends on the combination of different aspects of relatedness, and when two business units relate on several dimensions simultaneously, it should be easier and less costly to implement a synergy program that offers great potential for economies of scope.

However, to develop such a synergy program, we must be able to measure the degree of relatedness—not only between two business units but also across all the different business units of a firm's portfolio. Therefore, in the next section, we review different measures used to operationalize and measure the level of relatedness in a diversified firm's business portfolio.

MEASURING RELATEDNESS

Early diversification studies relied mostly on SIC codes to measure the level of relatedness in a firm's business portfolio, but more recent research shows that such measures may be of limited use, because they only address relatedness in the form of production processes and product use, without considering other types (Pehrsson, 2006b; Robins & Wiersema, 1995; St John & Harison, 1999). In addition, such studies show that SIC codes account for potential relatedness, not actual relatedness, which may make them of limited value for measuring the relationship between relatedness and performance.

The issue of relatedness | 85

Yet the other ways developed to measure relatedness, even with their advantages over SIC measures, also suffer from some deficiencies, in particular because of the reliance on subjective judgment (Martin & Sayrak, 2003). Overall, three types of measures of relatedness exist: application of SIC codes or similar indices, assessments by researchers, and studies of managerial perceptions. These different methods all address the different attributes of relatedness, that is, product market, resources, and value chain, as Table 6.1 depicts.

Table 6.1 Typology of relatedness measurement methods

	Product market attributes	Resource attributes	Value chain attributes
SIC codes and similar 'objective' indices	Amit & Livnat, 1988a Capron, 1999 Caves et al., 1980 Ding & Caswell, 1995 Hall & St John, 1994 Hoskisson et al., 1993c Jacquemin & Berry, 1979 Lubatkin et al., 1993 Lubatkin et al., 1997 Merchant & Schendel, 2000 Montgomery, 1982 Montgomery & Hariharan, 1991 Montgomery & Wernerfelt, 1988 Palepu, 1985 Pennings et al., 1994 Robins & Wiersema, 2003 Sharma, 1998 Simmonds, 1990 Szeless et al., 2003 Wernerfelt & Montgomery, 1988 Wood, 1971	Breschi et al., 2003 Bryce & Winter, 2009 Farjoun, 1994, 1998 Lee & Lieberman, 2010 Lien & Klein, 2009 Piscitello, 2000	Fan & Lang, 2000
Researcher assessments	Bergh, 1995 Bruton et al., 1994 Chatterjee & Blocher, 1992 Lubatkin et al., 1997 Palich et al., 2000 Pitts & Hopkins, 1982 Ramaswamy, 1997 Rumelt, 1974, 1982 Wrigley, 1970	Brush, 1996 Harrison et al., 1993 Lemelin, 1982 Markides & Williamson, 1994, 1996 Montgomery, 1982 Robins & Wiersema, 1995 Teece et al., 1994	Galbraith & Kazanjian, 1986 Ilinitch & Zeithaml, 1995 Rumelt, 1974, 1982 St John & Harrison, 1999 Tsai, 2000
Managerial perceptions	$\longleftarrow$	Grant, 1988 Keats, 1990 Nayyar, 1992 Pehrsson, 2006a $\longrightarrow$ Prahalad & Bettis, 1986 Stimpert & Duhaime, 1997 Tanriverdi & Venkatraman, 2005	

Source: Updated from Pehrsson (2006b)

The issue of relatedness

Table 6.1 also lists the key diversification studies that empirically measure relatedness. Despite their numerous critics, SIC based measures of relatedness remain popular and often used. In addition, because the studies in Table 6.1 use different conceptualizations, and thus different measures, of relatedness, their results are not always comparable, which represents an important limitation for the further development of diversification research and management.

Measures of relatedness based on product market attributes

Diversification studies based on industrial organization economics mostly use product market attributes to conceptualize and measure relatedness according to two general approaches: continuous measures derived from the SIC system and categorical measures based on the researchers' assessments.

Product market relatedness measure using researcher assessments

Most categorical measures, starting with the foundation provided by Wrigley (1970) and Rumelt (1974), are based on product market and technology attributes. Defining a business unit as a product, product line, or set of product lines with strong market interdependencies, both Wrigley and Rumelt use two broad dimensions to classify diversification strategies: *the specialization ratio*, which is a firm's sales in its major activity area as a proportion of its total sales, and *the related ratio*, or the proportion of the firm's total sales related to one another (see Box 1.2 in Chapter 1).

Rumelt (1974) refined Wrigley's classification by introducing additional dimensions of relatedness: *constrained diversification*, when a firm's activities relate to one another; *linked diversification*, which exists when each activity relates to at least one other activity but not all other activities; and *vertically integrated diversification*, such that firms' businesses can be classified into a separate, dominant vertical category, resulting in eight types of diversification strategies (see Table 6.2).

Rumelt's typology continues to be widely used because it exhibits high consistency between the definition and the measurement of the relatedness concept (i.e., high content validity) (Pehrsson, 2006b). Furthermore, in assessing the validity of the typology, Montgomery (1982) finds that Rumelt's classification correlates strongly with SIC based measures. Among others, Grant and Jammine (1988) and Hill (1988) have used Rumelt's measures in their diversification studies.

Table 6.2 Rumelt's classification of diversification strategies

Single business	SR > 95%
Dominant vertical	Vertically related sales > 70%
Dominant constrained	95% < SR < 70%, majority of other businesses related to one another through a core asset or skill
Dominant linked	95% < SR < 70%, majority of other businesses related to at least one other business within the firm
Dominant unrelated	95% < SR < 70%, majority of other businesses unrelated
Related constrained	SR < 70%, 70% + of businesses related to one another
Related linked	SR < 70%, RR > 70%, majority businesses related to at least one other business within the firm
Unrelated business	SR < 70%, RR < 70%

Note: SR = specialization ratio; RR = related ratio
Source: Adapted from Rumelt (1974)

However, measures based on researchers' assessments may be too subjective, which prevents a comparison of results across studies and replications. Moreover, as pointed out by Martin and Sayrak (2003), such a subjective classification scheme is also difficult to be accepted, given research norms in finance. Furthermore, Hoskisson et al. (1993c) note that these categorical measures should be regarded as measures of diversification types rather than of the degrees of relatedness, because the different diversification strategies Rumelt (1974) identifies actually differ conceptually rather than representing varying levels of relatedness. Measures based on the SIC classification attempt to palliate these limitations.

SIC codes and indices

Similarities in product technology provide the overarching criterion for the conceptualization of business relatedness used by SIC based measures of diversification and relatedness (Pehrsson, 2006b). Product technology, primarily pertaining to raw materials and assemblies, categorizes business units into industries and then, hierarchically, into industry groups. As discussed in Chapter 3, SIC based classifications rely on the assumption that if two businesses share the same SIC, they must have common input requirements and similar production/technology attributes, which makes them related to each other (Caves et al., 1980; Jacquemin & Berry, 1979; Palepu, 1985).

Of the several measures based on SIC codes, the most commonly used are (1) the *narrow spectrum* measure, developed by Wood (1971) and often used in merger contexts (Lubatkin et al., 1997), as well as its alternative, the *simple product count* measure (Lubatkin et al., 1993; Merchant & Schendel, 2000), which is based on the classification of business units into four digit industry groupings, according to their primary activity; (2) *concentric indices* (Montgomery & Hariharan, 1991; Montgomery & Wernerfelt, 1988; Wernerfelt & Montgomery, 1988); and (3) the *entropy index* (Capron, 1999; Caves et al., 1980; Ding & Caswell, 1995; Jacquemin & Berry, 1979; Palepu, 1985), which is based on a classification of three digit manufacturing businesses. The two SIC based measures of relatedness most widely used currently are the entropy index and the concentric index (Davis & Duhaime, 1992; Robins & Wiersema, 1995).

NARROW SPECTRUM MEASURE AND OTHER SIMPLE PRODUCT COUNT MEASURES

In an early study, Wood (1971) used SIC data to distinguish two distinct patterns of firm level diversification. She defined narrow spectrum diversification (NSD) as expansion, other than vertical integration, outside a four digit SIC industry but within a two digit SIC grouping. She also defined broad spectrum diversification (BSD) as expansion, other than vertical integration, into a different two digit SIC industry. Therefore, NSD represents diversification closely related to a firm's core expertise, whereas BSD is diversification less closely related to it (Varadarajan & Ramanujam, 1987). Because for a given two digit SIC code, a firm may be active in many or few four digit SIC code levels, Varadarajan and Ramanujam (1987) created a modification of the NSD, called mean narrow spectrum diversification (MNSD), by dividing NSD (the number of four digit SIC industries) by BSD (the number of two digit SIC industries).

Variations on Wood's product count diversification and relatedness measures include weighted average measures, such as the concentric and entropy indices that consider the importance of involvement in each SIC for a particular firm. The sophistication of product count measures thus ranges from simple counts of the number of SIC codes in which a firm participates to detailed weighted average measures (Montgomery, 1982). The weighted average measures require detailed business level information, such as a breakdown of sales by SIC codes at both two and four digit levels, so they are far more difficult to use (Palepu, 1985; Jacquemin & Berry, 1979). However, Montgomery (1982) argues that these weighted measures are superior to (i.e., more precise than)

The issue of relatedness

unweighted measures for describing a firm's diversification level. The two weighted measures of relatedness that currently are most widely used are the entropy index and the concentric index (Davis & Duhaime, 1992; Robins & Wiersema, 1995).

ENTROPY INDEX (ALSO KNOWN AS THE SHANNON INDEX)

A major failing of several simple count, SIC based measures is that they do not distinguish between related and unrelated diversification. Rumelt's (1974) classification is rich and captures the subtleties of a firm's diversification strategy, but it also is subjective and very time consuming. To resolve both these issues, the entropy index distinguishes between related and unrelated diversification and thus combines the advantages of using a product count measure with the essential richness of Rumelt's classification scheme (Palepu, 1985). It was originally proposed by Jacquemin and Berry (1979) to analyze the relationship between corporate diversification and growth.

The Jacquemin-Berry entropy measure entails three elements of the diversity of a firm's operations: (1) the number of product segments in which the firm operates, (2) the distribution of the firm's total sales across the product segments, and (3) the degree of relatedness among the various product segments (Palepu, 1985). What distinguishes the entropy measure from other diversification indices is its ability to consider the third element. This consideration means the entropy measure overcomes the limitations of previous diversification indices and allows for the decomposition of a firm's total diversity (DT) into two additive components: (1) an 'unrelated' component (DU) that measures the extent to which a firm's output is distributed in the form of products across unrelated industry groups and (2) a related component (DR) that measures the distribution of the output among related products within industry groups. Each component can be calculated using the following formula (Jacquemin & Berry, 1979):

$$E = \sum_i P_i \ln(1/P_i),$$

where E is an entropy measure, and P_i is the proportion of a firm's sales in the SIC industry i. The measure can be calculated using the distribution of sales across four, three, or two digit SIC levels, with the four digit SIC level typically representing total diversification (DT), whereas the two digit measure reflects unrelated diversification. To derive the related portion of the measure, modelers take the difference between total and unrelated diversification:

$$E_R = E_T - E_U = \sum_i P_T \ln(1/P_T) - \sum_i P_U \ln(1/P_U),$$

where:

E_R = related component of entropy
E_T = entropy defined at the four-digit SIC level
E_U = entropy defined at the two-digit SIC level
P_T = percentage of sales in each four-digit SIC industry
P_U = percentage of sales in each two-digit SIC industry

An intuitive explanation of the measure proposed by Palepu (1985, p. 244) indicates:

> The related diversification arising out of operations within an industry is the weighted sum of the shares of each of the product segments in the firm's sales in that industry. If the firm operates in several industries, the net related diversification is the weighted sum of the related diversification within each of these industries. In addition to the related diversification, a firm

operating in several industries has unrelated diversification. This is computed as the weighted sum of the shares of each of the industries in the firm's total sales. The measure thus provides three indices for each firm: (1) the index of related diversification; (2) the index of unrelated diversification and (3) the index of total diversification which is equal to the sum of (1) and (2).

The SIC in this measure defines the related and unrelated product groups. Products that belong to different four digit SIC industries within the same two digit group are related; products from different two digit SIC industry groups are unrelated. Although this calculation does not employ an explicit weighting factor for SIC levels—such as the weight d_{il} in the concentric index, as we discuss in the next section—it uses distinctions among SIC levels in a similar fashion. That is, SIC levels are treated as homogeneous, and all four digit SIC categories effectively appear equidistant from all two digit SIC categories on some underlying, quantitative scale of relatedness.

CONCENTRIC INDEX

The concentric index represents an adaptation of the Herfindhal index that Caves et al. (1980) developed to study industry concentration levels. Montgomery and colleagues (Montgomery & Hariharan, 1991; Montgomery & Wernerfelt, 1988) in turn adapted this measure of industry concentration to perform research on corporate level strategy and study the relationship between diversification and performance. To compute the concentric index, we first take the product of shares of sales for each pair of businesses at the bottom level of the industry hierarchy, then multiply that result by a weight that represents the relationship between the two businesses in the SIC system. That is:

$$FDIVERS_k = \sum P_{ki} \sum P_{kl} d_{il},$$

where:

P_{ki} = percentage of sales for firm k in industry i
P_{kl} = percentage of sales for firm k in industry l
d_{il} = weight, such that $d_{il} = 0$ when i and l are four digit products within the same three digit SIC category, $d_{il} = 1$ when they belong to different three digit SIC groups but the same two digit group, and $d_{il} = 2$ when i and l are in different two digit SIC categories

The index therefore is simply a weighting based on intra-portfolio relatedness distances, which increases with diversity and ranges in value from a minimum of 0 (when the firm's products all fall within a single three digit industry) to a maximum of 4 (many four digit products, with no two in the same two digit industry) (Caves et al., 1980).

These SIC based continuous measures of relatedness offer several features that make them very attractive for quantitative research. In particular, they provide variables at a high level of measurement and a wider range of techniques for analysis. Perhaps even more important, they use data classified according to standard categories, which facilitates the comparison of results across different studies and makes research both replicable and cumulative (Hoskisson et al., 1993c). Because of these advantages, the concentric and entropy indices are the most often used measures of diversification and relatedness. For example, Ding and Caswell (1995) use the entropy index to assess changes in the diversification level of large manufacturing food manufacturers in the 1980s; Szeless et al. (2003) use it to assess the portfolio relatedness of European firms in the 1990s.

Despite their extensive use though, the measures of relatedness based on SIC codes and sales data suffer widespread criticisms. The primary problem noted with these indices is their imposition of unsupported and extremely difficult assumptions on the SIC system. In constructing the measure, the two, three, and four SIC digit levels of classification implicitly get treated as points on an underlying scale of relatedness among businesses, with arithmetic values assigned to the distances between the points. This procedure requires two very strong and deeply problematic assumptions about the SIC system: first, that industries are homogeneous within category levels, and second, that the assigned relatedness scale accurately reflects quantitative distinctions between the category levels (Rumelt, 1982). The failure to meet either of these assumptions can be an important source of error.

Furthermore, the SIC code measures assume two businesses within the same two digit code are related, whereas two businesses with different two digit codes must be unrelated. This assumption can have limitations for strategy research in general; it is certainly too liberal for any effective assessment of relatedness (Pehrsson, 2006b; St John & Harrison, 1999). Robins and Wiersema (1995, p. 281) also argue that "the SIC system is a weak source of information on substantive relationships among industries," and thus, measures such as the entropy or concentric indices lack content validity. In addition, SIC measures use inconsistent criteria to assess the distance between industries and fail to acknowledge a firm's unique history and strategy (Montgomery, 1982; Rumelt, 1974). The SIC classification system simply might not be consistent across industries with regard to its ability to measure the degree of product relatedness; it might not even be consistent in its ability to measure performance differences with slightly different forms of measurement, even with the same samples (Ilinitch & Zeithaml, 1995).

Lemelin (1982) posits that the inadequate conceptualization of relatedness is responsible for the low overall explanatory power of diversification studies. For example, the oil refining (SIC 29) and chemical (SIC 28) businesses appear unrelated according to the two digit SIC code classifications, but in fact, they are vertically related, Most oil companies in the U.S. and other parts of the world own chemical segments (Fan & Lang, 2000). Furthermore, Lemelin cites the importance of additional sources of relatedness, not taken into account by SIC codes, such as complementary product use, similarity of differentiation techniques, shared technical knowledge, and the degree of vertical relatedness. Using such conceptual refinements improves the ability of diversification variables to explain variations in firm performance.

Resource-based approaches to relatedness

The RBV of the firm offers a broader based and more rigorous approach to the analysis of business relatedness, focused on the identification and analysis of common resources and capabilities (Robins & Wiersema, 1995). If the primary source of value creating in diversification is economies of scope in resources and capabilities, the ability to deploy common resources and capabilities must provide the very basis for relatedness between businesses (Farjoun, 1994).

This RBV of synergies or scope economies argues for the use of measures of relatedness that link to underlying forms of resources, knowledge, or capability, which might be the sources of corporate value creation for diversified firms (Robins & Wiersema, 1995). An index of business portfolio interrelationship for individual firms, developed by Robins and Wiersema (1995), uses measures of resource based similarities between pairs of industries. For each combination of two industry categories, i and j, in a firm's portfolio, the sales weighted measure of interrelationship R_{ij} can be calculated as:

$$R_{ij} = P_i r_{ij} + P_j r_{ij},$$

where:

P_i = percentage of sales in industry category i

P_j = percentage of sales in industry category j

r_{ij} = structural equivalence similarity (correlation) of i and j

Summing these weighted measures of similarity between paired industries (R_{ij}) over all possible combinations of pairs of industries in the firm's business portfolio results in an aggregate index of the interrelationship between the businesses of the firm:

$$M_k = \sum R_{ij} = \sum r_{ij} (P_{ki} + P_{kj}),$$

where i and j represent any two different industries in which firm k is active. A correction takes into account the total number of industries in which a firm is active (see Robins & Wiersema, 1995). The adjusted index ranges from +1.0 to −1.0, such that a positive score indicates a firm has a positively interrelated portfolio of businesses, whereas a negative score indicates a negatively interrelated portfolio.

Although this index bears substantial resemblances to the concentric or entropy measures, it differs in very important ways. The most significant difference is its stronger conceptual link to the underlying strategic theory of the multibusiness firm. The use of additional data about the position of SIC industries within the overall structure of the manufacturing sector substantially increase the information incorporated into this index, and patterns of technology usage have good content validity as indirect indicators of less transferable capabilities or know-how. By moving away from the use of the SIC hierarchy to determine interrelationship among businesses, this approach also avoids problems associated with transforming the categorical scheme of the SIC into a set of quantitative measures. At the same time, it preserves the capacity to analyze the economic activity reported in SIC categories.

Other resource based approaches are available as well. For example, Coff (2002) categorizes industries on the basis of the similarity of the human resource expertise they require. Farjoun (1998) adopts a skills based, rather than a product based, approach to attempt a greater level of detail in relation to the concept of industry relatedness. Markides and Williamson (1996) also focus on the deployment of similar, nontradable, nonsubstitutable, hard to accumulate assets in different markets. With this focus, they identify five types of assets: *customer* (e.g., brand recognition, customer loyalty, installed base), *channel* (channel access, distributor loyalty), *input* (knowledge of factor markets, supplier loyalty, financial capacity), *process* (proprietary technology, functional capabilities), and *market knowledge* (see Box 6.4) assets.

More recently, Lien and Klein (2009) proposed a new resource based measure of relatedness focusing on patterns of competition. Bryce and Winter (2009) have introduced another resource based relatedness index based on firms' inputs and outputs that may facilitate the opportunity to explain the direction of diversified expansion, the development of capabilities over time as industries and firms co-evolve, and the role of knowledge in the growth of the firm. In a similar vein, Lee and Lieberman (2010) also have developed a dynamic measure of relatedness.

Managerial perceptions

Accurate managerial judgments about the relatedness between business units remain central to diversification decisions in industrial firms (Pehrsson, 2006b). Another line of research (Nayyar, 1992; Stimpert & Duhaime, 1997; Pehrsson, 2006a) questions the objective measurements approach, based on SIC codes and resource similarities, and instead supports the use of managerial perceptions of business relatedness. The major rationale for this argument is that assessments made by managers underlie strategic decisions, including core competence determination, investments in products and markets, mergers, acquisitions, the formation of strategic alliances, and divesture. Therefore, managerial perceptions also should be used as input for the

BOX 6.4 RESOURCE BASED MEASURES OF RELATEDNESS

Studies by Markides and Williamson (1994) and Robins and Wiersema (1995) suggest that traditional measures of relatedness provide an incomplete and potentially exaggerated picture of the scope at which a corporation can exploit interrelationships between divisions. Traditional measures consider relatedness only at the industry or market level, whereas the relatedness that really matters is that between strategic assets. Although the advantages of the strategy of related diversification usually are cast in terms of the cost and differentiation benefits that arise from the cross-utilization of the firm's underlying assets, traditional measures of relatedness often fail even to consider the underlying assets that reside in these businesses.

The traditional measures might be acceptable proxies for what they are trying to measure if they were not biased. However, they suffer from a systematic bias. Consider a firm using a strategy of related diversification to exploit the relatedness of its business unit–level assets. Suppose, however, that these assets are not 'strategically important' (as we define subsequently). If the assets Firm X is trying to cross-utilize are ones that any other firm could easily obtain in the open market through purchase, even if Firm X achieves a short term competitive advantage from exploiting economies of scope, it cannot really achieve any sustainable competitive advantage over time, because other firms quickly achieve similar positions just by purchasing similar assets. Therefore, any measure of relatedness should take into consideration not only whether the underlying business unit–level assets of a firm are related but also whether those assets are important. Even when traditional measures of relatedness capture the relatedness of the underlying assets, they consistently ignore any evaluation of whether those assets are the 'right' ones.

It is not broad market relatedness that matters. Two markets may be closely related, but if the opportunity to build assets rapidly using competences from elsewhere in the corporation does no more than generate asset stocks that others can buy or contract for at similar cost, no competitive advantage ensues from a strategy of diversification. The 'strategic relatedness' between two markets—in that they value nontradable, nonsubstitutable assets with similar production functions—is a requirement before diversification can yield super normal profits in the long run. By failing to take into account the variance in the opportunities to build strategic assets offered by different market environments, traditional measures suffer from an exaggeration problem: They wrongly impute a benefit to related diversification across markets when the relatedness actually occurs primarily among nonstrategic assets.

Source: Markides (2002, pp. 104–105)

development of business relatedness measurements. Furthermore, this research stream stresses the multidimensionality of relatedness, in that it reflects combinations of business attributes.

Prahalad and Bettis (1986) propose an alternative approach to the analysis of relatedness in diversification (see Chapter 3). They use the term *dominant logic* to refer to "a mind set or world view or conceptualization of the business and the administrative tools to accomplish goals and make decisions in that business" (Prahalad & Bettis, 1986, p. 491). This concept of relatedness rests not on the presence of economies of scope in resources and capabilities but rather on top management's perception of similarity between businesses (Grant, 1988). Although Prahalad and Bettis (1986) develop this idea of the dominant logic as a common cognitive schema, through which corporate level managers can understand the nature of their firm and its strategic rationale,

The issue of relatedness

the operationalization of the concept requires a specification of the common strategic characteristics of the different businesses that enable the firm to apply its management capabilities and common corporate management systems to create value (Grant, 1988). Without such a specification, the danger arises that the dominant logic may not be underpinned by any true synergies.

The linkage between the dominant logic and corporate value creation most likely depends on the implications of the dominant logic for the overall portfolio of businesses, spanning corporate strategy, resources and capabilities, organizational structure, and management systems (Collis & Montgomery, 2005). Those companies that possess a stable consensus when it comes to their dominant logic should be better able to achieve fit among their resources, strategy, structure, systems, and style.

A key theme arising from several publications has been the emphasis on *strategic* rather than *operational* level linkages among the businesses of the diversified firm. Most traditional analyses of relatedness in diversification emphasize commonalities in technology and markets, which relate primarily to relatedness at the operational level, whether in manufacturing, marketing, or distribution activities (see Chapter 5). Although Porter (1985) suggests these operational level commonalities, which involve shared activities across businesses, require the closest integration between businesses, this point does not necessarily mean they offer the greatest potential for yielding economies of scope. Moreover, the sharing of activities typically imposes substantial coordination costs (Gulati & Singh, 1998), pertaining not simply to management time and effort to coordinate the linkages across businesses but also to the loss of clarity in financial control and performance monitoring that results from the presence of shared costs (Grant, 2002).

If the dominant logic rests ultimately on the resources and capabilities of the top management team, the domain across which the resources and capabilities can be deployed also depends on a set of common, strategic characteristics of the various businesses. Grant (1988) argues that the essence of these strategic linkages is the ability to apply similar strategic planning processes, resource allocation procedures, and control systems. Table 6.3 thus illustrates some of the features of strategic similarity that may facilitate the application of common corporate management systems.

Several researchers thus have concluded that managers' understandings of relatedness and strategic variety likely differ significantly from the conceptualization of relatedness that appears in existing measures (Keats, 1990; Nayyar, 1992; Prahalad & Bettis, 1986).

Table 6.3 **Determinants of strategic relatedness between businesses**

Corporate tasks	*Determinant of strategic similarity*
Resource allocation	• Similar sizes of capital investment projects. • Similar time spans of investment projects. • Similar sources of risk. • Similar general management skills required for business unit managers.
Strategy formulation	• Similar key success factors. • Similar stages of the industry lifecycle. • Similar competitive positions occupied by each business within its industry.
Targeting, monitoring, and control of business unit	• Goals defined in terms of similar performance variables. • Similar time horizons for performance targets.

Source: Grant (1988)

In contrast with the emphasis on sales revenues, SIC codes, and other archival data, a managerial or behavioral perspective focuses attention on managers, their perceptions and understandings, and their influence on decision-making. From a managerial perspective then, existing diversification measures seem incapable of capturing the relatedness that managers perceive and attempt to exploit when they formulate and implement their firms' diversification strategies. On the one hand, bounded rationality likely prevents managers from perceiving and exploiting many possible sources of relatedness (Simon, 1961). On the other hand, managers could develop novel understandings of relatedness from their ongoing management experiences. Over time, these novel understandings may become reinforced by the success of strategic initiatives that follow from their comprehension. That is, managers may develop conceptualizations of relatedness that move beyond economic and technical criteria and include additional, and possibly very different, beliefs about how their firms' businesses relate. Studying managers' views of relatedness, Stimpert and Duhaime (1997) note the multidimensional elements of the construct. Managers themselves hold varying conceptualizations of relatedness, such that some even think of it in terms of similarities in products, markets, or technologies, consistent with traditional economic theories about diversification. Managers' perceptions of relatedness in terms of product market similarities across their firms' portfolios businesses correlate closely with commonly used SIC based measures of relatedness. However, managers tend to hold several, additional conceptualizations, including some based on differentiation characterized by a common emphasis on product design, brand name products, R&D, and the development of new products.

CONCLUDING REMARKS

This chapter focuses on the concept of relatedness and its importance for the study of a firm's diversification strategy. A thorough understanding of this concept is critical because relatedness is a condition *sine qua non* for the realization economies of scope. Such an understanding also is particularly important because relatedness is subjective. Even when potential synergies abound, actual synergy is difficult. Relatedness, when managed properly, should result in tangible and intangible synergies that allow the corporate strategy to equal more than the sum of its individual business units' strategies (Kanter, 1989; Porter, 1985; St John & Harrison, 1999). Slack resources that might not be used otherwise could be put to good use (Penrose, 1959; Teece, 1980), and scarce resources could be bargained through the intercession of the larger, more powerful, synergistic organization (Porter, 1985). The firm's performance should surpass that of its sole business competitors when the combination of its businesses offers preferential access to the types of strategic assets that underpin its cost or differentiation advantage (Markides & Williamson, 1996).

In Chapter 5, we reviewed the different mechanisms that lead to the creation of corporate value through diversification. With Chapter 6, we discussed the issue of relatedness as a potential source of corporate value creating synergies. Next, Chapter 7 deals with the relationship between the level of diversification and performance and asks: does increasing the level of firm diversification (and relatedness between business units) always lead to better performance, or is there some limit to the scope of a firm's diversity?

Chapter

7

DIVERSIFICATION AND PERFORMANCE

LIMITS TO THE SCOPE OF THE FIRM

■ ■ ■ ■ ■ ■

> Intuitively, it would seem that in a world in which transaction costs are not assumed to be unimportant, there must be a limit to how much a firm can grow in size … Were this not the case, the world would be dominated by a single megafirm.
>
> (Markides, 1992, p. 399)

In Chapter 2 we discussed different motives for diversification, and in Chapter 5 we presented different strategies that diversified firms use to create corporate value. In this chapter we focus in turn on the relationship between the level of diversification and firm's performance. As an important objective, this chapter aims for a better understanding of the limits of diversification. Therefore, we seek to demonstrate how diversification increases a firm's performance—up to a point, after which diseconomies of scope reduce its performance.

THE DIVERSIFICATION–PERFORMANCE RELATIONSHIP

The relationship between diversification and performance has attracted significant research attention in a wide variety of business disciplines (Grant, 2002; Nippa et al., 2011; Palich et al., 2000). For example, industrial organization economists initially considered the relative performance of diversified and undiversified firms (e.g., Gort, 1962; Lang & Stulz, 1994; Markham, 1973), followed by studies in strategic management (e.g., Bettis, 1981; Christensen & Montgomery, 1981; Itami et al., 1982; Markides & Williamson, 1994; Nayyar, 1992; Rumelt, 1974, 1982) and finance (e.g., Higgins & Schall, 1975; Levy & Sarnat, 1970; Lewellen, 1971) that focused more specifically on the performance differences sparked by related versus unrelated diversification strategies.

Rumelt's (1974, 1982) research represented a watershed for the study of diversification strategies. Prior research in the corporate level strategy and organizational structure fields had conceived of the trends as moving from specialization to diversification and from closely related to unrelated diversification, with the seemingly natural conclusion that broadly diversified corporations were superior, in terms of strategy, to more focused ones. By introducing financial performance into his analysis, Rumelt provided an explicit linkage between a diversification strategy and profitability and offered the key finding that in fact it was related diversification that was superior to unrelated diversification. Firms that diversify into businesses more closely linked to their core activities are more profitable than are those that diversify in less related businesses.

Many empirical studies initially supported this claim of superiority of related over unrelated diversification strategies (Bettis, 1981; Christensen & Montgomery, 1981; Lecraw, 1984; Rumelt, 1982), though as the volume and sophistication of empirical work on this relationship has grown, the findings have become increasingly inconsistent (Palich et al., 2000). Some studies find no significant relationship between relatedness in diversification and profitability (e.g., Grant et al., 1988), whereas others indicate unrelated diversification is more profitable than related diversification (David et al., 2010; Lubatkin, 1987; Luffman & Reed, 1982; Michel & Shaked, 1984). More recently, studies indicate a curvilinear (i.e., inverted U-shaped) relationship between profitability and the extent of diversification, such that diversification provides benefits up to a point, but after that point, the costs of complexity grow larger than the benefits of diversification (Grant et al., 1988; Lubatkin & Chatterjee, 1994; Markides, 1992; Palich et al., 2000; Singh et al., 2010).

BOX 7.1 DIFFERENT TYPES OF DIVERSIFICATION STRATEGIES

Most of the studies we discuss in this chapter focus only on one particular type of diversification, namely, product or horizontal diversification. Other types of diversification strategies produce rather less confusing empirical findings. That is, in contrast with the contradictory findings that mark horizontal diversification, research is generally consistent when it comes to vertical integration (see Chapter 10) and international diversification strategies (see Chapter 14). Rumelt's (1974) finding that vertically integrated firms underperform both specialized and diversified firms has been corroborated by subsequent empirical findings. Furthermore, with regard to international diversification, multinational corporations tend to outperform nationally focused firms (Grant, 1987; Grant et al., 1988; Hitt et al., 1997).

In the next sections, we review three main literature streams pertaining to the relationship between diversification and firms' profitability: one proposing a positive linear relationship between diversification and performance, another proposing a negative linear relationship, and the third arguing in favor of an inverted U-shaped relationship. The final section considers factors that may limit the scope of a firm.

LINEAR RELATIONSHIP MODELS

Beginning with Gort (1962), industrial organization (I/O) economics has spawned decades of research that relies on the premise that diversification and performance are linearly and positively related. As we discussed at length in Chapter 5, diversification creates corporate value and increases a firm's profitability through three broad mechanisms: (1) operational economies of scope; (2) financial economies of scope; and (3) anticompetitive economies of scope (e.g., Barney, 2007; Collis & Montgomery, 2005; Dess et al., 2006; Goold & Campbell, 1998; Goold et al., 1994; Hitt et al., 2005; Markides, 2002; Porter, 1985, 1987). However, this position rests upon several assumptions, including those derived from market power theory and internal market efficiency arguments (Grant, 1998; Scherer, 1980).

Many studies have concluded that diversified firms gain significant financial benefits from using internal markets for their capital and other resources, (e.g., Grant, 1998; Ravenscraft & Scherer, 1987; Rumelt, 1982; Taylor & Lowe, 1995; Williamson, 1986), yet support for this position is not universal. Bhide (1990; see also Comment & Jarrell, 1995; Markides, 1992; Matsusaka, 1993) argues for example that internal capital market advantages from diversification may have been prevalent in the 1960s, but the information asymmetries that produced this edge diminished during the 1970s and 1980s due to economic, technological, and regulatory changes. The stock market's verdict, as exemplified in the price–earnings ratios attached to conglomerates during the 1960s, have been replaced by a conglomerate discount (Villalonga, 2004b). Berger and Ofek (1995) found a diversification discount of 13 to 15 percent during the 1986–1991 period by comparing the sum of the stand-alone values of a firm's business units to the firm's actual value. Diversified companies came under attack from leveraged buyout (LBO) specialists that sought to add value by dismembering the firms. One of the most emblematic example of these attacks was the $25 billion takeover and dismembering in 1989 of the tobacco and food giant RJR Nabisco by Kohlberg Kravis Roberts' (Burrough & Helyar, 2003). The trend toward acquisition announcements that would generate abnormal stock market returns for the acquiring firms in the 1960s and 1970s reversed during the 1980s (Jarrell et al., 1988). According to Markides (1992), refocusing announcements by diversified firms often were accompanied by abnormal stock market returns.

Whether these superior returns remain stable over time remains to be seen though. Further empirical evidence suggests that on average, the costs of diversification outweigh its benefits. Berger and Ofek (1995a), Lang and Stulz (1994), and Servaes (1996) report significant value losses associated with corporate diversification strategies. Moreover, Comment and Jarrell (1995) show that many diversified firms fail to take advantage of the potential or expected benefits of diversification. In addition, Berger and Ofek (1995), Comment and Jarrell (1995), and John and Ofek (1995) report a trend toward increased corporate focus in the 1980s and demonstrate that this increase is associated with significant increases in shareholder value.

Although sharing activities and resources can lead to unit cost savings and enhanced differentiation, exploiting interrelationships through diversification also may induce several categories of costs, namely, the cost of coordination, as influenced by the potential for greater complexity in a shared activity; the cost of compromise, because businesses may have to perform an activity in a suboptimal manner to share it with other units; and the cost of inflexibility (Porter, 1985). Furthermore, corporate headquarters may suffer from limited information processing capabilities (bounded rationality), especially in the face of the enormously complex information needs required for the strategic management of a large range of businesses (Hill, 1994). As the diversified company becomes more complex, the likelihood of political maneuvering and tactical self-interested behavior by business management teams inevitably increase (Campbell & Sadtler, 1998). Generally, corporate staff have moved far away from the real business and lack direct exposure to their customers and the market. Therefore, the service they provide tends to be unresponsive or uncompetitive—or both.

THE INVERTED U-SHAPED MODEL

In contrast with the preceding arguments, some researchers posit a curvilinear diversification–performance relationship. This argument recognizes that increasing diversification may not be associated with concomitant increases in performance, at least not across the entire diversification continuum. The inverted U-shaped model therefore indicates that some diversification (i.e., moderate levels or related constrained diversification) is better than none (i.e., single business) and than too much (i.e., unrelated diversification) (see Figure 7.1).

According to this inverted U-shaped model, with limited diversification, the firm focuses on a single industry, which limits its opportunities to leverage its resources and capabilities across divisions. Lubatkin and Chatterjee (1994) argue that single business firms also lack the opportunity to exploit synergies or portfolio effects, because these overly focused firms do not have multiple businesses, and they cannot benefit from scope economies. Furthermore, these firms bear greater risk, because they cannot combine revenues from multiple businesses. This tactic has negative implications for their debt capacity, cost of capital, and market performance (Lubatkin & Chatterjee, 1994; Shleifer & Vishny, 1991).

In contrast to single business firms and firms with limited levels of diversification (e.g., dominant

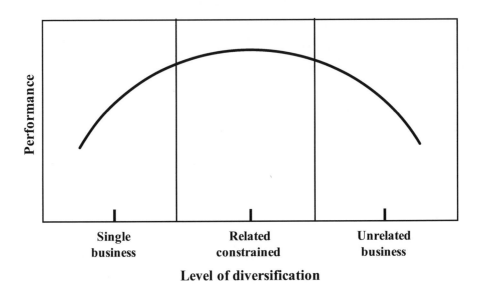

Figure 7.1 Curvilinear relationship between diversification and performance
Source: Adapted from Palich et al. (2000)

business firms), related diversifiers become involved in multiple industries with businesses that can employ a common pool of corporate resources (Lubatkin & O'Neill, 1987; Nayyar, 1992), which yields corporate advantages. Theoretical rationales that suggest the superiority of related diversification have proliferated, but perhaps the most common focuses on the advantages derived from economies of scope, as discussed in Chapter 5. Beyond the economies of scope that derive from activity sharing though, related firms can benefit from learning curve efficiencies, intrafirm product and process technology diffusion, and restricted access to factors of production that are necessary for operations in a specific industry (Barney, 2007).

Although these benefits may accrue to diversifying firms, at some point, their diversification efforts also invoke major costs. Grant et al. (1988) recognize the growing strain on top management that tries to manage an increasingly disparate portfolio of less and less related businesses. Markides (1992) delineates other costs, such as control and effort losses (i.e., due to managerial opportunism), coordination costs, and diseconomies related to the organization, as well as inefficiencies from conflicting 'dominant logics' between the various businesses and internal capital markets. In summary, the marginal costs of diversification increase rapidly when diversification hits high levels, such that on either side of an optimal level of diversification, performance decrements occur. Related diversification is superior to diversification that is unrelated or conglomerate in nature, implying an inverted U-shaped relationship between diversification and firm performance. Palich et al. (2000) meta-analysis of 55 studies published between 1971 and 1997 provides empirical support for this inverted U-shaped relationship. Similarly, Bausch and Pils (2009) meta-analytically integrate empirical data from 104 studies published between 1970 and 2005 and found that there is no such thing as a universally valid diversification strategy–performance linkage.

In sum, the above review of the literature reveals that there is no clear empirical evidence of an unconditional advantage or disadvantage of corporate diversification (Bausch & Pils, 2009; Nippa et al., 2011; Palich et al., 2000) (see Table 7.1). To date, the inverted-U model seems to have the most support in empirical studies and meta-analyses.

Table 7.1 Theoretical rationales and empirical evidence of the diversification–performance link

Value enhancing models	*Inverted U models*	*Value destroying models*

Theoretical rationales

• Market power advantages such as cross-subsidization	• Synergies and parenting advantage can be exploited to only a certain degree of diversification	• Internal power struggles increase influence costs
• Economies of scale and scope regarding multiple-use resources	• Competitive advantages restricted to related diversification	• Inefficient internal capital markets
• Capital market advantages and more efficient allocation	• The less related the diversification the more costs outlast benefits	• Inappropriate expansion due to agency problems
• Corporate diversification reduces risk, or volatility of return		

Empirical evidence

• Schoar (2002)	• Rumelt (1975, 1982)	• Lang & Stulz (1994)
• Mathur et al. (2004)	• Itami et al. (1982)	• Berger & Ofek (1995)
• Jandik & Makhija (2005)	• Grant et al. (1988)	• Servaes (1996)
• Yan (2006)	• Wernerfelt & Montgomery (1988)	• Rajan et al. (2000)
• David et al. (2010)	• Palich et al. (2000)	• Maksimovic & Philips (2002)
	• Singh et al. (2010)	• Denis et al. (2002)
	• Villalonga (2004a)	• Best et al. (2004)

Source: Palich et al. (2000) and Nippa et al. (2011)

LIMITS ON THE SCOPE OF THE FIRM

Can an appropriately organized, diversified firm continue to expand indefinitely, as Penrose (1959) has suggested, or are there organizational limits to its scope? In the introductory quote to this chapter, Markides (1992) acknowledges that intuition implies there should be some limit, and empirical support for the inverted U-shaped relationship between profitability and the extent of diversification (Palich et al., 2000) provides research support for such limits. Moreover, in his seminal article, Coase (1937) indicated that limits to scope take the form of diminishing returns to management; otherwise, all production conceivably would be organized within the confines of one really big firm.

According to RBV (Penrose, 1959; Teece, 1982), diversification is prompted by the excess capacity of less than perfectly marketable resources. Wernerfelt and Montgomery (1988) argue that such resources provide diminished returns when used outside the initially chosen industry. That is, marginal returns decrease as firms diversify farther afield. This claim is consistent with Schmalensee's (1985) argument that widely diversified firms cannot transfer their competence to a host of different markets, which in turn implies limits to the scope of the firm.

From an agency theory perspective, Jensen (1996) proposes that managers of a diversified firm may be inclined to invest free cash flows in projects that are unlikely to increase the firm's profitability (Berger & Ofek, 1995; Bolton & Scharfstein, 1990; Stulz, 1990). In a diversified firm, the costs of controlling for such managerial opportunism outweigh the benefits of diversification, so shareholders limit the scope of their firms (Jensen, 1986).

Transaction cost literature also focuses on factors that determine the bureaucratic costs of internal governance (Williamson, 1985), that is, the costs of managing exchanges within the firm, which represent internal organizational equivalents of transaction costs. These costs include not just the costs of hierarchy but also the inefficiencies that arise within hierarchies due to information processing problems in complex organizations (Hill & Hoskisson, 1987; Jones & Hill, 1988), internal politics (Milgrom & Roberts, 1990), and incentive distortions (Williamson, 1985). We discuss these three limiting factors in turn.

Information processing constraints

Agency theory suggests that the internal incentives and control structure of the firm are of critical importance (Jensen & Meckling, 1976; Fama, 1980). Within a diversified firm, top managers located at corporate headquarters represent the principals, and divisional managers are the agents (Hill, 1994). In the absence of adequate monitoring by corporate management, the agents have a tendency to engage in opportunistic behavior (e.g., shirking, free riding, pursuing subgoals that do not achieve efficiency maximization) (Demsetz, 1983). Accordingly, one of the basic functions of corporate management is to monitor the performance of divisional managers and ensure that they perform adequately (we discuss this function in more detail in Chapter 8). However, even in the perfectly organized firms, the ability of top management to perform a monitoring function depends on information processing capabilities—which ultimately are limited by managers' bounded rationality (Simon, 1961)—as well as the amount of information that managers must process to reduce opportunism to acceptable levels (Hill, 1994). When corporate managers' information processing capabilities are insufficient to process the necessary amount of information and reduce opportunism, they suffer a loss of control, increased opportunistic behavior, and suboptimal corporate value creation. In such a situation, the management costs are likely higher than the potential benefits earned from diversification.

The amount of information necessary to reduce opportunism to acceptable levels depends on both the number of divisions (or business units) in the firm's portfolio and the interdependencies among those divisions (Hill, 1994; Hill & Hoskisson, 1987; Jones & Hill, 1988). Because the amount of information needed to make meaningful capital investment decisions in highly diversified firms exceeds the information processing capabilities of the top management team, corporate management often allocates large budgets to different divisions with competing claims, solely on the basis of a superficial investment analysis (Bettis & Hall, 1983; Haspeslagh, 1982). That is, highly diversified firms may reach a point of diminishing returns to their diversification. Information processing constraints also make the firms' internal capital markets less efficient than are external capital markets, which limit the efficient scope of these firms.

Internal politics and influence costs

Another important source of management costs relates to the inefficiencies associated with organizational politics and conflicts between divisions (Hill, 1994). Milgrom and Roberts (1990, p. 58) coined the term 'influence costs' to describe these inefficiencies and define them as "the losses that arise from individuals within an organization seeking to influence its decisions for their private benefit (and from their perhaps succeeding to do so) and from the organization's responding to control this behavior."

Diversification and performance

According to Milgrom and Roberts (1990), influence costs arise in diversified firms because division managers expend time and effort to influence the decisions of corporate management. Their objective is to convince corporate management to make decisions that are consistent with the subgoals of the division managers. Therefore, influence costs actually are agency costs that arise because inefficient decisions result from these efforts or, less directly, from attempts to control them. As an implicit assumption, this perspective holds that the subgoals of division managers diverge from those of corporate managers when the latter act to maximize corporate value creation. Such influence is inevitable, because corporate decision makers must rely on division managers for information, which gives the division managers frequent opportunities to distort or withhold information (i.e., gatekeeper phenomenon).

Hill (1994) also argues for a direct relationship between corporate management's information processing constraints and influence costs, which contribute to limits on the scope of firms. When the extent of firm diversification is limited, the information processing capabilities of corporate management exceed the information processing capabilities required to control division managers. Although influence problems may occur, they remain limited, because corporate managers can cross-check the validity of any information provided by division managers. Corporate management can exploit this control method by assigning its corporate staff to undertake independent audits of operating divisions suspected of withholding or distorting information (Chandler, 1962; Williamson, 1970, 1975). The knowledge of the possibility of such an audit might be enough to reduce division managers' opportunism and minimize influence costs. However, when the information processing requirements vastly exceed the information processing capabilities of corporate managers, influence may become a serious problem that further limits the scope of the firm.

Incentive problems

Finally, to reduce business unit managers' opportunism and limit monitoring costs, corporate management may design an incentive system that aligns business unit managers' goals with those of corporate managers (Hill, 1994). However, such an incentive system is likely to be costly and can create its own set of incentive problems. According to Williamson (1985), the incentive problems that arise within a management hierarchy constitute a major source of bureaucratic costs; he finds incentive problems any time corporate management tries to impose market incentives on the firm.

To motivate divisional managers to improve the performance of their business unit, corporate management may provide incentives based on performance, such as a share of the profit generated by their division in the form of bonuses. Business unit managers also receive an implicit promise of promotion if they maximize their business unit performance. However, because business unit managers' tenure in their job is likely to be limited—the incentive system pushes them into new promotions and increased income categories—they may underinvest in assets and upgrades, which maximizes the current and short term profits of their business unit at the cost of long term efficiency and profits (Hill, 1994; Hoskisson & Hitt, 1988). Results of a study of 124 large U.S. firms by Hoskisson and Hitt (1988) suggest that less diversified firms invest more heavily in R&D than more diversified firms after controlling for size and industry effects.

This short term profit maximization problem appears endemic to highly diversified firms (Baysinger & Hoskisson, 1989; Hayes & Abernathy, 1980; Hill et al., 1988; Hoskisson & Hitt, 1988). As long as corporate management has sufficient information processing capacity, it can attenuate the problem by monitoring the business units and ensuring business unit managers do not opportunistically underinvest in asset upgrades. However, if the scope and complexity of the firm stretches the information processing capabilities of corporate management to and beyond their limit, the problem may become severe (Hill, 1994).

In addition to the short term profit maximization problem, performance based incentive systems for business unit managers may encourage another form of opportunism. That is, by gearing bonus

Diversification and performance

pay to business unit performance and allocating capital among the business units on the basis of relative yields, the firm reinforces business unit managers' incentive to maximize their performance. The system therefore likely produces competition among the divisions for more capital (Williamson, 1975) (see Box 7.2). This type of rivalry can impair the transfer of skills and knowledge across business units and reduce cooperation, which eliminates economies of scope. In contrast, the firm could encourage cooperation by implementing incentive systems that emphasize interunit cooperation rather than each business unit's performance as an independent unit (Gupta

BOX 7.2 COMPETING SUBSIDIARIES: THE ENEMY WITHIN

Sometimes global firms with large business portfolios face an unexpected enemy: themselves. Recent reports reveal that Coca-Cola was being sold in Spain without the blessing of the U.S. soft drink giant's local subsidiary, which saw its market being invaded by the same product—at a lower price! Coca-Cola España was surprised to discover the recent arrival of these import products and quickly found that independent consignments had been sent to hotel management firms, which then marketed them in Catalonia, a northeastern region with easy and inexpensive access to the rest of Europe. Using the Internet, distributors and hotel management firms acquired massive quantities from Coca-Cola subsidiaries in foreign countries, such as Egypt and Poland, for between 26 and €30 cents, whereas Coca-Cola bottled in Spain sells for about €45 cents. In 2009, the imported bottles accounted for approximately 4 percent of Coca-Cola sales in Spain, which reduced the Spanish subsidiary's €3 billion annual revenues by about 2 percent. How should Coca-Cola's corporate headquarters in Atlanta respond to this rivalry between its subsidiaries?

There is no easy or straightforward answer for headquarters. In the EU, firms cannot prevent the free circulation of goods across national borders. The EU imposes severe fines on firms that try to restrict competition within its borders. Legally, firms also cannot prohibit parallel imports and marketing policies. Because trade restrictions are illegal, corporate headquarters cannot exert influence over or even negotiate with the distributors. This restriction poses a serious concern for firms such as Coca-Cola with local production facilities in each country and agreements with national bottlers.

In fact, Coca-Cola is a collection of nationally localized firm; its corporate headquarters in Atlanta is 'nothing more than the brand.' The corporate headquarters sells the syrup to its national bottlers, but the beverage itself is manufactured in each country independently. In Spain, to prevent customers from buying products imported from other countries, Coca-Cola has begun an advertising campaign to boost consumption of the locally produced soft drink. The campaign reminds Coca-Cola drinkers that their consumer rights to information are guaranteed, so the retail price they pay is the same, regardless of where the soft drinks are produced. It also points out that by consuming soft drinks bottled locally, customers are helping the environment.

However, a similar issue occurred in Switzerland in 2014, when a large retailer started to import Coca-Cola soft drink from the Czech Republic. Coca-Cola Swiss subsidiary reacted first by coining a 'Made in Switzerland' logo with the Swiss map and flag on the labels and caps of its bottles and cans and then negotiated price discount with the retailer to stop parallel imports in September 2015.

Source: Universia Knowledge@Wharton (www.wharton.universia.net/index.cfm?fa=print Article&ID=1772&language=English) and Blick (www.blick.ch/news/wirtschaft/ schluss-mit-tschechen-brause-denner-siegt-im-cola-krieg-id3982129.html)

& Govindarajan, 1986; Kerr, 1985; Lorsch & Allen, 1973; Pitts, 1974; Salter, 1973). Such an incentive system might rely on profit bonus schemes for business unit managers that are linked to corporate rather than business unit profitability. Because corporate profitability depends on interunit cooperation, these reward systems provide business unit managers with a good incentive to cooperate. However, a corporate performance based incentive system also may induce opportunism in the form of free riding. The business unit managers' rewards depend on the efforts of the other business unit managers, as well as their own, so a savvy business unit manager might reduce his or her own efforts, because doing so does not strongly affect individual bonuses.

Because no incentive system can completely eliminate the risks of business unit managers' opportunism, some other forms of control must be installed. The costs of these alternative control systems are in proportion to the level of diversification of the firm, which once more means a limit on its diversification.

DEMAND FOR BUSINESS RESPONSIVENESS

Another factor that limits the scope of the firm is the potential incompatibilities between the firm's corporate level strategy and its business units' competitive strategies. When business units need to be highly responsive to their competitive environment, functioning as part of a diversified firm may constrain them. Responsiveness entails an ability to react to the competitive demands of a specific business area in a timely and adequate manner. That is, a business unit is responsive if it has the capability to match its strategic behavior to the competitive dynamics in its business. If a business unit does not focus its strategy on the conditions in its direct environment, nor organize its value adding activities and management systems to fit with the business characteristics, it will soon suffer a competitive disadvantage compared with more responsive rivals. Business responsiveness thus is a key demand for successful corporate level strategy. Yet in diversified firms, the responsiveness of the business units comes under constant pressure, such as when the firm seeks to create synergies among its various business units. Therefore, the need for responsiveness by the firm's business units, related to their business level strategies, creates some limits to the overall scope of the firm.

CONCLUDING REMARKS

The inverted U-shaped relationship in Figure 7.1 represents the research consensus, but studies often disagree, particularly those that find variations over time and across countries (see Mayer & Whittington, 2003; Chakrabarti et al., 2007) (see Box 7.3). In Latin America and other emerging economies such as China, Korea, and India, highly diversified conglomerates continue to dominate national economies (Fauver et al., 2003; Keister, 2000; Khanna & Palepu, 1997a; Khanna & Rivkin, 2001; Wan & Hoskisson, 2003). For example, in Taiwan, the largest 100 corporate groups produce one third of the gross national product (GNP) (Chung, 2001). Typically family controlled, these groups also account for the largest percentage of firms in India (Manikutty, 2000). Challenges to the viability of these large, diversified groups (Chang & Hong, 2002; Ferris et al., 2003; Lins & Servaes, 2002) are especially pertinent in developed economies such as Japan (Dewenter et al., 2001), though existing evidence suggests that if capital markets and legal system are underdeveloped, high levels of diversification still produce better performance (Fauver et al., 2003).

In this chapter, we have investigated the relationship between firm performance and the extent of diversification. Recent empirical evidence suggests that the form of this relationship is an inverted U, which implies a limit to the scope of firms. We highlight that this limit largely is determined by the information processing constraints that corporate management suffers, as well as

BOX 7.3 THE INSTITUTIONAL CONTEXT OF DIVERSIFICATION

In an empirical study, Mayer and Whittington (2003) have examined the stability of diversification performance relationships in three European countries (France, Germany, and the U.K.) for two time periods (1982–84 and 1992–94). At an aggregate level (i.e., combining the three countries and two time periods), a related constrained diversification strategy achieves the best performance, in support of Palich et al. (2000) findings. However, disaggregated analyses demonstrate sharp variations across the different countries and time periods. In the U.K., no statistically significant diversification–performance relationships mark British firms. The authors attain the same results for France in 1983, though by 1993, related constrained strategies had emerged as the most positive and significant business approaches. For Germany in 1983, only related linked diversification strategies exhibited a significant positive relationship to performance. Just as in France though, related constrained strategies were associated with statistically significant performance effects in 1993.

Two theoretical arguments may explain these differences. First, the relationship between diversification and performance could vary across countries, because of institutional effects (Khanna & Rivkin, 2001); second, it could vary across time because of learning effects (Grant & Jammine, 1988).

Variations across countries

Mayer and Whittington (2003) argue that two primary factors lead to cross national variations in the relationship between diversification and performance. In particular, the efficiency of external markets for products, capital, and labor varies across countries (Khanna & Rivkin, 2001; Ramaswamy et al., 2002). In areas where external markets work inefficiently, the relative advantage of internal hierarchies may be greater and lead, for example, to greater advantages derived from membership in an unrelated conglomerate. Yet differences between efficient and inefficient strategies also may be lower due to agency problems (Eisenhardt, 1989). Countries vary widely in the discipline that the market exerts over managerial agents when it comes to corporate control and other mechanisms of corporate governance (Shleifer & Vishny, 1997). These differences alter the ability of agents to expropriate the benefits of effective strategies for themselves, rather than as profits passed on to owners (Fligstein & Brantley, 1992; Li & Simerly, 1998). When agents can expropriate such benefits, the relative advantage of diversification strategies likely diminishes.

Variations across time

According to Mayer and Whittington (2003), the expectation that diversification–performance relationships vary over time relies on three main concepts. First, firms may become more adept at extracting potential advantages as managers learn over time (Eisenhardt & Martin, 2000). Second, the institutional foundations for local diversification–performance relationships may shift, such as when external markets become more efficient in some nations (Shleifer & Vishny, 1997). Third, performance differences may be attenuated over time, because a movement toward equilibrium prompts firms that are unsuited to certain strategies to abandon them, leaving only more efficient firms in place (Armour & Teece, 1978).

the risks of divisional managers' opportunism. In the next two chapters, we pursue a better understanding of how to manage both these factors. Specifically, in Chapter 8 we discuss the role of the corporate parent in managing and controlling business units, and in Chapter 9 we discuss the organizational structure of diversified firms and how it can help corporate managers implement their corporate strategy and reduce division managers' opportunism.

Chapter

8

THE ROLE OF THE PARENT

MANAGING THE MULTIBUSINESS FIRM

If a multibusiness corporation is to be viable, the additional profits generated by bringing several businesses together under common ownership and control must exceed the costs of establishing and running the corporate headquarters. Certainly, corporate parents have critical effects—they account for 1–2 percent (Rumelt, 1991), 4 percent (McGahan & Porter, 1997), or 5–15 percent (Brush et al., 1999) of the aggregate variance in profitability, depending on which study we trust (Armstrong & Shimizu, 2007). But how exactly does corporate headquarters create such value, and what are its main tasks? To explore the potential promise of corporate management as a means to add value, we must start by defining what is a corporate headquarters and considering its role and functions. Collis et al. (2007, p. 385) define the corporate headquarters as "the staff functions and executive management with responsibility for, or providing services to, the whole of (or most of) the company, excluding staff employed in divisional headquarters." In Chapter 5, we argued, in line with Goold et al. (1994), that corporate headquarters should serve as an intermediary between shareholders and the businesses. Corporate management is critical for providing goals, directions, guidelines, structures, and control systems to business unit managers (Burgelman, 1983) that facilitate the performance of their assigned tasks and responsibilities (Collis & Montgomery, 1998; Goold et al., 1994, Kownatzki et al., 2013; Nell & Ambos, 2013).

However, what are the specific roles and functions of a multibusiness firm's corporate headquarters? And, how are these roles and functions affected by the corporate level strategy of the firm? These questions are particularly relevant given the astounding variation in the size, structure, and performance of various corporate headquarters (Collis et al., 2007). In 2014, the LBO firm KKR & Co. (Kohlberg Kravis Roberts) controlled more than $101 billion in assets with fewer than 140 staff members at its corporate headquarters, whereas Coca-Cola needs nearly 13,000 corporate employees to handle less than $46 billion in revenues. Even within a single industry and one country, the differences can be notable. In Germany in 1999, before its merger with French Rhône-Poulenc, the German chemical and pharmaceutical firm Hoechst employed 180 people to run its corporate headquarters, whereas its competitor Bayer hired close to 7,000 (Bühner, 2000). In a survey designed to determine the structure and staffing of more than 600 corporate headquarters in Europe, the U.S., Japan, and Chile, Collis et al. (2007) found that the smallest have fewer than ten staff members, and the largest have many thousands. They also assert that the corporate headquarters must be designed to fit the corporate level strategy, whatever it is, for the firm to benefit from improved performance (see Box 1.4 in Chapter 1).

Through their survey, Collis et al. (2007) also found that almost all firms employed staff at the corporate headquarters in general management, legal, financial reporting and control, treasury, and taxation activities. Other functions appeared more discretionary, such as internal audits, payroll and benefits administration, human resource and personnel policies, training and education, government and public relations, corporate planning and development, R&D, marketing and commercial services, purchasing and inbound logistics, distribution and outbound logistics, and information systems and telecommunications. The centralization of such discretionary tasks at the corporate headquarters depends on the firm specific role of the headquarters and its corporate level strategies.

In his seminal book, *Strategy and Structure*, Chandler (1962, p. 9) argues that the division of activities between organizational levels should be clear: operating (business) units have authority over the activities needed to compete in their business; headquarters (or the center or parent) have two specific functions to perform: "coordinate, appraise and plan goals and policies" and "allocate resources." He later revisited the topic in light of economic research on economies of scope (Teece, 1980, 1982) and agency costs (Jensen & Meckling, 1976) and reclassified these functions or tasks as "entrepreneurial" (i.e., value creating) versus "administrative" (i.e., loss preventing) (Chandler, 1991, p. 31). Collis and Montgomery (2005) refined the typology and identified four tasks for corporate headquarters: (1) leadership, which consists of setting the goals and objectives of the firm's corporate level strategy; (2) managing the corporate portfolio of businesses, including defining the scope of the firm; (3) allocating resources across different businesses; and (4) administration, which consists of designing, implementing, and controlling the corporate structure, systems, and processes. Other scholars have developed similar classifications (e.g., Foss, 1997; Goold et al., 1994; Grant, 2013; Markides, 2002). Beyond these tasks, the main functions of the corporate headquarters are to manage the consistency or fit among the tasks themselves (Collis & Montgomery, 2005; Goold et al., 1994).

As argued by van Oijen and Douma (2000), corporate headquarters can perform its role in different ways, but the role should be consistent with the firm's corporate level strategy to create corporate value. The wrong choice, for example, could lead to excessive overhead costs or undermine the competitive strategies of the firm's business units. Collis and Montgomery (2005) recognize that a corporate advantage results from a harmonious combination of the three sides of the corporate triangle—resources, businesses, and organization (see Chapter 1)—which must align in the pursuit of a vision and be motivated by the appropriate goals and objectives (i.e., corporate value creation mechanisms). Their assertion receives empirical support from the results of Collis et al.'s (2007) survey.

Therefore, depending on the firm's main corporate value creation mechanism (e.g., sharing resources and activities, transferring skills, leveraging core competencies, creating an efficient internal capital market), the tasks of the corporate headquarters must differ (Markides, 2002). The level of diversification (i.e., focus, related, or unrelated diversification) represents a key element that influences the role of corporate headquarters, as the research summary in Box 8.1 details.

Whatever the level of firm diversification, the critical issue for creating corporate value is always the fit between the resources and capabilities of the firm and its corporate level strategy, business portfolio, resources, organization structure, and management systems. The resources and capabilities that reside with the corporate headquarters are fundamental determinants of the optimal configuration of different elements of the firm's corporate level strategy. To gain insight into these linkages, Goold et al. (1994, 1995) invoke the concept of parenting style to analyze the relationship between corporate headquarters and individual businesses of diversified firms. Box 8.2 describes how Philips delineates the role of its corporate headquarters.

The tasks and functions of the corporate headquarters also include designing and implementing a value creating, corporate level strategy, which means setting goals and objectives, managing the scope of the firm, allocating resources across business units, and organizing and controlling business units (Foss, 1997; Goold et al., 1994; Goold et al., 2001; Nell & Ambos, 2013). In Chapter 5, we already discussed how to create corporate value (i.e., the goals and objectives); in Chapter 9, we outline how headquarters should design the organizational structure to ensure coordination

BOX 8.1 DIVERSIFICATION STRATEGY AND THE TASKS OF THE CORPORATE HEADQUARTERS

In a study of 67 firms listed on the Amsterdam Stock Exchange, van Oijen and Douma (2000) found that the firms with the best performance also exhibited a better fit between their diversification strategies and their corporate headquarters' roles compared with firms with the poorest performance.

These authors identify seven different roles for corporate headquarters:

(1) *Planning:* Shaping the strategic plans for the business units;
(2) *Evaluation:* Assessing the investment proposals and results of the business units;
(3) *Selection:* Appointing key personnel to the business units;
(4) *Rotation:* Organizing the rotation of personnel across business units;
(5) *Motivation:* Providing business units managers with financial and career incentives;
(6) *Coordination:* Installing mechanisms that encourage cooperation among business units;
(7) *Support:* Performing services for the business units.

As the diversification level increases, firms with stronger financial performance became less involved in planning, relied more on financial criteria for evaluation, became less involved in selection, used more financially oriented motivations, and offered fewer centralized support services. Firms with weaker financial performance instead were more involved in selection, organized more rotations, and used more strategically oriented forms of motivation.

According to these findings, when the level of diversification increases and business units become more unrelated, headquarters should reduce their involvement in the operations of the business units, reduce coordination, and develop an efficient internal capital market. When the level of diversification decreases though and business units become more related, headquarters must be more involved in their business units' operations to achieve economies of scope through resource sharing or the transfer of skills and competencies.

BOX 8.2 THE TASKS OF PHILIPS' HEADQUARTERS

Koninklijke Philips Electronics N.V. is the corporate parent company of the Philips Group. The group activities in the field of health and well-being are organized on a sector basis, with each operating sector—Healthcare, Consumer Lifestyle and Lighting—being responsible for the management of its businesses worldwide. The corporate headquarters aims, through the Innovation & Emerging Businesses sector, to invest in projects that are not currently part of the operating sectors, but which will lead to additional organic growth or create value through future spin-offs. The Group Management & Services sector provides the sectors with support through shared service centers. Furthermore, country management supports the creation of value, connecting Philips with key stakeholders, especially employees, customers, government and society. This sector also includes global service units, pensions and global brand campaign activities.

Source: Philips 2008 Annual Report (www.annualreport2008.philips.com)

and control; and in Chapters 11 and 12, we detail how to manage the scope of the firm through internal development, M&A, strategic alliances, and restructuring. For this chapter though, we focus on two critical functions of the headquarters: maintaining control and achieving coherence (fit).

To understand the necessary fit between a firm's diversification strategy and the role of the corporate headquarters, we discuss ways to manage an unrelated diversified firm through resource allocations and a related diversified firm by managing the linkages among businesses through sharing and transferring resources and capabilities.

THE TASKS AND RESPONSIBILITIES OF CORPORATE MANAGEMENT

The main responsibilities of corporate management include administrative and leadership tasks to implement the firm's corporate level strategy, participation in the business units' competitive strategy formulation, the allocation of resources across business units, coordination of the relationships of the different divisions, and fostering overall cohesion, identity, and direction within the company. These responsibilities may be regrouped into four value adding activities for corporate headquarters: (1) *managing the corporate portfolio*, including M&A, divestments, and restructuring; (2) *legal and public representation*, which includes external tax and financial reporting; (3) *exercising guidance and control* over individual businesses, such as exerting influence over business strategy formulation, allocating resources, and managing financial performance; and (4) *managing linkages* among businesses by sharing and transferring resources and capabilities.

Managing the corporate portfolio

Managing the scope of the corporate portfolio requires consideration of activities such as M&A, divestments, and restructuring, as we discuss in detail in Chapters 11 and 12. For this chapter, it is only important to understand that the role of corporate headquarters is to make decisions about the scope of the firm's portfolio. Corporate headquarters may decide to increase the firm's scope by adding new divisions to its business portfolio through internal development, mergers, or acquisitions. It also might reduce the scope by closing or divesting itself of some business units. Finally, it could restructure its business portfolio by splitting or combining existing business units.

Public and legal representation

Corporate headquarters is the legal representative of the firm (Collis et al., 2007). As such, it must perform all the obligatory reporting and compliance functions, whether legal, financial, or regulatory, to demonstrate due diligence on behalf of shareholders and other stakeholders (as discussed in Chapter 15 on corporate governance).

Exercising guidance and control: Three parenting styles

It is also the task of corporate headquarters to guide and control the activities of its business units. Agency theory provides a framework for understanding the operations of the corporate control function of the multibusiness firm (Eisenhardt, 1985, 1989; Jensen & Meckling, 1976), because it highlights the adverse consequences of delegation and explains that without appropriate control systems, corporate headquarters lose the ability to develop and implement corporate level strategies effectively (see Chapter 2). Business units need to operate autonomously to maximize their own performance, but there also must be some sort of corporate control to prevent them from pursuing solely their self-interest, at the expense of the firm as a whole (Collis & Montgomery,

2005). This demand is even more critical when the firm seeks to achieve operational synergies across business units.

The control system adopted by diversified firms focuses mostly on three dimensions: the outcome (i.e., financial), the behavior (i.e., operational), and the content of the business strategy (i.e., strategic planning), such that business unit managers get evaluated on their performance and their actions (Collis & Montgomery, 2005; Eisenhardt, 1985; Kownatzki et al., 2013; Ouchi, 1979). The information needed for these two control systems differs greatly and has important implications for the tasks performed by corporate headquarters (Hill et al., 1992).

In multibusiness firms, *outcome control*, which is sometimes also referred to as financial control (Chung et al., 2000; Goold & Campbell, 1987) or budgetary control (Goold & Quinn, 1990), consists in corporate headquarters establishing short term, objective, and predominantly financial goals for business units, such as return on invested capital, and monitoring business unit performance against those goals (Collis & Montgomery, 1998; Goold et al., 1994; Hill & Hoskisson, 1987; Kownatzki et al., 2013). Corporate headquarters using outcome control tend to not formally review long term strategic plans, and responsibility for strategy formulation is usually delegated to business unit management (Chung et al., 2000). Outcome control motivates business unit managers to focus on improving their financial performance and abandoning ineffective strategies (Kownatzki et al., 2013). As such, it indirectly influences business units' strategic decisions by aligning business unit managers' incentives with corporate goals. The disadvantages of outcome control are limited flexibility and a bias against long term goals and strategies and risk taking (Goold & Campbell, 1987). Outcome control is relatively easier to implement, as it generally requires little interference by corporate headquarters compared to behavioral control, which demand that corporate headquarters monitor and even intervene in operational business decisions (Collis & Montgomery, 2005).

Behavior control, which is sometimes also referred to as strategic planning (Chung et al., 2000; Goold & Campbell, 1987) or budgetary control (Goold & Quinn, 1990), relies on subjective, strategically relevant criteria to assess business unit activity and measures performance in the context of progress toward the development of a long term strategy (Collis & Montgomery, 1998; Goold et al., 1994; Hoskisson & Hitt, 1988; Kownatzki et al., 2013). Corporate headquarters actively participates in and influences the strategy formulation process of the business units (Chung et al., 2000), but without imposing a specific strategy (Kownatzki et al., 2013). Behavior control not only provides checks and balances for business unit strategy development, but also provides a common organizational culture that facilitates collaboration between business units and fosters the creation of synergies. On the downside, behavior control places more demands, in terms of coordination, on an organization and generally leads to larger corporate headquarters (Collis & Montgomery, 1998). Behavior control can also lead to motivation problems at the business unit level, as the involvement of different hierarchical levels can make the process cumbersome, overly bureaucratic, frustrating, and costly (Goold & Campbell, 1987; Kownatzki et al., 2013).

Content control, which is also referred to as planning influence (Goold & Campbell, 1987), refers to the degree to which corporate headquarters exerts influence on the actual substance of strategy at the business unit level (Kownatzki et al., 2013; Muralidharan, 1997). On the one hand, retaining content autonomy at the business unit level is advantageous, as this level is most likely to have better access to the pertinent information necessary for strategic planning. On the other hand, when coordination, cooperation, and resource sharing are needed among business units, some degree of headquarters influence is required over the substance of business unit strategies (Gupta & Govindarajan, 1986; Hill et al., 1992; Hill & Hoskisson, 1987; Kownatzki et al., 2013).

These differences between control systems make their choice contingent on other elements of a firm's corporate level strategy and corporate value creation mechanisms. An unrelated diversification strategy that creates corporate value through financial economies of scope likely can be managed better with financial controls in a more decentralized manner than can related diversification, which would require much more active coordination and the use of behavior and content control mechanisms (Collis et al., 2007). This is, outcome control is most effective for highly diversified firms with unrelated business units that share few common resources (Goold & Campbell, 1987; Hill & Hoskisson, 1987; Jones & Hill, 1988; Vancil, 1978), but compete for resource allocations from the corporate headquarters (Hillet al, 1992). However, because it does not involve how goals are achieved, outcome control is less effective to realize and exploit synergies among businesses (Hill & Hoskisson, 1987). In contrast, behavior control is most effective for firms with low degrees of diversification and high level of relatedness between business units (Good & Campbell, 1987), in which business unit performance requires extensive cooperation, and resource sharing (Hill et al., 1992; Hill & Hoskisson, 1987; Lorsch & Allen, 1973; Vencil, 1978). Similarly, content control is also most effective for firms with related businesses and low level of diversification, in which coordination and centralization are critical to create value at the corporate level (Kownatzki et al., 2013).

Goold and Campbell (1987) similarly distinguish three general corporate control styles, each emphasizing different levels of planning and control influence (see Figure 8.1), then relate them to different corporate level strategies. Planning influence refers to the approach that the corporate headquarters takes to the formulation of plans, strategies, and budgets in businesses. It varies from low (highly decentralized) to high (headquarters is much more closely involved and influential). Control influence instead refers to the approach of the corporate parent to the control process. At one extreme, corporate parents emphasize the achievement of short term financial targets (i.e., tight financial outcome control), whereas at the other extreme, they are concerned primarily with strategic goals and underlying competitive strategies, which makes them more flexible with regard to the short term financial targets (i.e., flexible behavioral control). Finally, in the middle sit corporate parents that implement tight controls but also seek a balance between financial and strategic targets (i.e., tight strategic control).

Even if several combinations of planning and control influences appear within the organization, most firms' parenting style can be classified into one of the following styles (Goold & Campbell, 1987):

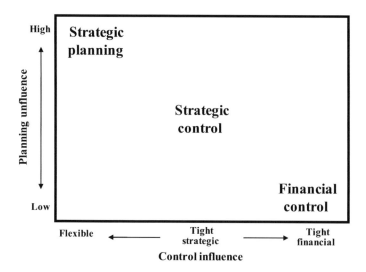

Figure 8.1 Parenting styles

Source: Adapted from Goold & Campbell (1987)

The role of the parent

1   **Strategic planning**: Parents are closely involved with their businesses to formulate plans and decisions. They provide a clear, overall sense of direction, from which their businesses develop strategies and take the lead on selected corporate development initiatives. Strategic business units have relatively little autonomy, and many key activities are centralized or standardized. Corporate headquarters also is heavily involved in securing cross business coordination and resource sharing. This control style is mostly used by focused firms or those with a limited level of diversification.

2   **Strategic control**: These parents basically decentralize all planning to the businesses but retain a role in checking on and assessing what those businesses propose. Thus, the businesses take responsibility for putting forward strategies, plans, and proposals in a 'bottom-up' fashion, though the corporate parent may sponsor certain themes, initiatives, or objectives and only sanctions those proposals that achieve an appropriate balance of strategic and financial criteria. In the strategic control style, the strategic business units have a closer relationship with the corporate center and rely on various central services, including some standardized systems and activities. Corporate headquarters explicitly tries to coordinate activities that reach beyond the boundaries of a single business unit to create economies of scope. This control style is mostly used by diversified firms with a portfolio of related businesses.

3   **Financial control**: Finally, these parents are strongly committed to the decentralization of planning: they structure their businesses as stand-alone units with as much autonomy as possible and with full responsibility for formulating their own strategies and plans. The business units are highly autonomous, with few centralized or standardized activities, except perhaps for the financial reporting system. Corporate headquarters does not explicitly attempt to coordinate activities across business units. This control style is mostly used by firms with unrelated diversification strategies.

The parenting style adopted depends strongly on the type of corporate value creation mechanisms it targets. The type of multibusiness synergies the firm seeks to achieve dictate the preferable parenting style, though the level of autonomy that the business units require to compete in their respective markets also has a key influence. On the one hand, corporate headquarters want to encourage integration and coordination, to benefit from maintaining several business units together under one corporate roof, which gives them a strong motivation to exert corporate headquarters control and stimulate cooperation between business units. On the other hand, corporate headquarters may be wary of heavy handed head office intervention, blunt centralization, rigid standardization, paralyzing coordination meetings, or excessive overhead costs. The business units need to be highly responsive to the specific demands of their own business area, so corporate headquarters are also inclined to grant them the freedom to maneuver and emphasize their own entrepreneurship and competitive strategies.

Table 8.1, which is adapted from Goold and Campbell (1987) and de Waal (2007), summarizes the main distinctions across the three parenting styles.

Managing linkages across business units

In addition to influencing the planning and control processes of its businesses, corporate headquarters needs to manage the linkages among its business units to achieve economies of scope and create corporate value. Goold et al. (1994) have developed a typology of four ways a corporate parent can influence its business units: (1) *stand-alone influence*, through which the corporate parent enhances the individual performance of the business units; (2) *linkage influence*, through which the corporate parent enhances the value of the linkages between the business units; (3) *functional and services influence*, through which the parent provides functional leadership and cost effective services for the business units; and (4) *corporate development activities*, which alter the scope of the

The role of the parent | 113

Table. 8.1 Characteristics of the three parenting styles

Aspect	Strategic planning	Strategic control	Financial control
Parent role	Headquarters is closely involved with business units in the formulation of plans and decisions. Clear sense of direction.	Planning is decentralized to business units. Parent role consists of checking, assessing, and sponsoring.	Headquarters insists that all decisions are 'owned' by the business units themselves.
Business role	Business units seek consensus with headquarters and other units to determine business initiatives (in line with strategic targets).	Business units have their own responsibility for strategies, plans, and budget proposals.	Business units are independent entities, sometimes working together to achieve mutual benefits.
Organizational structure	Large or powerful functional staff at the center. Shared service departments (marketing, R&D, etc.)	Decentralized with focus on the individual performance of business units. Headquarters operates as strategic controller.	Minimal staff at headquarters level; focused on support and financial control.
Planning process	Resource allocation driven by requirements of long term strategies. The planning influence of headquarters is high.	Negotiation of financial and strategic performance targets. Planning influence of headquarters is medium.	No formal strategic planning, process focuses on business unit's annual budget and financial targets. Planning influence of headquarters is low.
Control process	Headquarters puts low priority on monitoring monthly financial results; control is flexible.	Headquarters regularly compares actual results with planned financial and nonfinancial targets; control is strategic.	Headquarters concentrates on financial targets and results (contracting); control is strictly financial.
Corporate value creation mechanisms	Sharing resources through central function and services. Corporate development.	Transferring skills and competencies through the influence of linkages.	Portfolio management and efficient internal capital market.

Source: Chandler (1994); Goold et al. (1994); de Waal (2007)

business portfolio (Goold et al., 1994). Figure 8.2 graphically depicts these four types of influences, which represent both links between the corporate headquarters and its businesses, as well as those among business units themselves.

1   **Stand-alone influence**: The corporate parent can influence the strategies and performance of each of its businesses separately. In this case, each business unit is an independent profit center unrelated to the other business units. To manage an efficient internal capital market, the stand-alone corporate parent encourages competition among its business units for its attention and resources (Porter, 1987). Depending on the autonomy of the business units and the level of decentralization of the decision-making process, the influence of the corporate

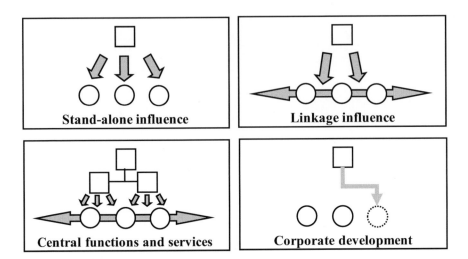

Figure 8.2 Managing linkages

Source: Adapted from Goold et al. (1994)

parent may be limited—such as when it determines performance targets, approves major capital expenditures, and selects and replaces business units' top managers—or more extreme, such that it takes over competitive strategies, pricing decisions, and human resource management (Goold et al., 1994). On September 2010, Nestlé announced the creation of a stand-alone health science division to tackle obesity and chronic disease (Simonian & Lucas, 2010). By setting up the new division as a stand-alone business unit, Nestlé seeks to avoid perceived conflicts between core product divisions, such as chocolate, and obesity. Regardless of its extensiveness, stand-alone influence manages each business unit separately, without seeking synergies with the other business units, which makes it most consistent with unrelated diversification. The results of a survey of corporate managers of 267 portfolio companies in 2007 by Landau and Bock (2013) show that corporate headquarters can create value through vertical stand-alone influence by reducing agency costs through governance mechanisms and by providing single businesses access to strategic resources during the course of their entrepreneurial activities.

2 **Linkage influence**: To create economies of scope, corporate parents seek to enhance linkages across their different business units. Corporate decision-making processes and structures, specific policies and guidelines, transfer pricing mechanisms, and personal pressures enable corporate parents to motivate relationships between business units that might not have occurred if the businesses were independent and lacked the pressure of corporate headquarters (Goold et al., 1994). The linking influence of the corporate parent may be required to create synergies between business units, because otherwise, they would not naturally collaborate, recognizing that some business units are likely to benefit more than others from such a collaboration. Linking influence seems most likely when the corporate parent seeks corporate value by transferring skills and competencies from one business unit to another.

3 **Functional and services influence**: Functional and services influence consists of centralizing some activities at the corporate level to achieve economies of scale and scope by sharing resources. These functions and services, performed by corporate staff, create value by providing functional leadership and cost effective services for the business units (Goold et

al., 1994). Supporting activities, such as human resources management, legal services, accounting, and R&D, might benefit from economy of scale effects when centralized at the corporate headquarters rather than being run independently in each business unit. Some relatedness between the business units is required, however, for sharing such functions and services.

4 **Corporate development activities**: As well as influencing the business units that already exist in the firm's portfolio, the corporate parent can determine the composition of the portfolio itself, that is, manage the portfolio, as mentioned previously. The corporate parent can buy or sell business units, create new businesses through internal development and corporate venturing, or redefine businesses by integrating or separating out units (Goold et al., 1994). Through such activities, the corporate parent does more than influence its existing business units; it restructures the portfolio by changing the relationships among the businesses that appear in that portfolio (Porter, 1987).

BOX 8.3 HEADQUARTERS' ROLE AND VALUE CREATION

In sum, corporate headquarters create value through two mechanisms (Nell & Ambos, 2013). First, headquarters "[create] value by preventing loss" (Foss, 1997, p. 314). This is, corporate headquarters control business units to ensure that, for instance, opportunistic behavior does not become problematic. Second, corporate headquarters create value through coordinating activities such as synergy management, knowledge sharing, and the organization of shared services. This has been referred to as the "positive role of parents" (Foss, 1997).

MANAGING THE DIVERSIFIED FIRM

According to organizational contingency theory (Donaldson, 2001; Lorsch & Allen, 1973) and following Chandler's (1962) observation that "structure follows strategy," we could argue that the roles and functions of the corporate headquarters should be conditional on the corporate level strategy of the firm (Hoskisson, 1987; Porter, 1987). As we discussed in the previous chapter, it also is important to distinguish between firms with a portfolio of related businesses and those that possess a portfolio of unrelated businesses (Hill et al., 1992). We already have argued that the corporate value creation mechanisms differ for these two types of firms; here, we note the need to understand the unique roles of the headquarters of these two types. A firm could seek to share resources between its businesses or transfer skills and competences from one to the other, or it might seek to create an efficient capital market or implement a restructuring strategy (Collis et al., 2007; Goold et al., 1994; Hill, 1988; Hill & Hoskisson, 1987; Hill et al., 1992; Markides, 2002; Varadarajan & Ramanujam, 1987). In one case, the corporate headquarters needs to motivate business units to collaborate to create synergies; in the other, it should push business units to compete for corporate funding. In the next sections, we discuss in turn how corporate headquarters can manage unrelated and related portfolios.

MANAGING THE UNRELATED–DIVERSIFIED CORPORATION

When a multibusiness firm possesses an unrelated business portfolio, it mostly creates corporate value by establishing an efficient internal capital market or using a restructuring strategy (i.e., acquire businesses at low prices, restructure them, and sell them at higher prices; Porter, 1987). In

The role of the parent

such situations, corporate headquarters pretty much does whatever is necessary to enable the firm to behave like an efficient capital market (Markides, 2002). These acts might include deciding which businesses to acquire and which to divest, as well as designing appropriate organizational contexts to facilitate the functions of the internal capital market (see Williamson, 1975).

Porter (1987) offers three tests, as we discussed in Chapter 6, to decide which businesses to acquire or divest, namely, the *attractiveness test*, *cost of entry test*, and *better off test*. If the parenting style focuses on financial controls, the internal capital market should become more efficient (Goold & Campbell, 1987). However, to function well, the internal capital market also requires a well balanced portfolio of businesses (e.g., Boston Consulting Group, 1972; Haberberg & Rieple, 2001).

Balance might be achieved across several dimensions, such as size (i.e., mix of small and large businesses), the life cycle of the industry (e.g., a young, fast growing business together with already mature businesses), the extent to which the businesses are net producers or consumers of cash flows, products and market characteristics, or even geographical locations (Haberberg & Rieple, 2001). A balanced portfolio reduces risk by minimizing the likelihood that all businesses face the same severe problems at the same time. Moreover, across a balanced portfolio of businesses, resources—especially financial resources—can be redistributed from those with excess to those that are in need of the resources (Boston Consulting Group, 1972).

One approach to this challenge relies on a set of techniques known as "portfolio analysis" or "portfolio planning" (Haspeslagh, 1982; Nippa et al., 2011). Developed primarily by management consultants in the 1960s and 1970s, these techniques compare the competitive position of different businesses in a company's portfolio on the basis of common criteria and thus assess the balance in a firm's portfolio. Although the popularity of portfolio analysis has declined since the 1970s and 1980s, when a majority of the largest firms in the world used it, by 1996, approximately 27 percent of Fortune 500 firms relied on it for their corporate strategy formulation (Reinmann & Reichert, 1996). More recently, a study of leading multibusiness firms worldwide conducted in 2009 found that top managers still perceive corporate portfolio management to be highly relevant and important (Pidun et al., 2011).

Furthermore, assessing the balance of a firm's portfolio remains useful for determining how and where corporate headquarters should allocate its cash flows and other resources; such an assessment becomes even more necessary when the firm's portfolio is unrelated. Perhaps the most common tools for analyzing business portfolios are the Boston Consulting Group's (BCG) Matrix and the General Electric (GE)/McKinsey Business Attractiveness Screen (see Boston Consulting Group, 1972; Campbell et al., 2014; Grant, 2013; Haberberg & Rieple, 2001; Hill & Jones, 2001; Pidun et al., 2011).

In their survey of Fortune 500 firms, Reimann and Reichert (1996) found specifically that 22.7 percent of the firms in their sample have used portfolio planning matrices (BCG, GE/McKinsey, or others) to make acquisition and divesture decisions, and 27.3 percent used these tools periodically to evaluate their strategy. Finally, 14.5 percent used them to decide about executive compensation. Pidun et al. (2011), through the 2009 survey, found that for 37 percent of the firms in their sample portfolio, planning matrices were a major part of their ongoing management process, 30 percent of them regularly used theses matrices for planning and strategic decisions, 28 percent of them used theses matrices in specific situations, and only 5 percent of them did not use portfolio planning tools at all.

The BCG matrix

The growth share matrix developed by BCG (1972) aims to help senior managers identify the cash flow requirements of different businesses in their portfolio and determine whether they need to change the mix of businesses in that portfolio (Hill & Jones, 2001). The matrix has two dimensions: the *relative growth rate* of the markets in which the firm's businesses compete, and the *relative market share* of the firm's businesses. Businesses can be represented on this two dimensional map by a circle, the center of which corresponds to the business's position on the two dimensions of the matrix. The size of the circle is proportional to the sales revenue generated by the business, so the bigger the circle, the greater is the business unit's revenue relative to total corporate revenues.

Along the two dimensions, the matrix consists of four cells. Business units in cell 1 are the stars, those in cell 2 are question marks (sometimes labeled problem children), firms in cell 3 represent the cash cows, and the ones in cell 4 are dogs (sometimes labeled cash dogs, if they are still profitable) (see Figure 8.3).

According to the rationales that support the matrix, these different types offer unique long term prospects and implications for the firm's cash flow.

- **Stars**. The leading business units in the firm's portfolio are its stars. They enjoy a high relative market share and often appear in high growth industries. Accordingly, they offer attractive long term profit and growth opportunities. However, because they are growing, they need more cash than they can generate by themselves.
- **Question marks**. These business units are relatively weak in competitive terms (i.e., they have low relative market shares), but because they are based in high growth industries, they may offer opportunities for long term profit and growth. A question mark can become a star if nurtured properly, though to do so, it usually needs substantial net injections of cash. Corporate headquarters therefore must decide if each question mark has the potential to become a star and if it is worth the capital investment necessary for it to achieve stardom.
- **Cash cows**. Business units that have a high market share in low growth industries and a strong competitive position in mature industries are cash cows. Their competitive strength

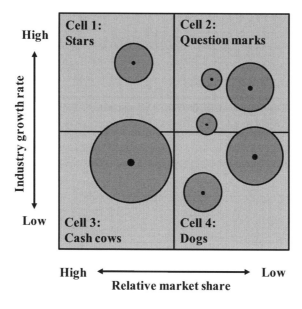

Figure 8.3 The BCG matrix

Source: Adapted from Boston Consulting Group (1972)

comes from being farthest along the experience curve. They are the cost leaders in their industries, which enables them to remain very profitable, but because their low growth implies a lack of opportunities for future expansion, their investment requirements are not substantial. Therefore, cash cows generate strong positive cash flows that can be used to fund the stars and question marks.

- **Dogs**. Business units in low growth industries with a low market share are dogs. Their weak competitive position in unattractive industries offers few benefits to the firm. The logic of the BCG matrix also suggests that dogs are unlikely to generate positive cash flows and may even require substantial capital investments, just to maintain their current market share.

The BCG matrix provides various insights into the balance and management of a portfolio of unrelated businesses (Haberberg & Rieple, 2001). For example, it enables firms to assess the risk profiles of their individual businesses (i.e., question marks are generally new, small, and untested, which makes them more risky than businesses that are older, have greater market share, and about which more is known), as well as formulate business unit strategies and set performance targets (Grant, 2013). It is not, however, a perfect source of information, as Box 8.4 notes. Yet the main objective of the BCG portfolio matrix remains to analyze a firm's portfolio balance and identify how corporate cash resources can be used best to maximize the firm's future growth and profitability.

BOX 8.4 MANAGING P&G'S PORTFOLIO

In the letter to shareholders of the P&G 2014 Annual Report, Alan G. Lafley, P&G chairman of the board, president and CEO, announced that to accelerate the firm's performance improvement, he was taking an important strategic step forward in the P&G's business and brand portfolio. P&G will become a simpler, more focused Company of 70 to 80 brands, organized into about a dozen businesses and four industry based sectors. The firm will compete in businesses that are structurally attractive and best leverage the firm's core capabilities. Within these businesses, it will focus on leading brands or brands with leadership potential. P&G will discontinue or divest businesses, brands, product lines, and unproductive products that are structurally unattractive or that do not fully play to the firm's strengths. Every brand P&G plans to keep will be strategic, with the potential to grow and deliver value creation. These core 70 to 80 brands should be leaders in their industries, businesses, or segments. They should offer differentiated products and have a track record of growth and value creation driven by product innovation and brand preference. They generate nearly 90 percent of current P&G sales and more than 95 percent of current profit. They have grown sales one point faster, with a higher profit margin than the balance of the firm during the past three years. The 90 to 100 brands P&G plan to exit have declining sales of −3 percent, declining profits of −16 percent, and half the average firm's margin during the past three years.

Source: P&G 2014 Annual Report

In general, the matrix recommends tactics for each category. First, the cash surplus from cash cows should go to support the development of selected question marks and nurture stars. The long term objective of this effort is to consolidate the position of stars and turn favored question marks into stars. Second, question marks with the weakest or most uncertain long term prospects should be divested from the portfolio to reduce the demands on the firm's cash resources. Third, the firm should exit any industry in which its business units are dogs. Fourth, if the firm lacks sufficient cash cows, stars, or question marks, it should consider undertaking acquisitions and divestments to build a more balanced portfolio. A portfolio also should contain enough stars and question marks to ensure healthy growth and profit outlooks for the firm and enough cash cows to support its investment requirements.

The GE/McKinsey matrix

Another popular portfolio management tool is the GE/McKinsey matrix (see Figure 8.4). The two dimensions of this matrix represent two key sources of superior profitability: *industry attractiveness* and *competitive advantage*. Unlike the dimensions of the BCG matrix, these dimensions reflect multiple criteria or factors. For example, industry attractiveness combines market size and growth rate, industry profitability, cyclicality, inflation recovery, and importance of overseas markets. A business unit's competitive advantage consists of measures of its market share; competitive position with regard to quality, technology, manufacturing, distribution, marketing, and costs; and return on sales relative to that of its leading competitors (Grant, 2013).

According to the position of business units on the two dimensional map, this approach develops strategy recommendations for three regions: (1) business units that rank high on both dimensions (winners), which have excellent profit potential, should be *grown*; (2) those that rank low on both

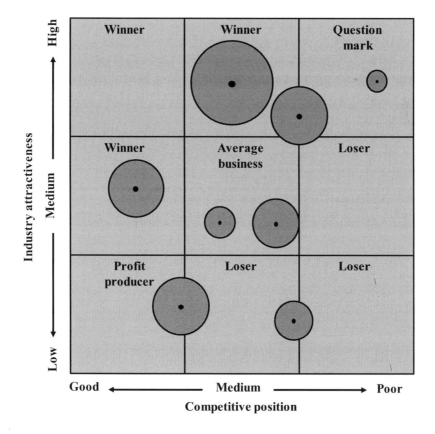

Figure 8.4 The GE/McKinsey matrix

BOX 8.5 LIMITATIONS OF THE BCG MATRIX

Although the rationales for portfolio planning techniques, such as the BCG matrix, sound reasonable, they contain several flaws that suggest the need for caution before using them. First, the BCG matrix is rather simplistic, and any assessment of a business unit in terms of just two dimensions is likely to be misleading. Other relevant factors should be taken into account, such as the core competence of the firm or the potential relatedness of the business units (Prahalad & Hamel, 1990). Although market share is undoubtedly an important determinant of a business unit's competitive position, firms can establish strong competitive positions by differentiating their products and thus serving the needs of a particular segment of the market (Porter, 1985). A business with a small market share still can be very profitable and enjoy a strong competitive position in certain segments. Similarly, industry growth is not the only factor that determines industry attractiveness. Many factors (e.g., level of entry barriers, mutual forbearance) determine competitive intensity in an industry and thus its attractiveness (Porter, 1985).

Second, the connection between relative market share and cost savings is not as straightforward as the matrix implies. Some industries may have less potential for economies of scale and shallower learning curves. Therefore, high market share does not always give a firm a cost advantage.

Third, a high market share in a low growth industry does not necessarily result in the large positive cash flow characteristic of cash cows. Specifically, it can be difficult to define the relevant market (Haspeslagh, 1982) and therefore the market share of a product or business. Does a health food firm have a 0.001 percent share of the global pharmaceuticals market (dog) or 25 percent of the French market for vitamins (star)? Moreover, the matrix relies on the questionable assumption that high market share implies good profits and low growth implies minimal investment needs. These assumptions clearly cannot always be true. Correlations may exist, but high market share is not always a direct path to high profits. There also are no objective rules for drawing the lines between large and small market share, or between high and low industry growth. And low growth markets can rebound. Many products and businesses never quite follow the predictable lifecycle of increase and decline; some dogs even remain profitable and viable for many, many years, which makes them unlikely candidates for divestment. Some cash cows also may require periodic injections of cash to sustain their competitiveness. The simple mapping of businesses according to two simple dimensions ignores any potential relations between products, such as the potential synergy between, say, dogs and stars. There is also little consideration of the potential for learning; dogs may be liable to divestment but also may be repositories of considerable learning and knowledge accrued over many years of operations. The implication that a question mark has a low market share also is unlikely to be universal, especially when the product constitutes a new market, for which total sales are likely small, and the company's few individual sales may represent a large percentage of the total market. The range of business types in a portfolio further may require very different management styles (Goold & Campbell, 1987), and the corporate parent may not be able to supply all of them. Managing highly innovative question marks demands very different skills and control systems than does managing dogs, but both need to be managed in the most cost effective way.

Fourth and finally, the matrix offers little consideration of the issues associated with motivating managers, especially those of cash cow businesses, who may be less than enchanted with seeing their hard-earned profits siphoned off to fund investments in high risk, and as yet unsuccessful, question marks.

Source: Adapted from Haberberg & Rieple (2001); Hill & Jones (2001)

dimensions have poor prospects and should be *harvested* (i.e., managed to maximize cash flows with little new investment); and (3) businesses in between (e.g., profit producers, average businesses, question marks) are candidates for a *hold* strategy (Grant, 2013).

In comparing the BCG and GE/McKinsey matrices, the GE/McKinsey matrix has several advantages over the BCG matrix, largely because it is based on more robust dimensions measured on several criteria, though most of the weaknesses and limitations of the BCG matrix still apply to the GE/McKinsey matrix. There is also less emphasis on the need for a 'balanced' portfolio in the GE/McKinsey matrix. Implicit in the application of the BCG matrix is the concept of cash flow balance. However, this idea is not critical to the GE/McKinsey matrix (Campbell et al., 2014).

While the BCG matrix advises corporate managers to "sell Dogs, grow or divest Question Marks, grow Stars and create a balances portfolio," the GE/McKinsey matrix advises managers to "restructure bottom left, and invest in top right." Businesses on the middle axis could be invested in if cash is available. But there is no explicit prescription for 'balance' (McKinsey, 2008). The implicit idea behind the GE/McKinsey matrix is that an attractive portfolio is one that provides "sustainable growth," with a mix of established and developing businesses (Campbell et al., 2014).

Together, the main limitation of the BCG and GE/McKinsey matrices remains that valid recommendations require the firm's portfolio to be composed of businesses that are unrelated (except for financially). Divesting a portfolio of a dog that shares some resources with a cash cow is likely to have dramatic consequences for the cash cow and its cash flow generation. Managing related diversified firms thus appears to require different management tools.

MANAGING THE RELATED DIVERSIFIED CORPORATION

Firms diversify in related businesses to generate economies of scope. That is, they can share resources across businesses or transfer skills and competences from one business to the other. Economics literature and the RBV, which underlie corporate value creation mechanisms, also suggest that the necessary activities for corporate headquarters to perform to share and leverage resources and competences across its businesses vary according to the actual resources and competences (Collis & Montgomery, 2005; Markides & Williamson, 1996; Porter, 1987).

Prahalad and Hamel (1990) argue specifically that a firm's core competencies link the different businesses in a diversified firm in the form of managerial and technical know-how, experience, and wisdom. These resources offer a source of corporate value and should be centralized and managed by corporate headquarters. When a related diversified firm exploits its core competences, the operations of each of its different business units should be significantly affected by the knowledge, experience, and wisdom they gain from the firm's previous business activities, which means such knowledge needs to be coordinated by corporate headquarters (Markides & Williamson, 1994).

Yet transferring skills and competences, which often are tacit, is not easy in practice, despite its simplicity in theory (Darragh & Campbell, 2001). In many cases, it requires the transfer of key personnel from one business unit to another, and the deliberate exchange of staff across business unit boundaries can be achieved only when corporate headquarters is involved; business unit managers probably are reluctant to release some of their best staff to be transferred (Haberberg & Rieple, 2001). Knowledge and experience naturally tend to be business specific, and in some cases, moving people into situations in which they lack expertise represents an inefficient use of their time. These transfers would have little purpose unless the businesses are sufficiently related and their processes sufficiently standardized to benefit from such an exchange. Opportunities for sharing and transferring resources and capabilities therefore may require *ad hoc* organizational arrangement, such as cross unit task forces (Grant, 2013).

Transaction cost theory (Coase, 1937; Williamson, 1975, 1985) provides a complementary theoretical lens through which to examine the roles and functions of the corporate headquarters of related diversified firms. According to transaction cost economics (TCE), the existence of factor market failures, such as business unit managers' opportunism, determines when a corporate hierarchy efficiently replaces the market governance of resource transactions required to transfer skills and competences and share resources among business units (Collis et al., 2007). The presence of such market failures therefore determines the coordination roles and tasks of corporate headquarters.

Furthermore, CEOs can use their authority to launch corporate wide initiatives that encourage business unit managers to exploit interbusiness linkages and take into account corporate wide issues in their competitive strategies and operational decisions. These initiatives should provide key mechanisms for disseminating corporate level strategies, strategic changes, best practices, and management innovations (Darragh & Campbell, 2001).

Exploiting the links between related businesses requires careful management, which imposes costs (Williamson, 1975). The success with which the corporate headquarters manages these links depends on top management's understanding of the communalities among its different businesses (i.e., relatedness; see Chapter 6) and choices in terms of centralization, coordination, and standardization, as well as the business units' autonomy. **Centralization** is necessary to share resources and activities, and though the name implies they would be situated at the central corporate headquarters, centralized activities could reside at one of the business units or another location. Even when resources, activities, and product offerings are decentralized, economies of scope might be achieved through **coordination** across the business units. This orchestration of work across business units should minimize transaction costs and result in the ability to operate as if the various parts were actually one unit. Economies of scale and scope also might be realized by **standardizing** resources, activities, and/or product offering characteristics across business units. Similar resources (e.g., technologies, people), standardized activities (e.g., R&D, human resource management), and common product features (e.g., operating system, high tech positioning) produce advantages such as economies of scale and rapid competence development, without the need to centralize physically or continuously coordinate. Centralization, coordination, and standardization therefore should be the main tasks of corporate headquarters in related diversified firms. Box 8.6 describes how the corporate headquarters of Nestlé and Heineken handle such issues in their planning and control efforts.

BOX 8.6 THE ROLE OF HEADQUARTERS: CENTRALIZATION AND DECENTRALIZATION

Nestlé: At Nestlé's headquarters in Vevey, Switzerland, some 1600 employees from more than 70 countries oversee the global strategy of the Nestlé Group. Corporate headquarters sets the overall strategy and ensures that it is carried out. The approach can best be summed up as: "*Centralize what you must, decentralize what you can*" (source: www.nestle.com).

Heineken: Heineken's corporate level strategy attempts to build a strong portfolio that combines the power of local and international brands, with the Heineken brand at the center. The consistent growth of these brands requires solid, creative brand management, which Heineken coordinates centrally. By carefully balancing the brands' portfolios and achieving optimal distribution and coverage, Heineken headquarters aims to build and sustain strong positions in local markets. For the Heineken and Amstel brands, the headquarters develops and maintains central guidelines and standards for the brands' style, value, and development. At a central level, it also supports local management of the entire brand portfolio through benchmarking programs designed to optimize marketing, sales, and distribution (source: www.heinekeninternatinal.com).

CONCLUDING REMARKS

Merely controlling the operation of autonomous business units is rarely enough to justify the existence, and related costs, of corporate headquarters. Although business units need to be differentiated and specialized to achieve a competitive advantage in their respective markets, valuable resources and core competences also must be deployed and leveraged throughout the business units to provide coherence to the corporation (Collis & Montgomery, 2005). Goold et al. (1994) argue that such coherence is the essence of successful parenting and requires a good fit between the way the corporate headquarters operates (i.e., parent characteristics) and the improvement opportunities that the parent addresses for its business units (i.e., business characteristics) (see Figure 8.5). To avoid opportunity costs, the firm needs this fit to be better than it would be with any rival parents; otherwise, the firm would be better off selling the business unit to this rival parent (Porter, 1987).

Conversely, a misfit between the role of the corporate headquarters and the needs of the business units destroys corporate value. Goold et al. (1994) argue that fit today does not ensure fit tomorrow; therefore, corporate headquarters must continually address the changes and trends that take place in its external environment.

To maintain this dynamic fit over time, corporate level strategy should guide corporate headquarters' decisions. Decisions about the portfolio and its businesses, covering M&A, divestments, strategic alliances, business restructuring, and new business development, determine the role of the businesses in the portfolio and therefore the characteristics and opportunities they present. Decisions about the parent, including how to structure the corporate headquarters, what planning and control systems to use, and so on, determine the parent's characteristics and the degree to which they fit with the business units. These two outputs of corporate level strategy then feed back into the characteristics of both the parent and its business units.

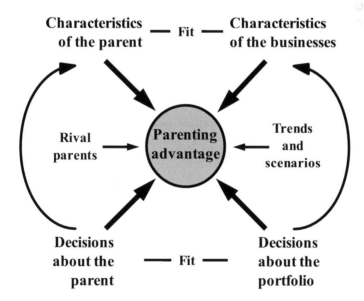

Figure 8.5 Parenting as fit

Source: Adapted from Goold et al. (1994)

In this chapter, we have discussed the role and tasks of corporate headquarters and show that they are contingent on the corporate level strategy of the firm. In the next chapter, we discuss how a firm's corporate level strategy can be implemented through the design of its organizational structure.

Chapter

9

ORGANIZING AND STRUCTURING THE MULTIBUSINESS FIRM

As early as 1962, Chandler was noting that the value creation potential of a diversification strategy largely depended on how it is implemented. Yet most research on corporate level strategies and diversification continually ignores the importance of organizational structure for the strategy–performance relationship (Hill et al., 1992). As Hill (1994) and Markides and Williamson (1996) remind us, diversification alone cannot produce value at the corporate level. Rather, to do so, the diversified firm must adopt an appropriate internal organizational structure. In this sense, organizational structure is a critical component of effective strategy implementation processes (Barkema et al., 2002), such that to create corporate value, the firm must maintain a proper match between its corporate level strategy and the organizational structure used to implement it (Hill et al., 1992). Strategy and structure influence each other (Amburgey & Dacin, 1994). If strategy initially has a more important influence on organizational structure, once in place, organizational structure more strongly influences strategy (Keats & O'Neill, 2001).

In Chapter 2, we mentioned that strategy implementation moderates the effect of a firm's level of diversification on its performance; in Chapter 7, we argued that a limit to diversification was imposed, in part, by organizational constraints. In Chapter 13, we outline how, in a multipoint competition context, a firm's organizational structure can weaken the relationship between the number of multipoint contacts and the intensity of rivalry.

In this chapter, we present, using an historical perspective, different types of organizational structures used by multibusiness firms to implement their diversification strategies. We also argue that multibusiness firms must change their organizational structure as they grow over time and diversify their business activities. From a theoretical perspective, we further discuss the advantages and disadvantages of the main organizational structure implemented by multibusiness firms, that is, the multidivisional structure. Finally, we argue that different types of organizations must be used to implement different corporate level strategies.

ORGANIZATIONAL STRUCTURE: A HISTORICAL PERSPECTIVE

Organizational structure refers to the design of the firm's organization and includes the lines of communication and authority across administrative offices, as well as the information that flows among them (Chandler, 1962). A firm's organizational structure specifies its formal reporting relationships, procedures, controls, and authority and decision-making processes (Galbreath, 1995; Keats & O'Neill, 2001). In response to wider changes in multibusiness firms' external environments and modifications of their strategies, different types of organizational structures have come to dominate the business landscape. Figure 9.1 offers a graphical representation of some of these organizational structures.

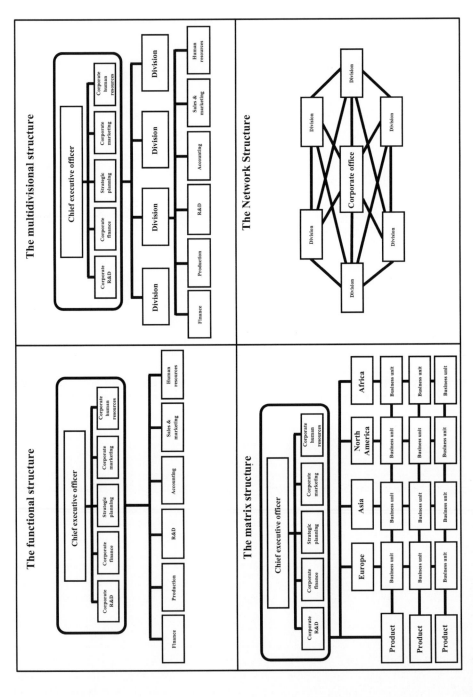

Figure 9.1 Types of organizational structures

Following the Industrial Revolution, three forms of organizations emerged as dominant in their time (Chandler 1962, 1977). The vertically integrated *functional* organization (or *F*-form) grew prominent in the late nineteenth and early twentieth centuries, when firms' competitive advantages were based largely on high volume, standardization, low costs, and a production orientation. Firms such as DuPont de Nemours, Sears Roebuck, and Royal Dutch Shell managed multiple, separated operating units using large functional departments that conducted sales, finance, R&D, legal affairs, or other specialist activities (Grant, 2013). In contrast, other large firms maintained unrelated business portfolios and organized as holding companies (*H*-form), including Standard Oil (U.S.), Mitsui (Japan), and the British South Africa Company, which resulted from series of acquisitions (Grant, 2013).

Following World War I and the example set by DuPont de Nemours (Chandler, 1962) and General Motors (Sloan, 1963), the *multidivisional* organizational structure (or *M*-form) rapidly came to replace the *F*-form (Fligstein, 1985). For example, at DuPont, the increased size and a widening product range strained the functional structure and overloaded top management: "the operations of the enterprise became too complex and the problems of coordination, appraisal and policy formulation too intricate for a small number of top officers to handle both long-run, entrepreneurial and short-run, operational administrative activities" (Chandler, 1962, pp. 382–383). The solution developed by Pierre Du Pont was to decentralize and create ten product divisions, each with its own sales, R&D, and support activities. The corporate headquarters, headed by an Executive Committee, took responsibility for coordination, strategy, and resource allocation.

Almost simultaneously, General Motors, which had grown through acquisitions into a loose holding company, adopted a similar structure as a solution to the problems of weak financial control and confused product lines. The new structure relied on two principles: the CEO of each division was fully responsible for its operation and performance, and the general office, headed by the president, was responsible for the development and control of the firm as a whole, including monitoring returns on capital invested within the divisions, coordinating the divisions (e.g., establishing terms for interdivisional transactions), and establishing product policy (Sloan, 1963).

The multidivisional form thus allowed firms to be more market and product oriented, which made it much better suited to a business environment characterized by rapidly changing customer preferences (see Box 9.1).

After the end of World War II, multibusiness firms continued to modify their structures at a rapid pace. This increased scope and complexity moved the *M*-form into a *matrix organization*, with separate hierarchies coordinated around products, functions, and geographical areas (Egelhoff et al., 2013). In the 1960s and 1970s, the matrix organization, with its emphasis on lateral relationships and dual lines of responsibility and authority, became popular among large diversified firms, especially those with a multinational scope (Qiu & Donaldson, 2012; Stopford & Wells, 1972). Many diversified, multinational firms, including Philips, Nestlé, and Unilever, adopted matrix structures during the 1960s and 1970s (Grant, 2013). The *M*-form also helped firms align their marketing functions more closely with their R&D departments and thereby improved coordination among the firm's functions. A matrix structure was also considered as the best way to organize multinational corporations to deal with increasingly complex international diversification strategies (Egelhoff et al., 2013).

However, the matrix structure was not a particularly successful innovation. Dow Chemical, one of the pioneers of the matrix structure, returned to a more conventional structure, with clear lines of responsibility for geographic managers in 1995 (Egelhoff et al., 2013) (see Box 9.2). Citibank, once a textbook example of the matrix, also discarded its dual reporting relationships after a few years of highly publicized experimentation (Bartlett et al., 2008). Most firms that tried to manage their multinational activities through the complex and rather bureaucratic matrix structure encountered similar problems.

Specifically, the matrix amplifies differences in perspectives and interests because it forces all

BOX 9.1 THE SPREAD OF THE MULTIDIVISIONAL FORM

Chandler (1962), among others, argues that the multidivisional (*M*-form) structure is the most appropriate for diversified firms. Empirical evidence indicates that the *M*-form spread very quickly among diversified firms. Once developed, it diffused throughout not only the U.S. but also other countries. Invented by DuPont de Nemours and General Motors in the 1920s, the *M*-form made its appearance in the 1930s in U.K., where it altered the structure of Imperial Chemical Industries (Hannah, 1976), and in Japan, where Matsushita was a pioneer (Bartlett & Ghoshal, 1989). By the 1960s and 1970s, the *M*-form had become the dominant organizational structure for large diversified firms in every developed country (Chang & Choi, 1988; Channon, 1973; Chenall, 1979; Franko, 1974; Hill & Pickering, 1986; Kono, 1984; Pavan, 1972; Rumelt, 1974; Suzuki, 1980; Thanheiser, 1973; Wrigley, 1970).

Fligstein (1985) has studied the causes of the dissemination of this organizational structure among large firms from 1919 to 1979. In his literature review, he shows that five theories of organizational change have been proposed as possible explanations for the dominance of the *M*-form: (1) strategy–structure (Chandler, 1963); (2) transaction cost analysis (Williamson, 1975); (3) population ecology theory (Hannan & Freeman, 1977, 1984); (4) control theory based on power (Perrow, 1970, 1981; Pfeffer, 1981); and (5) institutional or organizational homogeneity theory (DiMaggio & Powell, 1983).

First, Chandler (1963) argues that structure follows strategy. When firms chose diversification strategies to respond to changing market conditions, their main organizational issue is the coordination of multiple product lines. He argues that the *F*-form failed as a mechanism to control these multiple product lines, so some firms changed their organizational structure, which caused them invent the *M*-form.

Second, using a transaction cost perspective, Williamson (1975) argues that continuous expansion of the *F*-form creates cumulative control loss effects, which then exert internal efficiency consequences. As firms increase in size, managers reach their limits of control due to their bounded rationality. Opportunism therefore becomes more likely within the firm, and organizational efficiency and profitability are threatened. By reproducing the organization within divisions, the *M*-form resolves the problems of control, and the firm can continue to grow.

Third, based on population ecology theory, Hannan and Freeman (1984) argue that adaptation of organizational structures occurs principally at the population level. That is, firms occupy a niche in their wider environment, and once they have been selected by that environment, they tend to develop inertia. Overall, as firms age and achieve success, they lean toward structural inertia. Although Hannan and Freeman do not specifically cite the *M*-form, Fligstein (1985) argues that their argument is applicable to the *M*-form, such that younger and smaller firms should be more likely to adopt the *M*-form than are older and larger ones, which are more likely to disappear because of their ill adapted organizational structure.

Fourth, Pfeffer (1981) argues that all firms must allocate scarce resources, but the optimal allocation is not always clear. Therefore, power influences every important decision; it derives from some organizational claim over resources. An actor with control over valued resources, such as capital, information, organization, and outside ties, has significant power. In turn, the *M*-form results from the acts of certain key actors whose bases of power are consistent with that form. If the *M*-form provides a mechanism for growth through diversification, its implementation should be favored by managers who stand to gain the most from growth and diversification strategies (i.e., sales, marketing, and finance personnel) (Perrow, 1970, 1981). Therefore, firms managed by CEOs with sales, marketing, or finance backgrounds are more likely to implement a *M*-form.

Fifth, DiMaggio and Powell (1983) argue that large firms come to resemble one another due to isomorphic pressures from their environments. Thus, the *M*-form has spread across various firms as a mimetic response to other firms' behavior. The examples of successful firms such as DuPont de Nemours and General Motors provided role models for other firms.

Fligstein's (1985) empirical results show that the spread of the *M*-form among large firms between 1919 and 1979 resulted when managers in control of large firms acted to change their organizational structure, under three specific conditions: (1) when they were pursuing a multiproduct strategy (i.e., strategy structure theory); (2) when their competitors shifted structures (i.e., institutional theory); and (3) when they had a background that implied their interests would reflect those of the sales or finance departments (i.e., control theory based on power).

BOX 9.2 THE RISE AND FALL OF DOW CHEMICAL'S MATRIX STRUCTURE

For years Dow Chemical's managers claimed that part the firm's performance should be attributed to its matrix organizational structure. Dow's organizational matrix had three elements: functions (e.g., R&D, manufacturing, marketing), businesses (e.g., ethylene, plastics, pharmaceuticals), and geography (e.g., Spain, Germany, Brazil). Managers' job titles incorporated all three elements—for example, plastics manufacturing manager for Brazil—and most managers reported to at least two bosses. The plastics manufacturing manager in Brazil might report to both the head of the worldwide plastics business and the head of the Brazilian operations. The intent of the matrix was to make Dow operations responsive to both local market needs and corporate objectives. Thus, the plastics business might be charged with minimizing Dow's global plastics production costs, while the Brazilian operation might be charged with determining how best to sell plastics in the Brazilian market.

When Dow introduced the matrix structure in the 1970s, the results were less than promising; multiple reporting channels led to confusion and conflict. The large number of bosses made for a cumbersome bureaucracy. The overlapping responsibilities resulted in turf battles and a lack of accountability. Geographic area managers disagreed with managers overseeing business sectors about which plants should be built and where. In short, the structure did not work. However, instead of abandoning the structure, however, Dow decided to see if it could be render more flexible. Dow's decision to keep its matrix structure resulted from its diversification into the pharmaceuticals industry, which firm realized was very different from the chemicals business. To make the matrix structure more flexible, a small team of senior executives at headquarters was appointed to set priorities for each business unit. After priorities were identified one of the three elements of the matrix—function, business, or geographic area—was given primary authority in decision-making.

Dow claimed this flexible system worked well. However, by the mid-1990s, Dow had refocused its business on the chemicals industry, divesting itself of the pharmaceutical industry. Reflecting the change in corporate level strategy, in 1995, Dow finally decided to abandon its matrix structure in favor of a more streamlined structure based on global business divisions. The change was also in part driven by realization that the matrix structure was just too complex and costly to manage in an intense competitive environment.

Source: Adapted from Hill (2010)

Organizing the multibusiness firm

issues through dual chains of command, such that even a minor difference can become the subject of heated internal conflicts. As Bartlett et al. (2008) describe the situation, dual reporting led to confusion on many levels: the proliferation of channels created informational logjams, conflicts could be resolved only by escalating the problem, and overlapping responsibilities resulted in turf battles and a loss of accountability. Separated by barriers of distance, time, language, and culture, managers found it virtually impossible to clarify such confusion and resolve conflicts. As a result, most firms that had implemented a matrix structure switched back to a multidivisional structure or developed a new form of organizational structure: the network organization.

However, a matrix organization might advantageous to implement related diversification strategies requiring high levels of integration between business units (Egelhoff et al., 2013; Qiu & Donaldson, 2012). Today, there is some evidence that managers in multinational corporations are again increasingly interested in matrix structures, especially in Germany, where there seems to be a general belief on the part of managers that some forms of matrix structures are inevitable for firms that seek to implement complex international strategies (Egelhoff et al., 2013; Qiu & Donaldson, 2012).

Whereas Stopford and Wells (1972) recommended the use a matrix structure for firms with both high levels of foreign product diversification and geographic diversification, Qiu and Donaldson (2012) demonstrate that it is not the level of product diversification that matters, but the level of corporate integration. They argue that a matrix structure is the most appropriate structure for firms with high levels of geographic diversification but only when they also pursue high level of corporate integration to implement a related diversification strategy. If corporate integration and economies of scope are not the dominant corporate value creation mechanism, a matrix structure might be too costly in terms of coordination costs, and a network structure might be better suited and less costly (Egelhoff et al., 2013).

In the 1980s, attention began to move toward a 'new' organizational form, the *network* organization (or *N*-form) (Hedlund, 1994; Powell, 1990). For example, in the transnational firms studied by Bartlett and Ghoshal (1989), organizational structures are based on three main characteristics: dispersion, specialization, and interdependence (see Chapter 14). However, with the rise of Japanese global firms (see Box 9.3), it became increasingly apparent that many of these competitive advantages actually were external to the firm and interorganizational in nature (Achrol, 1997).

Within the firm's boundaries, the *N*-form is a melded network of relationships and functions. Across firms' boundaries, it entails a loose federation of partners that participate in the network's operations on a flexible basis (Hitt et al., 2004). Such interorganizational networks can be implemented through various forms of strategic alliances, as we discuss in Chapters 9 and 11.

The preceding history explains how at the population level, the dominant form of organizational structure can evolve over time to adapt to changing environmental conditions and new corporate level strategies. Box 9.4 presents a similar evolution at the firm level: as individual firms grow and diversify, they also need to adapt their organizational structures to implement their changing strategy successfully.

THE THEORY OF THE MULTIDIVISIONAL STRUCTURE

Even over the course of the failure of the matrix structure and the rise of the network organization, the *M*-form is still the most widely used structure among firms around the world (Hoskisson et al., 1993a).

In the multidivisional structure, each business is managed as a separate division. As discussed in Chapter 4, different firms may use different names for these divisions and different criteria to define their boundaries (e.g., customer needs, customer groups, or product technology). Whatever their names and boundaries, divisions in the *M*-form are profit and loss centers that must be large

Organizing the multibusiness firm | **131**

BOX 9.3 MITSUBISHI: A NETWORK ORGANIZATION

Q1: Is Mitsubishi a single company?

A1: No. 'Mitsubishi' is a community that consists of a multitude of independent companies. The names of most—but not all—of those companies contain the word 'Mitsubishi.' And many of the companies use the three-diamond Mitsubishi mark. But none calls itself simply 'Mitsubishi.'

Q2: You say Mitsubishi is "a multitude of independent companies." How do you define Mitsubishi and how many companies are there?

A2: Here at mitsubishi.com, we speak of 'Mitsubishi' in terms of the member companies subject to the company search on this website, which counts to approximately 200. But that is not the one and only definition of Mitsubishi. Another example of definition is the 29 members of the Kinyokai (Kinyokai, or Friday Club, is an informal association composed of the heads of core Mitsubishi companies that meet for lunch once a month). The independence of the Mitsubishi companies makes the 'Mitsubishi' all but impossible to define and thus a clear number the group consists of cannot be stated. If we simply count the number of companies with 'Mitsubishi' in their names existing world wide, that would be around 400. But there are also hundreds of Mitsubishi companies that do not have 'Mitsubishi' in their names.

Q3: Why do the Mitsubishi companies undertake joint endeavors like the 'mitsubishi.com' website if they are separate and independent companies?

A3: The companies conduct their business activities independently and even compete with each other in many fields. But as they share the same founding management philosophy, they cooperate in areas of common interest, such as sporting, cultural events and public-interest activities. The companies established a Mitsubishi portal on the Internet, 'mitsubishi.com,' to provide a broad perspective on 'Mitsubishi.'

Q4: Do the Mitsubishi companies have some kind of decision-making body that determines overall policy for the companies?

A4: No. But all the companies honor the Three Principles prescribed by Koyata Iwasaki, the Fourth and final president of the old Mitsubishi organization: (1) Corporate Social Responsibility, (2) Integrity and Fairness, and (3) International Understanding through Trade.

Q5: How did the Mitsubishi companies begin?

A5: The companies trace their origin to a shipping company started in 1870 by a man named Yataro Iwasaki. Yataro also established businesses in mining, shipbuilding, banking, and insurance. He thus laid the foundation for the subsequent growth and development of the Mitsubishi companies.

Source: www.mitsubishi.com/e/group/about.html

---

enough to represent identifiable business activities but small enough to enable division managers to manage them effectively (Barney, 2007).

Williamson (1975, 1981) also identifies four key efficiency advantages of the *M*-form: (1) adaptation to bounded rationality, (2) allocation of decision-making rights, (3) minimization of coordination costs, and (4) avoidance of goal conflicts.

1 **Adaptation to bounded rationality**. If managers are limited in their cognitive, information processing, and decision making capabilities (Simon, 1961), they cannot be responsible for

BOX 9.4 ORGANIZATIONAL STRUCTURE AND THE GROWTH OF THE FIRM

Chandler (1963) suggests that firms experience a certain pattern of relationships that link strategy and structure. In Figure 9.2, growth creates coordination and control problems that the existing organizational structure cannot handle. Over time, organizational growth creates the opportunity for the firm to change its strategy and improve its performance further. However, the existing structure may be adequate to implement the new strategy, after which the new structure can be adopted (Churchill & Lewis, 1983; Galbraith & Kazanjian, 1986; Greiner, 1972).

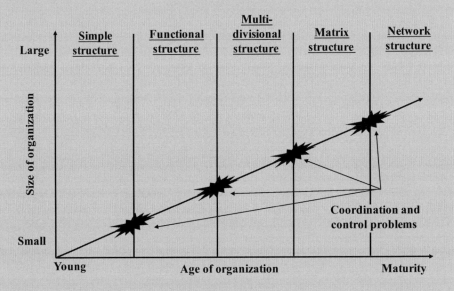

Figure 9.2 Strategy and structure growth pattern

Source: Adapted from Greiner (1972) and Churchill & Lewis (1983)

Five major types of organizational structures often appear successively in the effort to implement new strategies as the firm grows: simple structure, functional structure, multidivisional structure, matrix structure, and network structure.

The simple structure (also called the unitary or U-form) is often the first organizational structure implemented by a newly created entrepreneurial firm. The owner-manager makes all major decisions and monitors all activities; the staff serve as an extension of the manager's authority. Very efficient for small firms, this structure becomes problematic as the firm grows and the amount and complexity of information increases. The larger size of the firm requires more sophisticated workflows and better integration and coordination mechanisms.

The functional structure consists of a CEO and a limited number of corporate staff, with line managers in dominant functional areas, such as production, marketing, R&D, and human resource management. This structure allows for functional specialization (Keats & O'Neill, 2001) and thereby facilitates knowledge sharing within functional areas. However, as the firm continues to grow, this functional orientation can limit communication and coordination across the different functions. If the functional structure supports the implementation of business and corporate level strategies with only limited levels of diversification, it becomes problematic for larger and more diversified firms that require better coordination and control. Greater levels of diversification also require the analysis and coordination of greater amounts of information, such as when the firm offers the same products in different geographic markets or different products for different customer markets. Thus, higher levels of diversification require a new organizational structure (Chandler, 1963).

The multidivisional structure consists of multiple operating divisions, each of which represents a separate business to which corporate headquarters delegates responsibilities for operations and business level strategy to the division managers. Each division is a separate business, with its own functional hierarchy. Developed to implement diversification strategies, the multidivisional structure helps firms efficiently manage the increased demand for coordination and control (Chandler, 1994).

As discussed above, two other organizational structures—the matrix and network structures—can be implemented as the firm continues to grow and diversify.

all coordination and decision making within a large diversified firm (see Chapter 8). The *M*-form disperses and delegates decision making to divisional managers.

2 **Allocation of decision-making rights**. The *M*-form takes into account the distinction between business level strategy and corporate level strategy (discussed in Chapter 1). Decision-making responsibilities can be separated according to the strategic level of the decisions and then allocated to the adapted organizational level. Through the *M*-form, business level strategy decisions can be delegated to divisional level managers, while corporate level strategy decisions should be made at the headquarters level.

3 **Minimization of coordination costs**. In the functional organization, business level decisions must move up to the top of the firm, where all the relevant information and expertise can be integrated. In the multidivisional firm, as long as close coordination across different divisions is not necessary, most decisions that face a particular business can be made at the divisional level, which eases the information and decision-making burdens on corporate management.

4 **Avoidance of goal conflicts**. When a company organizes by function, department managers emphasize functional goals over those of the firm as a whole. The classic conflicts across functions follow a familiar pattern: marketing wants to please customers, production hopes to maximize output, R&D aims to introduce radically new products, and finance only cares about profits and losses. In the *M*-form though, incentive systems can be installed to push divisional managers, as the general managers of their division, to pursue profit goals consistent with the goals of the firm as a whole, rather than just their own personal or functional goals (Hitt et al., 2004).

Because of these advantages, the *M*-form can help solve two key problems of large, diversified firms: resource allocation and agency problems.

- **Allocation of resources**. Resource allocation within any hierarchical structure is a political process, in which power, status, and influence can come to dominate purely economic rationality (Bower, 1970). To the extent that the *M*-form can create a competitive internal capital market that allocates budgets on the basis of financial and strategic criteria, it can avoid much of the politicization inherent to purely hierarchical systems (Hill et al., 1992). The *M*-form attains this status by operating an internal capital market in which budgets get linked to past and projected divisional profitability, and individual projects are subject to a standardized appraisal and approval process (Bower, 1970).

- **Resolution of agency problems**. A related shortcoming of the modern corporation is that shareholders want to maximize the firm's market value, whereas managers are more interested in salaries, job security, and personal power (Jensen & Meckling, 1976). Because dispersed shareholders have limited power to discipline and replace managers, whereas top management often tends to dominate the board of directors (see Chapter 15), the M-form may act as a partial remedy to the agency problem. By providing an interface between the shareholders and divisional managers, corporate management can require and enforce adherence to common profit goals (Williamson, 1981). With divisions organized as profit centers, it becomes easier for corporate headquarters to monitor financial performance and hold divisional managers responsible for performance failures. As long as corporate management focuses on shareholder value, the M-form can be designed appropriately to support profit maximization goals at the divisional level (Williamson, 1981).

Problems of the multidivisional structure

As discussed, the M-form reconciles the benefits of decentralization with those of coordination (Williamson, 1981). However as Mintzberg (1983) points out, in practice, the M-form often suffers from two important rigidities that limit its desired decentralization and adaptability:

- **Constraints on decentralization**. Although business level decisions in the M-form are delegated to the divisional level, the individual divisions often feature highly centralized power that largely reflects the divisional manager's personal accountability to corporate headquarters. In addition, the freedom to make business level decisions can be preserved by division managers only as long as corporate headquarters is satisfied with divisional performance. For example, monthly financial reviews typically mean that variance in divisional performance precipitates speedy corporate intervention. Alternatively, divisional freedom might be reduced if related divisions need to coordinate to achieve synergies and economies of scope.
- **Standardization of divisional management**. In principle, in the divisional form, divisional management can be differentiated according to business needs. In practice though, powerful forces push to standardize control systems and management styles, which may prevent the individual divisions from achieving their full potential. The difficulties that large, mature firms experience in their efforts to develop new businesses often result from the application of management systems designed for existing businesses to new businesses (Birkinshaw & Campbell, 2004).

Bettis (1991) goes one step further to argue that the M-form is an "organizational fossil" that is becoming increasingly irrelevant in a world of global matrix organizations, multiple reporting relationships, virtual corporations, and networks. Yet almost 20 years after this prediction, the M-form persists as the most widely used strategy by firms around the world; evidence also suggests that the M-form is still an effective form for organizing diversified firms (Hoskisson et al., 1993a).

ORGANIZATIONAL STRUCTURE AND CORPORATE LEVEL STRATEGIES

The multidivisional structure is not one unique organizational form; it appears in several variations (Hill & Hoskisson, 1987). Empirical studies reveal that diversified firms using the M-form may exhibit substantial differences in their internal arrangements with regard to centralization, integration, and internal control mechanisms (Allen, 1978; Hill & Pickering, 1986; Lorsch & Allen, 1973; Vancil, 1978).

Organizing the multibusiness firm

As we argued in Chapter 5, different diversification strategies are associated with different value creation mechanisms and economic benefits. Within a multibusiness firm, corporate value can emerge through operational, financial, and anticompetitive economies of scope. Yet the realization of these different economic benefits demands different organizational arrangements (Hill et al., 1992). Hill and colleagues (Hill 1994; Hill & Hoskisson, 1987; Hill et al., 1992; Jones & Hill, 1988) argue that operational economies of scope demand organizational arrangements that stress cooperation across divisions. In contrast, realizing financial scope economies, achieved through an efficient internal capital market, requires organizational arrangements that emphasize the competition between divisions (Hill & Hoskisson, 1987; Hoskisson et al., 1993a).

Cooperative organizational structures

The cooperative M-form (see Figure 9.3) is an organizational structure in which horizontal integration induces interdivisional cooperation (Hitt et al., 2004; Markides & Williamson, 1996).

Within a diversified firm that adopts a multidivisional structure, cooperation between divisions is a prerequisite of operational economies of scope (Markides & Williamson, 1996). By coordinating the activities of the divisions, the firm ensures skills and knowledge can be transferred and/or resources shared (Porter, 1987). Child (1984) argues that some centralization is necessary to achieve such coordination; similarly, Mintzberg (1983) notes that interdependencies among divisions encourage corporate headquarters to retain some control over their common functions to ensure coordination and avoid duplication. Some degree of centralized control, especially over the strategic and operational decisions of interdependent divisions in related diversified firms, is required to realize economies of scope. For example, interdivisional sharing of technological resources through the centralization of R&D activities can create corporate value (Berg, 1973; Pitts, 1977). In addition to centralization, coordination between divisions also requires specific *integrating mechanisms* that can achieve lateral communication, that is, communication among the divisions. The complexity of these mechanisms depends on the extent of interdependence between divisions and can vary from simple liaison roles and temporary task forces to permanent coordination teams (Child, 1984; Galbraith, 1977; Lawrence & Lorsch, 1967). When there is an even higher need for coordination and control, the cooperative M-form might even evolve into a matrix structure (Hitt et al., 2004).

According to Hitt et al. (2004), the main structural characteristics of the cooperative M-form are as follows: (1) structural integration devices create links among all divisions; (2) corporate headquarters emphasizes centralized strategic planning, human resources, and marketing to foster cooperation among divisions; (3) R&D likely is centralized; (4) reward systems tend to emphasize overall firm performance in addition to divisional performance; and (5) organizational culture emphasizes cooperative sharing (see Figure 9.3).

The effectiveness of this cooperative M-form depends on how well the information can be processed among divisions. But because cooperation among the divisions also implies a loss of managerial freedom and autonomy, division managers may not readily commit to the type of integrative information processing activities that this structure requires (Hitt et al., 2004). Moreover, coordination among divisions can lead to an unequal flow of financial benefits to divisional managers. In other words, when managerial bonuses and rewards are based on the performance of individual divisions, the division manager that benefits the most from shared resources might be viewed as receiving gains at the expense of the other division managers (i.e., free-riding).

Performance ambiguities also might create problems for a firm trying to achieve coordination between interdependent divisions (Govindarajan & Fisher, 1990; Gupta & Govindarajan, 1986; Hill & Pickering, 1986; Lorsch & Allen, 1973; Vancil, 1978). This concern is essentially the problem of team production (Alchian & Demsetz, 1972), just occurring within rather than between firms. When divisions lack complete autonomy with regard to operating decisions and business level

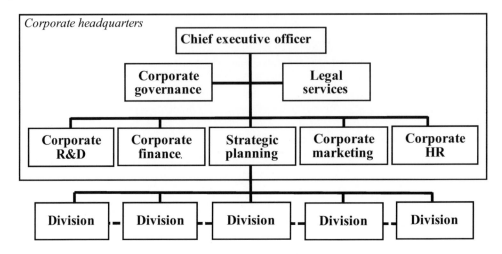

Figure 9.3 Cooperative M-form

strategies, then objective financial performance measures, such as the rate of return, cannot constitute unambiguous indicators of divisional efficiency. The poor financial performance of some divisions might be due to inefficiencies within that division, inefficiencies in another division with which it is tightly coupled, or even poor input from corporate headquarters that affects key business level decisions. Without access to more information, it would be difficult to assign real accountability to division managers.

The firm can overcome these performance ambiguity problems by increasing the amount of information it processes (Daft & Lengel, 1986). More precisely, as interdivisional coordination increases, the firm might de-emphasize financial performance measures and emphasize more strategic methods for evaluating performance (Govindarajan & Fisher, 1990; Hill, 1988; Ouchi, 1980). In a cooperative M-form, the corporate headquarters should base its assessment of divisional performance on a wide range of criteria that align with its dominant corporate value creation mechanisms. These criteria might include subjective measures of divisional performance, such as the ability to innovate, as well as objective measures other than financial criteria, such as labor productivity, capacity utilization, market share, or growth. Moreover, corporate management can allocate cash flows between competing claims using these multiple criteria.

Finally, coordination may improve if reward and incentive schemes emphasize interdivisional cooperation rather than the performance of each division as an independent profit center (Gupta & Govindarajan, 1986; Kerr, 1985; Lorsch & Allen, 1973; Pitts, 1974; Salter, 1973). The bonuses used to encourage divisional managers in related diversified firms should be linked to corporate rather than divisional performance. Because corporate performance depends on the success of interdivisional cooperation, such a reward system provides divisional managers with incentives to cooperate. It then follows that in related diversified firms, there is a need to emphasize incentive schemes based on corporate performance to reinforce the structural coordination that underlies the cooperative M-form.

Competitive organizational structures

Similar to firms that attempt to realize economies of scope, firms pursuing an unrelated diversification strategy (i.e., conglomerates) want to realize benefits from efficient internal governance and thus may require an adapted M-form structure (Chandler, 1962; Rumelt, 1974). The internal organizational arrangements of unrelated diversified firms are quite different from those of related diversified firms (Hill & Hoskisson, 1987; Mintzberg, 1983; Vancil, 1978). Therefore, to implement an unrelated diversification strategy based on value creation—whether through an efficient internal capital market or restructuring by buying and selling businesses—firms should use the competitive form of the multidivisional structure (Hoskisson & Hitt, 1990; Porter, 1987).

The competitive M-form favors complete independence among the firm's divisions (Hitt et al., 2004). Unlike the divisions in the cooperative M-form, the divisions that constitute the competitive M-form do not share common corporate competencies, and nor do they develop integrating devices. Moreover, the efficient capital market, which provides the rationale for implementing such a structure, emphasizes competition between divisions rather than cooperation.

According to Hitt et al. (2004), the competitive M-form exhibits the following primary characteristics: (1) corporate headquarters has a small staff; (2) finance and auditing are the main functions undertaken by corporate headquarters; (3) divisions are independent and separate for financial evaluation purposes; (4) divisions retain strategic control at the business level, but cash flows are managed by the corporate headquarters; and (5) divisions compete for corporate resources (see Figure 9.4).

Williamson (1975) argues that to implement a corporate, value creating, unrelated diversification strategy, the organizational structure of conglomerate firms must possess specific organizational features. First, each division should be autonomous with regard to its operating and business level decisions, so divisional managers can be held accountable for divisional performance (i.e., operating and business level decisions should be decentralized). Second, to preserve their autonomy, the relationship between the corporate headquarters and divisions should remain at arm's length. The corporate office cannot intervene in divisional affairs except to audit operations, discipline opportunistic or incompetent divisional managers, and correct performance shortfalls (Williamson, 1975). Third, corporate headquarters should exercise control over divisions by setting objective financial performance targets and monitoring outcomes. Fourth, incentive systems for divisional managers should be linked to divisional performance rather than corporate performance. And fifth, corporate headquarters should allocate cash flows across divisions on a competitive basis, rather than simply returning them to their source divisions.

Within the competitive M-form, these features seek to replicate the relationship between shareholders and firms in the stock market, though still overcome the limitations associated with the

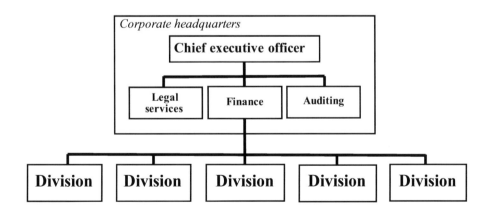

Figure 9.4 Competitive M-form

Organizing the multibusiness firm

stock market (Williamson, 1985). In such a structure, divisional managers are responsible for operational and business level decisions and therefore accountable for the performance of the divisions under their control. This accountability provides a strong incentive to maximize the efficiency of divisional operations. The structure also makes clear to divisional managers that promotional opportunities and job tenure are contingent on their attainment of specific objective performance targets. Linking bonuses to divisional performance and allocating cash flows and budgets among divisions on the basis of relative performance reinforces the incentive to maximize divisional performance.

Because the system is designed to produce competition among divisions (Williamson, 1975), it offers three main benefits: (1) flexibility, such that each division can develop the specific competencies it needs to compete best in its respective market; (2) challenges to the status quo and inertia, because division managers know that future resource allocations depend on their current performance and expected future performance; and (3) motivation, in that competing against internal peers can be as great a challenge as vying against external competitors (Birkinshaw, 2001).

Strategic business unit organizational structures

Because of the radical differences between cooperative and competitive *M*-form structures, it might be difficult for diversified firms to realize economic benefits simultaneously from operating and financial economies of scope (Hill, 1994). The lack of commonalties between divisions in unrelated conglomerates precludes operational economies of scope. Related firms also may find it difficult to realize simultaneous benefits from operational economies of scope and an internal capital market, because performance ambiguities arise from substantial interdependencies among divisions.

Thus, when a firm's diversification strategy involves a portfolio of related and unrelated businesses, neither the collaborative nor the competitive *M*-form is suitable to create corporate value. Rather, such a firm likely requires a strategic business unit (SBU) approach to the multidivisional structure (Hitt et al., 2004). This organizational structure consists of three different levels: the corporate headquarters level, the SBU level, and the SBU division level (see Figure 9.5). In this structure, the divisions within each SBU relate to each of the others in their shared products, markets, or both, but the divisions of one particular SBU are unrelated to the divisions of another SBU. Within each SBU, divisions share product and market competencies to develop economies of scope and scale, using integration mechanisms similar to those used by cooperative *M*-forms. At the same time, each SBU acts as a profit center controlled and evaluated by the corporate headquarters in the same way as it would be in competitive *M*-forms.

Hitt et al. (2004) summarize the main structural characteristics of the SBU *M*-form as follows: (1) structural integration exists among divisions within SBUs, but independence marks the SBUs; (2) strategic planning is an important function of corporate headquarters, which must manage the approval process and confirm the strategic planning performed by the SBUs; (3) each SBU may have its own budget and staff to foster integration within the SBU; and (4) corporate headquarters serves as a consultant for its SBUs and divisions, rather than exerting its direct impact on the development of the business level strategies.

CONCLUDING REMARKS

The preceding description suggests that fundamentally different organizational philosophies are required to realize operational and financial economies of scope. Firms pursuing a related diversification strategy are better off implementing a collaborative multidivisional structure, whereas firms pursuing an unrelated diversification strategy benefit from a competitive multidivisional

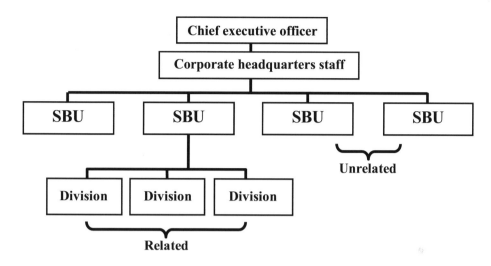

Figure 9.5 SBU M-form

structure. In addition, if the firm's portfolio combines related and unrelated businesses, a SBU multidivisional structure is more appropriate. The basic differences among these three organizational structures are summarized in Table 9.1, adapted from Hitt et al. (2004) and Hoskisson et al. (1993a).

Competitive and cooperative *M*-forms have different internal configurations with regard to centralization, integration, control practices, and incentive schemes. As a result, the internal management philosophies of cooperative and competitive organizations are incompatible (Hill, 1994; Hoskisson et al., 1993a). Cooperative organizations foster and encourage cooperation between divisions; competitive organizations foster and encourage competition between them. It is exceedingly difficult to simultaneously encourage competition and cooperation between

Table 9.1 The Characteristics of the different M-forms

Structural characteristics	Cooperative M-form	SBU M-form	Competitive M-form
Type of diversification strategy	Related constrained	Mixed related and unrelated	Unrelated
Degree of centralization	Centralized at corporate headquarters	Centralized in SBUs	Decentralized to divisions
Level of economies of scope	Extensive synergies	Moderate synergies	No synergies
Type of control	Planning and strategic control	Strategic and financial control	Financial control
Divisional incentive scheme	Linked to corporate performance	Linked to corporate, division, and SBU performance	Linked to divisional performance

Source: Adapted from Hitt et al. (2004) and Hoskisson et al. (1993)

divisions. However, it is not impossible; it can be done by adding a third organizational level. In the SBU *M*-form, competition is encouraged between SBUs even as collaboration is developed within SBUs.

The argument we have developed, that different organizational structures and control systems are needed to implement related and unrelated diversification strategies, is empirically supported by broad based research findings provided by Lorsch and Allen (1973), Mintzberg (1983), Pitts (1977), and Vancil (1978), among others (for reviews, see Hill & Hoskisson, 1987; Markides & Williamson, 1996). In particular, the results of Hill et al.'s (1992) survey of a sample of 184 Fortune 1000 firms indicate that the appropriate fit among strategy, structure, and control systems is associated with superior performance. Firms attempting to realize economies of scope perform better if their organizational arrangements stress cooperation between business units, whereas firms attempting to realize economic benefits from efficient internal governance perform better if their organizational arrangements stress competition between business units. Moreover, several studies have shown that the appropriate incentive systems for divisional managers depend on the degree of resource sharing (i.e., relatedness) among divisions (Gupta & Govindarajan, 1986; Kerr, 1985; Lorsch & Allen, 1973; Pitts, 1974; Salter, 1973).

In this chapter, as well as most of the preceding chapters, we have discussed horizontal diversification strategies. With such strategies, firms diversify across various activities at the same stage in the industry value chain. In the next chapter though, we discuss vertical integration, or a diversification strategy across stages of the industry value chain. Although vertical integration and horizontal diversification strategies share some communalities in terms of corporate value creation and economies of scope, they also differ on some aspects. For example, in terms of organizational structure, the main challenge for a horizontally diversified firm is to minimize agency costs, whereas the main challenge for a vertically integrated firm is to minimize transaction costs (Hill & Hoskisson, 1987; Jones & Hill, 1988).

Chapter

10

VERTICAL INTEGRATION

COORDINATING THE VALUE CHAIN

Vertical integration refers to the corporate level strategy by which a firm diversifies its activities along the industry value chain, whether by producing its own input (i.e., backward, or upstream, integration) or disposing of its own outputs (i.e., forward, or downstream, integration) (Grant, 2013; Harrigan, 1984, 1985a). Vertical integration increases a firm's value added margins for a specific processing chain (Harrigan, 1985a) (see Figure 10.1) and thereby enjoys scale or integration economies, as well as greater control over sources of raw material or distribution outlets (Pfeffer & Salancik, 1978; Scherer & Ross, 1990).

Vertical integration, as a corporate level strategy, is often one of the first diversification strategies that firms embrace (Harrigan, 1984). Vertical integration can be assimilated to a corporate level strategy because it refers to the scope of a firm when it chooses to compete in particular value-adding stages of an industry value chain (Hofer & Schendel, 1978). Yet vertical integration also constitutes an *internalization* strategy (Williamson, 1975), in transaction cost theory terms, because the firm performs activities itself instead of relying on external suppliers or buyers.

One of the famous examples of a fully vertically integrated firm is the Carnegie Steel Company during the late 1880s. At the height of its growth, the firm controlled not only the mills that manufactured the steel but also the mines from which the iron ore was extracted, the coal mines that supplied the coal, the ships that transported the iron ore to the factory, the railroads that transported the coal, the coke ovens that cooked the coal, and so on, along the entire value chain (Livesay, 1999).

Another example is Ford that at one time even owned a sheep farm to supply wool for car seats and a glass company (Achrol & Kotler, 1999). Other classic examples of vertical integration involve the oil industry, a context in which MNCs such as ExxonMobil, Royal Dutch Shell, and British Petroleum own everything from the oil drilling operations to the pipelines that transmit the crude oil, to the refining process, to distribution through their own retail stations.

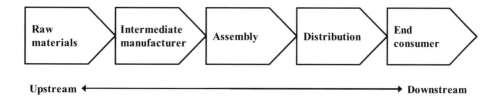

Figure 10.1 Stages in the industry value chain

Vertical integration

More recently, Apple can be considered as a mostly vertically integrated firm (Knowledge@Wharton, 2012): it designs its own computer hardware, accessories, operating systems, and much of its own software (Madden, 2013). And though its production has shifted to third party suppliers, Apple integrated downward in 2001 by launching its own retail outlets instead of relying on external sellers. As of December 2009, Apple had opened 294 of its own dedicated stores. The objective for Apple is to control the end to end customer experience as much as possible to deliver coherent experiences across multiple touch-points (Madden, 2013). And to meaningfully convert this control into consumer value, Apple decided to integrate backward into design. Design means Apple's retail environment must feel consistent with the way the brand is presented online, just as its industrial design supports its interactive experience to do vertical integration becomes necessary. However, as Box 10.1 demonstrate vertical integration can be a delicate strategy.

BOX 10.1 VERTICAL INTEGRATION WORKS FOR APPLE: BUT IT WON'T FOR EVERYONE

Google recently acquired mobile device maker Motorola Mobility and will soon manufacture smartphones and television set top boxes. Amazon's Kindle Fire tablet represents its bridge between hardware and e-commerce. Oracle bought Sun Microsystems and now champions engineered systems (integrated hardware and software devices). And even long standing software giant Microsoft now makes hardware for its Xbox gaming system. Technology titans are increasingly looking like vertically integrated conglomerates largely in an attempt to emulate the success of Apple.

Vertical integration dictates that one company controls the end product as well as its component parts. In technology, Apple for 35 years has championed a vertical model, which features an integrated hardware and software approach. For instance, the iPhone and iPad have hardware and software designed by Apple, which also designed its own processors for the devices. This integration has allowed Apple to set the pace for mobile computing.

The tech industry's success in this type of integration is mixed. Samsung, a large technology conglomerate, has thrived by making everything from LCD (liquid crystal display) panels to processors, televisions and smartphones. But Sony, which has attempted to meld content, TVs and game systems like the PlayStation, has yet to find a way to make the disparate parts gel. The technology industry's rush to vertical integration may be misplaced because they are harder to manage. Yet, with technology companies under increasing pressure to keep growth rates up, expanding into new areas is an attractive proposition for many firms.

Source: Knoweldg@Wharton (2012)

However, as the Apple example demonstrates though, vertical integration is not an either/or decision; a firm may integrate more or less vertically, depending on the number of value adding activities it performs internally. The degree or level of vertical integration therefore is a function of the number of activities in the industry value chain that a firm performs by itself (Box 10.2 describes a measure of a firm's degree of vertical integration). The greater the firm's ownership and control over successive (or adjacent) stages of the industry value chain, the greater is its degree of vertical integration. For example, Walt Disney is a highly integrated firm that produces its own movies, distributes them to cinemas and on its own TV networks, and uses images of its

BOX 10.2 MEASURING VERTICAL INTEGRATION

The extent of vertical integration can be measured as the ratio of the firm's added value to its sales revenue (Gort, 1962; Harrigan, 1986; Tucker & Wilder, 1977). As a percentage of sales, the value added measure pertains to the portion of a firm's sales generated by activities conducted within the boundaries of the firm. Therefore, a firm with a high ratio has internalized most of the value creating activities associated with its business, consistent with a high level of vertical integration (Barney, 2007). A firm with a small ratio between its value added and sales possesses a lower level of vertical integration. In mathematical terms, the degree of vertical integration equals:

$$\text{Vertical integration} = \frac{\text{Value added} - (\text{net income} + \text{income taxes})}{\text{Sales} - (\text{net income} + \text{income taxes})}.$$

The sum of net income and income taxes gets subtracted in both the numerator and the denominator to control for inflation and changes in the tax code over time. Net income taxes and sales can be taken directly from a firm's profit and loss statement. To calculate the value added, we can use the following equation:

$$
\begin{aligned}
\text{Value added} = &\ \text{Depreciation} + \text{amortization} + \text{fixed charges} \\
&+ \text{interest expense} + \text{labor and related expenses} \\
&+ \text{pension and retirement expenses} + \text{income taxes} \\
&+ \text{net income (after taxes)} + \text{rental expense.}
\end{aligned}
$$

Some studies indicate that value added as a percentage of sales may be an appropriate measure a firm's level of vertical integration in a wide range of situations (Maddigan, 1979), but this tactic also has also prompted criticism for being too sensitive to how far upstream the firm is integrated; it also may reflect some other diversification influences (Chatterjee, 1991), such as horizontal and geographic diversification.

---

movies' characters in both its own retail stores and its named theme parks. Nike is a much more vertically specialized (or disintegrated) firm: it is active in the design and marketing of it shoes and athletic apparel, but it outsources most other activities in its value chain, including manufacturing, distribution, and retailing. Davidow and Malone (1992) nicknamed such a kind of firm a "virtual corporation."

In terms of vertical integration strategies, two main questions are critical: (1) when should a firm integrate vertically? (Williamson, 1975, 1985); and (2) what are the alternatives to vertical integration? (Harrigan, 1984). In the reminder of this chapter, we seek to answer these two questions.

CREATING CORPORATE VALUE THROUGH VERTICAL INTEGRATION

Vertical integration is associated with several internal and competitive advantages and risks, which makes the decision to integrate vertically a difficult one for firms. Table 10.1, adapted from Harrigan (1984), summarizes these advantages and disadvantages.

These different advantages and disadvantages are relatively diverse and derive from different level of analysis and various theoretical frameworks. Four main theoretical frameworks rationalize

Vertical integration

Table 10.1 Some advantages and disadvantages of vertical integration

Advantages	Disadvantages
Internal benefits	*Internal costs*
• Integration economies reduce costs by eliminating staples, reducing duplicate overhead, and cutting costs. • Improved coordination of activities reduces inventory and other costs. • Can avoid time consuming tasks, such as price shopping, communicating design details, or negotiating contracts.	• Need for overhead to coordinate vertical integration increases costs. • Burden of excess capacity from unevenly balanced minimum efficient scale plants. • Poorly organized vertically integrated firms do not enjoy synergies that compensate for higher costs. • Lack of incentives for internal suppliers.
Competitive benefits	*Competitive risks*
• Avoid foreclosures to inputs, services, or markets. • Improved marketing or technological intelligence. • Opportunity to create product differentiation. • Superior control of firm's economic environment. • Create credibility for new products. • Synergies can be created by coordinating vertical activities efficiently.	• Obsolete processes may be perpetuated. • Create mobility (or exit) barriers. • Links firm to struggling adjacent businesses. • Lose access to knowledge and information from suppliers or distributors. • Synergies created through vertical integration may be overrated.

Source: Adapted from Harrigan (1984)

a firm's choice to vertically integrate: (1) transaction cost economics, (2) industrial organization economics and market power, (3) the resource based theory, and (4) real option theory. These theoretical frameworks have been introduced in Chapter 2; in this chapter, we focus on their arguments as they pertain to vertical integration.

Transaction costs and vertical integration

Transaction cost theory is the dominant theoretical framework that serves to explain firms' decisions to integrate vertically (Hennart, 1988; Jones & Hill, 1988; Williamson, 1975, 1985). From a transaction cost perspective (Williamson, 1975, 1985), a deal with a supplier or buyer that involves the transfer of goods or services is often accompanied by significant costs, related to the expenses of negotiations, drafting and signing contracts, financial transfers, packaging, distribution, and insurance (Arrow, 1974; Williamson, 1975). To these transaction costs, we need to add the search costs required to locate and analyze potential new suppliers or buyers and the monitoring costs incurred when the firm needs to determine contract fulfillment or take corrective actions against partners that shirk their contractual obligations. When a firm vertically integrates, it avoids many of these costs—for example, it should not need to monitor itself—which can create potential economies of integration (Harrigan, 1984).

In addition to eliminating these transaction costs, vertical integration also avoids the risk of opportunistic behavior by the transaction partner. In this sense, vertical integration enables the firm to protect and guarantee the quality of its products and services. By integrating backward, the firm gains control over its supply sources. By integrating forward, it gains control of distribution outlets and thus can maintain its required standards for after-sales service, which are particularly costly to control when performed by external parties (Anderson & Weitz, 1986).

In addition, Chandler (1977) argues that firms can gain competitive advantages through vertical integration because it becomes easier for them to plan, coordinate, and schedule adjacent value adding activities. For example, the enhanced logistics and scheduling that vertical integration makes feasible may enable the firm to respond better and faster to sudden changes in demand or to introduce its product into the market faster.

Vertical integration also helps the firm reduce its operational coordination costs. In different industries, various stages of the value chain must be tightly coordinated or even physically integrated to ensure that the right components, meeting the right specifications, are available in the right quantities, at the right moment (i.e., just in time processes). These capabilities in turn enable the firm to achieve high quality, low cost, and timely delivery. To realize this significant level of coordination, the firm may need to control key activities in the value chain instead of trying to convince independent suppliers and buyers to cooperate.

However, vertical integration is beneficial only if the economies, in terms of transaction costs, are higher than the administration (or bureaucratic) costs incurred by vertical integration to coordinate the activities along the industry value chain. This efficiency of this internal administration depends on several factors (Harrigan, 1984; Jones & Hill, 1988; Porter, 1980). For example, vertical integration suffers an important disadvantage when the optimal (or minimally efficient) scale differs at different stages of the industry value chain. In this case, a vertically integrated firm incurs supplementary costs due to the excess resources or suboptimal scales that occur at different stages of the value chain. Other important disadvantages of vertical integration include the incentive problem and reduced flexibility (e.g., Collis & Montgomery, 2005; Jones & Hill, 1988; Porter, 1980).

The incentive problem

Vertical integration alters the incentives between the vertically related businesses. For example, it might raise costs if the firm commits to purchasing inputs from its internal suppliers, even if less expensive external suppliers exist. In this case, vertical integration represents a disadvantage, because the firm's sources of supply demand higher costs than do those of independent suppliers. The high operating costs of internal supply sources might result because an internal supplier knows it can always sell its output to other parts of the firm. The lack of competition lessens the supplier's incentive to minimize its operating costs; the managers of the supply operation may even be tempted to pass on cost increases to other parts of the firm in the form of higher *transfer prices*, rather than looking for ways to lower those costs. Together, such disadvantages also increase administrative costs and limit the degree of vertical integration that a firm can achieve profitably.

Both transaction and administrative costs can be important but reflect different factors; therefore, to make a decision to integrate vertically, the firm first must understand when transaction costs are likely to be higher than administrative costs. According to Williamson (1985), transaction costs are usually high, and likely to be higher than administrative costs, when exchanges are subject to high threats of opportunism by the presence of transaction specific investments and/or high levels of uncertainty and complexity in the transactions. In this situation, the firm would benefit from vertical integration rather than transacting on the market.

Lack of flexibility

As discussed in Chapter 2, specialized assets are designed to perform a specific task, so their value declines significantly in their next best use (Williamson, 1985). Firms invest in specialized assets to lower the costs of value creation and/or differentiate their products from those of competitors. However, because of the specific nature of these assets and the related threat of opportunism (e.g., risk of holdup; Klein et al., 1978), a firm might have troubles finding partners in adjacent (upstream or downstream) stages of the industry value chain that agree to commit such investments (Subramani & Venkatraman, 2003). To realize the economic gains associated with investments, the firm might instead integrate vertically and internalize the investments.

In addition to transaction specific investments, the levels of uncertainty and complexity that mark transactions between two stages of the value chain can influence the extent of the threat of opportunism. When firms can anticipate all the different ways that an exchange partner might behave opportunistically, they can write a relatively complete contract that covers most risks. However, when the transaction consists of high levels of uncertainty and complexity, it becomes very difficult, or even impossible, to write a complete contract, and therefore, the risk of opportunism increases (Akerlof, 1970; Arrow, 1974). Vertical integration may be necessary to eliminate this risk.

A common example of such a scenario occurs when technological innovation requires the entire value chain to switch to a new technology, a new production method, or new standards. Such changes often can be implemented only if there is strong commitment and concerted efforts by all the firms across the different stages of the industry value chain. The risk is high, especially if the industry value chain is highly fragmented, that some firms along the chain act opportunistically in a foreseeable future. Thus, vertical integration can give a dominant firm the formal control needed to push through the necessary changes.

Market power and vertical integration

In addition to reducing transaction costs, vertical integration can increase firms' market power (Edwards, 1953; Harrigan, 1984; Porter, 1980). From an industrial organization (I/O) economics perspective, integrating backward to gain control over a source of a critical supply element or integrating forward to gain control over distribution channels gives the firm the capability to build entry barriers for its industry and increase its market power (Chatterjee, 1991). By limiting competition in the firm's industry, vertical integration also enables the firm to find supplies at a lower price or charge end consumers a higher price than it could in a competitive market situation (Harrigan, 1984; Williamson, 1985).

Monopolistic firms have perpetually turned to vertical integration to extend their monopoly positions from one stage of the industry to another. Two classic cases are Standard Oil—which used its power in the transportation and refining industries to foreclose markets to independent oil producers—and Alcoa—which used its monopoly position in the aluminum production field to squeeze independent fabricators of aluminum products and give the advantage to its own fabrication subsidiaries (Hill & Jones, 2004).

Along similar lines, if a firm confronts particularly powerful suppliers or buyers, it might pursue vertical integration as a means to weaken or neutralize the other party (Edwards, 1953). By performing activities internally, the firm lessens its dependence on a strong buyer or supplier (Pfeffer & Salancik, 1978; Scherer & Ross, 1990); it might even strive to acquire the other party and avoid a bargaining situation altogether (see Chapter 12). Thus, in an industry characterized by high levels of rivalry between incumbents and low entry barriers, a viable means to increase bargaining power is through the vertical integration of activities along the industry value chain.

Resources and vertical integration

A further input for the vertical integration decision, beyond transaction costs and market power, involves the resources and capabilities that differentiate firms. According to RBV, a firm should vertically integrate when it possesses valuable, rare, and costly-to-imitate resources and capabilities (Argyres, 1996). It should not (generally) integrate when other firms possess the same critical resources, even in the presence of a threat of opportunistic behavior (Barney, 1999).

Barney (1999) argues that because of resource heterogeneity within an industry value chain, some firms may be particularly skilled in some activities (e.g., R&D), whereas others may have distinctive capabilities in other activities (e.g., manufacturing, marketing). A firm that specializes in just a few activities can develop distinctive capabilities in those realms. Because a vertically integrated firm must spread its resources across the different stages of the value chain, it is more difficult for it to develop distinctive capabilities in any specific stage or stages. Therefore, by vertically integrating its activities, a firm may lose the advantages of specialization. Furthermore, the competitive environments at the different stages of the industry value chain often require different competencies or unique strategies. Managing strategically different businesses along the value chain may prove both difficult and costly for vertically integrated firms, so Barney (1999) argues that a firm should make its decision by considering the potential value of collaborating with specialized firms that have their own distinctive capabilities (i.e., valuable, rare, costly to imitate, and costly to acquire resources), beyond taking into account the threat of opportunism.

Barney's (1999) argument pertains to the vertical integration decision when other firms possess valuable, rare, costly to imitate, and costly to acquire resources; from the opposite perspective, Argyres (1996) argues that a firm should vertically integrate into those activities in which it possesses a competitive advantage because of its control over valuable, rare, and costly to imitate resources and competencies. Argyres (1996) lists three main reasons a firm should vertically integrate. First, vertical integration increases the possibility that a firm can retain the sources of its competitive advantage for itself. If the firm turns to outside suppliers to perform activities, the chances are greater that the source of its competitive advantage could spill over to its competitors. Second, by vertically integrating, a firm increases its chances of appropriating more or all of the profits generated by the source of its competitive advantage, without having to share them with outside suppliers. Third, a competitive advantage based on valuable, rare, and costly to imitate resources and competences is likely to be socially complex and have been built up over long periods of time. Therefore, this firm specific resource cannot be transferred easily to outside suppliers.

Real option theory and vertical integration

Vertical integration affects the flexibility of the firm, especially in uncertain environments. Real option theory takes these influences into account to suggest the answer to the question of whether to vertically integrate (Kogut, 1991). As discussed in Chapter 3, an option is the right, but not the obligation, to buy or sell a specified asset at a specified price on a pre-specified date in the future (Amram & Kulatilaka, 1999). Real option logic therefore focuses on the firm's ability to adjust its strategy in the future, depending on how that uncertain future evolves (Barney, 2007). The importance of the ability to adjust strategies over time means that significant uncertainty about the ultimate value of a particular investment should prompt the firm not to vertically integrate, assuming that doing so provides it with less flexibility (Kogut, 1991). In general, less hierarchical solutions (e.g., market exchanges, strategic alliances, and joint ventures) are more flexible than vertical integration (Barney, 2007), because investments tend to be sunk costs, which are difficult to recover if necessary.

Vertical integration also may be more risky in unstable or unpredictable demand conditions (see Box 10.3). When demand is stable, higher degrees of vertical integration can be managed with relative ease, because stable demand allows for better scheduling and coordination of production flows across activities. However, when demand conditions are unstable or unpredictable, achieving close coordination among vertically integrated activities may be difficult. Yet in this case, vertical integration provides firms with valuable options to learn in the future. When several vertically linked business units work closely together, exchanging knowledge and personnel, they can learn quickly and efficiently, more so than if these business units were independent. Especially if they initiate joint R&D projects and collaborate on business process improvement efforts, significant learning curve advantages can be realized.

BOX 10.3 DELTA AIR LINES' VERTICAL INTEGRATION INTO THE REFINERY OF OIL

In 2012, Delta Air Lines bought an oil refinery. No other airline owns a refinery. But Delta executives, led by CEO Richard Anderson, thought it was time to do something radical about the painful cost of fuel. Back then oil prices were stubbornly high–more than $90 a barrel. Its planes were burning the equivalent of 260,000 barrels a day, representing a third of total costs. At the time, Delta figured, $2.2 billion of the $12 billion a year it was spending on fuel went to refiners as profit. By making jet fuel in the company's own refinery, Anderson and his team figured Delta could keep some of that profit for itself. So they plunked down $180 million for an aging plant near Philadelphia.

Two and a half years later, Delta has sunk $420 million of capital into the refinery, which has generated roughly $100 million of losses. Is Delta at least getting cheaper jet fuel? Yes, it expects to pay about 50 cents a gallon less this year. But that's only because oil prices have plunged, which has nothing to do with owning a refinery. Besides, the real test is to compare Delta's fuel costs to other big airlines. Before the acquisition Delta was sourcing fuel for 9 cents a gallon cheaper than its peers. Its edge today: still 9 cents. Meanwhile, much of its rationale for owning a refinery has disappeared: refiners' margins have declined, while American crude no longer sells as such a wide discount to imported barrels. Even if you can run the operation as well as anyone else, the opportunity cost of the fuel is still determined by the global market. It only makes sense if you can run the operation better than others firms, which unlikely for an airline, compared to a specialized oil company.

Source: Helman (2015)

Recall the example of rapidly changing technology that we mentioned previously. In this case, vertical integration poses a hazard, because the firm might become tied to an obsolescent technology (Harrigan, 1985c). In this sense, vertical integration inhibits the firm's ability to change its suppliers or distribution systems to match the requirements of the market, with its changing technology. But rapidly changing technology also implies that a vertically integrated firm, which controls the compete value chain, can switch more easily to the new technology, without having to coordinate that switch with multiple suppliers or buyers across the different stages of the industry value chain (see Box 10.4).

ALTERNATIVES TO VERTICAL INTEGRATION

The disadvantages associated with vertical integration raise a key question: is it possible to reap the benefits of vertical integration without having to bear the associated bureaucratic costs? Four alternative arrangements attempt to achieve this ideal: taper integration, short term contracts, long term contracts (i.e., strategic alliances), and outsourcing.

Taper (or partial) integration

In addition to differentiating between forward and backward integration, we can distinguish full integration from *taper integration* (see Figure 10.2). A firm achieves full integration when it produces all of a particular input that it needs for its processes or disposes of all its output through its own operations. Taper integration instead combines vertical integration with spot bid contracts.

Vertical integration

BOX 10.4 VERTICAL INTEGRATION AND TECHNOLOGICAL CHANGE

Both Harrigan (1984, 1985a) and Balakrishnan and Wernerfelt (1986) have shown that the benefits of vertical integration decline considerably in the face of a technological change that renders upstream capabilities obsolete. They therefore argue that in industries with a high rate of technological change, firms are better off if they avoid vertical integration. Hill and Hoskisson (1987) and Jones and Hill (1987) support this conclusion.

Other researchers have suggested otherwise. Because greater uncertainty in the relationship with its suppliers increases the chances that the firm will integrate vertically and begin producing its own input (Monteverde, 1995; Monteverde & Teece, 1982; Pisano, 1990; Williamson, 1985), the obsolescence of upstream capabilities due to technological change simply may suggest more vertical integration.

Afuah (2001) argues that these seemingly divergent views actually represent two sides of the same coin: following a technological change that destroys the competences of firms and their suppliers, firms that are integrated vertically in the new technology perform better than do those that are not. Firms that instead are vertically integrated in the old technology perform worse than those that had not been so integrated.

Therefore, the firm might buy a particular input from outside suppliers, in addition to making it in-house (Harrigan, 1984; Porter, 1980). Taper integration requires the firm to manage its own production while also maintaining a relationship with its outside suppliers (Heriot & Kulkarni, 2001). The use of taper integration decreases the bureaucratic costs associated with full vertical integration and reduces the incentive problem.

Specifically, taper integration creates an incentive for internal suppliers to reduce their operating costs and increases the firm's ability to respond to changing demand conditions. In this way, it reduces some of the organizational inefficiencies that increase bureaucratic costs. By using taper integration, firms might, for example, monitor the R&D development of outside suppliers, reduce their vulnerability to strikes and shortages, and examine the products of competitors while also enjoying the lower costs and corporate advantages (and profit margins) of vertical integration (Harrigan, 1984). The results of a survey of a sample of 209 plant managers by Kirk and Kulkarni

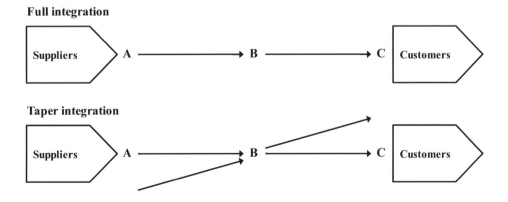

Figure 10.2 Full and taper integration

Vertical integration

(2001) indicate that firms use taper integration, as well as long term supplier relationships, more frequently than they do vertical integration or competitive spot bidding. Rothaermel et al. (2006) also found that a careful balance of vertical integration and strategic outsourcing helps firms achieve superior performance when they organize for innovation.

Competitive spot bidding and short term contracts

Short term contracts last for one year or less. Many firms use such short term contracts and competitive bidding to purchase inputs or sell their outputs. The presence of competition provides a strong incentive for suppliers to improve their offering by reducing the price, increasing the quality, or improving delivery time. However, such a strategy also signals a lack of long term commitment, which should be reciprocated by the suppliers, leading eventually to reduced cooperation between the firms and lowered investments in specialized assets. When the need for close cooperation and coordination is high, such competitive spot bidding and short terms contracts may have significant drawbacks, and long terms contracts may be an interesting alternative.

Long term contracts and strategic alliances

Long term strategic alliances help firms benefit from the coordination advantages associated with vertical integration, without bearing the administrative costs. As we discuss in Chapter 12, strategic alliances refer to cooperative relationships between two independent firms. Vertical alliances are long-term contractual arrangements, in which a firm agrees to supply a partner that agrees to continue purchasing from that supplier. In long term alliances, both firms make significant commitments, such as by investing in transaction specific (i.e., specialized) assets, jointly seeking ways to lower costs, or together increasing product quality. To mitigate the risk of opportunism that arises when firms invest in specialized assets, they can take some specific measures to ensure long term cooperative relationships. For example, firms might exchange hostages; both firms make investments in specialized assets that prevent either from exploiting its position (as Box 10.5 describes). Another method is to establish credible commitments on both sides and thus build trust (Dyer, 1997; Williamson, 1985). The mutual dependence that results from long term strategic alliances creates vulnerability for both parties, and though trust can alleviate some risks of opportunism, firms also should reinforce their vertical relationships and discourage opportunism through equity stakes and profit sharing arrangements. In these long term relationships, firms share the value created by quasi vertical integration but avoid many bureaucratic costs linked to their ownership of adjacent stages. In this sense, long term alliances can substitute for vertical integration (Harrigan, 1984).

BOX 10.5 KOREA'S *CHAEBOLS*

The Korean economy is dominated by a relatively small number of family dominated, large *chaebols*, which are similar to Japanese *keiretsu*. The four most prominent are Samsung, LG, Hyundai, and Daewoo. After the Korean War, these *chaebols* took advantage of subsidized loans and tax breaks from the Korean government and grew very quickly into strong vertical monopolies. Recently, Samsung and LG announced plans to vertically integrate even further: both firms plan to make investments in the production facilities for end customer products such as cell phones and digital TVs. For example, LG Electronics plans to invest 30 trillion won (€ 18 billion) in its production capabilities by 2010.

Source: www.wtec.org/loyola/kei/welcome.htm; Korean Times, 2004.

Outsourcing and the virtual corporation

The contrast to vertical integration is outsourcing. Consistent with RBV arguments, firms often outsource their non-core activities and keep their core activities in-house (Davidow & Malone, 1992). The outsourcing process usually starts when the firm identifies value creating activities that form the basis of its competitive advantage. It keeps performing these core activities, but it assesses other, non-core activities to determine if they can be performed more efficiently by external independent suppliers, as long as the risk of opportunism is not too high and too costly. The resultant relationships between a firm and its suppliers then can be structured as long term strategic alliances.

The extent to which firms pursue outsourcing and vertical deintegration has given rise to a new organizational form, the 'virtual corporation.' Davidow and Malone (1992) coined this term to describe firms whose primary function is to coordinate the activities of a network of suppliers. Often as a result of international cost differences, outsourcing has extended beyond the production of components and manufacturing to a wide range of services, including payroll, IT, training, and customer service and support. At Nike, a firm well known for its outsourcing strategy, manufacturing is subcontracted, many product innovations come from external design houses, and Nike clothing is licensed to other firms. In 2014, Nike earned $27.8 billion in revenues and $3.2 billion in operating income with 56,500 employees; a much more integrated firm, Philips needed 105,400 employees to generate $24.4 billion in revenues and $554 million in operating income the same year.

But the disadvantages of outsourcing are clear as well. Consistent with the RBV, by outsourcing an activity, a firm loses its ability to learn from that activity and the opportunity to transform it into a distinctive competency.

CONCLUDING REMARKS

The four theoretical perspectives that inform vertical integration decisions, as outlined in this chapter—transaction costs, market power, resources and capabilities, and real options—have mostly developed independently and may be difficult to integrate (see Figure 10.3). Even if their recommendations tend to be consistent, in some cases, they conflict, which requires managers to make difficult trade-offs. As Barney (2007) recognizes, there is no "unified field theory" of vertical integration choices. Further research is needed.

Vertical integration strategies also have been subject to shifting fashions. For most of the twentieth century, the prevailing wisdom held that vertical integration was beneficial because it allowed for superior coordination and increased market power. However, following Rumelt's (1974) study, which announced that vertically integrated firms systematically underperformed both specialized and horizontally diversified firms, a profound change of opinion in the past 40 years has pushed many firms' emphasis to the pursuit of benefits through outsourcing and strategic alliances.

During the 1980–1990s, a growing diversity of collaborative relationships has attempted to reconcile the flexibility and incentives of market transactions with the close collaboration provided by vertical integration (Grant, 2013). The period was marked by a massive shift from arm's length, supplier relationships to long term collaborations with just a few suppliers. In many instances, competitive bidding and multiple sourcing have been replaced by single supplier arrangements.

The pace of outsourcing also has intensified because firms continue to search for benefits from international cost differences. Some evidence suggests the 20 year outsourcing vogue is reaching its end, in respond to increased volatility. Consider the following examples:

Vertical integration

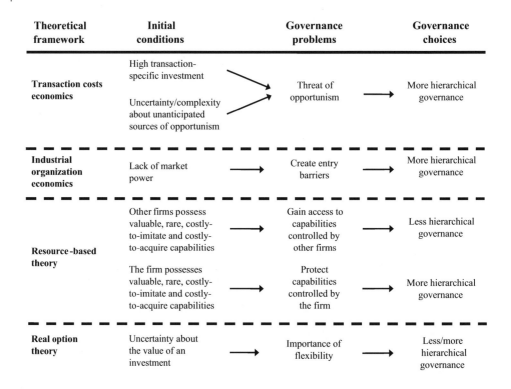

Figure 10.3 Integrating theoretical approaches to vertical integration decisions
Source: Adapted from Barney (2007)

- Rising commodity prices force firms that depend on materials to find more secure sources of supply. ArcelorMittal announced in May 2008 that it would increase its stake in Australia's Macarthur Coal in an effort to increase its self-sufficiency (*Financial Times*, 2008a).
- PepsiCo. recently announced its desire to reunite with its U.S. bottlers, a decade after it spun off the operations, to gain better control over prices (*Financial Times*, 2009).
- The German firm BASF has long been renowned for its vertical integration, from oil and gas to finished products. It recently announced its intention to vertically integrate even further. The company's CEO Jürgen Hambrecht cites three essential firm strategy elements in volatile environments (*Financial Times*, 2008b): first, pursue integration, both vertical and horizontal, to cushion against cost pressures and allow for diversification. Second, make close customer contacts. Third, develop a reputation for innovation.
- In its bid to meet demand for LCD televisions and increase its market power, Matsushita, which owns the Panasonic brand, will build a Y300 billion ($2.8 billion) LCD factory in Japan in 2010. This decision also pits it in head to head competition with leading LCD makers like Samsung, Sharp, and Sony (*Financial Times*, 2008c).
- Boeing, two years behind on the launch of its new Dreamliner, was forced to buy a component manufacturer in June 2009, for at least $580 million, in its efforts to fix its complex, disparate supply chain (*Financial Times*, 2009).

More recently, technology, and more specifically the e-business infrastructure, had critical effects on firms strategic decision to vertically integrate or not. The results of a study by Lajili and Mahoney (2006) suggest that suggest that changes in information technology are changing the nature of transaction costs leading to more efficient management through an electronic integration solution thus favoring contracting and outsourcing than would have been technologically possible 40 years ago when Williamson developed his transaction cost theory. Lajili and Mahoney (2006) found that transaction cost economics principles are still valid but that advances in information technology, especially in the past decade, have comparatively favored lower transaction costs of markets over hierarchies.

Chapter

11

THE GROWTH OF THE FIRM

INTERNAL DEVELOPMENT, MERGERS AND ACQUISITIONS, AND STRATEGIC ALLIANCES

In prior chapters, we have discussed rationales for firms' diversification (Chapters 5–7) and ways to manage diversified firms (Chapters 8–10). In this chapter, we address the means by which firms can implement a diversification strategy. Specifically, the objective of this chapter is to answer a key question: how can firms become diversified? Answering this question is critical, because the choice of a proper entry mode can reduce the chances and hazards of failure (Chang & Sing, 1999) and increase the firm's profitability (Chang, 1996). In addition, research indicates that entry modes, once established, are difficult to change or correct, suggesting long term consequences for the firm (Pedersen et al., 2002).

Firms could implement a diversification strategy through three basic means: (1) internal development, (2) M&As, and (3) strategic alliances (e.g., contractual alliances, joint ventures) (Collis & Montgomery, 2005; Dess et al., 2008; Geykens et al., 2006; Hill & Jones, 2004). These three basic diversification modes are also referred to as 'market entry strategies' (e.g., Chang & Singh, 1999; Mitchell & Singh, 1992; Porter, 1980) or 'growth strategies' (Andrews, 1971; Ansoff, 1965; Wernerfelt, 1984).

To implement their diversification strategy, firms first must pass the cost of entry test (see Chapter 5). That is, the cost of entry into a new business must not equal or exceed all future profits from the entry (Porter, 1987). Therefore, firms must choose an entry mode that makes it possible for them to recoup the investments required to do so. Although important for internal development and alliances, this requirement is even more critical for acquisitions, which are generally more expansive, because of the premium required for a tender offer. A diversification strategy creates value only if the firm purchases or develops businesses for less than the value of their marginal productivity (Makadok, 2001).

CHOOSING AN ENTRY MODE

Each of the three modes of expansion—internal development, M&As, and alliances—entails specific advantages and pitfalls, so choosing among them involves unavoidable trade-offs (Collis & Montgomery, 2005). Six sets of criteria should be taken into account when choosing a mode of entry: (1) the extent of market failures (e.g., Brouthers & Hennart, 2007; Williamson, 1975, 1985, 1991); (2) the level of entry barriers (e.g., Bain, 1956; Porter, 1980; Yip, 1982); (3) resource commitment and exit barriers (Chang & Singh, 1999; Hill et al., 1990); (4) the risk of managerial opportunism (e.g., Yip, 1982); (5) the availability of attractive partners (e.g., Brown et al., 2003); and (6) the types of and motives for the firm's diversification strategy (e.g., Ansoff, 1965; Chatterjee, 1990). In an international context, a seventh factor also influences the choice of an entry mode, namely, (7) cultural distance (e.g., Barkema et al., 1996; Kogut & Singh, 1988; Zhao et al., 2004).

Market failures

As we discussed in Chapter 4, market failures enable a firm to create corporate value through its diversification. Without market failures, the firm would be better off transacting through markets rather than diversifying and bearing the coordination costs itself (Williamson, 1975, 1985). Assuming the presence of market failures, the choice of an entry mode depends on the extent of these failures and the inherent trade-off between transaction and coordination costs (Williamson, 1985, 1991). In general, internal development involves minimal transaction costs but a high level of coordination costs, whereas M&As create hierarchies and benefit from reduced transaction costs, though to a lesser extent than does internal development due to the risks of adverse selection (Akerlof, 1970). Furthermore, the coordination costs for M&As, which must include integration costs (Haspeslagh & Jemison, 1991), are high. Strategic alliances enable the firm to reduce its coordination costs but involve higher levels of transaction costs, which reflect the possibility of opportunistic behavior by a partner (Poppo & Zenger, 2002; Williamson, 1991).

The extent of market failures also pertains to three characteristics of transactions: *asset specificity*, *uncertainty*, and *transaction frequency* (Williamson, 1975, 1985).

Transaction specific assets are tailored to a particular transaction and cannot be easily redeployed outside the relationship of the parties to a transaction (Geyskens et al., 2006). An example of physical asset specificity is the significant investment made by an automobile parts supplier (e.g., Fisher Body in the 1920s) in stamping equipment and molds for automobile bodies that are specialized to the needs of a particular auto manufacturer (e.g., General Motors in the 1920s) and that have little or no value to other firms (Klein et al., 1978). Their idiosyncratic nature creates a safeguarding problem, because market competition cannot restrain the opportunistic exploitation of such assets (Williamson, 1975). A possible solution to this safeguarding problem is vertical integration (as discussed in Chapter 10); unlike market controls, vertical relationship control procedures offer greater safeguarding capabilities (Hill et al., 1990; Williamson, 1985). From a transaction cost perspective, asset specificity may be the most critical influence on the choice between market and hierarchy (David & Han, 2004; Shelanski & Klein, 1995; Williamson, 1985).

Uncertainty arises when the contingencies surrounding a transaction are too unpredictable to be specified in a contract (*environmental uncertainty*) or when performance cannot be easily verified (*behavioral uncertainty*). The primary consequence of environmental uncertainty is an adaptation problem, pertaining to the difficulties with and the costs of adjusting the terms of the contract, which can be addressed through hierarchical governance. However, high environmental uncertainty also should encourage firms to maintain their flexibility, which conflicts with hierarchical governance (Klein, 1989). Walker and Weber (1984) distinguish two types of environmental uncertainty: *volume uncertainty* (an inability to forecast the volume requirements in a transaction accurately) and *technological uncertainty* (the inability to forecast the technical requirements in a transaction accurately). Unlike volume uncertainty, which provokes a hierarchical governance structure and thus facilitates adaptation, technological uncertainty can be managed more efficiently through a strategic alliance or market governance structure (Walker & Weber, 1987). If they use the market, firms can retain some flexibility to terminate their relationships and switch to partners with more appropriate technological capabilities (Balakrishnan & Wernerfelt, 1986); they also avoid getting locked in to a technology that may become obsolete (Heide & John, 1990).

Behavioral uncertainty instead creates a performance evaluation problem—that is, it is difficult to ascertain ex post whether the contract as been respected. To solve the performance evaluation problem, firms usually apply hierarchical integration, which offers a greater degree of control and thus stronger evaluation capabilities. In addition, the benefits of hierarchical integration involve

The growth of the firm

not only ownership or integration per se but also the ability to exercise decision control in the face of uncertainty (Anderson & Gatignon, 1986; Heide, 1994; Hill et al., 1990).

Finally, **transaction frequency** refers to the extent to which transactions recur regularly over time. This variable provides an additional incentive for a firm to adopt a hierarchical governance structure, because the overhead cost of hierarchical governance is easier to recover from recurring transactions, whereas transaction costs get multiplied over repeated interactions (Williamson, 1985).

Entry barriers

The choice of a diversification mode also reflects the barriers that may limit entry into new businesses or markets. Entry barriers entail resources owned by incumbents (i.e., firms already present in the business or market) that a new entrant must obtain at a cost (Chatterjee, 1990). As discussed in Chapter 5, the greater scope of a diversifying firm deepens its pockets, which mean reduced entry barriers. However, if entry barriers remain high, M&As and alliances, rather than internal development, can help the diversifying firm overcome. A diversifying firm is particularly likely to confront two main types of entry barriers: *structural* and *strategic* (Bain, 1956; Besanko et al., 2007; Porter, 1980).

Structural entry barriers reflect incumbents' natural cost or marketing advantages, as well as potential benefits from favorable regulations. We note six key types of structural entry barriers: (1) control of key resources, (2) economies of scale, (3) marketing advantages from differentiation, (4) capital requirements, (5) switching costs, and (6) government policies.

1   **Control of key resources**. Incumbents are protected from new market entrants because they control the resources that represent sources of competitive advantage in a market, especially if they can use those resources more effectively than can new entrants. For example, incumbents might erect entry barriers by obtaining a patent for a new product or production process. Other examples of key resources that incumbents might control include access to distribution channels, proprietary product technology, access to raw materials, desirable locations, and government subsidies. In markets in which incumbents control key resources, internal development is unlikely to result in a successful entry, so M&As and strategic alliances are required.

2   **Economies of scale**. When economies of scale are significant, established firms with large market shares likely have a substantial cost advantage over new entrants. Therefore, M&As and strategic alliances are critical methods for firms to move quickly along the learning curve and benefit from sufficient market share more rapidly. In contrast, internal development is less likely, because of the potential cost disadvantages that would result from a subscale entry, as well as the risk of retaliation in response to a large scale entry.

3   **Marketing advantages from differentiation**. In businesses in which brand names and reputations are important, a strong brand name can act as an entry barrier that protects incumbents against new entrants. Their strong brand name gives incumbents a reputational advantage over new entrants, and the entrant must spend significant sums on advertising and promotion to develop similar levels of credibility among consumers, retailers, and distributors. Diversifying firms therefore should seek the benefits of an existing brand and rely on M&As and alliances rather than suffering the likely high costs of developing their own reputation.

4   **Capital requirements**. Entering a new business requires a firm to possess resources it can invest. In addition to physical facilities, the new entrant needs capital for inventory, marketing activities, and other functions. Even if the new business is attractive, the capital required for entry may not be available, such that internal development and M&As are not options, and a strategic alliance is the only possibility for the diversifying firm.

The growth of the firm | **157**

5   **Switching costs**. Customers incur one time switching costs when they change suppliers. These costs involve purchasing new equipment, learning to use the products of the new supplier, and coming to terms with the end of a relationship with an old supplier. Depending on the industry, switching costs might be lower or higher; in the latter case, they provide significant entry barriers, because customers are less likely to overcome them to switch to the products of the new entrants. To lower entry barriers, diversifying firms could use M&As and alliances, but likely not internal development.

6   **Government policy**. Licensing and permit requirements are the tactics governments exert to erect entry barriers. Banking, telecommunications, weaponry, and healthcare industries all require government approval in most countries. Entering through internal development in regulated industries may be difficult, especially for foreign firms. A strategic alliance may be required, particularly in countries that forbid full ownership by foreign firms.

Strategic entry barriers instead result from incumbents' strategic actions. Two examples of such strategic actions designed to deter entry are *limit pricing* and *capacity expansion*. Limit pricing refers to a practice whereby an incumbent firm charges a low price before the diversifying firm's entry can occur (Bain, 1956). Through capacity expansion, the incumbent instead creates excess capacity in the industry, which eliminates any demand for the new entrant. The incumbent's ability to expand its output and charge a relatively low price makes the entry far more risky for the diversifying firm. In such a scenario, entering through M&As offers the advantage of not adding new capacity in the market, which should limit the impact on prices, unlike entry through internal development. Box 11.1 recounts an existing summary of these characteristics of entry conditions.

BOX 11.1 BAIN'S TYPOLOGY OF ENTRY CONDITIONS

In a seminal study, Bain (1968) argued that businesses and markets could be characterized according to whether their entry barriers are structural or strategic and whether incumbents can profit from entry deterring strategies. Bain described three entry conditions:

Blockaded entry. Structural barriers are so high that the incumbent need not do anything to deter entry. For example, production may require large fixed investments, or the entrant may sell an undifferentiated product for which it cannot raise the price above marginal cost.

Accommodated entry. Structural entry barriers are low, and either (1) entry deterring strategies are ineffective or (2) the cost to the incumbent of trying to deter entry exceeds the benefits it could gain from excluding the new entrant. Accommodated entry is typical in markets with growing demand or rapid technological improvements.

Deterred entry. The incumbent can keep the entrant out by employing an entry deterring strategy, and employing the entry deterring strategy boosts the incumbent's profits.

Source: Adapted from Bain (1968) and Besanko et al. (2007)

When they face entry barriers, diversifying firms may find the acquisition of an established firm more effective than simply entering the industry as a new competitor that offers products with which customers are unfamiliar. The higher the entry barriers, the greater the probability that a firm will acquire an existing firm to overcome them is (Hitt et al., 2004). Although such an acquisition can be expensive, it provides the diversifying firm with immediate market access.

Yet with a high extent of market failure, diversifying firms need an entry mode that can provide them with more control over the new business unit. Various entry modes imply different levels of control (Anderson & Gatignon, 1986; Hill et al., 1990), including the authority over operational and strategic decision making. The level of control is lowest for contractual alliances and highest for wholly owned subsidiaries and internally developed ventures. A contractual alliance, such as a license agreement, grants control over operations and strategy to the licensee, usually in exchange for a lump sum payment, a per unit royalty fee, and a commitment to abide by any terms set out in the licensing contract. In an internally developed or acquired wholly owned subsidiary, control over day to day operations and certain strategic decisions is delegated to the business unit managers, but the ultimate control always resides at the corporate headquarters office. Control in joint ventures depends on the ownership split and the number of parties involved, but in any case, it is shared.

Resource commitment and exit barriers

Each entry mode requires different levels of resource commitments, among which are those transaction specific assets that cannot be redeployed to an alternative use without costs (Anderson & Gatignon, 1986; Hill et al., 1990). The amount of transaction specific assets required for the diversifying firm to enter a new business then creates exit barriers and limits its strategic flexibility, which makes the entry more risky (Harrigan, 1981). That is, when faced with exit barriers, the firm must stay in the market, even when the prevailing conditions are such that the firm would not have entered in the first place (Harrigan, 1981, 1985b). Examples of exit barriers include specialized assets, fixed costs of exit (e.g., labor agreements), strategic interrelationships and partnerships with distributors and suppliers, and government and social restrictions. To reduce the risks associated with high exit barriers, firms may choose to adopt an entry mode that minimizes these exit costs.

For example, in a contractual alliance, the partner might accept a significant portion of the costs associated with opening and serving the new market. The level of resource commitment required from the diversifying firm therefore would be relatively low. In the case of internal development and M&As, the diversifying firm must bear all of the costs, so its level of resource commitment is correspondingly high; again, the resource commitment demanded by a joint venture falls somewhere between these two extremes, depending on the ownership split and resource sharing (Hill et al., 1990). Chang and Singh (1999) show that a firm's choice of entry mode affects the exit barriers it confronts and consequently the firm's exit mode (i.e., whether it will sell the business to another firm or dissolve) (see Box 11.2). Several studies have observed higher rates of exit out of acquired businesses than from internally developed businesses. For example, Porter (1987) notes that 44 percent of new internally developed businesses eventually are divested, whereas 53.4 percent of acquisitions had been divested during the same time period. Ravenscraft and Scherer (1991) also observe that acquired business units exhibit significantly higher divestiture rates than do internally developed units. Chang and Singh (1999) argue in turn that the internal development of a new business results in a longer time before market entry, which requires a higher degree of firm specific investment within the business than does the case of acquisition. According to transaction cost theory, these idiosyncratic assets reduce the range of prospective buyers and can depress the value of the business unit for other firms (Williamson, 1975). In contrast, by definition an acquired business already has been packaged for sale at least once, so it seems likely to be more suitable for sale than is an internally developed business, such that its exit barriers are lower.

BOX 11.2 REDUCING EXIT BARRIERS

In 1996, Matsushita Electric Industrial Co. sold off MCA, the Hollywood entertainment group it had spent $6.1 billion to acquire just six years earlier. Although the exact terms were not disclosed, Matsushita recorded a one time, non-operating loss of $1.5 billion on the sale in its 1996 annual report. That is, Matsushita reduced the losses it incurred from a failed attempt to diversify into entertainment business by selling MCA back to an interested buyer. This move was possible because the acquired business had not yet become closely integrated into the company's core activities. If Matsushita had tried to enter the industry through internal development, its losses could have been much greater, because of the difficulty associated with trying to sell a closely integrated business. Furthermore, Matsushita could have used a strategic alliance or joint venture first to assess its capabilities to operate profitably in the entertainment business. Terminating such an alliance would have been less costly than its MCA experiment turned out to be.

Source: Chang and Singh (1999)

Managerial opportunism

Managerial opportunism, from an agency theory perspective (Jensen & Meckling, 1976), also influences the choice of a diversified entry mode. Internal development and acquisition entries differ in their managerial implications, with different risks and opportunities for individual managers (Yip, 1982). Entry through internal development tends to be more risky, because it offers no guarantee of achieving the requisite scale or profitability. The usually lengthy, initial start up period also exacerbates career risk. However, despite its speed, entry through acquisition involves its own managerial risks and demands, including the pressure to achieve rapid synergy or turnaround (Yip, 1982).

According to Roll (1986), top managers typically prefers M&As over other types of entry modes, primarily because of their sense of hubris, such that rising to the top of a corporation gives them an exaggerated sense of their own capabilities (see Box 11.3). Roll (1986) does not claim that the hubris hypothesis can explain every M&A, but he posits that it represents the important human element of any choice of entry mode. Acquiring a target business may result solely from a manager's desire to maximize stockholder wealth—but it also might reflect a desire to enter a target's industry or become 'the largest firm in the business.' The extent of influence of such motives varies from acquisition to acquisition.

Availability of attractive partners

Another important factor when it comes to selecting a new business entry mode is the availability of investment partners (Brown et al., 2003). Attractive acquisition candidates and alliance partners reflect the market structure, and the number and strength of competitors are functions of both market concentration and market growth rates (Yip, 1982). When few attractive potential alliance partners exist, the diversifying firm cannot use alliances to enter the market. Furthermore, if the diversifying firm decides to work with less attractive partners, such as those that seem unqualified or untrustworthy, it opens itself to opportunism by those partners. Attractive, available investment partners instead enable the entrant to rely on entry modes that demand less equity participation, including contractual alliances (Anderson & Gatignon, 1986). In markets without attractive acquisition targets or alliance partners though, the only entry mode remaining is direct entry through internal development.

BOX 11.3 THE HUBRIS HYPOTHESIS OF TAKEOVERS

The hubris hypothesis implies that managers seek to acquire firms for their own personal motives and that pure economic gains for the acquiring firm cannot constitute the sole, or even the primary, motivation for an acquisition. Roll (1986) uses this hypothesis to explain why managers might pay a premium for a firm that the market has already correctly valued at a lower price. These managers, he claims, have superimposed their own valuation over that of an objectively determined market valuation, because their pride is such that they believe that their valuation is superior to that of the market.

Several studies confirm that an acquiring firm's announcement of a takeover pushes down the value of the acquirer's stock. Dodd (1980) finds statistically significant negative returns for an acquirer following an announcement of a planned takeover, as does Eger (1983). Yet not all studies support this conclusion; Paul Asquith (1983) notes no consistent pattern of declining stock prices following the announcement of a takeover.

More widespread agreement surrounds the positive price effects for target stockholders, who experience wealth gains following takeovers. Bradley et al. (1989) show that tender offers provide gains to target firm stockholders, though admittedly, the hostile nature of ten-der offers should produce greater changes in the stock price than do friendly takeovers. Yet most studies maintain that target stockholders can earn gains following both friendly and hostile takeover bids. Varaiya (1988) shows that bidders tend to overpay; in a study examining the relationship between a bid premium and the combined market values of the bidder and the target, the premium paid by bidders emerges as too high relative to the value of the target to the acquirer.

Research on the combined effect of the upward movement of the target's stock and the downward movement of the acquirer's stock does not quite confirm the hubris hypothesis. Malatesta (1983, pp. 178–179) examines the combined effects and finds that "the evidence indicates that the long-run sequence of events culminating in merger has no net impact on combined shareholder wealth." Yet Malatesta's failure to find positive combined returns does necessarily support the hubris hypothesis, even as more recent research seems to do so (Hayward & Hambrick, 1997). Using a sample of 106 large acquisitions, Hayward and Hambrick reveal that CEO hubris is positively associated with the size of premiums paid; they measure hubris according to variables such as the firm's recent performance and CEO self-importance (e.g., media praise, compensation relative to the second highest paid exec-utive). Their study also includes independent variables, such as CEO inexperience (measured by years in that position) and board vigilance (number of inside versus outside directors).

Diversification strategy

The decision to enter a new business can also be analyzed according to a resource-based view (Chang & Singh, 1999; Chatterjee, 1990; Lee & Lieberman, 2010). That is, firms considering entry into new businesses or markets make their decisions about entering through the acquisition of existing concerns or new internal developments. Yip (1982) argues that for an internally developed business, the closeness of the relation of the firm to the new business in the entered market sig-nificantly reduces the costs due to entry barriers. However, such market relatedness cannot reduce the cost of entry through acquisition, because the price of an acquisition mostly depends on the market. Thus, firms tend to enter related businesses through internal development but unrelated businesses by acquisition. Extending Yip's argument, Chatterjee (1990) suggests that diversifying entrants incur two types of costs to enter. Not only do they invest whatever excess resources they currently possess into a newly entered business, but they simultaneously acquire complementary resources to operate in a new market. In businesses related to their current operations, firms can reduce their entry costs by exploiting their excess resources, because the more related the new business is to the entrant's core activities, the greater the probability that its current excess resources can serve to mitigate these entry costs. Furthermore, the more closely related the businesses are, the fewer complements the firm needs to its existing resources. Therefore, internal development should reduce entry costs significantly in a related market, but entry through an M&A likely means purchasing unwanted assets, including redundant resources that come with the acquired business unit (Chatterjee, 1990). Therefore, acquisitive entry should be more attractive in unrelated markets, with their lesser probability of encompassing unwanted assets. Furthermore, the more distant or less related the acquisition is from the firm's current businesses, the greater is the possibility of acquiring complementary resources from the acquired firm (Chang & Singh, 1999).

Cultural distance

Finally, in an international diversification context, cultural distance affects the choice of entry mode. This variable refers to the difference in national cultures between the home country of the diversifying firm and that of the new market it wants to enter (e.g., Kogut & Singh, 1988). Zhao et al. (2004) suggest cultural distance is one of the most important factors, with country risk, that influences uncertainty. However, prior research provides mixed empirical evidence about the specific influence of cultural distance on the choice of an entry mode (Tihanyi et al., 2005). Overall, according to this stream of the literature, larger cultural differences push diversifying firms to search for more hierarchical control to minimize their risks in the form of opportunism and transaction costs (Hennart & Reddy, 1997). Greater control might be necessary in a culturally distant market, because transactions in those markets generate significant information costs and can make it more difficult to transfer competencies (Li & Guisinger, 1992). In a study of Western European multinational firms for example, Brouthers and Brouthers (2003) find that most firms prefer joint ventures to wholly owned subsidiaries when they enter uncertain Central and Eastern European markets. In addition, Gatignon and Anderson (1988) argue that cultural distance requires diversifying firms to maintain more flexibility, so they may prefer modes of entry that exert lower levels of control, such as licensing or joint ventures. By relying on joint ventures, these firms reduce their resource commitments and thus their risk exposure (Grosse & Trevino, 1996; Kim et al., 1993). Several empirical studies confirm that greater cultural distance is associated with entry modes that entail lower percentages of equity ownership (Barkema et al., 1997; Barkema & Vermeulen, 1998). Finally, the results of a meta-analysis by Tihanyi et al. (2005) indicate that cultural distance does not significantly predict entry mode choices in the presence of the other factors, but with regard to the effect of potential moderators, they find that cultural difference has a significant effect when they take the location of the diversifying firms into account. Other studies concur that for an entry mode choice, a firm's home base correlates with its risk propensity (Barkema & Vermeulen, 1998; Brouthers & Brouthers, 2003).

THREE ENTRY MODES

According to its assessment of the preceding criteria, a diversifying firm chooses a mode of entry into a new business or market from among three generic modes: internal development, M&As, and strategic alliances. Each mode represents a broad category with many specific and peculiar variations. However, each broad category possesses specific advantages and drawbacks that distinguish it from the other two categories.

Internal development

With an internal development, the firm creates a new business entity in a particular industry or market, including new production capacities, distribution relationships, sales forces, and so on (Burgelman, 1983; Porter, 1980). Internal development sometimes is referred to as a *greenfield investment*, that is, it is a start-up investment in new facilities (Kogut & Singh, 1988). Such an investment can entail a wholly owned subsidiary or a joint venture. To simplify the exposition, following Kogut and Singh (1988), we classify start-ups that are wholly owned as internal developments, whereas those that involve shared ownership or a joint venture represent strategic alliances.

Benefits of internal development

Internal development serves as the entry strategy when the firm possesses valuable resources and competences in its existing businesses that it considers in excess and that it can leverage or recombine to enter a new business (Penrose, 1959). Despite the inherent risks of internal development, many firms have discovered significant benefits (Collis & Montgomery, 2005). For example, internal development allows for incremental decision making that can accommodate changing environmental conditions and learning that may occur within the firm itself, consistent with a real option approach (see Chapter 3). In contrast with M&As, which demand a major commitment all at once, internal development can reduce risk by permitting the firm to delay some choices and extend them over a longer period of time. With high uncertainty, such flexibility, or the ability to change direction quickly and at low cost in response to unanticipated changes in the environment, is critical (Kogut, 1991).

In the early stages of an industry lifecycle, internal development may be not be just the best but the only choice. Even if a diversifying firm lacks resources to compete in a new business field, it may be forced to pursue an internal development strategy if no established firms possess the competences it requires. In this case, the option of acquiring or partnering with an established firm does not exist, so the firm may have no choice but to enter through internal development (Hill & Jones, 2004).

The most important benefit of internal development is the relative ease with which the firm can transfer its intangible resources and competences from the corporate headquarters or existing business units into the new business (Goold et al., 1994). Employees who understand the firm's culture and embody its tacit knowledge also can deploy those resources more easily in the new context. When a firm wants to stretch or leverage a particular resource such as an organizational capability or intangible asset, the preferred route therefore is internal development (Hamel & Prahalad, 1993; Montgomery & Hariharan, 1991; Penrose, 1959).

There are other benefits of internal development too. Through an in-house expansion, a firm can capture the externalities of its development process, including the learning and experience that it accumulates as the business grows. Over time, this tacit know-how can become a valuable resource in its own right and guide further expansion of the firm (Dierickx & Cool, 1989). By growing a business internally, management signals its commitment to developing and leveraging the firm's resources, which should foster an organizational culture in which *intrapreneurship* flourishes (Burgelman, 1983).

Pitfalls of internal development

Yet internal development failures also are common (Collis & Montgomery, 2005). Three reasons serve to explain the relatively high failure rate associated with internal development: (1) insufficient market entry, (2) poor commercialization of the new venture product, and (3) poor corporate management of the process (Biggadike, 1979; Block & Macmillan, 1993; Burgelman, 1983). First,

The growth of the firm

because it is incremental, internal development may be unworkable if the new venture's success demands a large scale entry (Biggadike, 1979; Block & Macmillan, 1993). Second, internal development often focuses the top management attention of on the firm's strengths and weaknesses, at the expense of the monitoring of the external environment. Internal new ventures often fail because the firms ignore or neglect the basic needs of the market, blinded as they are by the technological possibilities of their new products. Their new ventures fail because they lack sufficient commercialization or attempt to market a technology for which there is no real demand. Third, managing the new venture process raises several difficult organizational issues that top managers have to address (MacMillan & George, 1985): delimiting the scope of the venture, designing the structure of the venture and it relationship with the corporate headquarters, the provision of adequate support from corporate headquarters, and the appointment of a representative of the corporate headquarters to act as a sponsor of the venture. Without, top management full support, the new venture has almost no chance to succeed.

Mergers and acquisitions

Buying or merging with an existing firm may be the easiest way to diversify, but not the cheapest one. The firm immediately obtains a full set of resources that should grant it a competitive advantage in its new industry. Yet these corporate advantages often require synergies, which in turn demand post-acquisition or post-merger integration—both a necessary and a difficult and costly process. Mergers and acquisitions tend to be lumped together under the acronym M&As; however, despite their many similarities (and their combined treatment in this chapter), they exhibit some notable differences too. A merger occurs when two firms agree to integrate their operations on a relatively coequal basis (Hitt et al., 2004); there are few true mergers, because one party is usually dominant. In 1998, DaimlerChrysler AG was termed a 'merger of equals,' despite Daimler Benz's dominance in the automakers' transaction, because Chrysler managers would not accept the deal unless it received that terminology (Keeton, 2003). An acquisition involves one firm buying a controlling interest in another, with the intention of making the acquired firm a subsidiary business within its portfolio (Hitt et al., 2008). Most mergers are friendly transactions, but acquisitions also include unfriendly takeovers. Finally, a takeover refers to a special type of an acquisition, wherein the target firm does not solicit, and may even fight against, the acquiring firm's bid.

Benefits of mergers and acquisitions

Firms often use M&As to enter a business area that is new to them, especially if they lack important competencies (e.g., resources, capabilities) to compete in that area but have sufficient financial resources to purchase an incumbent firm with those competencies (Kogut & Zander, 1992; Ranft & Lord, 2000). For example, acquisition offers unique advantages to obtain technologies and technical knowledge that are often complex, tacit, based on accumulated experience, and embedded in relationships and ways of communication among multiple individuals, and therefore are difficult, costly and time consuming to develop internally (Graebner et al., 2010). Firms also tend to prefer acquisitions if they sense a need to move fast. A need for speed makes acquisition a favored entry mode, because acquisitions can rapidly position the firm in its new business. By purchasing an existing player, the firm does not need to take the time to establish its presence or develop resources it does not already possess, which can be a particularly important benefit when those critical resources are difficult to imitate or accumulate (Barney, 1986; Makadok, 2001).

Moreover, acquisitions seem somewhat less risky that internal developments, primarily because they involve less uncertainty regarding the viability of the venture, which already exist for a while. When a firm makes an acquisition, it buys a known entity, with established profitability, revenues, and market share (Ahuja & Katila, 2001; Hitt et al., 1990). In the case of an acquisition failure, the acquired ventures can be more easily divested than could internally developed businesses (Chang & Singh, 1999), because it already proved that it could survive autonomously and can be repackaged as a stand alone business.

Acquisitions also emerge as the preferred entry mode when the industry to be entered is well established and incumbent firms enjoy significant protection from entry barriers. When such barriers are substantial, entering the industry through internal development is relatively more difficult. The challenges might include constructing an efficient manufacturing plant, undertaking massive advertising to build reputation and overcome established brand loyalties, and rapidly expanding distribution outlets. In contrast, acquiring an established firm means the diversifying firm can circumvent most of these entry barriers. If it purchases a market leader, it benefits immediately from substantial scale economies and brand loyalty. The greater the barriers to entry, the more likely acquisitions are the favored entry mode.

In addition, acquiring an existing firm takes a potential competitor out of the market. Whereas the internal development required for a firm to reach minimum efficient scale can add substantial capacity to an industry, by acquiring a competitor, the firm prevents any increase in the level of rivalry. If the minimum scale of entry must be large, relative to the market size, acquisition again may be the preferred means to mitigate intense post-acquisition rivalry.

Pitfalls of mergers and acquisitions

Again, ample evidence reveals that acquisitions often fail to add value to the acquiring company and may even end up diminishing overall value. Most studies of acquisitions reveal a success to failure ratio (using accounting, finance, or managerial assessments) of approximately 50 percent (Hunt, 1990). In a major study of post-acquisition performance, Ravenscraft and Scherer (1987) identify many profitable firms that had been acquired whose average profits and market shares declined following the acquisition. They also noted that a smaller but substantial subset of profitable firms experienced traumatic difficulties, ultimately including being sold off by the acquiring company. More generally, research suggests that many acquisitions simply fail to realize the anticipated benefits (Brush, 1996; Caves, 1989; Jensen & Ruback, 1983).

Four major reasons dictate this outcome: (1) firms often experience difficulties when trying to integrate divergent corporate cultures (Cannella & Hambrick, 1993; Haspeslagh & Jemison, 1991; Walsh, 1988); (2) firms overestimate the potential economic benefits of an acquisition (Hayward & Hambrick, 1997; Roll, 1988); (3) acquisitions tend to be very expensive (Bazerman & Samuelson, 1983; Varaiya, 1988); and (4) firms often fail to screen their acquisition targets adequately (Haspeslagh & Jemison, 1991).

1 **Postacquisition integration**. Having made an acquisition, the acquiring firm must integrate the acquired business into its own organizational structure. Integration might involve adopting a common management and financial control system, combining operations, or establishing linkages for sharing information and personnel. Such forms of integration almost invariably create unexpected problems, generally based on the differences in the corporate cultures (Datta, 1991; Weber & Camerer, 2003). Furthermore, many acquired companies experience high turnover, possibly because employees do not like the acquiring firm's methods for doing things (Walsh, 1988). The loss of management talent and expertise can cause serious harm to the performance of the acquired business (Cannella & Hambrick, 1993).

   But not every M&A demands the same level of integration. Haspeslagh and Jemison (1991) posit that the appropriate form of post-acquisition integration depends on two principal characteristics: first, the corporate value creation mechanism determines the degree of *strategic interdependence* to establish between the acquired and acquiring firms. Resource sharing and skills transfer imply high or moderate strategic interdependence, respectively, whereas portfolio management and restructuring imply little or no interdependence. Second, the extent of maintained autonomy required by the acquired firm to preserve its distinctive skill determines the need for *organizational autonomy* (Cording et al., 2002, 2008). These two characteristics then suggest the appropriate form of post-acquisition strategy, as we illustrate in Figure 11.1.

Absorption acquisitions require a high degree of interdependence to create corporate value, but they have little need for organizational autonomy to achieve that interdependence. Integration in this case implies a full consolidation, over time, of the operations, organization, and culture of both firms. That is, in absorption acquisitions, the objective ultimately is to dissolve the boundary between the firms. *Preservation acquisitions* entail a high need for autonomy and a low need for interdependence, because the primary task of management is to keep the source of the acquired benefits intact; deterioration in the acquired firm's management, practices, or even motivation would endanger its success. Even though the needs for interdependence are low in preservation acquisitions, the autonomy and protection it implies tend to be difficult to provide. The acquired operations therefore may be managed with arm's length practices, outside any areas that would benefit from interdependence, such as financial risk sharing or general management capability transfers. *Symbiotic acquisitions* need both strategic interdependence (because substantial capability transfer must take place) and organizational autonomy (because the acquired capabilities must be preserved in an organizational context different than the acquirer's). In symbiotic acquisitions, the two organizations first must coexist and then gradually become increasingly interdependent. Finally, *holding acquisitions* have a low need for strategic interdependence and a low need for organizational autonomy; the acquired firm actually is not integrated into the acquired firm at all.

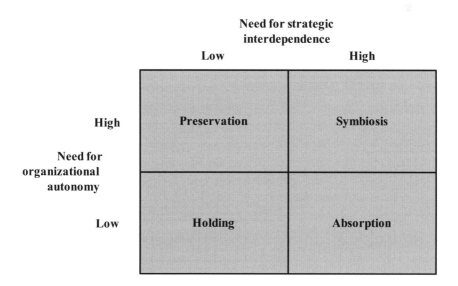

Figure 11.1 Types of acquisition integration approaches

Source: Adapted from Haspeslagh & Jemison (1991)

2 **Overestimating economic benefits**. Even when firms succeed in integrating, they often overestimate their potential for creating value together. In particular, the strategic advantages that can be derived from an acquisition may be less than anticipated, but the acquirer already has paid more for the target company than it probably is worth. As discussed previously, Roll (1986) attributes this tendency to hubris on the part of top management. They overestimate their ability to create value from the acquisition, primarily because their rise to the top has given them an exaggerated sense of their own capabilities (see Box 11.3).

3 **Cost of acquisitions**. Acquisitions of firms with publicly traded stock tend to be very expensive. When a firm bids to acquire a majority share of the stock of another company, the stock price frequently gets bid up during the acquisition process, particularly in the case of contested bids or takeovers, that is, when two or more firms simultaneously attempt to gain control of one target firm (see Box 11.4). The acquiring firm then must pay a premium, beyond the current market value of the target, to gain control of the popular business (Varaiya, 1988).

   The debt taken on to finance expensive acquisitions can later become a millstone around the acquiring firm's neck—particularly if it has taken out a loan to gain the acquisition and then interest rates rise. Moreover, if the market value of the target company prior to the acquisition was a true reflection of its worth, a premium beyond this value means that the acquiring company must improve the performance of the acquired unit by just as much, if it is to reap any positive returns on its investment. Such performance gains, however, can be very difficult to achieve.

4 **Inadequate pre-acquisition screening**. Haspeslagh and Jemison (1991) find that one of the most important explanations of acquisition failures is managerial inattention to pre-acquisition screening. Through the *due diligence* process, a potential acquirer should evaluate a target firm for its acquisition likelihood (Hitt et al., 2005). In an effective due diligence process, the acquiring firm examines hundreds of aspects, including the financing for the intended transaction, differences in cultures between the acquiring and target firm, the tax consequences of the transaction, and potentially necessary actions to meld the two workforces successfully. Any failure to complete effective due diligence is likely to result in the acquiring firm paying an excessive premium for the target firm. Rappaport and Sirower (1999) even show that without due diligence, the purchase price depends on the pricing of other, 'comparable' acquisitions rather than a rigorous assessment of where, when, and how management can drive real performance gains. In these cases, the price paid may have little to do with any form of meaningful value.

BOX 11.4 THE WINNER'S CURSE

The winner's curse, in the context of takeovers, holds that bidders who overestimate the value of a target likely win the contest, because they are more inclined to overpay and outbid rivals who value the target more accurately. This ironic result is not specific to takeovers; it is the natural result of any bidding contest (Bazerman & Samuelson, 1983). One of the more public forums in which it regularly occurs is the free agent markets that characterize professional sports, such as baseball and basketball (Cassing & Douglas, 1980). In a study of 800 acquisitions from 1974 to 1983, Varaiya (1988) shows that on average, the winning bid in takeover contests significantly overstates the capital market's estimate of any gains from that takeover by as much as 67 percent. His measure of overpayment consists of the difference between the winning bid premium and the highest bid possible, before the market responded negatively to the bid. In turn, his study supports not only the existence of the winner's curse but also the likelihood of the hubris hypothesis.

Strategic alliances

A strategic alliance is a voluntary, long term, cooperative relationship between two firms, designed to achieve specific objectives through the benefits of shared resources. Over the past several decades, we have witnessed enormous growth in alliance activity (Anand & Khanna, 2000; Dyer et al., 2001). However, strategic alliances still can be grouped into three broad categories: non-equity alliances, equity alliances, and joint ventures. In a non-equity alliance, the cooperating firms agree to work together, but they do not take equity positions in their partner's firm or form any independent organizational unit to manage their cooperative efforts. Rather, their cooperative relations function through the use of various contracts, such as cooperation, patent licensing, supply, or distribution agreements. In an equity alliance, the cooperating firms supplement their contracts with equity holdings in the alliance partners. In a joint venture, the cooperating firms create a legally independent firm in which they invest and from which they derive their share of any profits created. These different forms of strategic alliances represent hybrid governance forms, somewhere between market and hierarchy (Williamson, 1991), which vary in the level of interaction between the partners and the types of arrangement (Beamish, 1999).

In Figure 11.2 we classify these different types of strategic alliances according to the level of interaction they require, as well as the type of arrangement they demand between the involved partners. Low interaction between the partners reduces governance costs, but higher interaction levels produce high governance costs; competitive arrangements involve more transaction costs than do cooperative alliances. And of course, strategic alliances possess their own specific benefits and drawbacks, especially compared with M&As and internal development.

Benefits of alliances. A firm may prefer internal development to M&A but hesitate to commit itself to a completely internal development, because of the risks and costs of building a new operation from the ground up. This situation is common when a firm perceives the potential to establish a new business in an embryonic or growth industry but cannot afford to take the risks and costs

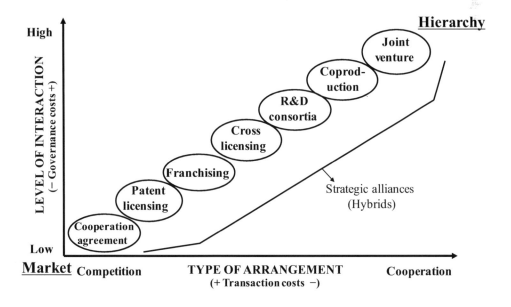

Figure 11.2 Classification of strategic alliances

Source: Adapted from Beamish (1999)

The growth of the firm

associated with the project on its own. In these circumstances, the firm might decide to enter into a strategic alliance with another firm and use that alliance as a vehicle to enter the new business. The arrangement enables the firm to share the substantial risks and costs involved with a diversification strategy; it also can increase the probability of success because it combines the forces and capabilities of two firms. If one firm possesses some of the skills and assets necessary to diversify, collaborating with another firm that has complementary skills and assets should increase the overall probability of success.

From a real option perspective, strategic alliances offer an intermediate step, before a merger or an acquisition. Kogut (1991) argues that the decision to invest or diversify into businesses or markets that are characterized by uncertain demand represents a fundamental firm; this problem becomes exacerbated when the new business is unrelated to the firm's current activities. A real option perspective depicts the firm's initial investments in new markets, such as in a joint venture, as options that grant that firm the right to expand in the future. Following Kogut's analysis, several authors similarly have investigated strategic alliances as real options (Folta, 1998; Nöldeke & Schmidt, 1998; Seth & Kim, 2001) and revealed alliances as options to grow, defer, or abandon the new business. Depending on the evolution of the new business, the firm may decide later to acquire its joint venture partner or else just dissolve the alliance.

Drawbacks of strategic alliances. Two thirds of all alliances experience severe problems, and their reported failure rates range as high as 70 percent (e.g., Das & Teng, 2000). Three main drawbacks stem from strategic alliance arrangements. First, a strategic alliance permits the firm to share the risks and costs of developing a new business, but it also requires that firm to share any profits if the new business succeeds. Second, a firm that enters into a strategic alliance always runs the risk of releasing critical know-how to its partner, which can use that know-how to compete directly with the company in the future (Hamel, 1991). Third, the alliance partners must share control. If they have different business philosophies, time horizons, or investment preferences, substantial problems can arise, including conflicts about how to run the joint venture that can eventually result in business failure. In Table 11.1, we summarize the benefits and drawbacks that mark each of the three diversification modes.

Table 11.1 Summary of the benefits and drawbacks of the different entry modes

Entry mode	Benefits	Drawbacks
Internal development	• Incremental • Compatible with culture • Encourage intrapreneurship • Internal investment	• Slow speed • Need to build new resources • Addition to industry capacity • Subscale entry • Unsuccessful efforts are difficult to recoup
M&As	• Speed • Access to complementary assets • Removal of potential competitor • Upgrade of corporate resources	• Cost of acquisition • Unnecessary adjunct businesses • Organizational clash that may impede integration • Major commitment
Alliances	• Access to complementary assets • Speed	• Lack of control • Assistance to a potential future competitor • Questionable long-term viability • Difficult to integrate learning

Source: Adapted from Montgomery & Collis (2005)

CONCLUDING REMARKS

In this chapter, we have discussed the three main diversification modes (internal development, M&As, and strategic alliances) and their comparative advantages and drawbacks. We also note the criteria that a diversifying firm should use to choose among these modes.

Regardless of the method used, diversification implies a growth strategy in which a firm seeks to expand its scope. In the next chapter, we consider the opposite side of the problem; that is, reducing the scope of the firm. As we discussed in Chapter 7, some firms may become overdiversified in time, which requires them to restructure their portfolios of businesses.

Chapter

12

RESTRUCTURING STRATEGIES

REDUCING THE SCOPE OF THE FIRM

So far we have focused on strategies for expanding the scope of the firm into new business areas. As noticed by Decker and Mellewigt (2007), although divestiture is an important corporate change initiative, the buyer's side seems to be more appealing to management scholars than the seller's because acquisitions imply growth (i.e., *success*). Managers might also resist exiting a business to avoid the stigma of *failure*, as it is often perceived as a result of poor corporate management (Decker & Mellwigt, 2007). To provide a fuller picture of corporate level strategy, we must however now turn in the direction of the restructuring strategies designed to reduce the scope of the firm by exiting specific business areas.

A restructuring strategy is a corporate level strategy by which a firm changes the set of its businesses or its financial or organizational structure (Bethel & Liebskind, 1993; Johnson, 1996). Reducing the scope of the firm through divestment and restructuring has become increasingly popular as a corporate level strategy, particularly among the firms that diversified into unrelated businesses during the 1960s, 1970s, and 1980s (Grant, 2002). A famous example is the case of RJR Nabisco (Burrough & Helyar, 2003). The company created by the merger of cigarette company RJ Reynolds Tobacco with biscuit seller Nabisco Brands in 1985, which was hailed by the managerial press as a great diversification deal. RJR Nabisco became the U.S. largest consumer products firm, with annual sales of more than $19 billion. However, a few years later in 1988, the firm was taken over by the private equity firm Kohlberg Kravis Roberts (KKR) through a leveraged buyout. The results was that burdened by debt used to fund the LBO, beset by cigarette pricing wars and facing an avalanche of smoking lawsuits, the tobacco business was separated out and sold off in 1999. This example highlights the risk that an over-diversified firm might perform poorly in new areas because managers do not understand them sufficiently well. If Nabisco's managers had a better view on the groundswell of smoking lawsuits, they would probably not have agreed to merge with a tobacco company. Aside from this risk, diverse businesses may suffer higher costs because they require more coordination efforts. As for RJR Nabisco case, most firms engaged in restructuring are divesting their diversified activities to refocus on their core businesses (Hatfield et al., 1996).

However, restructuring does not always mean a reduction of the scope of the firm; it also can encompass a broad range of transactions, such as selling business lines, making significant acquisitions, changing the capital structure through an infusion of debts, or altering the internal organization of the firm (Bowman & Singh, 1993). For example, in an effort to refocus its portfolio on the healthcare nutrition business, Nestlé completed a series of acquisitions and divestments with Novartis. Nestlé acquired for CHF3 billion ($3.3 billion), Novartis Medical Nutrition in 2006. Later in 2007, Nestlé bought from Novartis, Gerber, the baby food company, for CHF6.7 billion. Then, in 2008 and 2010, in a two stage operation, Nestlé sold to Novartis, respectively 24.8 and 52 percent of Alcon for a total value of about $40 billion.

To organize the wide range of existing restructuring activities, we can distinguish between three main types: organizational restructuring, financial restructuring, and portfolio restructuring (see Figure 12.1). Business portfolio restructuring (or downscoping) generally involves the sale of lines of business that appear peripheral to the long term strategy of the firm (Hoskisson & Hitt, 1994). Portfolio restructuring, as in the Nestlé example, might also involve a sequence of acquisitions and divestitures to change the configuration of the firm's businesses (Barkema & Schijven, 2008; Capron et al., 2001). Financial restructuring consists instead of changes to the financial structure of the firm and usually involves the infusion of large amounts of debt, whether to finance LBOs, buy back stock from equity investors, or pay large one time dividends. In August 2014, Nestlé revealed a CHF8 billion ($8.8 billion) share buyback program to improve shareholder value by increasing earnings per share. Finally, organizational restructuring attempts to increase the efficiency and effectiveness of the firm through significant changes in its organizational structure. It often is accompanied by downsizing and layoffs of employees. For example, in July 2014, Microsoft announced a restructuring plan to simplify its organization and align the recently acquired Nokia Devices and Services business with the firm's overall strategy. This organizational restructuring was expected to result in the elimination of up to 18,000 employees over the following year. Of this total, about 12,500 positions would be eliminated through synergies and strategic alignment of the Nokia Devices and Services business acquired by Microsoft in April 2014. Firms might simultaneously pursue a combination of several of these restructuring activities; as for example, restructurings involving organizational structure change often are accompanied by asset disposals or new acquisitions.

Restructuring is critical to corporate level strategy at several levels: at the macro or industry level, restructuring affects industry concentration, size, and competitive structure; at the firm level, restructuring influences performance, ownership, organizational structures, and the strategic content; and at the individual level, restructuring affects the motivation and commitment of both employees and managers (Brauer, 2006). By changing an industry structure, restructuring changes the power balance between multibuisness competitors and requires firms to adapt their corporate level strategy to new rules of the game. For example multibusiness firms might need to engage

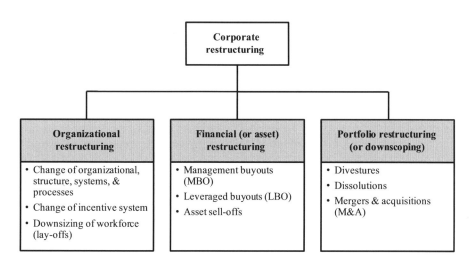

Figure 12.1 Structure and elements of corporate restructuring

Source: Adapted from Bowman & Singh (1993); Brauer (2006); Hoskisson & Hitt (1994)

in multipoint competition. By changing the firm's business portfolio, restructuring requires the multibusiness firms to realign the three slides of the corporate strategy triangle (see Chapter 1). Finally by changing the organizational structure of the firm, restructuring might require an adaptation of the incentive system to reduce agency costs.

From the 1970s into the 2000s, divesting businesses and downsizing accounted for a large percentage of firms' restructuring strategies (Hitt et al., 2004). With a meta-analysis of 52 restructuring studies published between 1986 and 1998, Bowman et al. (1999) identify financial and portfolio restructurings as more profitable, with higher proportions of positive returns than organizational restructurings. In 86 percent of financial and portfolio restructuring events, the impact on performance is positive, whereas the impact is positive in only half of the organizational restructuring cases. A more recent meta-analysis of 94 studies published between 1980 and 2007 by Lee and Madhavan (2010) shows that there is positive relationship between divesture and firm performance.

In the rest of this chapter, we focus on two critical questions related to corporate restructuring: (1) why do firms restructure? This is, what are the internal and external motivations and drivers of restructuring? And (2) what are the different restructuring strategies? This is, what are the different options available and how is their choice influenced by the firm's motives for restructuring?

WHY DO FIRMS RESTRUCTURE?

An important reason for restructuring is a firm's poor corporate performance. Such performance often results from managers' failure to maintain the alignment among a firm's corporate level strategy, structure, and objectives in a rapidly evolving and changing environment (Mellahi & Wilkinson, 2004; Sheppard & Chowdhury, 2005). As we argued in Chapter 1, an effective corporate level strategy demands the harmonious combination of four elements: a dominant logic; the firm's resources; its businesses; and the role of the headquarters (see the corporate level strategy triangle in Chapter 1). In addition to their alignment, the combination of these elements depends on, and therefore should fit with, the firm's external environment (Porter, 1980, 1987). A failure to align the firm's corporate level strategy with the threats and opportunities in the external environment may nullify any corporate advantages resulting from alignment among the elements of the triangle, in which case corporate performance is likely to suffer. When the firm's corporate performance falls below a critical threshold, it is sufficient to warrant the expenditure of turnaround costs, and a restructuring situation arises (Robbins & Pearce, 1992). According to this reasoning, restructuring occurs to overcome the firm's troubles and return it to a level at which it can match or exceed its prior performance.

The most frequent causes of corporate problems that induce restructuring are poor management, over-diversification, inadequate financial control, high costs, new competition, and unforeseen shifts in the external environment (Kaplan & Weisbach, 1992; Markides, 2002; Shleifer & Vishny, 1991) (see Box 12.1). These problems lead to misalignments among the three sides of the corporate strategy triangle or a misfit with the external environment, often due to organizational inertia (Hannan & Freeman, 1977, 1984; van Witteloosstuijn, 1998). Organizational inertia occurs when the external environment changes faster than the firm can adapt. When the gap between the required structure—organizational, financial, or portfolio—and the firm's actual structure becomes too large, restructuring becomes necessary.

Nine causes for corporate declines stand out as particular triggers for restructuring: managerial opportunism, over-diversification, inadequate financial controls, high costs, organizational inertia, the emergence of powerful new competitors, unforeseen shifts in demand, institutional changes, and managerial innovation (Hoffman, 1984; Schendel et al., 1976). As in Table 12.2, we can classify these various causes of misalignment into two categories, according to whether they result from internal problems or external issues (Filatotchev & Toms, 2006; Furrer et al., 2007a).

BOX 12.1 PRIMARY REASONS FOR DIVESTITURES

Kaplan and Weisbach (1992) analyze 271 large acquisitions completed between 1971 and 1982. A total of 43.9 percent (or 119) were divested by 1982. In investigating the reasons for these divestures, Kaplan and Weisbach find that diversified acquisitions are four times more likely to be divested than are non-diversified acquisitions. They also identify several motives for divestures: (a) a change of focus or corporate strategy; (b) an unprofitable or erroneous unit; (c) to finance other acquisitions or a leveraged restructuring; (d) antitrust legislation; (e) the need for cash; (f) to protect the firm against a hostile takeover; and (g) a good offer price for the sold unit. Among the 103 divestures for which they could determine the motives, Kaplan and Weisbach (1992) reveal that the first three motives—change of focus or corporate strategy, an unprofitable unit, or the need to finance acquisitions or a leveraged restructuring—are the more frequent, as the following table from their article demonstrates. We provide a more extensive list of motives for divestures subsequently.

Table 12.1 Divestitures

Motive	No. of divestitures
• Change of focus or corporate strategy	43
• Unit unprofitable or mistake	22
• Sale to finance acquisition or leveraged restructuring	29
• Antitrust	2
• Need cash	3
• To defend against takeover	1
• Good price	3
• Total	103

Source: Kaplan & Weisbach (1992)

Internal causes

Poor management and managerial opportunism

Poor management refers to a multitude of issues, ranging from sheer incompetence to simple neglect of core businesses. However, one particularly problematic concern related to poor management is managerial opportunism. As we explained in Chapter 2, managers are decision-making specialists with some latitude to make strategic choices that should support the interests of the

Table 12.2 Causes of corporate restructuring

Internal causes	External causes
• Poor management	• New competition
• Over-diversification	• Unforeseen shifts in demand
• Inadequate financial control	• Institutional (regulatory) change
• High costs	• Managerial innovation
• Organizational inertia	

firm's owners (Berle & Means, 1932; Chandler, 1977; Demesetz, 1983; Fama & Jensen, 1983). However, self-interested managers may make strategic decisions that maximize their own personal power and welfare instead, to minimize their personal risk rather than maximize shareholder value (e.g., Amihud & Lev, 1981; Berger et al., 1997; Jensen & Meckling, 1976; Jensen & Murphy, 1990). Thus, some opportunistic managers might engage the firm into a overly risky diversification strategy to increase their bonus in the short term, but which is likely to destroy corporate value in the long term.

In a review of empirical studies on restructuring and turnaround situations, Hoffman (1984) identified several other management defects common to restructuring firms. These include a lack of balanced expertise at the top (e.g., too many engineers, too many marketers), a lack of strong middle management that can implement corporate decisions, a failure to provide for managerial CEO succession, and a failure by the board of directors to monitor management's strategic decisions adequately. (We discuss control of managers extensively in Chapter 15.)

Different types of restructuring may be required to overcome poor management and managerial opportunism. For example, poor management likely establishes an inadequate organizational structure. Owners often implement financial restructuring to gain control over the risks of managerial opportunism (Gibbs, 1993). Managerial opportunism instead can mean an over-diversification of firm activities that demands portfolio restructuring.

Overexpansion

Overexpansion or over-diversification is diversification beyond the level that is optimal for shareholders (Markides, 1992). Strong empirical evidence indicates that in the heyday of corporate diversification, which began in the 1960s and lasted until the early 1980s, many firms over-diversified (Shleifer & Vishny, 1991). To reverse this situation, between 1981 and 1985, a firm like General Electric (GE), under the leadership of CEO Jack Welch, divested 117 business units, which amounted for 20 percent of GE's corporate assets (Dranikoff et al., 2002). As we argued in Chapter 7, the bureaucratic inefficiencies created by expanding the scope of the firm too far grew to outweigh the additional value created by diversification. As corporate performance declines, the stock prices of diversified firms are likely to fell, and over-diversified firms find themselves vulnerable to hostile takeover bids (Gibbs, 1993). Among the firms that over-diversified in the 1960s and 1970s, a large number were acquired in the 1980s and subsequently broken apart (Gaughan, 2011). As in the case of RJR Nabisco presented at the beginning of this chapter.

Hoskisson et al. (1994) outline two lines of thought about restructuring activities by over-diversified firms. One rationale holds that managers over-diversified firm activities because their governance systems were inadequate to restrain the diversification (Hoskisson & Turk, 1990). Another rationale states that the firms' managers formulated their strategy poorly, which resulted in over-diversification (Shleifer & Vishny, 1991). The first rationale suggests that governance structures, including boards of directors, ownership, and managerial incentives (see Chapter 15), have been inadequate to prevent over-diversification (Bethel & Liebeskind, 1993; Gibbs, 1993; Jensen, 1986). In this case, the use of financial restructuring strategies, such as LBOs, may provide necessary control mechanisms that reduce managers' tendency to over-diversify. The second rationale instead implies that top executives made significant strategic errors by pursuing unrelated diversification or too many avenues of related diversification simultaneously, so portfolio restructuring would be the solution.

As exemplars of this line of thought, Markides (1992), Shleifer and Vishny (1991), and Williams et al. (1988) argue that some managers create business portfolios with too much diversification, which can prompt poor strategy formulations in other areas, such as technology or financial strategy. Poor strategy formulation results from the loss of strategic control, because diversification expands and requires a restructuring of the business portfolio (Hoskisson & Hitt, 1988). Hill and Hoskisson (1987) further argue that over-diversification may lead firms to restructure their portfolios, as well as emphasize financial control over strategic control, because the information processing burdens and constraints on corporate executives increase with diversification.

Inadequate financial controls

A common element of inadequate financial controls is a failure to assign profit responsibility to key decision makers within the firm (Goold & Campbell, 1987). The lack of accountability for the financial consequences of their actions can encourage managers to employ excess staff or spend resources beyond the point of efficiency (Hill & Hoskisson, 1987). In such cases, the bureaucracy may balloon as costs spiral out of control. As we discussed in Chapter 8, one of the main tasks of corporate headquarters is to guide and control the activities of its business units and their managers. Although business units need to operate autonomously to maximize their own performance, there also must be some corporate controls to prevent them from pursuing only their self-interest, at the expense of the firm as a whole (Collis & Montgomery, 2005). Furthermore, the control system used by corporate headquarters should fit the corporate level strategy (Goold & Campbell, 1987). When there is a misalignment between the firm's corporate level strategy and its control system, organizational restructuring becomes necessary.

High costs

Inadequate financial controls can lead to high costs, but the most common cause of a high cost structure actually is low labor productivity (Hill & Snell, 1989). Such productivity weaknesses may stem from union imposed restrictions on working practices, management's failure to invest in new labor saving technologies, or some combination of the two. For example in France, despite evidence of low productivity, Nestlé had difficulties to restructure its Perrier subsidiary because of the resistance of labor unions and restrictive employment laws (Furrer, 2008). Other common causes include high wage rates (which are particularly important for firms competing on a cost basis in the global marketplace) and the failure to realize economies of scale because of relatively small market share.

In these scenarios, firms may restructure to relocate activities abroad in countries that grant them a cost advantage. Because different value creating activities, such as R&D, production, and marketing, require unique inputs to various degrees, a firm might gain cost advantages by reconfiguring its value chain and placing each activity in the country that induces the lowest costs for the most intensively used factors (Kogut, 1985). Thus, many firms locate labor intensive operations in low wage countries, such as China or Eastern European countries. Restructuring activities globally provides an opportunity to increase their scale and reduce their costs—motives for internationalization that we discuss further in Chapter 14.

Organizational inertia

Firms are often slow to respond to environmental changes, especially if they have enjoyed success (Hannan & Freeman, 1984). A firm's core competences tend to be the source of their strengths and guideposts for the future direction of their corporate level strategies. When firms are successful, they tend to stay committed to their core competences and continue to invest in them. However, events in the firm's external environment may create new conditions that turn the firm's core competencies into *core rigidities*, which implies organizational inertia (Leonard-Barton, 1992). A misalignment between a firm's resources or core competences and its corporate level strategy pushes that firm to restructure.

Chandler (1963) also suggests that firms tend to experience a pattern of relationships that link their corporate level strategy and their organizational structure (see Chapter 8). Growth creates coordination and control problems that the existing organizational structure cannot handle without loss of efficiency. Over time, organizational growth also creates the opportunity for the firm to change its strategy to improve its performance. However, the existing structure may not be adequate to implement the new strategy, in which case organizational restructuring is needed (Churchill & Lewis, 1983; Galbraith & Kazanjian, 1986; Greiner, 1972). This is before being able to implement a new corporate level strategy, firms might need to restructure their organization.

External causes

In addition to internal causes of restructuring, firms restructure in response to changes in their external environment. For example, new opportunities in the external environment might appear particularly attractive to the firm, in light of its core competencies. In such a case, restructuring may be appropriate to better position the firm against its external environment and thus create opportunities for additional corporate value. Four primary changes in firms' external environment likely trigger restructuring activities: the emergence of powerful new competitors, unforeseen shifts in demand, institutional (or regulatory changes), and managerial innovation (Hoffman, 1984; Schendel et al., 1976).

New competition

Many diversified firms find necessary to restructure their activity and to refocus on their core businesses while under attack from new competitors. Three main phenomena facilitate the entry of new competitors: technology convergence, industry deregulation, and international liberalization. When technologies converge, incumbents from different industries are likely to become new competitors. This is, for example, the case of the mobile phone industry, which is at the convergence point of hardware, software, and Internet technology development and which experience the rivalry of firms such as Apple, Microsoft, and Google, which come from very different origins. Firms that previously seemed insulated from competition because they functioned in a regulated industry may find themselves under attack from new competition when the industry undergoes deregulation. In many countries the deregulation of postal services forced former state monopolies to develop banking services to maintain their activities. Finally, international liberalization may place firms in competition with new foreign competitors, as in the airline industry. Top managers of firms that are thus attacked in their core business may decide to divest the firm of some noncore activities to devote more attention and resources to their troubled core business. In 2008, Ford sold Jaguar to Tata to refocus on its core brand.

Unforeseen shifts in demand

Unforeseen shifts in demand might result from major changes in technology, economic or political conditions, or social and cultural norms. Although such changes some times create market opportunities for new products, they also threaten the existence of many established enterprises and thus necessitate some restructuring. In a familiar example, both changes in technology and shifting cultural norms eventually led Sony to shift its focus away from the personal music device market, even though as the producer of the Walkman, it had previously enjoyed market dominance (Inagaki, 2015).

Institutional changes

As we argued in Chapter 2, government antitrust policies may require firms to restructure their activities (Lubatkin et al., 1997). Antitrust laws prohibit mergers that create increased market power, so firms may be forced to divest their noncore business units after they achieve a major acquisition to their reduce market power (see Box 12.2).

BOX 12.2 NESTLÉ'S ACQUISITION OF PERRIER

In 1992, Nestlé acquired Perrier, after a long struggle with its competitor BSN and the Italian Agnelli family. However, the European Commission (EC) challenged the agreement, on the grounds that it would give Nestlé a dominant position in the French bottled water market. To determine if the acquisition would create an overly dominant position for Nestlé, the EC examined several factors. First, it investigated the degree of supply concentration, because if Nestlé acquired Perrier, only two major suppliers would remain, each with massive market share in France. Second, the EC addressed transparency and prices in the market. The commission asserted that transparency would lessen if only two firms remained. Before the acquisition, three competitors monitored one another in terms of their prices and volumes sold. If only two large firms, with a combined market share of 68 percent, remained, they could easily increase prices without fear of offsetting volume losses. Third, the EC noted that consumers buy and drink mineral water on a daily basis and do not have access to perfect substitutes. Therefore, an increase of prices would have a relatively small impact on quantities demanded, which would lead to increases of total revenues and profits. The commission believed that this development would reinforce the likelihood of such a strategy, as well as encourage tacit collusion.

However, because the EC could not prove that Nestlé would use Perrier for tacit collusion or a disputable strategy, it approved the acquisition with one important condition: Nestlé had to restructure its bid with the provision that it would sell Volvic, one of the top brands in Perrier's portfolio, to BSN so that Nestlé and BSN would have an equal market share in France. As a result, Nestlé would control 36.8 percent of the French market and BSN 30.9 percent. The EC also demanded the condition that Nestlé would not control more than 20 percent of France's mineral water capacity, and it required the firm to sell eight smaller springs, including Vichy, Thonon, Pierval, and Saint-Yorre, to a single buyer. Furthermore, it could not buy back the brands for ten years.

Source: Furrer (2008)

The more inefficient the outside institutions, the greater the benefits that diversification confers. Markides (1992, 1993) argues that because outside institutions such as the capital and labor markets have improved in many countries, diversification has lost some of its beneficial effects (e.g., an efficient internal capital market). Therefore, many firms reduce their scope and restructure their activities, simply to gain back efficiencies (see Khanna & Palepu, 1997a).

Managerial Innovation

Finally, some innovations in management practices diminish the advantages of scope that a firm might gain through vertical integration or horizontal diversification. As we discussed in Chapter

11, new forms of strategic alliances permit firms to benefit from economies of scope without incurring the related administrative costs. In response, many firms have reduced their scope through restructuring, divestments, and outsourcing. For example, long term strategic alliances between a firm and its suppliers offer a viable economic alternative to vertical integration and competitive bidding, as in the automotive industry.

However, restructuring is not always cause by internal or external problems. For example, Capron et al. (2001) argue that resource redeployments and asset divestitures after an M&A might provide a means of reconfiguring the structure of resources within the firm and that asset divestiture could be considered as a logical consequence of this reconfiguration process.

RESTRUCTURING STRATEGIES

In Figure 12.1 at the beginning of this chapter, the restructuring strategies were organized into three categories: organizational restructuring, financial restructuring, and portfolio restructuring. Even without an exact one to one match between the causes of poor corporate performance and the type of restructuring strategy, specific restructuring strategies generally should be used to target particular causes.

Organizational restructuring

Organizational restructuring refers to significant changes in the organizational structure of the firm, including divisional redesign, changes to the management incentive system, and employee downsizing (Bowman & Singh, 1993; Bowman et al., 1999). Organizational restructuring therefore usually helps solve internal problems, such as poor management or high costs. Its main objective is to improve efficiency.

Change of organizational structure, systems, and processes

Organizational restructuring can be defined as any major reconfiguration of the internal administrative structure (Bowman & Singh, 1993). In Chapter 10, we argued that as firms grow and diversify, coordination and control problems and crises are likely, requiring changes in the organizational structure of the firm (Churchill & Lewis, 1983; Greiner, 1972). We also have contended that different corporate level strategies might require different organizational structures (e.g., Chandler, 1962). For example, related and unrelated diversification strategies need to be supported by different multidivisional structures (Hill & Hoskisson, 1987). Therefore, as firms diversify their activities or change their level of diversification, they also need to adapt their organizational structure.

Prior studies of organizational restructuring emphasize its ineffectiveness (Bowman & Singh, 1993). In particular, Hannan and Freeman (1984) call restructuring disruptive, so much so that that it usually increases the rate of corporate failure. They also argue that the selection pressures reward firms for being reliable and accountable, so an attempt to adapt to environmental changes, particularly through organizational restructuring, increases the firm's probability of failure. This line of argument is further developed by Amburgey et al. (1993), who argue that change is hazardous because it destroys some of the firm's existing routines, which often provide sources of the firm's core competences. This is because core competences are often causally ambiguous (Reed & DeFillippi, 1990), which is a reason why they are source of sustainable competitive advantage—if it easy to understand how its works, then competitors can easily imitate. However, because of their causal ambiguity they are also more likely to be damage during a restructuring.

Restructuring management incentives

As we discussed in Chapter 7, related and unrelated diversification strategies may require different incentive systems to control corporate and divisional managers. When shareholders' and corporate managers' interests are not aligned, the incentive systems demands modification. (We discuss this need further, with regard to corporate level managers' incentive systems and control mechanisms, in Chapter 15 on corporate governance.) In addition, at the divisional level, when the managerial incentive system is not aligned with the firm's dominant logic it should be restructured to achieve fit between the different parts of the corporate strategy triangle.

Divisional executives' compensation can be designed to attract and retain talent, encourage cooperation or competition, balance short and long term objectives, and control risk taking behaviors (Hoskisson & Hitt, 1994). Corporate managers may change the incentive structure at the divisional level to encourage different behaviors among their division managers. For example, division managers in an entrepreneurial division that needs to grow could receive a low salary with limited short term earnings incentives, complemented by the promise of significant 'phantom' stock options in the division if performance improves; these incentives should encourage more risk taking behaviors. On the contrary, a division in a later growth stage may emphasize salary and short term bonuses but play down stock options for their divisional managers to avoid too much risk taking (Hoskisson et al., 1993b).

Many executive compensation plans provide incentives for division managers to diversify, or even over-diversify, and increase their division's size and scope (Hoskisson & Hitt, 1994). For example, an incentive based on annual returns on investment (ROI) may enhance short term performance but reduce managers' risk taking. Long term incentives alone would be inadequate, because they imply trade-offs too (Hoskisson et al., 1993b). For example, long term incentives based on divisional performance may reduce cooperation among related divisions. To be most effective, a restructured managerial incentive system should occur together with other forms of restructuring, such as down-scoping, as we define in the next section (Hoskisson & Hitt, 1994).

Downsizing the workforce

Downsizing involves a reduction in the number of the firm's employees, but in a way that does not change the composition of the businesses in the firm's portfolio (Hitt et al., 2004). Firms use downsizing as their restructuring strategy for different reasons, though perhaps the most frequently cited is that the firm expects improved profitability from the associated cost reduction and more efficient operations (Cascio, 2005). Because of its quick results, downsizing is a widely preferred restructuring strategy among managers. For example, Cascio (2005) reports that in 2001 alone, firms in the U.S. announced layoffs of almost 2 million workers; American Express, Lucent, Hewlett-Packard, and Dell conducted multiple rounds of layoffs in that year. In 2005, General Motors announced it would lay off 25,000 employees to address its poor competitive performance, especially in the face of the improved performance by foreign competitors—even before the end of decade crises and near collapse the car company faced.

However, a downsizing strategy that is not accompanied by a diminution of the firm scope— that is, down-scoping—is likely to have negative long terms effects on the firm's financial performance (Hoskisson & Hitt, 1994). Downsizing alone might result in the loss of core competences in the form of human capital (Fisher & White. 2000). It also tends to have a negative effect on the morale of retained employees, who may be afraid that they will be the next to be laid off in future restructuring rounds (Cascio, 2005).

BOX 12.3 PRIMARY REASONS FOR DIVESTITURES

On July 17, 2014, Microsoft announced it was cutting 18,000 jobs or about 14 per cent of its full time workforce. It is the largest layoff in the company's history, and 12,500 of these jobs are related to Microsoft's acquisition of Nokia's mobile phone business earlier the same year. The layoffs were expected to hit almost all product groups across the nearly 130,000 person company across the world and to include not only engineers, but also a number of employees in sales and marketing in many product groups. Few, if any, entire product groups were expected to be eliminated completely in the current downsizing scheme. Microsoft's previous major round of layoffs occurred in 2009, when management eliminated 5,800 jobs over the course of two plus rounds. Then CEO Steve Ballmer attributed the cuts in 2009 to a 'response to the global economic downturn.'

Source: www.geekwire.com/2014/breaking-microsoft-cutting-18000-jobs-next-year-14-workforce/

Financial restructuring

Financial restructuring refers to significant changes in the capital structure of a firm, including LBOs, leveraged recapitalizations, and debt for equity swaps (Bowman & Singh, 1993; Bowman et al., 1999). The primary vehicles for financial restructuring are the LBO, management buyout (MBO), and asset sales.

Leveraged buyouts

Leveraged buyouts as a restructuring strategy attempt to correct for poor management or managerial opportunism (Bergh & Holbein, 1997; Jensen & Meckling, 1976; Markides & Singh, 1997). With a LBO, one party buys all of the firm's assets and thus takes the firm private (i.e., out of the stock market) (Gaughan, 2011). After this transaction, the firm's stocks no longer trade publicly, but a significant amount of debt usually has been incurred to finance the buyout (this is the leveraged part). A key assumption behind a LBO is that a high level of debts provides better control over managerial opportunism (Jensen & Meckling, 1976). That is, the pressure of high interest payments seemingly should force managers to focus on their core businesses, rather than wasting free cash flows earned from core businesses on projects with negative present values. However, because of this high pressure, the risk of bankruptcy is also high. Therefore, the idea is most applicable to mature businesses, for which cash flows are available. Indeed, mature firms rarely need to make investments in R&D and marketing that are large enough to absorb all the free cash flow generated by the businesses (Jensen, 1989).

Management buyouts

When a complete unit gets sold to its management, it is referred to as an MBO. Thus, MBOs are very similar to LBOs, except that the sale is to management, which generally finances the purchase through the sale of high yield bonds to external investors (Gaughan, 2011). Therefore, MBOs are particularly well suited to solve agency problems, because the managers become the owners of the division. The Virgin Group has undergone several management buyouts in its recent past. On September 24, 2008, Virgin Comics underwent a management buyout and changed its name to Liquid Comics. On 29 September 2008, Virgin Radio also underwent a similar process and became Absolute Radio. However, managers often lack the financial backup of being part of a large

Restructuring strategies

diversified firm and the risk of failure is high. On September 17, 2007, Richard Branson announced that the U.K. arm of Virgin Megastores was to be sold off as part of a management buyout, and from November 2007, will be known by a new name, Zavvi. However, the venture did not succeed as an independent firm and went into liquidation at the end of 2008.

Asset sell-offs

Unlike LBOs and MBOs, asset sell-offs only involve specific assets. Firms might undertake this form of restructuring for two primary reasons (Hovakimian & Titman, 2006). First, asset sales enable firms to restructure their operations to achieve higher operating efficiencies, because ideally they sell their assets to more productive users (Goold et al., 1994) or divest themselves of assets unrelated to their core business. Asset sales increase efficiency by transferring some assets to better uses outside the firm, and the seller can capture some of the resulting gains (Hite et al., 1987) (see the Nestlé example at the beginning of this chapter). In empirical support of this argument, John and Ofek (1995) show that asset sales lead to improved operating performance, especially if the firm also reduces its scope. Second, financial constraints may provoke a firm to undertake asset sales. By selling some assets, the firm can raise capital, even if debt and equity markets are unavailable or unattractive. Lang et al. (1995) show that firms that sell assets tend to be poor performers and/or suffer from high leverage ratios, which suggests that asset sales provide funds when alternative sources of financing are too expensive.

Portfolio restructuring (or down-scoping)

Portfolio restructuring demands a significant change in the configuration of the firm's portfolio of businesses through either acquisitions or divestitures (Bowman & Singh, 1993). Portfolio restructuring becomes down-scoping, using Hoskisson and Hitt's (1994) term, if it involves the divestiture, spin off, and or other form of elimination of businesses unrelated to a firm's core competence. In 2005, Sara Lee Corporation spun off its apparel business in a "massive restructuring that […] shed operations with annual revenues of US$8.2 bio" (Adamy, 2005, p. A5). The firm argued that it intended to focus on its strongest brands in bakery, meat, and household products. However, the restructuring trimmed revenues that previously had accounted for 40 percent of the firm's total sales (Adamy, 2005). Yet the savings the firm earned from the divestiture went into R&D for new products to support its top selling lines (Adamy, 2005). Compared with downsizing, down-scoping is more selective and thus has a more positive effect on firms' long term performance, because it enables firms to reduce their scope without losing their core competence or key human resources (Hoskisson & Hitt, 1994).

Divestures

Divestitures refer specifically to a firm's adjustments in its business portfolio structure, using spin offs, equity carve outs, split ups, or unit sell offs (Brauer, 2006; Mulherin & Boone, 2000). In practice, divestitures have proven critical for many firms (see Box 12.4), independent of their scope, size, age, or industry background (Hoskisson & Johnson, 1992; Markides, 1992). The basic idea of a divesture is to sell a business unit to the highest bidder.

Weston et al. (1998) have identified 14 motives for divestures, rather than other restructuring strategies: dismantling conglomerates, abandoning the core business, changing corporate level strategies, adding corporate value by selling to a better parent, requiring large additional investment, harvesting past success, discarding unwanted businesses from prior acquisitions, financing prior acquisitions, warding off hostile takeovers, meeting governmental requirements, selling businesses to their managers, taking a position in another firm, reversing mistakes, and learning.

BOX 12.4 DIVESTURE: THE LESSON FROM THE APPLE FARMER

Dranikoff et al. (2002, p. 74) draw an important lesson for manager from the of apple farmers. They argue:

> [s]mart apple farmers routinely saw off dead and weakened branches to keep their trees healthy. Every year, they also cut back a number of vigorous limbs—those that are blocking light from the rest of the tree or otherwise hampering its growth. And, as the growing season progresses, they pick and discard perfectly good apples, ensuring that the remaining fruit gets the energy needed to reach its full size and ripeness. Only through such a careful, systematic pruning does an orchard produce its highest possible yield.

The three types of buyers of divestitures are independent investors, other firms, and the managers of the unit to be divested. Selling a business unit to independent investors constitutes a spin off; a spin off is most likely to succeed when the unit to be sold is profitable and the stock market is moving upward. However, spin offs are usually not an option when the business unit is unprofitable and unattractive to independent investors or if the stock market is contracting. Selling a unit to another firm is more likely if that purchasing firm already is in the same line of business as the unit for sale. In such cases, the purchaser might be willing to pay a premium for the opportunity to increase the size of its business, create economies of scope, or reduce its competition. Finally, as we already discussed, selling a business unit to its management is an MBO. Box 12.5 summarizes a recently released review of extant divesture literature.

Dissolutions

Eventually, the liquidation or dissolution of a business unit might occur if the firm cannot sell the unit for a good price. This restructuring strategy is not very attractive; it requires the firm to write off its investment in a business unit, often at a considerable cost. However, in the case of a poorly performing business unit, for which a sell off or spin off is unlikely and an MBO cannot be arranged, liquidation may be the only viable alternative to reduce costs and improve long-term performance.

Mergers and acquisitions

However, portfolio restructuring does not always mean a reduction in the scope of the firm. Firms may restructure by adding new businesses through M&As, as we discussed as a growth strategy in Chapter 11. Although M&As are effective vehicles to restructure a firm's portfolio, their effects on corporate value are relatively unclear (Bowman & Singh, 1993). When the consequences also include measures such as management turnover and loss of human capital, there is evidence of significant negative impacts, even years after the event (Walsh, 1988).

CONCLUDING REMARKS

This chapter concludes our description of the growth cycle of firms' corporate level strategy: firms grow by diversifying their activities to a point at which they become over-diversified and

BOX 12.5 RESEARCH ON DIVESTURES

In a review of existing literature, Brauer (2006) finds that two major research questions have dominated divestiture research: (1) what are determinants of firm divestitures? And (2) what are the implications of divestitures on firm performance? Research into the divestiture process has been less frequent.

In relation to the first question: the contingencies that trigger divestitures can be broadly categorized into *industry specific determinants* and *firm and unit specific determinants*. Industry specific factors, such as industry concentration, industry growth, technological change, environmental uncertainty, and changes in the industry's institutional setting, likely constitute major drivers for divestitures. In addition, previous studies have generated a long list of firm and unit specific factors (e.g., poor performance, excessive diversification, size, age) that precipitate divestitures. The most popular contention in divestiture research holds that divestitures serve to restore corporate efficiency. Consequently, poor firm performance provides the strongest predictor of divestiture. In addition, weak performance at the business unit level and relative debt intensity trigger divestitures. The underperformance of certain units, or even the entire firm, have been associated with minimal relatedness between these units and the core business of the parent, which in turn creates interdependency between the units and perhaps even negative synergies. Consequently, excessive diversification may constitute an additional and closely associated trigger of divestitures. Finally, another determinant of divestiture is closely associated with the two preceding factors, that is, weak internal governance or agency problems.

In relation to the second question: although strategic management research acknowledges that divestitures have several important macro and industry level effects (e.g., increased industry concentration), the implications of divestitures have been much more commonly assessed at the firm or unit level. At the firm level, most studies deal with the implications of divestitures on a firm's financial performance. In strategy oriented divestiture research, divestiture success instead depends on a combination of accounting (industry adjusted return on assets [ROA] or return on sales [ROS]; earnings before interest, tax, depreciation, and amortization [EBITDA]) and market (Jensen's Alpha, Treynor, or Sharpe ratio) measures. Yet results regarding firms' post-divestiture performance based on these measures have been mixed. At the individual level, divestitures affect the motivation and commitment of employees in both the retained and the divested units, because company breakups almost invariably cause high levels of stress for employees.

their economies of scope turn negative. This point triggers the restructuring of their organizational structure, financial structure, or portfolio.

In the next chapters, we discuss three specific issues related to corporate level strategies: vertical integration and the reduction of transaction costs, multipoint competition and the management of market power, and internationalization of firms' diversification strategies. In the final chapter, we conclude with a discussion of pertinent corporate governance issues.

Chapter

13

MULTIPOINT COMPETITION

MANAGING MARKET POWER

In Chapter 2 we discussed market power as a potential rationale for the existence of multibusiness firms. Market power can provide multibusiness firms with the ability to create defensive positions against the competitive forces that confront them in the marketplace (Porter, 1980). In Chapter 10 we discussed how a firm could increase its market power through vertical integration. In the current chapter we demonstrate that horizontally diversified firms may also benefit from increased market power compared to non-diversified firms. This is, unlike single business firms that compete in only one business, multibusiness firms likely encounter the same competitors across several businesses (as in Figure 13.1). This situation is referred to as multipoint (or multimarket) competition, that is, "a situation where firms compete against each other simultaneously in several markets [or businesses]" (Karnani & Wernerfelt, 1985, p. 87). For example, Michelin and Goodyear compete in both the U.S. and European automobile tire markets. Disney and AOL-Time Warner both compete in the movie production and book publishing businesses. This situation provides firms with more strategic options and more market power, because they can choose in which business(es) they engage their rivals using resources from their different businesses (see Box 13.1).

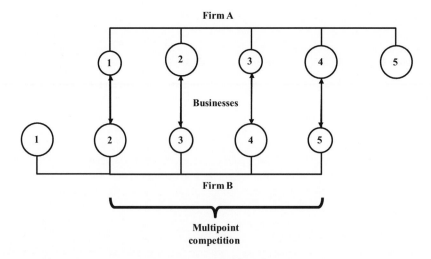

Figure 13.1 Multipoint competition between two hypothetical firms

Source: Adapted from Barney (2007)

BOX 13.1 CHOOSING WHERE TO COMPETE: THE 'MARLBORO FRIDAY'

MacMillan et al. (2003) provide a striking example of the power of multipoint competition. They report what analysts later caller the 'Marlboro Friday.' This is, on April 2, 1993, Philip Morris announced that it would reduce the U.S. price of its premium brand of cigarettes (Marlboro) by 20 percent. It also said it would substantially increase the budget for its advertising in the U.S. R.J. Reynolds, Philip Morris's biggest competitor, responded by matching the price cut on its own premium brands (Camel and Winston among them) and by pouring more money into its own domestic advertising. The pricing war that ensued cost both companies tens of millions of dollars.

However, domestic market share was not the real reason Philip Morris lowered the price of Marlboro cigarettes. The main reason was to push R.J. Reynolds to use its cash resources trying to keep up with its chief opponent in the U.S., while it was expanding aggressively into the Eastern European market, investing $800 million in Russia and neighboring countries. Having spent so much money to maintain its market share in the U.S., R.J. Reynolds was in no position to fight back, and Philip Morris easily won the battle for Eastern European market share.

Because multipoint competition, provide multibusiness firms with strong market power, multipoint rivals usually consider a balance of power as an attractive alternative to hyper-competition. Accordingly, the theory of multipoint competition suggests that mutual forbearance may reduce the business level intensity of competition between two firms when they simultaneously compete in several markets. In turn, reduced competition open the door to higher margins and profits for the competitors. These different businesses could be product markets, geographic markets for the same product, or national markets for different products (Ma, 1999).

MULTIPOINT COMPETITION AND INTERFIRM RIVALRY

The roots of the theory of multipoint competition can be traced to industrial organization economics (e.g., Bernheim & Whinston, 1990; Edwards, 1955) and sociology (Simmel, 1950). The focus of this theory is interfirm competition (Baum & Korn, 1996) and the balance of power (Porter, 1980). If the business portfolios of competing multibusiness firms overlap, the firms are said to engage in multipoint competition. The extent to which business portfolios overlap depends on the degree of multipoint contacts (Gimeno & Woo, 1996); a contact occurs when two firms compete in the same business and the level multipoint contact consists of the number of product markets shared with rivals divided by firm scope (Gimeno & Jeong, 2001). As the level of multipoint contact between two firms increases, they likely become more interdependent, such that the outcomes of actions initiated by one firm become more contingent on the actions and reactions of its rivals. Furthermore, increasing multipoint contacts provides firms with more opportunities to compete and retaliate in different businesses, which results in greater market power. The degree of rivalry (i.e., intensity of competition) reflects the aggressiveness and speed of the actions and reactions that firms initiate to compete in the market (Chen, 1996; D'Aveni, 1994). Measures of rivalry intensity generally depend on the frequency and aggressiveness of changes to strategic variables (Chen, 1996), such as prices and advertising intensity, that influence profit margins (Gimeno & Woo, 1996, 1999). Multipoint competitors also may enter one another's markets to threaten rivals (Baum & Korn, 1999; Ketchen et al., 2004). Although multipoint competition increases the opportunity for competition among rivals, greater overlap does not necessarily translate into more intense competition. On the contrary, the theory of multipoint competition suggests that competition intensity among firms with overlapping business portfolios may be dampened because of *mutual forbearance* (Baum & Korn, 1996, 1999; Clark & Montgomery, 1996; Edwards, 1955; Gimeno, 1994; Gimeno & Woo, 1996; Karnani & Wernerfelt, 1985).

Mutual forbearance

Mutual forbearance is a form of tacit collusion. Tacit collusion occurs as firms compete simultaneously in several businesses, which increases their interdependence. Tacit collusion, as opposed to explicit or direct collusion (which is illegal in most countries), implies two firms understand each other's motives and strategies and implicitly coordinate to avoid competing intensely (Jayachandran et al., 1999). Mutual forbearance as a result of multipoint competition appears in various industries; for example, Karnani and Wernerfelt (1985) describe mutual forbearance in the competitions between Michelin and Goodyear, Maxwell House and Folger's, Caterpillar and John Deere, and BIC and Gillette. Gimeno (1994; Gimeno & Woo, 1996) observed multipoint competition in the U.S. airline industry, Fuentelsaz and Gómez (2006) in the Spanish savings bank market, and Boeker et al. (1997) in the U.S. hospital industry.

Jayachandran et al. (1999) describe two processes leading to mutual forbearance: *familiarity* (Baum & Korn, 1999) and *deterrence* (Bernheim & Whinston, 1990; Edwards, 1955; Porter, 1980).

Familiarity refers to the extent to which tacit collusion may be enhanced by a firm's awareness of the capabilities and actions of its rivals. Familiarity between rivals influences the extent to which firms engage in actions and reactions with one another (Chen & Miller, 1994). In a complex environment, it is virtually impossible for firms to gather all necessary information about rivals to become familiar with them, because available information in a competitive environment rarely meets the information requirements for competing effectively (Furrer & Thomas, 2000). Therefore, firms must construct imperfect versions of the competitive reality, which in turn guide their decisions and strategies more than does *objective reality* (Porac & Rosa, 1996). The social construction of rivalry also implies that firms might not realize their actual interdependence with other firms, so they might engage in competitive actions with little consideration of how these actions influence their rivals or how their rivals might respond. For firms to realize that their strategic actions and performance are interdependent with those of other firms, they first must become aware of these firms and recognize that their business portfolios overlap. Firms gain familiarity with the strategies, capabilities, and actions of multipoint competitors because they encounter them more frequently across businesses. Multipoint contacts further facilitate mutual learning by providing firms with the opportunity to become familiar with each other and recognize their interdependence. However, mere familiarity may not be sufficient to engender mutual forbearance; firms also need the ability to deter each other (Chen, 1996). Otherwise, powerful firms have no incentive to refrain from engaging in very aggressive rivalries with relatively weaker competitors (Teece et al., 1997).

Deterrence is the extent to which a firm can prevent rivals from initiating aggressive actions that may harm its interests. Thus, deterrence is a consequence of the firm's ability to cause its rivals serious financial loss by retaliating aggressively in response to their actions. Deterrence results from the ability to cause financial damage to rivals, particularly when firms can issue credible threats of retaliation against rivals. In such conditions, firms refrain from competing aggressively because the expected gains from their aggressive moves are likely to be less than the potential future losses due to the competitive retaliation. Furthermore, in contrast with familiarity, which derives from prior interactions with a rival, deterrence requires future interactions between the firms to enable a response to a current attack. The possibility of repeated interactions in the future allows for retaliation and creates a link between the future payoffs for a firm and its present actions. This link, called *the shadow of the future*, implies that "the future casts a shadow back upon the present, affecting current behavior patterns" (Parkhe, 1993, p. 799). The knowledge that competitors can and will retaliate in the future against current attacks may prevent firms from undertaking aggressive actions (Heide & Miner, 1992). For deterrence to be effective, firms should believe that their rivals have the *ability* and the *opportunity to retaliate* aggressively and hurt them.

This **ability to retaliate** in multiple businesses implies that future losses from multipoint warfare would be considerably larger than those generated in a single point context (Edwards, 1955). A firm's action in a particular business context (e.g., a price cut, increased advertising intensity) may result in gains for that business but also cause much greater losses in other businesses. The possibility of larger losses arises because rivals could retaliate across the many different businesses to a specific action that the focal firm initiates in just one business. Therefore, relative to a single business context, the more severe rivalry in multipoint competition may inflict much heavier losses on firms.

Although the ability to harm competitors is a necessary condition to cause deterrence, a firm also must perceive its rivals as having the **opportunity to hurt** through retaliation (Chen, 1996; Gimeno, 1999). In a single business context, retaliation is possible only in future interactions in that same market, such as when a competitor introduces a new product in the market. If a firm enjoys a powerful position in the attacked business line, its future retaliation may induce significant costs. In a multipoint competition scenario however, more common markets provide more areas for retaliation against competitive attacks (Jayachandran et al., 1999). Therefore, relative to the single business competitive context, multipoint competition increases opportunities for retaliation by extending the interdependence of firms from the time dimension (future) to both time and space dimensions (future and multiple markets). This extension enables firms to retaliate in businesses in which their response may be less costly or more convenient for them.

As game theory suggests, the basic condition for sustaining mutual forbearance is that each firm must perceive the payoff for engaging in tacit collusion to be greater than what they might gain from breaking the implicit agreement (Schelling, 1960). By increasing the ability of firms to deter competitors, multipoint competition makes the payoff of mutual forbearance more attractive than the payoff of aggressive rivalry. Moreover, by increasing familiarity among firms, multipoint competition makes it easier for them to realize that they share the same beliefs about the beneficial nature of mutual forbearance and thus (implicitly) coordinates their competitive behavior. As Schelling (1960) notes, what deters firms is not the aggressive retaliation that might arise when a rival initiates an action in a multipoint context but rather the expectation that such retaliation would occur. If the firms involved in multipoint competition share this expectation (due to increased familiarity), they may eschew aggressive competitive behavior. Figure 13.2, adapted from Jayachandran et al. (1999), depicts this discussion about the process by which multipoint competition influences interfirm rivalry graphically.

Though support for the negative relationship between the level of multipoint contact and intensity of competition has not always been consistent (e.g., Mester, 1987; Rhoades & Heggestad, 1985), strong empirical evidence supports the mutual forbearance hypothesis (e.g., Baum & Korn, 1996; Gimeno & Woo, 1996; Parker & Röller, 1997). Recent studies provide some support for an inverted U relationship between the level of multipoint contact and the intensity of rivalry (Baum & Korn, 1999; Haveman & Nonnemaker, 2000; Stephan et al., 2003) (see Figure 13.3). When the level of contact is low, firms might not perceive each other as competitors and the intensity is likely to be low; as the level of contact increases, firms pay more attention to the other firm and start to react to each other competitive moves, the intensity of rivalry increases as rivals seek to establish their market position. The intensity of rivalry increases up to a point when the level of contact is high enough for the rivals to become dangerous because of their ability and opportunities to hurt, and then mutual forbearance enter in action and the intensity of rivalry starts to decrease.

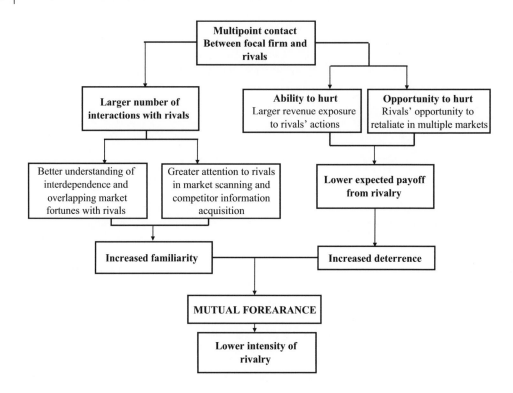

Figure 13.2 Multipoint competition and intensity of rivalry
Source: Adapted from Jayachandran et al. (1999)

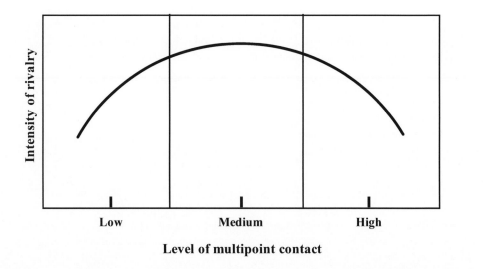

Figure 13.3 The relationship between the number of multipoint contacts and the intensity of rivalry

MULTIPOINT CONTACT AND INTENSITY OF COMPETITION: A CONTINGENCY MODEL

Several moderating variables may affect the relationship between the number of multipoint contacts and intensity of competition. We focus on the effects of six factors: spheres of influence, resource similarity, organizational structure of competing firms, seller concentration, opportunities for scope economies, and CEO tenure. The moderating effect of these factors is graphically represented in Figure 13.4.

Spheres of influence

Spheres of influence refer to the extent to which different multipoint competitors take dominant positions in different businesses (Edwards, 1955). A firm's sphere of influence consists of three general dimensions: market share dominance, market dependence, and resource centrality (Gimeno, 1999). Spheres of influence thus occur when firms engaged in multipoint competition dominate different businesses in which they overlap (D'Aveni, 2004; Edwards, 1955; Ma, 1999; McGrath et al., 1998). When firms are involved in multipoint competition, their competitive positions may not be similar in all common businesses, for example due to differing areas or levels of technological knowledge, specialization, and varied transportation costs because of more distant plant locations (Bernheim & Whinston, 1990; Gimeno, 1999). If firms with multipoint contacts also have different spheres of influence, it may accentuate the negative relationship between multipoint contacts and intensity of competition (Baum & Korn, 1996).

Spheres of influence also may enhance deterrence, because firms want to protect their key businesses from retaliatory moves by rivals and therefore may refrain from taking actions that

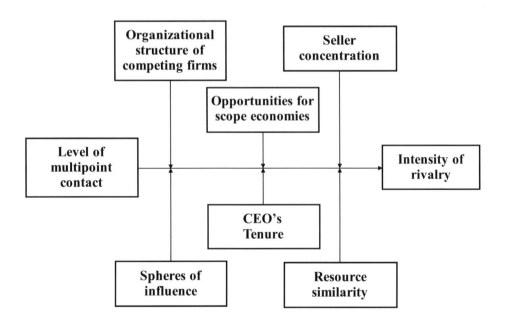

Figure 13.4 Multipoint contact and intensity of rivalry

Source: Adapted from Gimeno & Woo (1999); Jayachandran et al. (1999), and Stephan et al. (2003)

could provoke reactions in those particular businesses (Bernheim & Whinston, 1990). This argument receives empirical support from Gimeno (1999), who finds that when firms have reciprocal relationships (e.g., Firm A has greater strategic interest in business 1 than does Firm B, but Firm B has greater interest in business 2), they are less likely to engage in intense rivalry than when their relationships are nonreciprocal (e.g., Firm A has a greater interest than Firm B in both businesses).

Resource similarity

Resource similarity entails the extent to which competing firms are comparable in their possession of resources critical for success in the market (Chen, 1996). Such resource similarity may affect their interfirm rivalry, because competitive advantage comes from the ability to develop and sustain valuable resources that differ from those of its competitors (Teece et al., 1997). Firms with similar resources likely have similar strategic strengths and weaknesses (Chen, 1996), so they may compete using similar strategies (Fuentelsaz & Gómez, 2006; Gimeno & Woo, 1996).

As mentioned previously, rivalry results from social constructions of the competitive environment. Firms with similar resources should view each other as significant competitors because they are more alert to the other's actions (Porac & Thomas, 1990). However, such an increased focus also implies these firms can understand each other's strategies and capabilities better and that they are more familiar with each other than are firms with less similar resource bundles. In addition, firms with similar resource bundles can better sustain a cooperative arrangement, including mutual forbearance, because they can issue credible threats of retaliation (Chen, 1996). That is, firms with similar resource bundles should be able to deter each other better because they can match competitive actions, which renders actions invalid (Teece et al., 1997). Regardless of the number of contacts, if one firm has a resource advantage over its rival, it may not be motivated to avoid aggressive competition, because it perceives it can outmaneuver the competitor on the basis of its superior resources. The likelihood of multipoint contacts to reduce the intensity of competition between firms thus is greater when the firms are similar in their resource endowments.

Empirically, Baum and Korn (1999) find that resource dissimilarity interacts with multipoint contacts to influence the rate of entry and exit in a market. The more dissimilar the resources of competitors, the higher is the rate of entry into and exit out of rivals' markets. Young et al. (2000) also reveal that resource dissimilarity pushes firms to undertake more actions and do so more quickly, though these effects appear mitigated by the level of multipoint contact.

Organizational structure of competing firms

Organizational structure refers to the extent to which a firm is able to control and coordinate its actions jointly across multiple businesses. Appropriate coordination and control among the different organizational units that manage the activities in different businesses are critical for the effectiveness of multipoint strategies (Gimeno & Woo, 1999). For example, consider Firm A and Firm B, which compete in businesses X and Y, such that different administrative units manage the operations of those firms in each business. For mutual forbearance to take place, the administrative units of both firms must be willing and capable of coordinating their strategies across the two businesses. That is, multipoint competition leads to mutual forbearance and less intense competition only if each firm achieves effective coordination between its administrative units tasked with managing operations across businesses. In the absence of such intrafirm coordination, competition converges into business by business competition. Therefore, organizational structures that provide firms with the ability to coordinate their actions (see Chapter 9) may improve their ability to deter rivals in a multipoint context. Golden and Ma (2003) posit that firms with efficient between-unit

Multipoint competition

integrating mechanisms and reward structures that encourage between unit cooperation are the most likely to recognize and exploit opportunities for mutual forbearance. Such firms also are more likely to hire unit managers willing to make sacrifices in their own unit to benefit the firm.

Opportunities for economies of scope

Firms that have resource sharing **opportunities for economies of scope** likely meet other firms in multiple markets, as their rivals also attempt to gain similar scope economies (Gimeno & Woo, 1999). If managers attempt to exploit economies of scope between their business units, decisions about these units must be coordinated across the firm's decision-making process. This coordinated decision-making facilitates perceptions of interdependence with multipoint competitors. Even with different administrative units, the presence of strong resource sharing opportunities should lead to the formation of coordinating roles and mechanisms (Hill et al., 1992) and thus the recognition of interdependence. However, the failure to perceive extended interdependence or a lack of effective coordination still reduces the ability to synchronize responses to rivals across units and thus undercuts incentives for mutual forbearance (Collis & Montgomery, 1997, p. 166). That is, unless the opportunities for resource sharing among business units are strong and easy to recognize, the coordination needed to induce forbearance will be largely absent.

Gimeno and Woo (1999) also argue that the gains from tacit collusion among multipoint competitors are more limited in businesses that do not benefit from economies of scope; in the absence of economies of scope, multipoint competitors lack any efficiency advantage over single business incumbents or potential entrants. Thus, an attempt by multipoint incumbents to collude, perhaps by raising their prices over their costs, may be self-defeating, because single business incumbents and potential entrants can do the same and bring the market back into competitive equilibrium. In contrast, when multipoint competitors benefit from economies of scope, they obtain a cost advantage over single business incumbents or potential entrants, in that they can raise prices to a level that does not allow for output expansion by single point incumbents and potential entrants. Therefore, the opportunity to reduce rivalry using tacit approaches is greater when multipoint competitors meet in multiple businesses marked by strong opportunities for resource sharing and scope economies.

Seller concentration

Seller concentration, which is the number of competing firms in a business and the pattern of dispersion of total industry sales across theses competitors, is important predictor of competitive behavior (Jayachandran et al., 1999). When seller concentration is low, firms cannot deter each other, because no firm has a sufficient stake in the business. Furthermore, the difficulty that firms encounter in gaining familiarity with each other when there are many competitors suggests that multipoint contacts may not be effective as learning mechanisms that encourage tacit collusion. Retaliatory moves in less concentrated businesses also likely influence many firms, which may escalate rivalry.

In conditions of high seller concentration, because a significant share of total market revenues is dispersed across fewer firms, these firms should be more likely to refrain from intense rivalry, because doing so puts their sizable revenues and market shares at stake. For example, the absolute financial losses from an aggressive price war may be higher than they would be in conditions of low seller concentration. Therefore, the potential for higher losses, which already exists when seller concentration is high, combined with increased opportunities for retaliation provides a strong motivation for deterrence in multipoint competition. Furthermore, firms should be more familiar with each other, because with fewer competitors, they can monitor those competitors better. An implicit coordination of activities between firms may be easier, in that their familiarity enables them to recognize their interdependence. In effect, firms likely do not even require multipoint contacts to become familiar with each other or attain a position in which they benefit by refraining from intense competition. Concentrated markets may provide firms with necessary and sufficient conditions (i.e., familiarity and deterrence) for mutual forbearance, just as multipoint contacts do, and thereby substitute for multipoint contacts in creating conditions for tacit collusion. Multipoint contacts in turn may have little additional effect on forbearance in concentrated businesses.

Finally, in businesses marked by moderate concentration, firms may lack the necessary power to deter rivals or the familiarity to coordinate activities tacitly. Hence, multipoint contacts may provide the best means to foster mutual forbearance. That is, multipoint contacts should be more likely to ensure mutual forbearance in businesses with moderate concentration (Bernheim & Whinston, 1990) compared with businesses of high or low concentration. Empirical support for this argument comes from both Alexander (1985) and Feinberg (1985). Furthermore, Gimeno et al. (1998) outline interaction effects of focal business concentration and multipoint contacts on intensity of competition, such that multipoint contacts appear most effective for enforcing mutual forbearance when the businesses are moderately concentrated.

CEO tenure

The length of the **CEO's tenure** on the job (Stephen et al., 2003) may affect the CEO's ability to foster (or hinder) strategic change in an organization. Stephan et al. (2003) observe that the attention paid to multipoint concerns changes over a CEO's tenure, such that newer CEOs experience different influences than do longer tenured CEOs with regard to their preferences for particular competitive actions. If their firm's multipoint contact levels are relatively low, longer tenured CEOs likely understand the advantages of entering into additional markets that contain current competitors, including the possibility of gaining a functional deterrent capability. Thus, longer tenured CEOs are likely to build additional multipoint ties. If the firm already has established a deterrent capability, these CEOs likely are aware of the negative consequences, should their firm's actions violate the tacit collusion implicit in these relationships, and thus they refrain from doing so. Overall, longer tenured CEOs are more sensitive to the implications of multipoint contacts and institute organizational actions consistent with firm specific levels.

Newer CEOs, in contrast, appear less sensitive to the potential reduction in aggressive competitive behavior that should accompany higher levels of multipoint contacts between firms. Three explanations relate to why newer CEOs do not act consistently with mutual forbearance theory. First, newer CEOs is more likely to be unaware of the benefits that stem from engaging in mutual forbearance when the firm has high levels of market overlap with its rivals. Second, new CEOs may misperceive his or her firm's position in its competitive network and thus conclude that the likelihood that a competitor will respond to an aggressive act is lower than it actually is. Third, the failure may be an example of executive hubris in action. Hayward and Hambrick (1997) note that hubris, the unrealistic perception of one's own capabilities, comes from several sources, including the media attention that newer CEOs may receive after attaining a position or their previous successes. In combination with their likely mandate to bring change to their organizations, these effects lead newer CEOs to reject the premise that violating the tacit interfirm agreement of mutual forbearance inevitably results in costly competitive retaliation. If newer CEOs believe that their firm can engage rivals directly and earn beneficial results in the long term, they move into markets that already have been ceded to their multipoint rivals but that they believe offer untapped potential.

BOX 13.2 MULTIPOINT CONTACT'S ASYMMETRY

In addition to multipoint contact, there is one other factor that affects a firm's competitive behavior: firm scope, or the number of product markets in which a firm has presence (Upson & Ranft, 2010). Scope is important because multipoint contact consists of the number of product markets shared with rivals divided by firm scope (Gimeno & Jeong, 2001). When rivals have different scopes, although the number of common product markets between them may be equal, their multipoint contact and resulting views of competition are asymmetric and will differ.

Upton and Ranft (2010, p. 51) provide an interesting example of the consequences of such an asymmetry: consider the rivalry between Hewlett-Packard (HP) and Dell. HP and Dell both compete in the desktop computer, laptop computer, and printer product markets, and also meet as rivals in several other product markets. However, their scopes differ. Dell's scope is relatively narrow, and centers mainly on computers and peripherals. HP's scope is broad, and includes computers and peripherals like Dell, but also includes such product markets as calculators, business services, commercial printers, and networking solutions. Between them, Dell meets HP in exactly the same number of product markets that HP meets Dell.

However, differing scopes indicate a difference in multipoint contact. Given the number of common product markets shared with Dell, HP's broad scope suggests that it has relatively low multipoint contact with Dell. Dell's multipoint contact with HP, however, is relatively high because of Dell's narrower scope. This affects competition because if Dell's multipoint contact is sufficiently high, it will seek mutual forbearance with HP. Meanwhile, if HP's multipoint contact is in the mid-range, it will seek to compete aggressively against Dell.

MULTIPOINT COMPETITION: STRATEGIC OPTIONS

Mutual forbearance is not the only behavioral result of multipoint competition; studies also investigate strategic options available to multipoint competitors. For example, multipoint competitors might reduce the price of their products in some markets, launch new products, increase their advertising spending, and enter new markets and businesses to gain footholds in their rivals' spheres of influence. They also might exit from businesses to avoid competitive escalations or reestablish the balance of power.

Multipoint competition and business/market entry or exit

A firm may benefit from entering a business and/or market because doing so holds a multipoint competitor in check, especially if that competitor has either entered one of its businesses or exhibits the potential to do so. For example, if a multipoint competitor enters a firm's business and tries to gain share by cutting prices, the firm can respond in kind and diversify into the attacker's home industry, in which it cuts prices. Recent consideration of entry rates into and exit rates from common markets (Ketchen et al., 2004) consistently shows that the relationship between multipoint contacts and market entry depicts an inverted U shape (Baum & Korn, 1999; Haveman & Nonnemaker, 2000; Stephan et al., 2003). According to Haveman and Nonnemaker (2000), consistent with the pattern shown in Figure 13.3, with fewer multipoint contacts, a firm attempts to obtain information about competitors by engaging them in many businesses. It also works to gain foootholds in multiple businesses so that it appears to pose a credible threat. Thus, low multipoint contacts speed entry into new businesses. However, as the multipoint contacts increase, each firm suffers vulnerability in multiple arenas, which should prompt managers to recognize the benefits of avoiding fierce competition. As a result, entry rates decline.

BOX 13.3 MICROSOFT'S ENTRY INTO THE HOME VIDEO GAME INDUSTRY

An example of market entry, designed primarily to keep a potential competitor in check, comes from the late 1990s, when Microsoft recognized that Sony could emerge as its rival (Hagiu, 2007). Although Sony functioned in a different industry (i.e., consumer electronics rather than software), Microsoft noted that the Sony PlayStation was, in essence, nothing more than a specialized computer and, even worse, one that did not use a Microsoft operating system. Microsoft thus worried Sony might use the PlayStation II, which came equipped with web browsing potential, as a 'Trojan horse' that would gain control of consumers' web browsing and computing habits from their living rooms, ultimately taking those customers away from PCs with Microsoft operating systems. The desire to keep Sony's ambitions in check was a significant part of the rationale for Microsoft's diversification into the video game industry, with the launch of its Xbox (Hill & Jones, 2004).

Haveman and Nonnemaker (2000) also note that multipoint contact effects are greater when businesses or markets are controlled by a few dominant multipoint firms. Single business firms also act with the awareness that they earn spillover benefits when their competitors are engaged in multipoint contacts. For example, to avoid attacking its multipoint competitors, a multipoint firm could decrease its level of advertising, which would benefit single business firms in addition to the multibusiness rivals. Finally, Baum and Korn (1999) find that rivals' size and scope influence business entry, such that a firm is more likely to enter a small firm's markets or the markets of firms with which they share only a few markets.

In contrast, the results pertaining to multipoint contact and market exit remain inconsistent. Boeker et al. (1997) show that a firm is less likely to exit a market that contains firms it competes with in other markets. These authors offer three dynamics that may lessen the likelihood of market exit: (1) lower rivalry (which decreases the need to exit) due to mutual forbearance, (2) the firm's desire to stay in the mutual market to maintain multiple venues from which to attack other firms, and (3) a firm's desire to stay in the market to gain more information about its competitors. However, Baum and Korn (1999) argue that multipoint contacts and market exit exhibit an inverted U shaped relationship, in which low multipoint contacts mean limited rivalry and limited incentive to exit. As multipoint contacts increase, firms experience stronger pressure to jockey for position and define which markets they should continue to hold and which they should sacrifice. Thus, exit rates increase. With greater multipoint contacts, market exit also may decline because of the resulting competitive stability.

Multipoint response strategies

Karnani and Wernerfelt (1985) have developed a predictive model of behavioral responses (or competitive moves) in multipoint competition contexts. They argue that a firm attacked in one business may choose to counterattack in another business, which increases the complexity of the decision situation (Furrer & Thomas, 2000). In turn, they identify four alternative competitive responses: do nothing, defend, counterattack, and total war. Karnani and Wernerfelt use the deregulation of the U.S. airline industry during the 1980s—which engendered greater competition and a shift of emphasis from non-price to price competition—as a case example to present their model. They note that in this context, there have been several instances of the following scenario:

> [A]n airline, say A, competes directly with another airline, B, on several routes. Airline A initiates an attack with a drastic price cut on one or more routes. How should airline B respond to this move? Airline B has, broadly speaking, four options: (1) do nothing, (2) cut prices on those routes on which airline A has cut prices, (3) cut prices on some other routes on which it competes with airline A or (4) cut prices on all routes on which it competes with airline A. In other words, the options are, respectively, do nothing, defend, counterattack and declare a total war.
>
> (Karnani & Wernerfelt, 1985, p. 88)

Doing nothing likely signals weakness and is unlikely to result in peace; rather, it probably means a loss of competitive position for Airline B. Declaring total war can be dangerous and costly for both airlines, leaving them vulnerable to attacks from other firms (e.g., Airline C). Because an airline's profitability depends on its market share in the routes for which it competes rather than on its share of the airline industry as a whole, an ignored price cut likely leads to a loss for the more expensive airline. Thus, the best option for Airline B probably is to defend its competitive position directly on the routes that Airline A attacks. This choice should stabilize in what Karnani and Wernerfelt (1985) call a 'limited war' equilibrium, such that the fighting remains within small or isolated regions. Alternatively, Airline B might counterattack by cutting prices on other routes for which it competes with Airline A, in which case it signals that it is ready for a total war if Airline A does not adopt a less aggressive posture. This latter option leads to what Karnani and Wernerfelt call a 'mutual foothold' equilibrium, such that each firm maintains a foothold in the other firm's market and thus has a 'stick' it can use to discipline the other firm. These different options and their respective equilibria appear in Table 13.1.

Karnani and Wernerfelt (1985) further argue that when the defender has reasonable alternatives, a mutual foothold equilibrium is likely in response to an attack by a competitor, because doing nothing signals weakness and encourages the attacker to increase competitive pressures. A total war is unlikely because of the threat of mutual destruction. If an attack strategy offers significant first mover advantages, a mutual foothold, rather than total peace, effectively becomes the stable equilibrium.

Table 13.1 Overview of responses in Karnani and Wernerfelt's model

Response	Illustrative action	Expected equilibrium	Expected stability
Do nothing	No price change	Implicit	Unstable
Defend	Match entrant's price, respondent's market	Limited war	Stable
Counterattack	Match entrant's price in one of entrant's markets	Mutual foothold	Stable
Total War	Underprice entrant in more than one market	Victory or mutual destruction	Unstable

Source: Adapted from Karnani & Wernerfelt (1985) and Smith & Wilson (1995)

BOX 13.4 TOTAL WAR BETWEEN WALT DISNEY AND AOL-TIME WARNER

Sometimes multipoint competition does not lead to mutual forbearance. Consider the conflict between the Walt Disney Company and AOL-Time Warner in the early 1990s. Disney operates in the theme park, movie and television production, and television broadcasting industries; AOL-Time Warner operates in the theme park and movie and television production industries, while also operating a significant magazine business (publishing *Time*, *People*, *Sports Illustrated*, and others). Disney spends millions of dollars to advertise its theme parks in AOL-Time Warner magazines. Despite this substantial revenue though, AOL-Time Warner initiated an aggressive advertising campaign, aimed at wooing customers away from Disney theme parks to its own. Disney retaliated by canceling all of its advertising in AOL-Time Warner magazines. Then AOL-Time Warner responded by canceling a corporate meeting that was to be held at Disney World. Disney in turn responded to AOL-Time Warner's meeting cancellation by refusing to broadcast AOL-Time Warner theme park advertisements on its Los Angeles television station. As suggested by Karnani and Wernefelt (1985), when multipoint rivals are not able to achieve mutual forbearance, competition is likely to turn into total war.

Source: Adapted from Barney (2007)

Smith and Wilson (1995) empirically tested the predictions from Karnani and Wernerfelt's (1985) model using a sample of 10 major domestic U.S. airlines for the period of 1983–1984. In 57 percent of the cases, firms did not respond at all to an attack. The defend strategy appeared in 10 percent of the cases, counterattack in 9 percent, and total war in 2 percent. Yet these authors also identify two additional responses: price leadership in the attacked market, which entails increasing prices after a competitor enters it (22 percent of the cases), and price leadership in another market (1 percent).

McGrath et al. (1998) suggest that a firm's resource allocation in multipoint competition can divert competitors' resource allocation patterns, which may enhance the firm's own sphere of influence without triggering an all out war. Specifically, they cite three competitive strategies, *thrust*, *feint*, and *gambit*, that should influence competitors' resource allocations. Their discussion of the three stratagems adds variations to and elaborates on Karnani and Wernerfelt's (1985) model and other extant work on strategic options in multipoint competition. *Thrusts* describe a significant, direct attack on a specific business, the purpose of which is to make competitors withdraw their resources because they determine that their further commitments in that business would be too difficult or expensive. A *feint* involves an attack on a focal business that is important to the competitor but not vital to the aggressor (i.e., not its true target business). The feint is followed or accompanied by the commitment of resources to the actual target business. To prevent a rival from dedicating resources to the target business, the firm engaged in a feint therefore tries to compel its opponent to divert resources to defend the focal arena. The third stratagem is what chess players call a gambit: a firm visibly sacrifices a position in a focal business, with the intention of enticing the competitor to divert resources into that business to enhance its sphere of influence there. The firm executing the gambit then can focus its resources on increasing its sphere of influence in another target business (in which the opponent concomitantly may be reducing its resource commitments). The result of a gambit, if accepted, is that both players attain enhanced spheres of influence, just in different businesses (McGrath et al., 1998).

As exemplified in Box 13.5, rivalry can be exacerbated when three, rather than two, rivals become multipoint competitors.

BOX 13.5 THREE RIVALS MULTIPOINT COMPETITION

In some industries, multipoint competition does not occur between two but three rivals. In such a situation, the intensity of rivalry is likely to relatively high, as tacit collusion is more difficult to achieve with two rather than one competitor. Ketchen et al. (2004, p. 779) provide an example of such a situation. As they explain, a flurry of competitive moves occurred in the shaving products industry in August 2003. Market leader Gillette launched a new three blade disposable razor. Its main rival, Schick, a subsidiary of battery giant Energizer Holdings, followed by introducing a four blade razor backed by a large advertising campaign. Gillette then sued Schick for patent infringement. Meanwhile, Rayovac Corporation acquired Remington Products, a third major shaving products firm, possibly allowing Rayovac to better compete with both Gillette (owner of the Duracell battery line) and Energizer in two different industries.

CONCLUDING REMARKS

As discussed in Chapters 4 and 6, market power is an important rationale for the existence of the multibusiness firms and an important motive for a firm diversification. Diversification provides market power not only to vertically integrated firms, as discussed in Chapter 10, but also to horizontally diversified firms, through mutual multipoint competition.

It is also interesting to notice that if diversification increases a firm's market power, this does not necessary lead to more rivalry. On the contrary, diversified firms are most likely to refrain themselves from using their power as it could be too damaging. Indeed, mutual forbearance between multipoint competitors is most likely to reduce the intensity of rivalry.

Another important implication of multipoint competition is the interrelationship between corporate level and business level strategy. When a multibusiness firm is engaged in multipoint competition, corporate level decisions, such as entering a new business or market, have important business level implications for its existing businesses, as its multipoint rivals may retaliate by reducing their prices or increasing their advertising in different businesses, with implications for the respective competitive advantages of the rivals in these markets.

Chapter

14

INTERNATIONAL DIVERSIFICATION

GLOBAL INTEGRATION AND LOCAL RESPONSIVENESS

In addition to the horizontal diversifications and vertical integration presented in Chapters 5 and 10, a firm may also diversify its activities internationally. An internationally diversified firm often is referred to as a multinational enterprise (MNE) or multinational corporation (MNC), for which the definition requires a firm that has substantial direct investment in more than one country (e.g., Bartlett et al., 2008; Caves, 1996; Peng, 2006). For example, CEMEX, a construction and material firm headquartered in Mexico employs 66 percent of its workforce and operates 35 of its 48 subsidiaries outside its home country (Hitt et al., 2006).

In this chapter, we argue that an international diversification strategy represents a special case of a more general diversification strategy (Dastidar, 2009: Denis et al., 2002; Fouraker & Stopford, 1968). As we described in Chapters 1 and 4, a firm is diversified when it is active in more than one business, such as according to the types of technology, customer needs, or customer groups (including customers from different geographic markets) it serves (Abell, 1980; Ansoff, 1965). Therefore, an international diversification can simply be seen as a diversification strategy in which the businesses are defined in geographic (i.e., country) terms.

The nations of the world possess different formal and informal institutions (North, 1990; Peng, 2003; Scott, 1995), as well as different factor endowments (Dunning, 1981; Porter, 1990), and such differences can provide firms with opportunities to benefit through unrelated diversification. Current globalization trends also enable firms to capitalize on similarities across countries through related diversification (see Chapter 5). The combination of forces that encourage related and unrelated international diversification strategies gives firms four generic value creating strategies (Bartlett & Ghoshal, 2000). However, if an international diversification strategy has the potential to create corporate value through economies of scale and scope and risk diversification, firms may easily over-diversify their international activities and thus destroy corporate value (Dastidar, 2009: Denis et al., 2002). Additionally, in contrast to product diversification, however, international diversification also offers new means for corporate value creation through access to foreign stakeholders, resources, and institutions (Hitt et al., 2006). Although doing business abroad increases uncertainty, international diversification is increasingly used by firms because it allows them to leverage their existing core competencies, gain unique knowledge, and access substantial growth opportunities in foreign product markets (Hitt et al., 2006).

In this chapter (see Figure 14.1), we first review some of the motivations that induce a firm to internationalize its activities, as identified in previous literature, and systematically compare those motivations with the rationales for diversification discussed in Chapter 4. We also describe the forces for global integration and coordination or local differentiation and responsiveness and relate them to a firm's related or unrelated diversification goals. Finally, we discuss the four alternative

International diversification

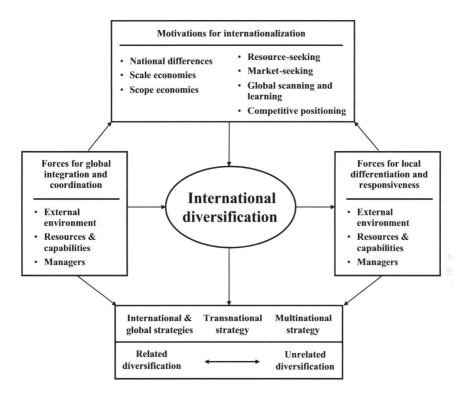

Figure 14.1 Internationalization framework

strategies developed by Prahalad and Doz (1987) and Bartlett and Ghoshal (1989, 2000) and compare them with the value creating strategies discussed in Chapter 5.

MOTIVATIONS TO INTERNATIONALIZE

If internationalization can be seen as a special case of diversification, the motivations for a firm to diversify internationally can be compared to the different rationales for diversification that we discussed in Chapter 2. That is, the main motivations for international diversification should be increased market power (Hamel & Prahalad, 1985; Teece, 1981b), the use of excess resources and intangible assets (Bartlett & Ghoshal, 1989, 2000; Caves, 1971, 1996; Mishra & Gobeli, 1998; Morck & Yeung, 1991; Peng, 2001), spreading risks (Doukas & Travlos, 1988; Garrod & Rees, 1998; Gomes & Ramaswamy, 1999), reducing transaction costs (Buckley & Casson, 1976; Dunning, 1977; Hennart, 1982a; Kogut, 1985; Rugman, 1979; Saudagaran, 2002; Teece, 1986), achieving economies of scale and scope (Eun et al., 1996; Grant, 1987; Levitt, 1983; Porter, 1985), and managerial hubris (Eun et al., 1996; Mishra & Gobeli, 1998; Saudagaran, 2002) (see Hitt et al., 2006 for a recent literature review of these motivations). Operating in an international rather than a domestic environment presents managers with supplementary opportunities, but the diversification logic remains the same.

The motivations for international diversification further are based on two fundamental mechanisms that provide the basis of any MNE's corporate advantage: exploiting differences in sourcing and market potential across countries and exploiting synergies through economies of scale and scope (Ghoshal, 1987).

National differences

In the absence of efficient markets, different nations' varied factor endowments (e.g., labor, land, materials) lead to inter-country differences in factor costs (Dunning, 1981; Kogut, 1985; Porter, 1990). Because different value creating activities, such as R&D, production, or marketing, use various factors to unique degrees, a firm might gain cost advantages by configuring its value chain and placing each activity in the country that represents the least cost for the most intensively used factors (Kogut, 1985). This is why many firms locate the labor intensive production operations in low wage countries such as China and those of Eastern Europe, despite the fact most of their customers are located in more developed countries. National differences also exist in output markets, marked by varying customer tastes and preferences, unique distribution systems, differing government regulations, and changing effectiveness for different advertising strategies. Consequently, a firm can earn higher prices for its output if it tailors its offerings to fit the unique requirements of each national market (Hout et al., 1982).

Scale and scope economies

International diversification provides firms with the opportunity to increase their scale and scope and thus reduce their costs. For example, firms successfully that developed highly differentiated products or proprietary assets for their home markets, can choose to go abroad by leveraging their products and assets to expand their markets and benefit from economies of scale (Caves, 1996; Douglas & Craig, 1989). The resulting higher volume should help these firms accumulate knowledge, which reduces their costs as they progress along their learning curve (Ghemawat, 1985). That is, the learning curve entails cost reductions that occur as *cumulative* volume rises. Unlike experience effects, scale effects, in principle, can be replicated quickly by, for example, building a larger plant, but experience must be built through time (Lieberman, 1984) and therefore provide a longer lasting competitive advantage. Furthermore, international diversification influences a firm's scale and learning economies through the presence of cost saving opportunities across countries. International economies of scope exist when it is less costly to serve two or more businesses or markets (i.e., countries) together than it is to serve them separately (Panzar & Willig, 1981). Firms like Coca-Cola and McDonalds are able to benefit form economies of scope by selling the same products in the same way under the same brands across a large number of countries. As we discussed in Chapter 4, economies of scale and scope provide two strong motivations for diversification, including international diversification (Chandler, 1990; Douglas & Craig, 1989).

Following Bartlett and Ghoshal's (2000) work, which builds upon these two mechanisms, we can classify the motivations for a firm's internationalization into four broad categories.

Resource seeking motives

Among the most important motivations that push firms to diversify their activities internationally is the need to secure key supplies (e.g., Caves, 1971). Behind this motivation lies the objective of reducing transaction costs (Teece, 1986). By investing abroad, firms can secure key supplies and protect themselves against the opportunism of foreign suppliers, by reducing the risks inherent to price volatility on open exchange markets (Bartlett & Ghoshal, 2000), as the oil market continually demonstrates. This motivation is similar to the rationales for vertical integration discussed in Chapter 10.

Another important trigger pertains to the ability to exploit factor cost differences and access low cost factors of production (Vernon, 1966). For example, in December 2008, Electrolux announced it would cut 3,000 jobs (5 percent of its global workforce) in different locations. These cuts represent part of a long term program to shift factory work from high cost countries to lower cost nations such as China and Mexico. Since 2001, Electrolux has been shutting down plants in Australia, the U.S., Denmark, Germany, and Spain while also opening new ones in Mexico, Poland, China, Thailand, Hungary, and Russia. Its plan was to enhance its operating earnings by shifting 50 percent of total production to low cost countries by 2010 (Marsh, 2008).

Market seeking motives

Internationalization may also reflect a search for new markets for the firm's products and services (Douglas & Craig, 1989; Perlmutter, 1969; Vernon, 1966). This motivation is particularly important for firms that have some intrinsic advantage, such as a technology based patent or strong brand image, that gives them a competitive advantage in foreign markets (Mishra & Gobeli, 1998; Morck & Yeung, 1991). Such fungible, intangible resources can be used across market and thus provide economies of scope (Furrer et al., 2004; Penrose, 1959; Teece, 1986). Furthermore, when confronted with market saturation at home, firms might internationalize their activities to use up their excess resources (Douglas & Craig, 1989; Vernon, 1980), which is consistent with a resource based argument for diversification (Peteraf, 1993; Teece, 1986). Finally, many firms internationalize their activities to reap additional sales that enable them to exploit further economies of scale and scope (Douglas & Craig, 1989).

Worldwide scanning and learning

Another factor that often appears critical to a firm's internationalization strategy is its *worldwide scanning and learning* capability (Vernon, 1980). A company with a presence abroad is more likely to be aware of alternative, low cost production sources around the globe, as well as new technologies or market needs that may stimulate new product development (Bartlett & Ghoshal, 1989, 2000). With a worldwide presence, a MNE gains an informational advantage that could encourage it to relocate sources more efficiently or develop more advanced product and process technologies (Kogut, 1985; Porter, 1990). For example, an information technology firm, regardless of its country of origin, that locates its R&D activity in the Silicon Valley benefits from a dynamic and stimulating environment that increases the likelihood that the firm will be able to identify technology and market trends at an early stage.

Competitive positioning

International diversification provides firms with important competitive positioning and market power advantages. For example, one controversial competitive strategic action taken by MNEs relies on the cross-subsidization of markets (see Chapter 2). Firms may also move abroad to pre-empt markets or resources, in order to secure a competitive advantage before the competitors (Bartlett & Ghoshal, 2000; Kim et al., 2004); or to match the competitive advantages of their rivals if those already moved abroad. More adaptable firms can capitalize on the potential advantages derived from international operations and use these strengths to play a strategic game, a type of *global chess* (Bartlett & Ghoshal, 1992; MacMillan et al., 2003). Firms that manage their worldwide operations as interdependent units and implement a coordinated worldwide strategy are the competitors in this competitive, strategic game, which is based on the assumption that a firm's competitive position in all markets is linked through financial and strategic interdependence (see Chapter 13).

BOX 14.1 PFIZER'S NEW GLOBAL STRATEGY

New York, March 5, 2009 – Pfizer announced plans to capture greater revenue in emerging markets in Latin America, Eastern Europe and Asia. The company will leverage its global scale and breadth of products to provide health solutions to the growing and untapped market of middle-income patients living in these markets. The Company pointed out four drivers that will help it expands in the $47 billion emerging Asian pharmaceutical market. Pfizer expects to reinforce its market leadership, increasing market share to 6% by 2012, up from 4% today. These drivers include expanding its existing presence in high growth markets, building leadership in oncology, tailoring portfolio offerings to local market needs and taking greater advantage of global manufacturing and R&D in Asia. For example, Pfizer plans to expand operations in China from the 110 cities it now serves to more than 650 cities. Growing established products (medicines that have lost or will soon lose patent protection), launching new products and reaching more patients will enable Pfizer to continue to capitalize on its strong base in China, a country expected to be one of the world's top five healthcare markets as early as 2010.

Forming Dedicated Business Unit for Established Products. The Company recently formed an Established Products Business Unit within Worldwide Pharmaceutical Operations, with the goal of achieving double-digit growth in the global market for established medicines. The newly formed unit will execute growth strategies tailored to the unique needs of branded emerging markets (such as China, India, Brazil and Russia), branded traditional markets (such as Japan, Western Europe, and South Korea), and intellectual-property-driven markets (such as the U.S. and Canada). The Company expects to increase market share by leveraging its existing portfolio through product enhancements and reformulations, pursuing new indications for niche markets, and intensifying late-stage lifecycle plans for its established medicines.

Source: www.pfizer.com

Beyond these motivations, which are based on the corporate advantages that a firm may gain from the international diversification of its activities, there are managerial motives for internationalization, similar to those for diversification (Saudagaran, 2002). Agency theory suggests that managers' choice to diversify internationally could result in an international diversification discount: A poorly performing firm may decide to diversify internationally to avoid greater scrutiny by shareholders in its home markets. Monitoring managers internationally is more difficult, and weak governance in host countries may facilitate value destroying investments, which would result in lower firm value (Dastidar, 2009). Jensen (1986) also points out that because managers' compensation often is based on the size of the assets they control, rather than the profits they earn, they might expand the size of the firm beyond that which maximizes shareholder wealth. Through international diversification, such managers can quickly increase the size of their firms. For example, foreign M&As might be an excellent tactic for managers who pursue growth and diversification at the expense of shareholders' interests. In an empirical study, Eun et al. (1996) find that the managers of the British firms in their sample often undertook negative net present value projects when they acquired U.S. firms, in support of this agency theory argument. However, when firm internationalization is based on managerial motives rather than economic motivations, its performance likely suffers compared with that of purely national firms (Eun et al., 1996; Mishra & Gobeli, 1998).

CHOICE BETWEEN RELATED AND UNRELATED INTERNATIONAL DIVERSIFICATION

An international diversification strategy may be a response to similarities among countries (i.e., related diversification strategy) or be motivated by differences among countries (i.e., unrelated diversification). For managers, the choice between related and unrelated international diversification depends on three sets of factors: environmental, internal (resource based), and managerial. Each set of factors may push a firm toward global integration and coordination of its activities or else toward local differentiation and responsiveness. The choice between related and unrelated international diversification also has consequences for the role the corporate headquarters as discussed in Chapter 8 (Ambos & Mahnke, 2010).

Forces for global integration and coordination

For global integration, a firm coordinates its activities across countries in an attempt to build efficient operations networks and take maximum advantage of similarities across locations, which enable it to benefit from economies of scale and scope (Kobrin, 1991; Luo, 2001). The forces that may push toward global integration and coordination, or external, internal (resource based), and managerial forces, are interlinked in what Bartlett and Ghoshal (2000) call an *expanding spiral of globalization* and Dicken (2007) refers to as *global shift*.

External forces

The external forces pushing toward global integration and coordination include the following:

- *Technological forces*, such as industrial development, improved transportation, and improved information management, which decrease the costs of global integration and coordination.
- *Social forces*, such as rising levels of income and consumer credit facilities, which contribute to worldwide consumerism and an increasing demand for global products and services.
- *Political and legal forces* that increase world trade and globalization by reducing barriers to international trade. Under the provisions of the World Trade Organization (WTO) and the General Agreement on Tariffs and Trade (GATT), barriers to trade have fallen substantially. Tariffs imposed by the developed countries fell from an average of more than 40 percent in 1948 to approximately 3 percent in 2005 (Griffin & Pustay, 2010). Furthermore, regional integration agreements such as the EU, North American Free Trade Agreement (NAFTA), the Southern Cone Customs Union (MERCOSUR), the Association of Southeast Asian Nations (ASEAN) Free Trade Area, and others have also dramatically reduce trading barriers between countries.
- *Competition* in many industries and markets increasingly is becoming global as the role of governments diminishes and free market forces play more significant roles.

Internal forces

To respond effectively to these external forces, firms develop corporate advantages on a worldwide basis using their resources and capabilities. In the pursuit of global efficiency, multinational flexibility, and worldwide learning, these resources and capabilities become internal forces that reinforce global integration and coordination. In a global environment, a globally integrated and coordinated firm can enhanced its *global efficiency* by increasing the value of its outputs (i.e., securing higher revenues), lowering the value of its inputs (i.e., lowering costs), or both. Furthermore, in a globalized environment, firms face an operating environment characterized by diversity and volatility. Therefore, a key element of worldwide competitiveness is *multinational flexibility*, which enables firms to manage the risks and exploit the opportunities that arise from the diversity and volatility of their global environment (Kogut, 1985, 1989). Finally, the diversity of a global environment exposes firms to multiple stimuli, through which they can develop diverse capabilities, and thereby this provides them with broader learning opportunities (Ghoshal, 1987). *Worldwide learning* then becomes a goal that pushes firms to coordinate and integrate their activities globally.

Managerial forces

In addition to external and internal forces, managerial motives may also push toward global integration and coordination. As discussed in Chapter 4, agency theory suggests that because managers' compensation tends to depend on the size of the assets they control, rather than the profits they earn, they likely integrate and coordinate worldwide activities beyond the point at which shareholder wealth would be maximal (Jensen, 1986).

Forces for local differentiation and responsiveness

National environments differ on many dimensions, and again, three sets of forces may encourage local differentiation and responsiveness across these environments. Such forces push firms to differentiate their activities to be more locally responsive and thus create corporate value. Local responsiveness represents an attempt to respond to specific needs in a variety of host countries (Luo, 2001).

External forces

Even when globalizing forces are strong, counterbalancing localization forces can be important (Bartlett & Ghoshal, 1989). National environments differ on many dimensions, such as per capita gross national product or industry specific technological capabilities. They also differ in terms of political systems, government regulations, social norms, and the cultural values of their citizens. These differences force managers to be sensitive and responsive to the national, social, economic, and political characteristics of the host countries in which they operate. Specifically, *cultural differences* across countries result in wide variations in social norms and individual behavior, which influence the effectiveness of different organizational forms and management systems (Hofstede, 2001). Cultural differences also appear in the form of nationally differentiated consumption patterns, including the way people dress or the foods they prefer. To build a corporate advantage in a world with such diversity, firms must find ways to respond to the local needs and opportunities created by cultural differences. The diverse *government demands* and expectations of home and host governments remain among the most severe constraints on the global strategies of many firms.

Internal forces

Two internal factors lead firms to differentiate their activities locally and to be more responsive: *transportation and coordination costs* and *new flexible technologies*. Although the benefits of global integration must outweigh the added costs involved in supplying markets from a central location, firms often forget that transportation costs consist of more than just freight charges. In particular, the administrative costs of coordinating and scheduling worldwide demand among various global scale facilities usually are quite significant. For some products, lead times are so short or market service requirements so high that scale economies may well be offset by other costs—fresh food and dairy products being an example of such products. However, developments in computer aided design and manufacturing, robotics, and other advanced production technologies have made the concept of flexible manufacturing a more viable reality. When linked to consumers' growing disenchantment with homogenized, global products, flexible production technology may offer MNEs a means to respond effectively to localized consumer preferences and national political constraints without compromising their economic efficiency. Dell, for example, launched build to order and mass customization trends in the computer industry, which traditionally sold only standard models. Dell allows customers to adapt their computers to their personal needs, which has significantly contributed to the company's worldwide success.

Managerial forces

A firm's senior managers may have strong beliefs that favor local differentiation and responsiveness (i.e., a dominant logic, in the sense of Prahalad & Bettis, 1986). This dominant logic might be based on their history, cultural orientation, or managerial philosophy (Devinney et al., 2000; Kobrin, 1994).

The role of the MNC headquarters

Consistent with the corporate strategy triangle presented in Chapter 1 and the role of the parent discussed in Chapter 8, it is critical to also ask the question: How do MNCs' headquarters add value (Ambos & Mahnke, 2010)? If we consider that international diversification is only a special case of corporate diversification, then the question of how headquarters add value to MNCs is closely linked to the concept of parenting advantage (Campbell et al., 1995). In other words, to justify its position as an intermediary between the local subsidiaries and the firm's shareholders, an MNC's headquarters, like any other corporate parent, should add value to the operations of its local subsidiaries. According to Campbell et al. (1995), parenting advantage depends on two crucial questions: (1) does the parent understand the business of its local subsidiaries? And (2) can the parent contribute to the resource and capability endowment of the local subsidiaries?

Parents that neither understand the local businesses nor are in a position to contribute to local operations in any meaningful way carry a high risk of value destruction. On similar grounds, a mere understanding of the local business without possession of the means to improve local operations is unlikely to produce value for the MNC (Mahnke & Pedersen 2004). Therefore, Campbell et al. (1995) conclude that parenting advantage requires both knowledge of the local context and the capabilities necessary to add value to the local units.

Moreover, depending on the choice between a related or an unrelated international diversification strategy, the role of the MNC headquarters will differ. Related international diversification will require high levels of coordination and strategic control, whereas unrelated international will require much a lower level of coordination and a more financial control. Accordingly, the role of the MNC headquarters and the way it creates value depend on the implementation of one of four worldwide corporate level strategies.

FOUR WORLDWIDE CORPORATE LEVEL STRATEGIES

A dominant conceptualization used to examine strategy in an international context is the integration responsiveness (IR) framework (Bartlett & Ghoshal, 1989; Devinney et al., 2000; Johnson, 1995; Prahalad & Doz, 1987; Roth & Morrison, 1990), which suggests that the forces for global integration and coordination and those for local differentiation and responsiveness simultaneously confront a firm that competes internationally. Therefore, the strategy to secure a corporate advantage in an international context must be framed by the response to or management of two imperatives: meeting local demands and capitalizing on worldwide competitive advantages (Roth & Morrison, 1990).

Figure 14.2 graphically depicts the IR framework. The vertical axis represents the potential benefits from the global integration of activities—benefits that largely translate into lower costs through scale and scope economies. The horizontal axis represents the benefits of national responsiveness—those that result from the country by country differentiation of product, strategies, and activities. These benefits essentially translate into better revenues due to more effective differentiation in response to national differences in tastes, industry structures, distribution systems, and government regulations. From these two dimensions, we can derive four generic corporate level strategies: an international strategy, a multinational strategy, a global strategy, and a transnational strategy (according to the terminology developed by Bartlett & Ghoshal, 1989).

International strategy

In early internationalization stages, many MNEs tend to think of their overseas operations as appendages whose main role is to support the domestic parent by, for example, contributing incremental sales to domestic manufacturing operations. Bartlett and Ghoshal (1898) label this approach the *international strategy*.

The strategy is consistent with Vernon's (1971) international product cycle theory. At an early stage of internationalization, product development for the domestic market creates items that subsequently are sold abroad; technology and other knowledge get transferred from the parent company to the overseas operators; and offshore manufacturing represents a means to protect the company's home market. This approach was and still is common among U.S. based MNEs such as Kraft, Pfizer, Procter & Gamble, and General Electric (Bartlett & Ghoshal, 1989). Although

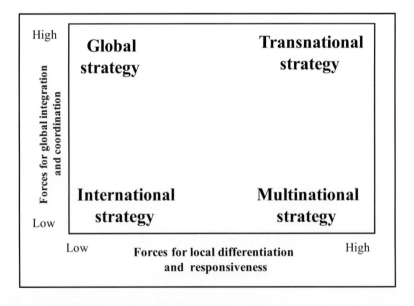

Figure 14.2 The integration responsiveness framework

Source: Adapted from Prahalad & Doz (1987) and Bartlett & Ghoshal (1989)

firms following this strategy have built some considerable strengths from their ability to create, leverage, and protect innovations developed in their home country, they often suffer from deficiencies of both efficiency and flexibility, because they do not benefit from either centralized, high scale operations or from high degrees of local responsiveness.

In the international strategy, key knowledge and skills moves from the home headquarters to foreign subsidiaries, which makes it the international equivalent of Porter's (1987) 'transferring skills' corporate strategy. Both share the same corporate level value mechanisms and the belief that lessons learned in one country can be transferred to another country to achieve synergy. As discussed in Chapter 5, transferring knowledge and skills between countries leads to a corporate advantage only if the similarities (i.e., types of relatedness) between countries meet three conditions (Porter, 1987): (1) the activities are similar enough that sharing expertise is meaningful; (2) transferring knowledge and skills pertains to activities important to a competitive advantage; and (3) the knowledge and skills transferred represent an significant source of competitive advantage for the receiving national subsidiary. If these three criteria are not met, the advantages of the transfer will be lower than the cost of transferring and coordinating them across countries. Thus, there will be no international diversification advantage.

Multinational strategy

A *multinational strategy* (also called multidomestic or multicentric) is implemented by firms that recognize and emphasize differences between national markets and operating environments. Firms following this strategy adopt a flexible approach to their international operations by modifying their products, strategies, and management practices country by country. The multinational strategy also relies on multiple, nationally responsive, business level strategies that have been developed and implemented by a portfolio of local subsidiaries worldwide.

The multinational strategy focuses primarily on national differences to develop a corporate advantage. Firms therefore tend to focus on the revenue side, usually differentiating products and services in response to national differences in customer preferences, industry characteristics, or government regulations. Conducting their activities within each country on a local basis also allows these companies to match costs and revenues on a currency by currency basis. Historically, many European companies such as Unilever, ICI, Philips, and Nestlé have followed this strategic model (Bartlett & Ghoshal, 1989); many of them still follow a similar multinational strategy in the modern era. The assets and resources of these firms are widely dispersed, which enables the overseas subsidiaries to conduct a wide range of activities, from development and production to sales and services. Their self-sufficiency typically means considerable local autonomy. Although these independent national units tend to be unusually flexible and responsive to their local environments, they also inevitably suffer from inefficiencies and an inability to exploit the knowledge and competencies of other national units.

Thus, the multinational strategy, which involves managing a portfolio of independent, locally responsive subsidiaries, is the international equivalent of Porter's (1987) 'portfolio management' corporate strategy, with which it shares the same corporate level value mechanisms. Local subsidiaries remain separate and independent to diversify risks. Furthermore, headquarters can subsidize cash poor subsidiaries with cash flow collected from cash rich subsidiaries. Firms following a multinational strategy often use M&As rather than internal development; as in Chapter 5, the MNE uses its expertise and analytical resources to attract firms with competent national managers who agree to stay on board but that lack the financial resources to become national leaders. The MNE therefore provides capital on favorable terms that reflect its corporate wide fundraising ability. It also introduces professional management skills and discipline. Finally, it provides high quality review and coaching, unencumbered by national and cultural biases (Porter, 1987).

International diversification

BOX 14.2 TOYOTA TAPS JAPAN FOR EXPORTS TO SMALL MARKETS

The persistent weakness of the yen has encouraged Toyota Motor Corp. to make Japan an export center that it can use to meet growing demand for automobiles in small markets around the world. According to Mitsuo Kinoshita, Toyota's executive vice president, meeting demand for autos in emerging markets can be difficult. Markets in the Middle East, Africa, and Central America are just too small for Toyota to justify opening plants to serve them, so even though "We're committed to producing vehicles where demand exists … you can't honor that in a market where we sell only 10,000 vehicles a year." Toyota's solution has been to combine demand in small emerging markets and produce cars in Japan, where the company already had excess capacity because of poor and lingering domestic demand.

Source: Reuters (2007)

Global strategy

Although the multinational strategy typically results in very responsive marketing approaches in different national markets, it also gives rise to an inefficient manufacturing infrastructure. Plants provide local marketing advantages or improve political relations rather than maximizing production efficiency (Bartlett & Ghoshal, 2000). Similarly, the proliferation of products designed to meet local needs decreases efficiency in design, production, logistics, distribution, and other functional tasks (Levitt, 1983). In a global operating environment with improved transportation and communication infrastructures and falling trade barriers, firms may benefit from creating products for a world market and manufacture them on a global scale in a few highly efficient plants. This approach is called a *global strategy*. The underlying assumption is that national tastes and preferences are more similar than different or that they can be made more similar by providing customers with standardized products for an adequate cost and that offer quality advantages over national varieties (Douglas & Craig, 1989; Levitt, 1983).

This global strategy therefore requires central coordination and control. Headquarters generally manages the R&D and manufacturing activities, and most strategic decisions also take place at the center. Firms adopting a global strategy depend heavily on their global efficiency, so they pursue various means to achieve the best cost and quality positions for their products. Many Japanese companies, such as Toyota, Canon, Komatsu, and Matsushita (Bartlett & Ghoshal, 1989), reflect this efficiency, as well as the related compromises in flexibility and learning. For example, concentrating manufacturing to capture global scale may result in a high level of inter-country product shipments, which could increase the risks of governmental intervention. Similarly, companies that centralize their R&D for efficiency reasons often find they are constrained in their ability to capture new developments in countries outside their home markets or leverage innovations created by foreign subsidiaries in the rest of their worldwide operations. Finally, the concentration (usually through centralization) of activities such as R&D and manufacturing to achieve a global scale exposes companies to high sourcing risks, particularly in terms of the exchange rate.

The global strategy of global integration and coordination to obtain benefits from economies of scale and scope, which involves shipping and marketing the same products all over the world, is the international equivalent of Porter's (1987) 'sharing activities' corporate strategy. The ability to share activities may provide a corporate advantage by lowering costs or increasing differentiation, but not all sharing leads to corporate value creation. Many MNEs encounter deep country resistance to even beneficial sharing possibilities. Thus, any sharing should involve activities that are significant for enhancing corporate advantage, not just any activity (Porter, 1987).

BOX 14.3 GLOBALIZING AND LOCALIZING MANUFACTURING AT TOYOTA

Since 1957, when Toyota began exporting the Crown to the United States, we have expanded the scope of our automobile sales across the entire globe. During the almost 50 years since we first began exports, Toyota vehicles have found their way to over 170 countries and regions throughout the world. As our exports have continued to develop so has the localization of our production bases, in line with our policy of "producing vehicles where the demand exists." Currently there are 52 bases in 27 different countries and regions. In addition, there are design and R&D bases in seven locations overseas, showing that "from development and design to production, sales and service, Toyota has now achieved consistent globalization as well as localization."

There are a number of hurdles that this globalization of production has to overcome. Among these the most important is "quality assurance," which requires that "no matter where Toyota vehicles are made, they have the same quality." To put it another way, we don't put a label on our vehicles which says "Made in such and such a country;" we put the same label on all vehicles which reads "Made by TOYOTA."

This means that we need to spread Toyota's manufacturing philosophy—the "Toyota Way"—to all of our overseas bases. And on top of this it is important that we minimize the necessary support that comes from Japan and let each of our overseas bases become self-reliant. For example, the Toyota plant that recently commenced production in Texas made maximum use of the know-how which has been cultivated over the past 20 years by the Toyota plant in Kentucky. This is just the latest example of how the localized "Toyota Way" is being passed on overseas.

Toyota believes that the way to achieve "quality assurance" and to "spread the Toyota Way" is by educating people: "Making things is about developing people." So, in 2003, we established the Global Production Center (GPC) within the Motomachi Plant in Toyota City. Furthermore, in 2006, we established regional GPCs in the United States, the United Kingdom and Thailand to carry out corresponding activities in the North American, European, and Asia-Pacific regions respectively.

Source: Senior managing director, Koichi INA, www.toyota.co.jp/en/vision/globalization/index.html

A strong corporate culture is also necessary to keep the national subsidiaries together and achieve synergies.

Transnational strategy

When both globalization and local adaptation pressures are strong, the dual imperatives become critical simultaneously (Bartlett & Ghoshal, 1989, 2000; Doz & Prahalad, 1991; Kobrin, 1991; Roth & Morrison, 1991). The MNE must be responsive to local needs but also capture the benefits of global efficiency. In such firms, key activities and resources can be neither centralized in headquarters nor decentralized for each country subsidiary that conducts its own local tasks. Instead, their resources and activities get dispersed and specialized to achieve efficiency and flexibility at the same time. These dispersed resources also may be integrated into an interdependent network of worldwide operations. To achieve worldwide corporate advantages, the firms need to manage costs and revenues simultaneously, recognize the importance of both efficiency and innovation,

International diversification

and acknowledge that innovations can arise in many different parts of the worldwide organization. This strategy is a *transnational strategy* (Bartlett & Ghoshal, 1989).

Instead of focusing on any specific subpart of issues, a transnational company focuses on exploiting each and every goals–means combination to develop layers of corporate advantage and exploit efficiency, flexibility, and learning simultaneously. To achieve this ambitious strategy, the transnational firm must develop a sophisticated, differentiated configuration of assets and capabilities (Bartlett & Ghoshal, 2000). It first decides which key resources and capabilities can be centralized within the home country operation, not only to realize scale economies but also to protect certain core competencies and provide the necessary supervision of corporate management. Basic research, for example, often appears as such a capability, so core technologies remain at home for reasons of strategic security as well as competence concentration. Other resources may be concentrated but not necessarily at headquarters; for example, world scale production plants for labor intensive products might be built in a low wage country such as Mexico or Malaysia. Or the advanced state of a particular technology may demand the concentration of relevant R&D resources and activities in countries with technological skills. Such flexible specialization complements the benefits of scale economies with the flexibility of access to low input costs or scarce resources, as well as the responsiveness associated with accommodating national political interests. Some other resources instead may function better if they are decentralized on a regional or local basis, either because the potential economies of scale are small or the MNE needs to create flexibility by avoiding an exclusive dependence on a single facility. Local or regional facilities can not only afford protection against exchange rate shifts, strikes, natural disasters, and other disruptions but also reduce transportation and coordination costs.

In this sense, the transnational strategy, which involves the pursuit of global integration as well as local responsiveness, combines the four corporate strategies identified by Porter (1987): an efficient internal capital market (worldwide transfer of cash flow from corporate headquarters), restructuring (activities may be centralized in a foreign subsidiary), sharing resources (to gain global economies of scale), and transferring skills (to achieve worldwide learning). However, even though this strategy offers great potential to increase corporate value, it also entails the great risk of getting stuck in the middle, because global integration and local responsiveness often require different skills and capabilities.

Table 14.1 summarizes the relationships between Porter's (1987) four generic corporate level strategies and Bartlett and Ghoshal's (1989) worldwide strategies.

Table 14.1 Relationships between internationalization and diversification strategies

	International strategy	*Multinational strategy*	*Global strategy*	*Transnational strategy*
Value creation mechanisms	Economies of scope	Local responsiveness	Economies of scale	Scale, scope, & responsiveness
Perceived level of relatedness between countries	Medium	Low	High	Varying
Sources of corporate advantage	Transferring skills and knowledge	Portfolio management	Sharing resources	Restructuring, sharing, & transferring
Main type of diversification	Related linked	Unrelated	Related constrained	Both related and unrelated

CONCLUDING REMARKS

In this chapter, we argue that worldwide strategy is primarily a special case of a diversification strategy. It is special in that it involves crossing national boundaries (which implies the need to deal with cultural differences and political actors), though these boundaries often are similar to the organizational cultural differences that appear when firms cross industry boundaries in their product diversification tasks. Worldwide strategies may be related or unrelated, depending on cultural distances and the assumptions made by the firms about the extent of these national or cultural differences. For example, the Netherlands and Belgium may be considered two related markets, where the Netherlands and Japan represent two unrelated markets. Yet the opposite also may be true, depending on the firm's perception of relatedness, as discussed in Chapter 6.

Chapter

15

CORPORATE GOVERNANCE

CONTROLLING TOP MANAGERS AND MEETING CORPORATE RESPONSIBILITIES

Corporate governance refers to "those administrative monitoring and incentive mechanisms that are intended to reduce conflicts among organizational actors due to differences in incentives" (Lubatkin et al., 2007, p. 43). In other words, governance concerns the structure of rights and responsibilities among the parties with a stake (i.e., stakeholders) in a firm (Aguilera & Jackson, 2003; Aoki, 2000; Usunier et al., 2011). Corporate governance organizes the relationships among stakeholders, which in turn determine and control the corporate level strategies and performance of firms.

Modern corporations, characterized as they are by the separation of ownership and managerial control, use managers as decision-making specialists who act on behalf of the firm's owners (Berle & Means, 1932; Chandler, 1977; Demsetz, 1983; Fama & Jensen, 1983). As such, they have some latitude (i.e., discretionary power) to make strategic choices that should be in the best interest of the firm's owners (Jensen & Meckling, 1976). They also are primarily responsible for the performance and sustainability of the firm (Barnard, 1938; Fligstein & Shin, 2007). However, self-interested managers may make corporate level strategic decisions that maximize their own personal power and welfare and minimize their personal risk rather than maximizing shareholder value (e.g., Amihud & Lev, 1981; Berger et al., 1997; Jensen & Meckling, 1976; Jensen & Murphy, 1990). In this chapter, we argue that in addition to shareholders, top managers are responsible to other stakeholders and, to some extent, to society at large (Carroll, 1999; Freeman, 1984). In this sense, corporate governance requires controlling the risk of opportunism by top managers as well as ensuring that the firm meets its corporate social responsibilities.

Agency theory pertains to the conflict of interest between shareholders and top managers (Berle & Means, 1932); it provides the dominant theoretical perspective on corporate governance systems. The potential areas of conflict between shareholders and managers include the election of directors, the supervision of CEO pay, and the firm's overall structure and corporate level strategies (Fama & Jensen, 1983). As we have discussed in several chapters of this book, diversification is one such corporate level strategic decision that may reflect an influence of managerial opportunism (Denis et al., 1997, 1999). For example, corporate diversification might enhance a firm's value, which would serve the interests of both shareholders and top managers. But it also might result in benefits only to top managers that shareholders do not share, in which case managers prefer more diversification than do shareholders (Hoskisson & Hitt, 1990; Montgomery, 1994) (see Chapter 2). Specifically, diversification likely increases the size of the firm, and size often relates positively to top managers' compensation (Cordeiro & Veliyath, 2003; Gray & Cannella, 1997; Wright et al., 2002). Moreover, diversification increases the complexity associated with managing the firm and its portfolio, such that managers might demand increased pay to deal with this complexity (e.g., Geletkanycz et al., 2003). Because increased diversification gives top managers a means to increase their compensation, they may be motivated to engage in ever more diversification (Finkelstein & Hambrick, 1989; Wright et al., 2002).

Several studies provide empirical support for this managerial compensation motive (Brenner & Schwalbach, 2003; Denis et al., 1997, 1999). As mentioned in Chapter 2, shareholders tend to prefer riskier strategies and more focused diversification, because they can reduce their risks in other ways, such as holding a diversified portfolio of equity investments. In contrast, managers cannot diversify their employment risk by working for a diverse portfolio of firms (Fama, 1980), which should cause them to prefer a higher level of diversification that increases their compensation and reduces their employment risk. According to agency theory then, shareholders must control the work of top managers to avoid self-serving opportunistic behaviors, which would be detrimental to their interests (Denis et al., 1997, 1999).

However, this argument relies on a key, but also controversial, assumption of agency theory—that is, managerial opportunism (Ghoshal, 2006; Ghoshal & Moran, 1996). In management literature, as well as economic and strategic literature, several assumptions persist about the goals managers pursue. For example, neoclassical economists (e.g., Jensen & Meckling, 1976; Williamson, 1975, 1985) assume that managers are opportunistic and only motivated by self-interest, but this assumption has been subject to frequent challenges. Davis et al. (1997) hold that most managers actually are highly responsible stewards of the assets they control and do not behave opportunistically. With this alternative view of managers' motives, they propose stewardship theory, according to which shareholders should install more flexible corporate governance systems to avoid frustrating their benevolent managers with unnecessary bureaucratic controls.

By focusing on the relationship between shareholders and managers, agency theory also takes a narrow view of corporate governance and the responsibilities of top managers. Stakeholder theory broadens this view by arguing that managers are responsible not only to shareholders but to the larger group of stakeholders (e.g., Freeman, 1984; Mitchell et al., 1997). However, when multiple stakeholders' interests represent ends to be pursued, managers must make strategic decisions that balance these multiple goals rather than just maximize shareholder value. Stakeholder theory in turn proposes that managers' goals should be developed in collaboration with a diverse group of internal and external stakeholders, even if they support potentially conflicting claims (Freeman, 1984; Mitchell et al., 1997). Furthermore, with regard to corporate governance, the stakeholder perspective asserts that managers should be controlled not just by shareholders but by other stakeholders as well.

Again, according to agency theory, managers are solely responsible to shareholders, so their actions must aim to maximize shareholder value: They should be accountable only for making a profit (Fligstein & Shin, 2007; Friedman, 1970). In this scenario, as Daily et al. (2003) outline it, corporate governance identifies ways to ensure effective strategic decisions, regardless of potential agency problems. However, if the number of stakeholders to whom managers are accountable increases, the scope of a firm's corporate responsibilities also increases. Carroll (1979, 1991) therefore argues that not one but four types of corporate social responsibilities exist: economic, legal, ethical, and discretionary (or philanthropic).

These four responsibilities also can be classified into two broad types: social (discretionary, ethical, and legal) and economic (Aupperle et al., 1985; Furrer et al., 2010). Carroll (1979) identified the environment as a social issue for businesses, but stakeholder theory (Freeman 1984; Mitchell et al., 1997) instead calls the environment a third dimension that pertains to firms' responsibilities to maintain ecologically sustainable relationships with biophysical and societal environments (Shrivastava, 1996). Managers' strategic choices therefore must reflect a compromise between various considerations—of which shareholder value is just one (McWilliams & Siegel, 2001).

Corporate governance also is a vast subject that could be (and has been) the object of a book on its own. In this chapter, we therefore limit ourselves to only those issues that pertain to corporate level strategies. Specifically, this chapter focuses on corporate governance as a mechanism designed to control managerial opportunism (Furrer, 2013). We start by presenting corporate governance based on an agency theory perspective and draw implications from its main assumptions. Then we start relaxing some of those assumptions. First, we mitigate the idea that every manager is opportunistic and present stewardship theory. Second, we relax the assumption that the ultimate goal of a corporate level strategy and managers' sole responsibility is the maximization of shareholder value and therefore offer stakeholder theory as an alternative. Finally, we discuss how to expand a firm's corporate responsibilities from making a profit to encompass broader economic, social, and environmental responsibilities.

CORPORATE GOVERNANCE: CONTROLLING MANAGERIAL OPPORTUNISM

The comparison of two broad approaches to corporate governance requires a global perspective: the Anglo-American versus continental European approaches (Becht & Röell, 1999; Hall & Soskice, 2001; La Porta et al., 1998). The Anglo-American approach gives power to investors and other stakeholders through legal protections, such as protections of minority rights and legal prohibitions against managerial self-dealing (Shleifer & Vishny, 1997). The continental European approach instead is based on ownership by large investors but participation by other stakeholders, which matches significant control rights with significant cash flow rights. Shleifer and Vishny (1997) argue that a good corporate governance system should combine both approaches, with both ownership concentration and legal protection of the rights of all stakeholders. Corporations in the U.S., Germany, and Japan rely on somewhat different combinations of legal protections and concentrated ownership, but they generally possess at least some elements of both; in stark contrast, countries with weak governance systems usually lack at least one of these two elements (Shleifer & Vishny, 1997).

Diversified firms in particular commonly use three internal and one external governance mechanism: (1) ownership concentration, as represented by the types of shareholders and their different incentives to monitor managers, (2) the board of directors, and (3) executive compensation, as well as (4) the market for corporate control, as we discussed in Chapter 2.

Internal governance

Ownership concentration

The relative amount of stock owned by individual shareholders and institutional investors determines the ownership concentration (Hitt et al., 2004). In general, diffuse ownership, characterized by a large number of shareholders, each of which owns a few shares, produces weak monitoring of managers' decisions, because these diffuse shareholders cannot effectively coordinate their actions. Without sufficient monitoring, managers might pursue strategic decisions that harm shareholder value, such as over-diversification. Empirical evidence confirms that ownership concentration is associated with lower levels of firm product diversification (Chen & Ho, 2000; Hoskisson et al., 1994). That is, higher degrees of ownership concentration, marked by the presence of large block shareholders that own more than 5 percent of the firm's shares, increase the likelihood of effective controls on managers' strategic decisions to maximize shareholder value.

Ownership concentration as a governance mechanism has recently received considerable interest, because large block shareholders, such as institutional owners (e.g., financial institutions, pension funds) have become increasingly active, especially in their demands that firms adopt effective governance mechanisms to control managerial decisions (Coles et al., 2001).

The board of directors

This group of elected individuals is primarily responsible to support owners' interests by formally monitoring and controlling the firm's top level executives (Rebeiz, 2001; Seward & Walsh, 1996). Boards have the power to direct the affairs of the firm, punish and reward managers, and protect shareholders' rights and interests (Mallette & Hogler, 1995). Thus, boards of directors must be structured appropriately to protect shareholders from managerial opportunism.

Generally, there are three types of board members or directors:

- Insiders are active top managers of the firm, elected to the board because they are a source of information about the firm's operations (Baysinger & Hoskisson, 1990; Hoskisson et al., 2002).
- Related outsiders have some relationship with the firm or its managers, contractual or otherwise, but they are not involved with the operational activities of the firm.
- Outsiders provide independent counsel to the firm and may hold top level managerial positions in other firms.

Recent criticisms regarding failures by boards of directors to protect shareholders effectively suggest that insiders dominate boards. When boards contain a significant percentage of insiders, they may tend to provide relatively weak monitoring and control of managerial decisions (Westphal & Milton, 2000). Proposed reforms would ensure that independent outside directors represented a significant majority of the total membership of a board.

Executive compensation

This governance mechanism aims to align the interests of managers and shareholders through salaries, bonuses, and long term incentive compensation, such as stock awards and options (Gomez-Mejia & Wiseman, 1997; Miller et al., 2002). As we discussed in Chapter 10, the use of longer term pay helps reduce potential agency problems by aligning the time horizon of managers and shareholders (McGuire & Matta, 2003; Sanders & Carpenter, 1998). Similarly, by making managers part owners of the firm, stock option plans can align their interests with those of their co-owners, the shareholders.

External governance

The market for corporate control

This external governance mechanism becomes active when a firm's internal controls fail (Coff, 2002; Hitt et al., 1996; Walsh & Kosnik, 1993). It involves potential owners seeking to acquire undervalued firms, replace ineffective top management teams, and thereby earn above average returns on their investments (Hitt et al., 1996). Because ineffective managers of the undervalued firms will be replaced after a firm takeover, they have a constant incentive to work to support the best interest of the actual shareholders and maximize the firm's stock market value.

Williamson (1975) argues that a multidivisional structure also could be a governance device for ensuring the efficient management of large firms with diffuse shareholdings. However, Hoskisson and Turk (1990) suggest that even if multidivisional structures are adequate to govern division managers (see Chapter 9), corporate managers in such firms may still realize weak governance features, such as diffuse shareholdings and compensation plans that shift risk to managers. Because these managers have an incentive to increase firm size (to increase their compensation) and the other governance mechanisms have not adequately constrained them, excessive diversification may result (Hoskisson et al., 1994). In some cases, such as Enron and WorldCom, these mechanisms were proven relatively inefficient, which triggered various governments to develop more restrictive legislations to control managers. In the U.S., one of the laws intended to exert such control is the Sarbanes-Oxley Act of 2002 (see Box 15.1); other countries have taken similar initiatives.

BOX 15.1 SARBANES-OXLEY ACT OF 2002

The Sarbanes-Oxley Act was signed by President George W. Bush on July 30, 2002. Among other important clauses, the Act states that a firm's CEO and CFO (chief financial officer) must certify every report that contains financial statements. The certification acknowledges that both top managers have reviewed the report, which means they attest that the information does not include untrue statements or omit pertinent information. Furthermore, because it reflects these officers' knowledge, the report should be a reliable source regarding the firm's financial condition and operations for the period represented. The certification thus makes the officers responsible for establishing and maintaining internal controls, and therefore, they must be aware of any material information relating to the firm. The officers also must evaluate the effectiveness of internal controls within 90 days of the release of the report and present their conclusions. They have to disclose any fraudulent material, deficiencies in the reporting, or problems with the internal controls to the firm's auditors and auditing committee. Finally, these officers are responsible to communicate any changes to the firm's internal controls or factors that could affect them.

Strict penalties punish violations of the Sarbanes-Oxley Act. If a firm must restate its financial statements due to noncompliance, the CEO and CFO must relinquish any bonus or incentive-based compensation or realized profits they earned from the sale of securities during the subsequent 12-month period. Other forms of securities fraud, such as destruction or falsification of records, can result in fines and prison sentences of up to 25 years.

Source: Adapted from Pearce and Robinson (2007, pp. 60–63)

STEWARDSHIP THEORY: RELAXING THE OPPORTUNISM ASSUMPTION

Agency theory assumes, perhaps erroneously, that managers left on their own will behave opportunistically and reduce the wealth of their shareholders. But maybe most managers are highly responsible stewards of the assets they control (Davis et al., 1997). This alternative view is referred to as stewardship theory (Davis et al., 1997; Donaldson & Davis, 1991).

Stewardship theory derives from psychology and sociology rather than economics and suggests that when a manager has the choice between self-serving and pro-organizational behavior, this steward's behavior will not depart from the interests of the firm. Because most managers, as Davis et al. (1997) argue, act as stewards, they seek to improve their firm's performance, satisfy most stakeholder groups, and adopt pro-organizational motives that serve shareholders in the longer term (Angwin et al., 2004).

According to Davis et al. (1997), who developed stewardship theory, the rational steward's behavior is ordered such that pro-organizational, collectivistic behaviors offer greater utility than do individualistic, self-serving behaviors; agency theory instead assumes an economic manager who is self-interested and opportunistic. The behavior of the steward is collective and seeks to attain the objectives of the whole (e.g., sales growth, profitability) rather than just the objectives of the managers or even just their shareholders (e.g., stock market value). Furthermore, the potential multiplicity of stakeholders' objectives means a steward's behavior is organizationally centered, focused on the long term survival of the firm rather than the short term profitability preferred by managers and shareholders.

On several other dimensions, agency theory assumptions differ from those of stewardship theory, especially in terms of psychological factors and situational factors (Davis et al., 1997). The fundamental difference between agency and stewardship theories with respect to psychological factors derives from to the different 'model of man' they describe. The two models—self-serving versus collective serving—produce divergent assumptions about top managers' motivation, identification, and use of power. In terms of personal motivation, stewards are more likely to be motivated by higher order needs (i.e., growth, achievement, and self-actualization) and intrinsic factors, whereas agents are motivated by lower order and economic needs (i.e., physiologic, security, and economic) and extrinsic factors. Stewards also tend to identify with the organization and its owners; agents are more likely to identify with other top managers. In hierarchical relationships, stewards use personal sources of power, such as referent and expert power, and agents rely on institutional sources of power, such as legitimate, coercive, or reward based power.

Among the situational factors that differentiate agency and stewardship theories, differences in management philosophies are particularly important. Agency theory is better adapted to situations in which managers take a control perspective (i.e., require control mechanisms to reduce risks, have a short term perspective, or focus on cost control objectives); stewardship theory works better in situations that require managers to be involved (i.e., use trust to control risks, have a long term perspective, and focus on performance enhancements). Davis et al. (1997) also find cultural differences between CEOs' behaviors. That is, individualistic, high power distance cultures likely push managers to become agents, whereas collectivistic, low power distance cultures favor stewards, as Table 15.1 summarizes.

Table 15.1 Differences between agency and stewardship theories

	Agency theory	Stewardship theory
Model of man	Economic	Self-actualizing
Behavior	Self-serving/opportunistic	Collective serving
Psychological mechanisms		
Motivation	Lower order/economic needs (physiologic, security, economic) Extrinsic	Higher order needs (growth, achievement, self-actualization) Intrinsic
Social comparison	Other managers	Owners
Identification	Low value commitment	High value commitment
Power	Institutional (legitimate, coercive, reward)	Personal (expert, referent)
Situational mechanisms		
Management philosophy	Control oriented	Involvement oriented
• Risk orientation	Control mechanisms	Trust
• Timeframe	Short term	Long term
• Objective	Cost control	Performance enhancement
Cultural values	Individualism High power distance	Collectivism Low power distance

Source: Adapted from Davis et al. (1997)

Davis et al. (1997) argue that the choice between agency and stewardship relationships is similar to the decision in a prisoner's dilemma: Based on their psychological characteristics and the situational factors, both managers and owners influence the nature of the relationship. The owners make assumptions about managers' behaviors as agents or stewards, and managers decide to behave as agents or stewards based on their assumptions about the owners' behavior. We illustrate the nature of this dilemma in Figure 15.1.

When both the principal and the manager choose an agency relationship, the result is a true principal–agency relationship that is likely to achieve the expectations of both parties. The agency relationship minimizes potential losses to each party. The manager uses his or her discretion to act opportunistically and must be controlled by the owners, so the presence of controls ensures minimal agency costs. Both parties have similar (mistrustful) expectations of the relationship.

When both the principal and the manager choose a stewardship relationship, the result is a true principal–steward relationship that maximizes the performance of the relationship. In this situation, the manager works to fulfill the purposes and objectives of the organization. Likewise, the principal chooses to create a stewardship situation that is involvement oriented and empowering. Controls are not necessary and minimal, and the mutual gains are high.

The dilemma occurs due to the possibility of a divergent choice by either party. If the principal chooses an agency relationship but the manager selects a steward relationship, the result is a very frustrated manager who feels betrayed by the principal. When stewards are controlled as if they were agents, even though they are acting as stewards, they cannot enjoy the internal rewards they desire, which may prompt them to engage in anti-organizational behaviors. In contrast, if the

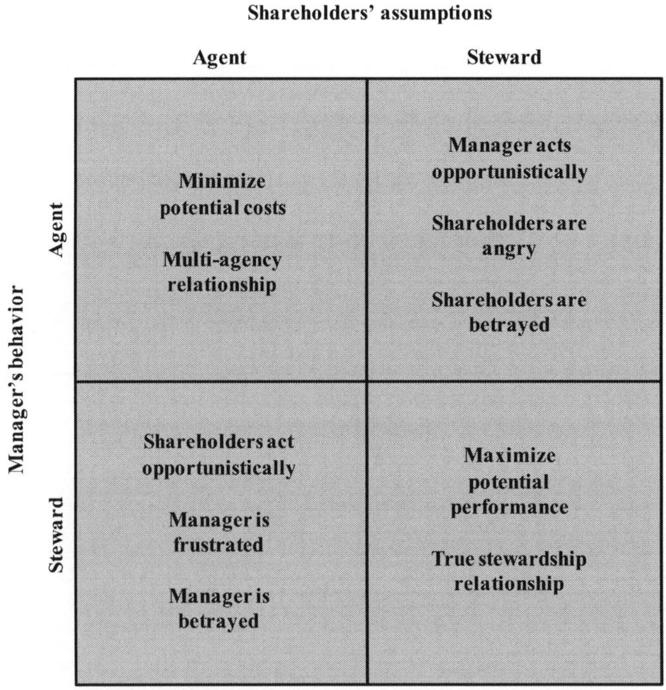

Figure 15.1 Owner–manager prisoner's dilemma

Source: Adapted from Davis et al. (1997)

principal chooses a steward relationship and the manager chooses an agency relationship, the manager acts opportunistically and takes advantage of the principal. The principal then feels betrayed and angry and likely increases controls radically, withdraws from the situation, or attempts to remove the manager.

Because the dilemma involves high levels of risk for both parties, a true stewardship relationship, the most beneficial form, often gets replaced by a suboptimal agency relationship, which is less risky for both parties. The highest joint utility derives from the principal–steward relationship, in which both parties choose the steward relationship, but the least risk of betrayal is in the principal–agent relationship.

STAKEHOLDER THEORY: RELAXING THE SHAREHOLDER VALUE MAXIMIZATION ASSUMPTION

In the mid-1980s, a stakeholder approach to strategy emerged, contesting the assumption that maximizing shareholder value should be the sole goal of corporate level strategy (Clarke, 1998; Freeman, 1984; Freeman & McVea, 2001). This approach argues that in developing the firm's corporate level strategy, managers must recognize the legitimate rights of all the firm's claimants, including not only shareholders but also other stakeholders affected by the firm's actions, such as employees, customers, suppliers, governments, unions, competitors, local communities, and the general public. Each of these interest groups has justifiable reasons to expect the firm to satisfy its claims in a responsible manner.

As Figure 15.2 shows, Freeman (1984, p. 46) also broadened the scope of corporate level strategy beyond its traditional economic roots by defining stakeholders as "any group of individuals who can affect or is affected by the achievement of [firm]'s objectives." This definition offers an extremely wide range of possibilities regarding who or what are really stakeholders. Despite the

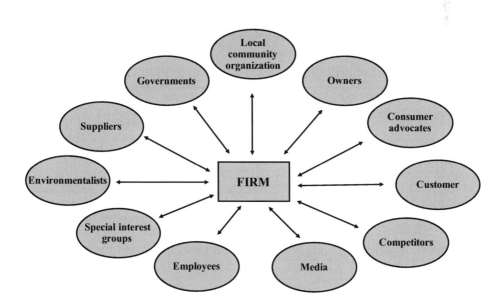

Figure 15.2 A firm's stakeholder groups

Source: Adapted from Freeman (1984)

use of different definitions by various authors (e.g., Clarkson, 1995; Mitchell et al., 1997), there are no fundamental disagreements about the kind of entity that constitutes stakeholders (Mitchell et al., 1997), such that a stakeholder can refer to persons, groups, neighborhoods, firms, institutions, societies, or even the natural environment.

The idea of stakeholder theory or a stakeholder approach to corporate level strategy suggests that managers must formulate and implement strategies that satisfy all, but only, those groups that have a stake in the firm's activities (Freeman & McVea, 2001). The central task in this strategic process is to manage and integrate the various relationships and interests of shareholders, employees, customers, suppliers, governments, unions, competitors, local communities, the general public, and the like. In doing so, stakeholder theory strongly challenges the assumption that the only goal of managers in developing and implementing the firm's corporate level strategies is to maximize shareholder value.

The main strategic issue then becomes the different claims of stakeholders, which often come into conflict. Shareholders require appropriate returns on their investment; employees seek broadly defined job satisfaction; customers want value in what they pay for; suppliers seek dependable buyers; governments demand adherence to legislation; unions seek benefits for their members; competitors require fair competition; local communities want the firm to be a responsible citizen; and the general public expects the firm to improve, or at least not harm, the overall quality of life.

From these definitions and assumptions, stakeholder theory developed as four management research streams: corporate planning, system theory, corporate social responsibility, and organization theory (Freeman & McVea, 2001). The corporate social responsibility stream is most relevant for our discussion of corporate governance. From this perspective, stakeholder theory asks: what responsibility do top managers have to stakeholders? (Freeman et al., 2004).

CORPORATE RESPONSIBILITIES: ECONOMIC, SOCIAL, ETHICAL, AND PHILANTHROPIC

In the neoclassical economic tradition, the only corporate responsibility is to make a profit (Friedman, 1970). However, it is important to recognize that more than ever before, stakeholders including customers, employees, investors, and local communities expect firms to play a role in contributing to the resolution of social and environmental issues, such as climate change, energy shortages, diversity, and health. These stakeholders' expectations create social responsibilities for firms (Freeman & McVea, 2001).

The concept of corporate social responsibility (CSR) has a long and diverse history in management literature (for overviews, see Carroll, 1999; Jamali & Mirshak, 2007; Michael, 2003; Moir, 2001; Wood, 1991), prompting several varied definitions and conceptualizations (Carroll, 1999). Following McWilliams and Siegel (2001), we define CSR as actions that attempt to further some social good, beyond the interest of the firm and the requirements of the law.

We also adopt Carroll's (1979, 1999) four types of corporate social responsibilities: economic, legal, ethical, and discretionary (or philanthropic). Economic responsibilities refer to the business's financial performance and the provision of goods and services. Legal responsibilities involve compliance with societal laws and regulations. Ethical responsibilities relate to adherence to societal moral codes of conduct. Discretionary responsibilities require voluntary involvement in and support of wider societal entities (see Figure 15.3).

Even if the broader stakeholder perspective establishes these different corporate responsibilities as important, they are not perceived as equally important by managers. Carroll's (1979, p. 499) graphical representation of the four types of corporate responsibilities suggests a weighting of 4-3-2-1 for economic, legal, ethical, and philanthropic responsibilities, respectively (see Figure 15.3). Using a forced choice scale, Aupperle et al. (1985) have empirically measured the relative

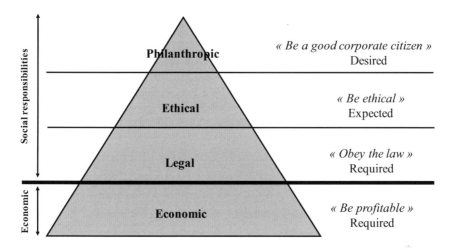

Figure 15.3 A pyramid of corporate social responsibilities
Source: Adapted from Carroll (1979, 1999)

importance of the four corporate responsibilities among a sample of U.S. CEOs and confirm Carroll's (1979) ranking; their respondents clearly place the most emphasis on economic responsibilities. When these authors regrouped the four responsibilities into broader social (discretionary, ethical, and legal) and economic dimensions, the non-economic responsibilities in combination took much greater weight than the singular economic responsibilities.

Pinkston and Carroll (1994) replicated Aupperle et al.'s (1985) study with a sample of managers from multinational subsidiaries located in the U.S. but with headquarters in France, Germany, Japan, Sweden, Switzerland, the U.K, and the U.S. They found similar rankings of the four corporate responsibilities across countries (in descending order: economic, legal, ethical, philanthropic), with the exceptions of Germany and Sweden, which accorded similar priority to legal and economic responsibilities. During the ten year span separating these two studies, the different corporate responsibilities appear to have retained the same priority, regardless of the firm's country of origin (though all were located in developed, Western countries), but the gap between economic and legal responsibilities appears to have become smaller (Pinkston & Carroll, 1996). Overall then, the perceived importance of social (i.e., non-economic) responsibilities has been increasing, or else the importance of economic responsibilities has been decreasing.

Later, Maignan et al. (1999) have revealed that U.S. marketing managers and executive MBA students perceive legal and ethical responsibilities as more important than economic responsibilities; their ranking prioritizes, in descending order, legal, ethical, economic, and philanthropic responsibilities. Furthermore, in a cross national study of consumers, Maignan and Ferrell (2003) determined that U.S. consumers rank the importance of corporate responsibilities in the following decreasing order of importance: (1) economic and legal, (2) ethical, and (3) philanthropic. This ranking differs significantly from that provided by French consumers: (1) legal, (2) ethical, (3) philanthropic, and (4) economic; and German consumers: (1) legal and ethical, (2) philanthropic, and (3) economic.

Although Carroll (1979) also identified the environment as a social issue for businesses, stakeholder theory (Freeman, 1984, Mitchell et al., 1997) considers environmental corporate responsibility a different dimension that pertains demands firms engage in ecologically sustainable relationships with both biophysical and societal environments (Shrivastava, 1996). Regarding these attitudes toward corporate environmental responsibilities, a few studies indicate their relative importance also may vary. Dunlap et al. (1993) show that respondents in industrialized countries are more likely to assert business and industry should have primary responsibility for solving environmental problems than are respondents in developing countries. These results receive support from Schnaiberg and Gould (1994), who find a higher level of pro-environmental attitudes and behaviors in advanced industrialized countries.

Taken together, these studies indicate that perspectives on the relative importance of the different types of corporate responsibilities appear to evolve over time. The perceived importance of non-economic (social and environmental) responsibilities is increasing, while the importance of economic responsibilities is decreasing. However, meeting its corporate social responsibilities requires managers and firms implementing a range of practices, including engagement in community activities, reducing environmental impact, and transparent corporate governance practices. Each of these practices may respond to different stakeholder groups' expectations and thus their implementation may have a separately identifiable impact upon firm performance (Brammer & Pavelin, 2006). For instance, Orlitzky et al.'s (2003) meta-analysis found that corporate environmental responsibility activities have a weaker relationship with firm performance than do all other dimensions of corporate social responsibility. Never the less, firms and their managers are entering in a new era where their integrity plays a larger role and their responsibility covers a larger spectrum.

CONCLUDING REMARKS

Corporate governance pertains to the structure of rights and responsibilities among the parties with a stake (i.e., stakeholders) in a firm (Aguilera & Jackson, 2003; Usunier et al., 2011). In this chapter, we have argued that beyond shareholders, managers are responsible toward various stakeholders and society at large (Carroll, 2001; Freeman, 1984). A just society is constructed only when people, acting rationally, realize that their self-interests are inextricably intertwined with those of others (Rawls, 1999), therefore, the assumption that managers' sole responsibility is the maximization of shareholder value should be relaxed (Furrer, 2013). Moreover, corporate governance must entail controls of the risk of opportunism by managers but also assurances that the firm will meet its corporate social responsibilities. Managers must make strategic decisions based on a compromise across a variety of considerations; shareholder value is just one of them. However, integrating integrity within firms' corporate governance systems requires managers and shareholders to change their view about corporate responsibilities and several assumptions in management theory to be relaxed.

In this chapter, we argued that managerial opportunism, shareholder value maximization, and managers' main responsibility toward shareholders are theoretical assumptions that might have negative side effects on managers' integrity and, as such, might need to be relaxed or replaced. Moreover, we argued that the four different theoretical perspectives we briefly reviewed—agency theory, stewardship theory, stakeholder theory, and CSR perspective—systematically differ on these three assumptions and accordingly have different goals for corporate governance systems. Table 15.2 juxtaposes the four perspectives with their assumptions, and goals of corporate governance systems.

Managerial opportunism, shareholder value maximization, and the main responsibility of managers being toward shareholders are three important assumptions of agency theory. In such a system, managers must be controlled by shareholders with the help of governance systems that protect shareholders' rights. Stewardship theory relaxes managerial opportunism as a key assumption, but maintains shareholder value maximization and managers' main responsibility toward shareholders. This implies that even if managers' responsibility is still toward shareholders, it should

Corporate governance

Table 15.2 Comparison of the different approaches

Assumptions	Agency theory	Stewardship theory	Stakeholder theory	CSR perspective
Managerial opportunism	Yes	No	No	No
Shareholder value maximization	Yes	Yes	No	No
Managers' main responsibility toward shareholders	Yes	Yes	Yes	No
Corporate governance systems …	should protect shareholders' rights	should protect shareholders' and managers rights	should protect stakeholders' rights	should insure sustainability

Source: Adapted from Furrer (2013)

be assumed rather than systematically controlled, because such control could trigger managerial opportunism. Accordingly, corporate governance systems should protect both shareholders' and managers' rights. On top of managerial opportunism, stakeholder theory also relaxes the assumption of shareholder value maximization. Even if some variations exist between various streams of stakeholder theory, most assume that shareholders are important stakeholders, whose interests should be satisfied or, at best, only be maximized under the constraint of the satisfaction of the interests of the other stakeholders. This implies that managers' responsibility should be toward all stakeholders, not only shareholders and that corporate governance systems should protect the rights of the different stakeholders. Finally, the CRS perspective challenges all three assumptions of managerial opportunism, shareholder value maximization, and managers' main responsibility being toward their shareholder and argues that managers' integrity refers to their responsibility toward society to create economic, social, and environmental value (the triple bottom line) and that corporate governance system should insure sustainability along these three value dimensions.

Corporate level strategy must reflect a compromise across a variety of considerations; shareholders' value is just one of these.

GLOSSARY

Acquisition. When a firm purchases another firm. Acquisition could be friendly or hostile (i.e., hostile takeover).

Acquisition premium. The difference between the current market price of a firm's shares and the price the acquirer offers to pay or paid for those shares.

Adverse selection. A market situation in which buyers are more likely to choose products (or suppliers) with higher prices or of lower quality because of information asymmetry between buyers and sellers (Akerlof, 1970).

Agency problems. An agency problem occurs when parties in an agency relationship differ in their objectives.

Agency relationship. An agency relationship refers to relationship in which a party delegates decision authority to a second party.

Ambidexterity. Ambidexterity refers to a dynamic capability that allows a firm to build future new businesses, while operating in matures ones (O'Reilly & Tushman, 2004, 2008).

Barriers to entry. See **entry barriers**.

Best alternative test. This is a test proposed by Goold et al. (1994) for firms to decide to keep or divest a business unit. The test is stricter than Porter's (1987) better off test. Goold et al. argue that the appropriate benchmark for corporate value creation is not what would happen without a parent, but what the best available parent would achieve. Each parent should create more value from its businesses than could be attained by any alternative parent. The firm will maximize it corporate value by divesting any business which posses a best alternative parent.

Better off test. It is a test proposed by Porter (1987) to help firms to make decisions about their business portfolio. The better off test requires that a business unit should gain competitive advantage from its link with the firm or vice versa. The business unit should be better off (i.e., create more value) within the firm's portfolio than as a stand alone business. Business units that do not meet the better off test should be divested. Similarly, potential targets should also meet the better off test to be acquired by the firm. See also **best alternative test**.

Board of directors. Individuals elected by a firm's shareholders to monitor top managers' strategic decisions (Hitt et al., 2004). The members of a board of directors assume legal responsibility for the firm's activities.

Bounded rationality. Bounded rationality refers to human behavior that is "intendedly rational, but only limitedly so" (Simon, 1961, p. xxiv). Three factors bound or constrain manager's rationality: (1) the availability of information, which is limited and often unreliable; (2) the limited capacity of human mind to evaluate and process information; and (3) the limited amount of time that is available to make a decision. Therefore, even managers who intend to make rational choices are bound to make satisficing (rather than maximizing or optimizing) choices.

Glossary | **225**

Broad spectrum diversification. Wood (1971) used the SIC data to distinguish two distinct patterns of firm level diversification. She defined narrow spectrum diversification, or NSD, as expansion, other than vertical integration, outside a four digit SIC industry but within a two digit SIC industry. She also defined broad spectrum diversification, or BSD, as expansion, other than vertical integration, into a different two digit SIC industry. NSD is viewed as diversification closely related to a firm's core expertise and BSD as diversification less closely related to it (Lubatkin et al., 1993; Varadarajan & Ramanujam, 1987).

Bureaucratic costs. Bureaucratic costs can be defined as the costs of managing exchange within the firm (Williamson, 1985). They are the internal organizational equivalent of transaction costs. They include not just the costs of hierarchy, but also the inefficiencies that arise within hierarchies due to information processing problems in complex organizations (Hill & Hoskisson, 1987; Jones & Hill, 1988), incentive distortions (Williamson, 1985), and internal politics (Milgrom & Roberts, 1990a).

Business-level strategy. A business level strategy is an integrated and coordinated set of commitments and actions the firm uses to gain a competitive advantage by exploiting core competences in specific product markets (Dess et al., 1995).

Business. A business can be define as a set of goods or services that serves similar functions, is created by the use of similar technology, and/or is used by similar consumers (Abell, 1980; Abell & Hammond, 1979).

Business unit. A business unit is an organizational element or segment of a firm designed to serve a particular business. It is also called department, division, or a functional area. See also **strategic business unit** (SBU).

Capability. A capability is the capacity for a set of resources to perform a task or an activity in an integrative manner.

Chaebols. The name means business association in Korean and refers to a South Korean form of business conglomerate. *Chaebols* are large, usually family controlled, business group characterized by strong ties with government agencies. Among the several dozen large *chaebols*, some are powerful global multinationals owning numerous international enterprises, such as Samsung, Hyundai, and LG.

Chairman of the board. The individual who presides over the board of directors.

Chief executive officer (CEO). The top manager of the firm to all business unit executives report to. The CEO is responsible toward the board of directors for the firm's strategy formulation and implementation.

Collusion. Situation created when two or more firms in an industry coordinate their strategic choices to reduce competition in that industry. Explicit collusion is illegal in most countries, whereas tacit is tolerated. In multipoint competition situations, tacit collusion often leads to mutual forbearance.

Configuration. Configuration refers to a firm' multimarket scope, including its product, geographic, and vertical boundaries (Collis & Montgomery, 2005).

Conglomerate. A conglomerate is a corporation that is made up of a number of different, mostly unrelated businesses. In a conglomerate, one firms owns a controlling stake in a number of smaller companies, which conduct business separately. Each of a conglomerate's business units is run independently of the other business divisions, but the business units' management reports to senior management at the corporate headquarters.

Conglomerate discount. The conglomerate discount refers to the degree to which the value of a particular conglomerate, and by extension any firm, is less than the sum of its parts.

Conglomerate merger. Unrelated merger or acquisition where there are no vertical, horizontal, product, or market links between the acquirer and the target firm.

Coordination. Coordination refers to how a firm manages the activities and business that lie within the corporate hierarchy (Collis & Montgomery, 2005).

Concentric index. It is a measure of diversification, the concentric index measures the degree of distance or relatedness between industries. Weights are given based on industry sales shares and its value depends on the relations between the industries (Montgomery & Hariharan, 1991; Montgomery & Wernerfelt, 1988; Wernerfelt & Montgomery, 1988). The concentric index is measured as follows:

$$FDIVERS_k = \sum_i P_{ki} \sum_l P_{kl} d_{il}$$

where: P_{ki} = percentage of sales for firm k in industry i, P_{kl} = percentage of sales for firm k in industry l, and d_{il} = weight, such that $d_{il} = 0$ when i and l are four digit products within the same three digit SIC category, $d_{il} = 1$ when they belong to different three digit SIC groups but the same two digit group, and $d_{il} = 2$ when i and l are in different two digit SIC categories.

Core capability. See **core competence**.

Core competence. A set of differentiated skills, complementary assets, and routines that provide the basis for a firm's competitive capacities and sustainable advantage in a particular business (Teece et al., 1997).

Core rigidity. Core rigidities are the flip side of core capabilities (Leonard-Barton, 1992, p. 118). They are core capabilities—i.e., values, skills, managerial systems, and technical systems— that served the firm well in the past, but that have become inappropriate (Leonard-Barton, 1992). As they are deeply embedded knowledge sets, they actively create problems, such as inertia.

Corporate headquarters. The staff functions and executive management with responsibility for, or providing services to, the whole of (or most of) the firm, excluding staff employed in divisional headquarters (Collis et al., 2007).

Corporate level strategy. Corporate strategy is the way a company creates value through the configuration and coordination of its multimarket activities (Collis & Montgomery, 2005).

Corporate restructuring. Corporate restructuring is defined by Hoskisson and Turk (1990) as a major change in the composition of a firm's assets combined with a major change in its corporate strategy. It usually involves selling off (or liquidating) businesses in M-form firms, either voluntarily through spin-offs or involuntarily through hostile takeovers. Restructuring also can occur once a leveraged buyout (LBO) of a firm has been completed. Thus, restructuring is viewed by Hoskisson and Turk (1990) as more than the simple divestiture of a single business unit.

Corporate structure. Corporate structure refers to the design of the organization and it includes the lines of communication and authority between administrative offices as well as the information that flows between them (Chandler, 1962, p. 14).

Corporation. Enterprise with a legal identity that is distinct from the individuals that own the firm.

Divestures. This refers to a firm's adjustments of its business portfolio structure via spin-off, equity carve-out, split-up, or unit sell-off (Brauer, 2006; Mulherin & Boone, 2000). Moschieri and Mair (2008, p. 399) define divestures as "the parent company's disposal and sale of assets, facilities, prouct lines, subsidiaries, divisions and business units."

Deep pockets. Deep pockets refer to a firm having strong financial resources from monopoly power in one of its business and which is able to engage in costly predatory activities, as price wars and cross-subsidization, to try to financially exhaust entrants (Poitevin, 1989; Saloner, 1987; Telser, 1966).

Dominant business firm. Firms with between 70 percent and 95 percent of their total sales in a single business (Rumelt, 1974).

Dominant logic. A dominant logic is defined as the way in which managers conceptualize the business and make critical resource allocation decisions (Prahalad & Bettis, 1986, p. 490).

Glossary

Downscoping. Downscoping refers to divestiture, spin-offs, or some other means of eliminating businesses that are unrelated to a firm's core businesses (Hitt et al., 2005).

Downsizing. Downsizing is a reduction in the number of employees, and sometimes in the number of operating units, but it may or may not change the composition of businesses in the corporate portfolio (Hitt et al., 2005).

Due diligence. Due diligence is a process through which a potential acquirer evaluates a target firm for acquisition (Hitt et al., 2005).

Economic value. The difference between the perceived benefits gained by a customer that purchases a firm's products and the full economic cost of theses products.

Economies of scale. Economies that result when the increased size of a single operating unit producing or distributing a single product reduces the unit cost of production or distribution (Chandler, 1990, p. 17).

Economies of scope (or economies of joint production or distribution). Economies of scope arise when the cost of combined production of several products or services are lower than the cost of producing each product or service separately (Chandler, 1990; Panzar & Willig, 1981).

Equity alliance. Alliance in which alliance partners supplement contracts with equity holdings in alliance partners.

Entrenchment. See **managerial entrenchment**.

Entropy index (also known as the **Shannon index**). This is a diversification measure, which distinguishes between related and unrelated diversification, and was originally proposed by Jacquemin and Berry (1979) to analyze the relationship between corporate diversification and growth. The Jacquemin-Berry entropy measure entails three elements of the diversity of a firm's operations: (1) the number of product segments in which the firm operates, (2) the distribution of the firm's total sales across the product segments, and (3) the degree of relatedness among the various product segments (Palepu, 1985). The entropy index decomposes a firm's total diversity (DT) into two additive components: (1) an 'unrelated' component (DU) that measures the extent to which a firm's output is distributed in the form of products across unrelated industry groups and (2) a related component (DR) that measures the distribution of the output among related products within industry groups. Each component can be calculated using the following formula (Jacquemin & Berry, 1979):

$$E = \sum_i P_i \ln(1/P_i)$$

where E is an entropy measure, and P_i is the proportion of a firm's sales in the SIC industry i. The measure can be calculated using the distribution of sales across four, three, or two digit SIC levels, with the four digit SIC level typically representing total diversification (DT), whereas the two digit measure reflects unrelated diversification. To derive the related portion of the measure, modelers take the difference between total and unrelated diversification:

$$E_R = E_T - E_U = \sum_i P_T \ln(1/P_T) - \sum_i P_U \ln(1/P_U)$$

where: E_R = related component of entropy, E_T = entropy defined at the four digit SIC level, E_U = entropy defined at the two digit SIC level, P_T = percentage of sales in each four digit SIC industry, and P_U = percentage of sales in each two digit SIC industry.

Entry barriers. They are attributes of an industry's structure that increase the cost of entry.

Excess capacity. This is a situation where a firm posses resources that are underutilized.

Executive compensation. Use of salary, bonuses, and long term incentives to align managers' interests with shareholders' interests (Hitt et al., 2004).

Experience curve. See **learning curve**.

Explicit collusion. See **collusion**.

Glossary

***F*-form.** See **functional structure**.

Financial economies. Financial economies are cost savings realized through improved allocations of financial resources based on investments inside or outside the firm (Bergh, 1997; Hill, 1994).

Free cash flow. Free cash flow is cash flow in excess of that needed to fund all projects with a positive net present value (when discounted at the relevant cost of capital (Jensen, 1986; Hoskisson & Turk, 1990).

Functional structure. A functional organization implies departmentalization along discrete task lines, such as sales, finance, R&D, legal affairs, or other specialist activities

Geographical structure (*G*-form). This is an organizational structure, which reflects businesses demarcated into departments along geographical divisions (Fligstein, 1985).

Global integration. This concerns the coordination of activities across countries in an attempt to build efficient operations networks and to take maximum advantage of similarities across location (Luo, 2001).

Golden parachutes. Incentive compensation paid to senior managers if the firm they manage is acquired. Initially developed as an anti-takeover measure, golden parachutes have recently been criticized by shareholder activists for the negative effects on managerial opportunism.

Headquarters. See **corporate headquarters**.

Herfindhal index (HI). The Herfindahl index is a measure of industry concentration equal to the sum of the squared market shares of the firms in the industry.

Holdup problem. A problem that arises when a party in a contractual relationship exploits the other party's vulnerability due to relationship specific assets (Besanko et al., 2007).

Holding company. A holding company is a firm that owns part, all, or a majority of other firms' outstanding stock. It usually refers to a firm that does not produce goods or services itself; rather its only purpose is owning shares of other companies. Holding companies are legal devices whereby small central offices act as portfolio managers, while each subunit is operated independently (Fligstein, 1985).

Hostile takeover. A hostile takeover is an acquisition in which the target firm did not solicit the bid of the acquiring firm and is fighting it.

Hubris. Hubris is an unrealistic belief held by top managers about their own capabilities. In the context of takeovers, hubris refers to managers' belief that they can manage the assets of the target firm more efficiently than the target firm's current management. Hubris often occurs when managers value and act upon their own interests more than those of the shareholders (Roll, 1986).

Incentive. Financial or non-financial motivators that can lead to certain action or behavior. In economic theory, incentives are often referred to by pay systems (Baker et al., 1988).

Influence costs. Influence costs are the losses that arise from individuals within an organization seeking to influence its decisions for their private benefit (and from their perhaps succeeding to do so) and from the organization's responding to control this behavior (Milgrom & Roberts, 1990, p. 58).

Initial public offering (IPO). An IPO refers to the first sale of stock by a private firm to the public.

Institutional owners. Pension funds, corporations, and others that professionally invest other people's money in firm equity. Institutional owners are generally more active shareholders than the general public and monitor more closely managerial opportunism.

Internal capital market. Williamson (1975, 1985) used this term to suggest that the multidivisional (*M*-form) structure was created to overcome external capital market failure (Hoskisson & Turk, 1990).

Internalization. Internalization refers to the process of conducting some operations with the firm rather then on the market. According to the 'Long-run Theory of the Multinational

Enterprise' by Buckley and Casson (1976), firms can circumvent the imperfections of international markets by internalizing business processes concerning tacit knowledge, perishable goods, intermediate products and raw materials. Similarly, Williamson's (1975) transaction costs theory suggests to internalize transactions that feature a high rate of repetition, are surrounded by uncertainty, and require specific investments.

International diversification. International diversification can be defined as the "number of different markets in which a firm operates and their importance to the firm," where markets refer to different geographic locations that cross national borders (Hitt et al., 1997, p. 767).

Joint venture. A type of strategic alliances in which alliance partners create a legally independent firm in which they invest and from which they share any created profits.

Learning curve. The learning curve refers to the cost reductions that occur as cumulative volume rises. The difference between scale and experience effects is that scale, in principle, can be quickly replicated by building a large plant, whereas experience must be built through time (Lieberman, 1984).

Leveraged buyout (LBO). A LBO is a restructuring action whereby the managers of the firm and/or an external party buys all of the assets of the business, largely financed with debt, and takes the firm private (Hitt et al., 2004).

Local responsiveness. This concerns the attempt to respond to specific needs within a variety of host countries (Luo, 2001).

Managerial employment risk. Managerial employment risk is defined as the risk of job loss, loss of compensation, or loss of managerial reputation (Amihud & Lev, 1981; Hoskisson & Turk, 1990).

Managerial entrenchment. Entrenchment describes the actions of managers who make investments that are more valuable under themselves than under alternative managers. Those investments might not maximize shareholder value. So shareholders have a moral hazard in contracting with managers. In other words, "managerial entrenchment occurs when managers gain so much power that they are able to use the firm to further their own interests rather than the interests of shareholders" (Weisbach, 1988, p. 435). Entrenchment is problematic from a shareholder's point of by because "by making manager-specific investments, managers can reduce the probability of being replaced, extract higher wages and larger prerequisites from shareholders, and obtain more latitude in determining corporate strategy" (Shleifer & Vishny, 1989, p 123).

Market attractiveness. Market attractiveness describes the characteristics of a market or industry with interesting profit possibilities. The attractiveness of a market can be assessed by calculating the average profitability of the competitors in the market (Campbell et al., 2014). If average profitability is significantly above the cost of capital, the market is attractive. If the profitability is significantly below the cost of capital, the market is unattractive. Porter's Five Forces framework can be used to identify the factors that drive average profitability.

Market failure. It entails a failure of the price-market system. Market failure occurs when a competitive market is unable to efficiently allocate its resources. Important sources of market failure are government interventions and opportunistic behavior (Bator, 1958; Datta-Chaudhuri, 1990; Williamson, 1975)

Market for corporate control. The purchase of a firm that is underperforming relative to industry rivals in order to improve the firm's strategic competitiveness (Hitt et al., 2004). The market for corporate control is an external governance mechanism that becomes active when a firm's internal controls fails (Coff, 2002; Hitt et al., 1996; Walsh & Kosnik, 1993). The market for corporate control works as a control mechanism as this market is a set of potential owners seeking to acquire undervalued firms and earn above average returns on their investments by replacing ineffective top level management teams (Hitt et al., 1996). Because, the ineffective managers of the undervalued firms are likely to be replaced if the firm is taken over, there is an incentive

Glossary

for managers to work in the best interest of the actual shareholders and to maximize the firm's stock market value.

Market imperfection. See **market failure**.

Market power. It is the ability of a market participants or group of participants (people, firms, partnerships, or others) to influence price, quality, and the nature of the product in the market-place (Shepherd, 1970, p. 3).

Minimum efficiency scale. The scale of operation necessary to reach the lowest cost per unit (Chandler, 1990, p. 24).

Modern corporation. Collection of operating units, each with its own specific facilities and personnel, whose combined resources and activities are coordinated, monitored, and allocated by a hierarchy of middle and top managers (Chandler, 1990). The main characteristic of modern corporations is the separation of ownership and managerial control. Shareholders own the firm and delegate the managerial tasks to professional managers. Thus, managers are decision-making specialists who act on behalf of the firm's owners (Berle & Means, 1932; Chandler, 1977; Demesetz, 1983; Fama & Jensen, 1983). As such, they have some latitude (i.e., discretionary power) to make strategic choices that should be in the best interest of the firm's owners (Jensen & Meckling, 1976). They are the primarily responsible for the performance and sustainability of the firm (Barnard, 1938). An important drawback of modern corporations is that shareholders want to maximize the firm's market value, whereas managers are more interested in salaries, job security, and personal power, creating agency problems (Jensen & Meckling, 1976).

Moral hazard. Moral hazard occurs when a party insulated from risk may behave differently from the way it would behave if it were fully exposed to the risk. Moral hazard is a special case of information asymmetry, a situation in which one party in a transaction has more information than another. The party that is insulated from risk generally has more information about its actions and intentions than the party paying for the negative consequences of the risk. More broadly, moral hazard occurs when the party with more information about its actions or intentions has a tendency or incentive to behave opportunistically from the perspective of the party with less information (Williamson, 1975).

Multidivisional structure (or *M*-form). The *M*-form is a decentralized organization structure. Firms are organized into product divisions and each division contains a unitary structure. In addition they possess a central office where long range planning and (financial) resource allocations are located (Fligstein, 1985).

Multimarket competition. Rivalry between firms competing against each other in several product or geographic markets; they are engaged in multimarket competition.

Multinational enterprise (MNE). An MNE is a company that consists of a group of geographically dispersed and goal disparate organizations that include its head quarters and the different national subsidiaries (Ghoshal & Bartlett, 1990). An MNE has substantial direct investment in foreign countries, not just an export business, and is engaged in the active management of these offshore assets, rather than simply holding them in a passive financial portfolio (Bartlett et al., 2008).

Multinational flexibility. This is the ability of a firm to manage the risks and exploit the opportunities that arise from the diversity and volatility of the global environment (Kogut, 1985).

Narrow spectrum diversification. Wood (1971) used the SIC data to distinguish two distinct patterns of firm level diversification. She defined narrow spectrum diversification, or NSD, as expansion, other than vertical integration, outside a four digit SIC industry but within a two digit SIC industry. She also defined broad spectrum diversification, or BSD, as expansion, other than vertical integration, into a different two digit SIC industry. NSD is viewed as diversification closely related to a firm's core expertise and BSD as diversification less closely related to it (Lubatkin et al., 1993; Varadarajan & Ramanujam, 1987).

Network structure (or _N_-form). A type of organizational structure in which several smaller firms representing different stages in the production process establish informal or contractual links with one another rather than joining together in vertical integration (Hedlund, 1994; Powell, 1990). Within the firm's boundaries, the _N_-form is a melded network of relationships and functions. Across firms' boundaries, it entails a loose federation of partners that participate in the network's operations on a flexible basis (Hitt et al., 2004). For example, in the transnational firms studied by Bartlett and Ghoshal (1989), network organizational structures are based on three main characteristics: dispersion, specialization, and interdependence.

Opportunism. Williamson (1975) defines opportunism as self-interest with guile. In a strategic alliance context, Luo (2007, p. 41) defines opportunism "as an act or behavior performed by a party to seek its own unilateral gains at the substantial expense of another party ... by breaching the contract or agreement, exercising private control, withholding or distorting information, withdrawing commitment, shirking obligation, or grafting joint earnings."

Organizational structure. See **structure**.

Outsourcing. This is the purchase of a value creating activity from an external supplier.

Overdiversification. This is a diversification beyond the level that is optimal for shareholders (Markides, 1992).

Overexpansion. See **overdiversification**.

Ownership concentration. The relative amount of stock owned by individual shareholders and institutional investors (Hitt et al., 2004).

Predatory pricing. Predatory pricing refers to a pricing strategy, in which prices are set below business costs, and which used by a dominant firm's to reduce competitive pressure by driving out of the market existing rivals or excluding from the market potential ones (Joskow & Klevorick, 1979).

Processes. Processes describe the informal elements of an organization's activities (Collis & Montgomery, 2005, p. 15).

Real options. An option is the right, but not the obligation, to buy or sell a specified asset at a pre-specified price on a pre-specified date (Amram & Kulatilaka, 1999). Options traditionally are written on financial assets, but they also can be written on real assets, such as physical, human, and organizational assets that a firm may use to implement its corporate strategy. The ability to delay the decision to buy or sell an asset at any point up until the pre-specified date introduces strategic flexibility.

Renewal. See **strategic renewal**.

Resources. Resources include assets (such as plants, patents and cash flows) and competencies, which represent the know-how to create a new asset or expand existing assets (Markides & Williamson, 1996).

Restructuring. Restructuring is a strategy through which a firm changes its set of businesses or financial structure (Bethel & Liebskind, 1993; Johnson, 1996).

Sarbanes-Oxley Act of 2002. U.S. Law that revised and strengthened auditing and accounting standards.

Scope. See **economy of scope**.

Shannon index. See **entropy index**.

SIC. See **Standard Industry Classification**.

Small numbers problem. Transaction costs are influenced by the number of potential transaction partners, known as the small number problem. The fewer the partners in the market, the stronger their individual power, and therefore their capability to increase transaction costs, are.

Spin-off. A spin-off is a new organization or entity formed by a split from a larger one. A spin-off is a pro-rata distribution of the shares of a firm's subsidiary to the shareholders of the company. No cash transaction takes place. After the spin-off, the shareholders of the parent firm hold shares in both the parent firm and the subsidiary (Veld & Yulia, 2004). A spin-off is one of the techniques used by firms to divest businesses when they conduct the restructuring of their portfolio.

Standard Industry Classification (SIC). The SIC code is a four digit number assigned to various, distinct business industries, and addresses the entire field of economic activities, including agriculture, forestry, fishing, hunting, and trapping; mining; construction; manufacturing; transportation, communications, electric, gas, and sanitary services; wholesale trade; retail trade; finance, insurance, and real estate; personal, business, professional, repair, recreation, and other services; and public administration. For instance, SIC Code 5021 represents furniture, 7372 refers to prepackaged software, and 8721 indicates accounting services. The SIC codes were developed to classify establishments according to the type of activity in which they engage, as well as to promote uniformity and comparability in the presentation of statistical data collected by various agencies of the U.S. government, state agencies, trade associations, and private research organizations. SIC codes are also used to measure a firm's level of diversification (see the **entropy index** and **concentric index**).

Strategic business unit (or SBU). An SBU is a business unit (see this term) of strategic importance for a firm. It is often organized as a profit center that focuses on product and/or market segment. SBUs typically have a discrete marketing plan, analysis of competition, and marketing campaign.

Strategic intent. This is the leveraging of a firm's resources, capabilities, and core competences to accomplish the firm's goals (Hamel & Prahalad, 1989).

Strategic renewal. Strategic renewal includes the process, content, and outcome of refreshment or replacement of attributes of an organization that have the potential to substantially affect its long term prospects (Agarwal & Helfat, 2009). Firms seek to achieve strategic renewal when they encounter poor performance in the core business and diversify to move away from the core business.

Structure. Structure refers to the way the corporation is divided into discrete units. It describes the formal organization chart that delineates the allocation of authority inside the corporate hierarchy (Collis & Montgomery, 2005, pp. 14–15). There are obviously many ways to classify or describe organizational structures. Seven forms are typically distinguished: unitary, functional, geographical, holding company, multinational, and network forms (Fligstein, 1985; Hedlund, 1994; Rumelt, 1974).

Sunk costs. Sunk costs are costs that have been incurred and that cannot be recovered to any significant degree.

Synergy. The term used to describe a situation where the final outcome of a system is greater than the sum of its parts.

Systems. Systems are the set of formal policies and routines that govern organizational behavior. They are the set of rules that define how tasks, from strategic planning to personnel evaluations, are to be fulfilled (Collis & Montgomery, 2005, p. 15).

Tacit collusion. See **collusion**.

Tacit knowledge. Knowledge that cannot be written down in a set of blueprints or equations (Polyani, 1962).

Transaction costs. Costs involved in the transfer of goods and services from operating unit to another. When these transactions are carried out between firms or between individuals, they usually involve the transfer of property rights and are defined in contractual terms. When they are carried out within the enterprise, they are defined by accounting procedures (Chandler, 1990, p. 17; see Williamson, 1975, 1985).

Transaction specific assets. Transaction specific assets are assets that are tailored to a particular transaction and cannot be easily redeployed outside the relationship of the parties to the transaction (Geyskens et al., 2006; Williamson, 1975). Their idiosyncratic nature gives rise to a safeguarding problem, because market competition will not restrain opportunistic exploitation.

Glossary

Transfer price. The price at which divisions of a firm transact with each other. Transactions may include the trade of supplies or labor between departments. Transfer prices are used when individual business units of a multibusiness firm are treated as separate units.

Unitary structure (or *U*-form). The *U*-form, also referred to the simple structure, is a organizational structure in which the owner-manager makes all major decisions and monitors all activities while the staff serves as an extension of the manager's supervisory authority (Hitt et al., 2004).

Value chain. A value chain is the set of discrete activities the must be accomplished to design, build, sell, and distribute a product of service (Porter, 1985).

Vertical integration. Vertical integration refers to the corporate level strategy by which a firm diversifies its activities along the industry value chain, whether by producing its own input (i.e., backward, or upstream, integration) or disposing of its own outputs (i.e., forward, or downstream, integration) (Grant, 2008; Harrigan, 1984, 1985a).

BIBLIOGRAPHY

Abell, Derek F. (1980). *Defining the Business: The Starting Point of Strategic Planning*. Englewood Cliffs, NJ: Prentice Hall.

Abell, Derek F. & John S. Hammond (1979). *Strategic Market Planning*. Englewood Cliffs, NJ: Prentice–Hall.

Achrol, Ravi S. (1997). "Changes in the Theory of Interorganizational Relations in Marketing: Toward a Network Paradigm," *Journal of the Academy of Marketing Science*, 25(1), 56–71.

Achrol, Ravi S. & Philip Kotler (1999). "Marketing in the Network Economy," *Journal of Marketing*, 63(SI), 146–163.

Ackoff, Russell L. (1974). *Redesigning the Future*. New York: Wiley.

Adamy, J. (2005). "Sara Lee to Spin Off Apparel Arm," *Wall Street Journal*, February 11, A5.

Afuah, Allan (2001). "Dynamic Boundaries of the Firm: Are Firms Better off Being Vertically Integrated in the Face of a Technological Change?" *Academy of Management Journal*, 44(6), 1211–1228

Agarwal, Rajshree & Constance E. Helfat (2009). "Strategic renewal of organizations," *Organization Science*, 20(2), 281–293.

Aguilera, Ruth V. & Gregory Jackson (2003), "The Cross-National Diversity of Corporate Governance: Dimensions and Determinants," *Academy of Management Review*, 28(3), 447–465.

Aguilera, Ruth V., Deborah E. Rupp, Cynthia A. Williams, & Jyoti Ganapathi (2007). "Putting the S Back in Corporate Social Responsibility: A Multilevel Theory of Social Change in Organizations," *Academy of Management Review*, 32(3), 836–863.

Ahuja, Gautam & Riitta Katila (2001). "Technological Acquisitions and the Innovation Performance of Acquiring Firms: A Longitudinal Study," *Strategic Management Journal*, 22(3), 197–220.

Akerlof, George A. (1970), "The Market for 'Lemons': Quality Uncertainty and the Market Mechanism," *Quarterly Journal of Economics*, 84(3), 488–500.

Alchian, Armen A. & Harold Demsetz (1972). "Production, Information Costs, and Economic Organization," *American Economic Review*, 62(5), 777–795.

Alexander, Donald L. (1985). "An Empirical Test of the Mutual Forbearance Hypothesis: The Case of Bank Holding Companies," *Southern Journal of Economics*, 52(1), 122–140.

Allen, Steve G. (1978). "Absenteeism and the Labor Market," Ph.D. dissertation, Harvard University.

Ambos, Björn & Volker Mahnke (2010). "How do MNC Headquarters Add Value?" *Management International Review*, 50(4), 403–412.

Amburgey, Terry L. & Tina Dacin (1994). "As the Left Foot Follows the Right? The Dynamic of Strategic and Structural Change," *Academy of Management Journal*, 37(6), 1427–1452.

Amburgey Terry L., Dawn Kelly, & William P. Barnett (1993). "Resetting the Clock: The Dynamics of Organizational–Change and Failure," *Administrative Science Quarterly*, 38(1), 51–73.

Amihud, Yakov & Baruch Lev (1981). "Risk Reduction as a Managerial Motive for Conglomerate Mergers," *Bell Journal of Economics*, 12(2), 605–617.

Amit, Raphael & Joshua Livnat (1988a). "Diversification and the Risk-Return Trade-Off," *Academy of*

Management Journal, 31(1), 154–166.

Amit, Raphael & Joshua Livnat (1988b). "A Concept of Conglomerate Diversification," *Journal of Management*, 14(4), 593–604.

Amram, Martha & Nalin Kulatilaka (1999). *Real Options: Managing Strategic Investment in an Uncertain World*. Cambridge, MA: Harvard Business School Press.

Anand, Bharat N. & Tarun Khanna (2000). "Do Firms Learn to Create Value? The Case of Alliances," *Strategic Management Journal*, 21(3), 295–315.

Anand, Jaideep & Harbir Singh (1997). "Asset Redeployment, Acquisition and Corporate Strategy in Declining Industries," *Strategic Management Journal*, 18(S1), 99–118.

Anderson, Erin & Hubert Gatignon (1986). "Modes of Foreign Entry: A Transaction Cost Analysis and Propositions," *Journal of International Business Studies*, 17(3), 1–26.

Anderson, Erin & Barton A. Weitz (1986). "Make-or-Buy Decisions: Vertical Integration and Marketing Productivity," *Sloan Management Review*, 27(3), 3–19.

Anderson, Ronald C., Thomas W. Bates, John M. Bizjak, & Michael L. Lemmon (2000). "Corporate Governance and Firm Diversification," *Financial Management*, 29(1), 5–22.

Andrews, Kenneth R. (1971). *The Concept of Corporate Strategy*. Burr Ridge, IL: Dow-Jones-Irwin.

Angwin, Duncan, Philip Stern, & Sarah Bradley (2004). "Agent or Steward: The Target CEO in a Hostile Takeover: Can a Condemned Agent be Redeemed?" *Long Range Planning*, 37(3), 239–257.

Ansoff, H. Igor (1957). "Strategies for Diversification," *Harvard Business Review*, 35(2), 113–124.

Ansoff, H. Igor (1965). *Corporate Strategy*. New York: McGraw–Hill.

Ansoff, H. Igor (1988). *The New Corporate Strategy*. New York: John Wiley & Sons.

Aoki, Masahiko (2000). *Information, Corporate Governance, and Institutional Diversity: Competitiveness in Japan, the USA, and the Transnational Economies*. Oxford: Oxford University Press.

Argyres, Nicholas (1996). "Evidence on the Role of Firm Capabilities in Vertical Integration Decision," *Strategic Management Journal*, 17(2), 129–150.

Armour, Henry O. & David J. Teece (1978). "Organizational Structure and Economic Performance: A Test of the Multidivisional Hypothesis," *Bell Journal of Economics*, 9(1), 106–122.

Armstrong, Craig E. & Katsuhiko Shimizu (2007). "A Review of Approaches to Empirical Research on the Resource-Based View of the Firm," *Journal of Management*, 33(6), 959–986.

Arnould, Richard J. (1969). "Conglomerate Growth and Public Policy," in L. Gordon (Ed.), *Economics of Conglomerate Growth*, pp. 72–80. Cornvallis: Oregon Sate University Department of Agricultural Economics.

Arrow, Kenneth J. (1974). *Limits of Organizations*. New York: Norton.

Asquith, Paul (1983). "Merger Bids, Uncertainty and Stockholder Returns," *Journal of Financial Economics*, 11(1), 51–83.

Attiyeh, Robert S. (1969). "Where Next for Conglomerates? Best Course: Effective Asset Management," *Business Horizons*, 12(6), 39–44.

Aupperle, Kenneth E., Archie B. Carroll, & John D. Hatfield (1985). "An Empirical Examination of the Relationship Between Corporate Social Responsibility and Profitability," *Academic of Management Journal*, 28(2), 446–463.

Bain, Joe S. (1956). *Barriers to New Competition*. Cambridge, MA: Harvard University Press.

Bain, Joe S. (1968). *Industrial Organization*. New York: Wiley.

Baker, George P., Michael C. Jensen, Kevin J. Murphy (1988). "Compensation and Incentives: Practice vs. Theory," *Journal of Finance*, 43(3), 593–616.

Balakrishnan, Srinivasan & Birger Wernerfelt (1986). "Technical Change, Competition and Vertical Integration," *Strategic Management Journal*, 7(4), 347–359.

Barkema, Harry G. & Mario Schijven (2008). "Toward Unlocking the Full Potential of Acquisitions: The Role of Organizational Restructuring," *Academy of Management Journal*, 51(4), 696–722.

Barkema, Harry G. & Freek Vermeulen (1997). "What Differences in the Cultural Backgrounds of Partners are Detrimental for International Joint Ventures," *Journal of International Business Studies*, 28(4), 845–864.

Barkema, Harry G. & Freek Vermeulen (1998). "International Expansion through Start-up or Acquisition:

A Learning Perspective," *Academy of Management Journal*, 41(1), 7–26.

Barkema, Harry G., John H. J. Bell, & Johannes M. Pennings (1996). "Foreign Entry, Cultural Barriers, and Learning," *Strategic Management Journal*, 17(2), 151–166.

Barkema, Harry G., Oded Shenkar, Freek Vermeulen, & John H. J. Bell (1997). "Working Abroad, Working with Others: How Firms Learn to Operate International Joint Ventures," *Academy of Management Journal*, 40(2), 426–442.

Barkema, Harry G., Joel A. C. Baum, & Elizabeth A. Mannix (2002). "Management Challenges in a New Time," *Academy of Management Journal*, 45(5), 916–930.

Barnard, Chester I. (1938). *The Functions of the Executive.* Cambridge, MA: Harvard University Press.

Barney, Jay B. (1986). "Strategic Factor Markets: Expectations, Luck, and Business Strategy," *Management Science*, 32(10), 1231–1241.

Barney, Jay B. (1991). "Firm Resources and Sustained Competitive Advantage," *Journal of Management*, 17(1), 99–120.

Barney, Jay B. (1999). "How Firm's Capabilities Affect Boundary Decisions," *Sloan Management Review*, 40(3), 137–145.

Barney, Jay B. (2007). *Gaining and Sustaining Competitive Advantage.* Second edition. Upper Saddle River, NJ: Prentice–Hall.

Barney, Jay B. & William G. Ouchi (1986). *Organizational Economics.* San Francisco: Jossey–Bass.

Bartlett, Christopher A. & Sumantra Ghoshal (1989). *Managing Across Borders: The Transnational Solution.* Boston, MA: Harvard Business School Press.

Bartlett, Christopher A. & Sumantra Ghoshal (1992). "What is a Global Manager?" *Harvard Business Review*, 70(5), 124–132.

Bartlett, Christopher A., Sumantra Ghoshal, & Paul W. Beamish (2008). *Transnational Management.* Fifth edition. Boston: McGraw–Hill.

Bator, Francis M. (1958). "The Anatomy of Market Failure," *Quarterly Journal of Economics*, 72(3), 351–379.

Baum, Joel A. C. & Helaine J. Korn (1996). "Competitive Dynamics of Interfirm Rivalry," *Academy of Management Journal*, 39(2), 259–291.

Baum, Joel A. C. & Helaine J. Korn (1999). "Dynamics of Dyadic Competitive Interaction," *Strategic Management Journal*, 20(3), 251–278.

Baumol, W. J., J. C. Panzer, & R. D. Willig (1982). *Contestable Markets and the Theory of Industry Structure.* New York: Harcourt Brace Jacanovich.

Bausch, Andreas & Frithjof Pils (2009). "Product Diversification Strategy and Financial Performance: Meta–Analytic Evidence on Causality and Construct Multidimensionality," *Review of Managerial Science*, 3(3), 157–190.

Baysinger, Barry & Robert E. Hoskisson (1989). "Diversification Strategy and R&D Intensity in Multiproduct Firms," *Academy of Management Journal*, 32(2), 310–332.

Baysinger, Barry & Robert E. Hoskisson (1990). "The Composition of Boards of Directors and Strategic Control: Effects on Corporate Strategy," *Academy of Management Review*, 15(1), 72–87.

Bazerman Max H. & William F. Samuelson (1983). "I Won the Auction but I Don't Win the Prize," *Journal of Conflict Resolution*, 27(4), 618–634.

Beamish, Paul W. (1999). "The Design and Management of International Joint Venture," in Paul W. Beamish, Allen J. Morrison, Philip M. Rosenzweig, & Andrew C. Inkpen (eds). *International Management: Text and Cases*, pp. 113–131. Boston (MA): Irwin–McGraw–Hill.

Becht, Marco & Ailsa Röell (1999). "Blockholdings in Europe: An International Comparison," *European Economic Review*, 43(4–6), 1049–1056.

Berg, Norman A. (1973). "Corporate Role in Diversified Companies," in Bernard Taylor and Keith Macmillan (eds). *Business Policy: Teaching and Research*, pp. 298–347 New York: John Wiley.

Berger, Philip G. & Eli Ofek (1995). "Diversification's Effect on Firm Value," *Journal of Financial Economics*, 37(1), 39–65.

Berger, Philip G., Eli Ofek, & David L. Yermack (1997). "Managerial Entrenchment and Capital Structure Decisions," *Journal of Finance*, 52(4), 1411–1438.

Bergh, Donald D. (1995). "Size and Relatedness of Units Sold: An Agency Theory and Resource–Based Perspective," *Strategic Management Journal*, 16(3), 221–239.

Bergh, Donald D. (1997). "Predicting Divesture of Unrelated Acquisitions: An Integrative Model of Ex Ante Conditions," *Strategic Management Journal*, 18(9), 715–731.

Bergh, Donald D. (2001). "Diversification Strategy Research at a Crossroads: Established, Emerging and Anticipated Path," in Michael A. Hitt, R. Edward Freeman, & Jeffrey S. Harrison (eds). *The Blackwell Handbook of Strategic Management*, pp. 362–383. Oxford, UK: Blackwell Business.

Bergh, Donald D. & Gordon F. Holbein (1997). "Assessment and Redirection of Longitudinal Analysis: Demonstration with a Study of the Diversification and Divestiture Relationship," *Strategic Management Journal*, 18(7), 557–571.

Bergh, Donald D. & Michael W. Lawless (1998). "Portfolio Restructuring and Limits to Hierarchical Governance: The Effects of Environmental Uncertainty and Diversification Strategy," *Organization Science*, 9(1), 87–102.

Bergh, Donald D. & Elizabeth Ngah-Kiing Lim (2008). "Learning How to Restructure: Absorptive Capacity and Improvisational Views of Restructuring Actions and Performance," *Strategic Management Journal*, 29(6), 593–616.

Berle, Adolf A. & Gardiner C. Means (1932). *The Modern Corporation and Private Property*. New York: Commerce Clearing House.

Bernardo, Antonio E. & Bhagwan C. Chowdhry (2002). "Resources, Real Options, and Corporate Strategy," *Journal of Financial Economics*, 63(2), 211–234.

Bernheim, Douglas & Michael D. Whinston (1990). "Multimarket Contact and Collusive Behavior," *RAND Journal of Economics*, 21(Spring), 1–26.

Berry, Charles H. (1975). *Corporate Growth and Diversification*. Princeton, NJ: Princeton University Press.

Besanko, David, David Dranove, Mark Shanley, & Scott Schaefer (2007). *Economics of Strategy*. Fourth Edition. New York: Wiley.

Best, Ronald W., Charles W. Hodges, & Bing-Xuan Lin (2004). "Does Information Asymmetry Explain the Diversification Discount?" *Journal of Financial Research*, 27(2), 235–249.

Bethel, Jennifer E. & Julia Liebeskind (1993). "The Effect of Ownership Structure on Corporate Restructuring," *Strategic Management Journal*, 14(SI), 15–31.

Bettis, Richard A. (1981). "Performance Differences in Related and Unrelated Diversified Firms," *Strategic Management Journal*, 2(4), 379–393.

Bettis, Richard A. (1991). "Strategic Management and the Straightjacket: An Editorial Essay," *Organizational Science*, 2(3), 315–319.

Bettis, Richard A. & William K. Hall (1981). "Strategic Portfolio Management in the Multibusiness Firm," *California Management* Review, 24(1), 23–38.

Bettis, Richard A. & William K. Hall (1983). "The Business Portfolio Approach: Where it Falls Down in Practice," *Long Range Planning*, 16(2), 95–104.

Bettis, Richard A. & C. K. Prahalad (1995). "The Dominant Logic: Retrospective and Extension," *Strategic Management Journal*, 16(1), 5–14.

Bhide, Amar V. (1990). "Reversing Corporate Diversification, 1990," *Journal of Applied Corporate Finance*, 3(2), 70–81.

Biggadike, Ralph E. (1979), "The Risky Business of Diversification," *Harvard Business Review*, 57(3), 103–111.

Birkinshaw, Julian (2001). "Strategies for Managing Internal Competition," *California Management Review*, 44(1), 21–38.

Birkinshaw, Julian & Andrew Campbell (2004). "Know the Limits of Corporate Venturing," *Financial Times*, August 9 [http://ashridge.org.uk].

Black, Fisher & Myron Scholes (1973). "The Pricing of Options and Corporate Liabilities," *Journal of Political Economy*, 81(3), 637–658.

Block, Zenas & Ian C. Macmillan (1993), *Corporate Venturing*. Cambridge, MA: Harvard Business School Press.

Boeker, Warren, Jerry Goodstein, John Stephan, & Johann Peter Murmann (1997). "Competition in a

Multimarket Environment: The Case of Market Exit," *Organization Science*, 8(2), 126–142.

Boston Consulting Group (1972). *Perspectives on Experience*. Boston, MA: Boston Consulting Group.

Bower, Joseph H. (1970). *Managing the Resource Allocation Process*. Cambridge, MA: Harvard University Press.

Bower, Joseph L. (1986). *Managing the Resource Allocation Process: A Study of Corporate Planning and Investment*. Boston, MA: Harvard Business Press.

Bowman, Cliff & Véronique Ambrosini (2007). "Firm Value Creation and Levels of Strategy," *Management Decision*, 45(3), 360–371.

Bowman, Edward H. & Constance E. Helfat (2001). "Does Corporate Strategy Matter?" *Strategic Management Journal*, 22(1), 1–23.

Bowman, Edward H. & Harbir Singh (1993). "Corporate Restructuring: Reconfiguring the Firm," *Strategic Management Journal*, 14(SSI), 5–14.

Bowman, Edward H., Harbir Singh, Michael Useem, & Raja Bhadury (1999). "When Does Restructuring Improve Economic Performance?" *California Management Review*, 41(2), 33–54.

Bradley, Michael, Anand Desai, & E. Han Kim (1989). "The Rationale Behind Interfirm Tender Offers: Information or Synergy," *Journal of Financial Economics*, 11(1), 183–206.

Brammer, Stephen J. & Stephen Pavelin (2006). "Corporate Reputation and Social Performance: The Importance of Fit," *Journal of Management Studies*, 43(3), 435–455.

Brauer, Matthias (2006). "What Have We Acquired and What Should We Acquire in Divesture Research? A Review and Research Agenda," *Journal of Management*, 32(6), 751–785.

Brenner, Steffen & Joachim Schwalbach (2003). "Management Quality, Firm Size, and Managerial Compensation: A Comparison between Germany and the UK," *Schmalenbach Business Review*, 55(4), 280–293.

Breschi, Stefano, Francesco Lissoni, & Franco Malerba (2003). "Knowledge-Relatedness in Firm Technological Diversification," *Research Policy*, 32(1), 69–87.

Brouthers, Keith D. & Lance E. Brouthers (2003). "Why Service and Manufacturing Entry Mode Choices Differ: The Influence of Transaction Cost Factors, Risk and Trust," *Journal of Management Studies*, 40(5), 1179–1204.

Brouthers, Keith D. & Jean-François Hennart (2007). "Boundaries of the Firm: Insights from International Entry Mode Research," *Journal of Management*, 33(3), 395–425.

Brown, James R., C. S. Dev, & Z. Zhou (2003). "Broadening the Foreign Market Entry Mode Decision: Separating Ownership and Control," *Journal of International Business Studies*, 34(5), 473–488.

Brush, Thomas H. (1996). "Predicted Change in Operational Synergy and Post–Acquisition Performance of Acquired Businesses," *Strategic Management Journal*, 17(1), 1–24.

Brush, Thomas H. & Philip Bromiley (1997). "What Does a Small Corporate Effect Mean?: A Variance Components Simulation if Corporate and Business Effects," *Strategic Management Journal*, 18(10), 825–835.

Brush, Thomas H., Philip Bromiley, & Margaretha Hendrickx (1999). "The Relative Influence of Industry and Corporation on Business Segment Performance: An Alternative Estimate," *Strategic Management Journal*, 20(6), 519–547.

Brush, Thomas H., Philip Bromiley, & Margaretha Hendrickx (2000). "The Free Cash Flow Hypothesis for Sales Growth and Firm Performance," *Strategic Management Journal*, 21(4), 455–472.

Bruton, Garry D., Benjamin M. Oviatt, & Margaret A. White (1994). "Performance of Acquisitions of Distressed Firms," *Academy of Management Journal*, 37(4), 972–989.

Bryce, David J. & Sidney G. Winter (2009). "A General Interindustry Relatedness Index," *Management Science*, 55(9), 1570–1585.

Buckley, Peter J. & Mark Casson (1976). *The Future of the Multinational Enterprise*. London: Holmes and Meier.

Bühner, Rolf (2000). "Governance Costs, Determinants, and Size of Corporate Headquarters," *Schmalenbach Business Review*, 52(April), 160–181.

Burgelman, Robert A. (1983), "A Process Model of Internal Corporate Venturing in the Diversified Major Firm," *Administrative Science Quarterly*, 28(2), 223–244.

Burgers, Willem P., Charles W. L. Hill, & W. Chan Kim (1993). "A Theory of Global Strategic Alliances: The Case of the Global Auto Industry," *Strategic Management Journal*, 14(6), 419–432.

Burrough, Bryan & John Helyar (2003). *Barbarians at the Gate: The Fall of RJR Nabisco*. New York: Harper & Row.

Buzzell, Robert D. & Bradley T. Gale (1987). *The PIMS Principles: Linking Strategy to Performance*. New York: Free Press.

Calori, Roland, Gerry Johnson, & Philippe Sarnin (1994). "CEOs' Cognitive Maps and the Scope of the Organization," *Strategic Management Journal*, 15(6), 437–457.

Campa, Jose M. & Simi Kedia (2002). "Explaining the Diversification Discount," *Journal of Finance*, 57(4), 1731–1762.

Campbell, Andrew & David Sadtler (1998). "Corporate Breakups," *Strategy & Business – Booz Allen & Hamilton*, Third Quarter [www.strategy-business.com/policy/98306/html].

Campbell, Andrew, Michael Goold, & Marcus Alexander (1995). "The Value of the Parent Company," *California Management Review*, 38(1), 79–97.

Campbell, Andrew, Jo Whiehead, Marcus Alexander, & Michael Goold (2014). *Strategy for the Corporate Level: Where to Invest, What to Cut Back and How to Grow Organisations with Multiple Divisions*. San Francisco: Jossey-Bass.

Cannella, Albert A. & Donald C. Hambrick (1993). "Executive Departure and Acquisition Performance," *Strategic Management Journal*, 14(1), 137–152.

Capron, Laurence (1999). "The Long-Term Performance of Horizontal Acquisitions," *Strategic Management Journal*, 20(11), 987–1018.

Capron, Laurence & John Hulland (1999). "Redeployment of Brands, Sales, and General Marketing Management Expertise Following Horizontal Acquisition: A Resource-Based View," *Journal of Marketing*, 63(2), 41–54.

Capron, Laurence & Nathalie Pistre (2002). "When Do Acquirers Earn Abnormal Returns?" *Strategic Management Journal*, 23(9), 781–794.

Capron, Laurence, Pierre Dussauge, & Will Mitchell (1998). "Resource Redeployment Following Horizontal Acquisitions in Europe and North America, 1988–1992," *Strategic Management Journal*, 19(7), 631–661.

Capron, Laurence, Will Mitchell, & Anand Swaminathan (2001). "Asset Divestiture Following Horizontal Acquisitions: A Dynamic View," *Strategic Management Journal*, 22(9), 817–844.

Carroll, Archie B. (1979). "A Three-Dimensional Conceptual Model of Corporate Performance," *Academy of Management Review*, 4(4), 497–505.

Carroll, Archie B. (1991). "The Pyramid of Corporate Social Responsibility: Toward the Moral Management of Organizational Stakeholders," *Business Horizons*, 34(July–August), 39–48.

Carroll, Archie B. (1999). "Corporate Social Responsibility: Evolution of a Definitional Construct," *Business & Society*, 38(3), 268–295.

Carroll, Glenn R. (1993). "A Sociological View on Why Firms Differ," *Strategic Management Journal*, 14(4), 237–249.

Casadesus-Masanell, Ramon & Daniel F. Spulber (2000). "The Fable of Fisher Body," *Journal of Law and Economics*, 43(1), 67–104.

Cascio, Wayne F. (2005). "Strategies for Responsible Restructuring," *Academy of Management Executive*, 19(4), 39–50.

Cassing, James & Richard W Douglas (1980). "Implication of the Auction Mechanism in Baseball's Free Agent Draft," *Southern Economic Journal*, 47(July), 110–121.

Cavanagh, Edward D. (2001). "Reciprocal Dealing: A Rebirth?" *St. John Law Review*, 75(4), 633–647.

Caves, Richard E. (1971). "International Corporations: The Industrial Economics of Foreign Investment," *Economica*, 38(February), 1–27.

Caves, Richard E. (1981). "Diversification and Seller Concentration: Evidence from Change," *Review of Economics and Statistics*, 63(2), 289–293.

Caves, Richard E. (1989). "Mergers, Takeovers, and Economic Efficiency," *International Journal of Industrial Organization*, 7(1), 151–174.

Caves, Richard E. (1996). *Multinational Enterprise and Economic Analysis*. Second edition. Cambridge, UK: Cambridge University Press.

Caves, Richard E., & Ralph M. Bradburd (1988). "The Empirical Determinants of Vertical Integration," *Journal of Economic Behavior & Organization*, 9(3), 265–279.

Caves, Richard E., Michael E. Porter, Andrew M. Spence, & John T. Scott (1980). *Competition in the Open Economy: A Model Applied to Canada*. Cambridge, MA: Harvard University Press.

Chakrabarti, Abhirup, Kulwant Singh, & Ishtiaq Mahmood (2007). "Diversification and Performance: Evidence from East Asian Firms," *Strategic Management Journal*, 28(2), 101–120.

Champlin, Dell P. & Janet T. Knoedler (1999). "Restructuring by Design? Government's Complicity in Corporate Restructuring," *Journal of Economic Issues*, 33(1), 41–57.

Chandler, Alfred D., Jr. (1962). *Strategy and Structure*. Cambridge, MA: MIT Press.

Chandler, Alfred D., Jr. (1977). *The Visible Hand: The Managerial Revolution in American Business*. Cambridge, MA: MIT Press.

Chandler, Alfred D., Jr. (1986). "The Evolution of the Modern Global Corporation," in Michael Porter (Ed.) *Competition in Global Industries*, pp. 405–448. Boston, MA: Harvard Business School Press.

Chandler, Alfred D., Jr. (1990). *Scale and Scope*. Cambridge, MA: Harvard University Press.

Chandler, Alfred D., Jr. (1991). "The Functions of the HQ Unit in the Multibusiness Firm," *Strategic Management Journal*, 12(WSI), 31–50.

Chang, Sea Jin (1996). "An Evolutionary Perspective on Diversification and Corporate Restructuring: Entry, Exit, and Economic Performance During 1981–89," *Strategic Management Journal*, 17(8), 587–611.

Chang, Sea Jin & Unghwan Choi (1988). "Strategy, Structure and Performance of Korean Business Groups: A Transaction Cost Approach," *Journal of Industrial Economics*, 37(2), 141–158.

Chang, Sea Jin & Jaebu Hong (2002). "How Much Does the Business Group Matter in Korea?" *Strategic Management Journal*, 23(3), 265–274.

Chang, Sea Jin & Harbir Singh (1999). "The Impact of Modes of Entry and Resource Fit on Modes of Exit by Multibusiness Firms," *Strategic Management Journal*, 20(11), 1019–1035.

Chang, Yegmin & Howard Thomas (1989). "The Impact of Diversification Strategy on Risk-Return Performance," *Strategic Management Journal*, 10(3), 271–284.

Channon, Derek F. (1973). *The Strategy and Structure of British Enterprise*. Cambridge, MA: Harvard Business Press.

Chatterjee, Sayan (1986). "Types of Synergy and Economic Value: The Impact of Acquisitions on Merging and Rival Firms," *Strategic Management Journal*, 7(2), 119–139.

Chatterjee, Sayan (1990). "Excess Resources, Utilization Costs, and Mode of Entry," *Academy of Management Journal*, 33(4), 780–800.

Chatterjee, Sayan (1991). "Gains in Vertical Acquisition and Market Power: Theory and Evidence," *Academy of Management Journal*, 34(2), 436–448.

Chatterjee, Sayan & James Blocher (1992). "The Continuous Measurement of Firm Diversification: Is it Robust?" *Academy of Management Journal*, 35(4), 874–888.

Chatterjee, Sayan & Michael Lubatkin (1990). "Corporate Mergers, Stockholder Diversification, and Changes in Systematic Risk," *Strategic Management Journal*, 11(4), 255–268.

Chatterjee, Sayan & Jagdip Singh (1999). "Are Tradeoffs Inherent in Diversification Moves? A Simultaneous Model for Type of Diversification and Mode of Expansion Decisions," *Management Science*, 45(1), 25–41.

Chatterjee, Sayan & Birger Wernerfelt (1991). "The Link between Resources and Type of Diversification: Theory and Evidence," *Strategic Management Journal*, 12(1), 33–48.

Chatterjee, Sayan, Jeffrey S. Harrison, & Donald D. Bergh (2003). "Failed Takeover Attempts, Corporate Governance and Refocusing," *Strategic Management Journal*, 24(1), 87–96.

Chen, Ming-Jer (1996). "Competitor Analysis and Interfirm Rivalry: Toward a Theoretical Integration," *Academy of Management Review*, 21(l), 100–134.

Chen, Ming-Jer & Danny Miller (1994). "Competitive Attack, Retaliation, and Performance: An Expectancy-Valence Framework," *Strategic Management Journal*, 15(2), 85–102.

Chen, Sheng-Syan & Kim Wai Ho (2000). "Corporate Diversification, Ownership Structure, and Firm

Value: The Singapore Evidence," *International Review of Financial Analysis*, 9(3), 315–326.

Chenall, Robert H. (1979). "Some Elements of Organizational Control in Australian Divisional Firms," *Australian Journal of Management*, 4(1 Supplement), 1–36.

Child, John (1984) *Organization: A Guide to Problems and Practice*. Second edition. London: Harper and Row.

Christensen, H. K. & C. A. Montgomery (1981). "Corporate Economic Performance: Diversification Strategy versus Market Structure," *Strategic Management Journal*, 2(4), 327–343.

Chung, Chi-nien (2001). "Markets, Culture and Institutions: The Emergence of Large Business Groups in Taiwan, 1950s–1970s," *Journal of Management Studies*, 38(5), 719–745.

Chung, Lai Hong, Patrick T. Gibbons, & Herbert P. Schoch (2000). "The Influence of Subsidiary Context and Head Office Strategic Management Style on Control of MNCs: The Experience in Australia," *Accounting, Auditing & Accountability Journal*, 13(5), 647–668.

Churchill Neil C. & Virginia L. Lewis (1983). "The Five Stages of Small Business Growth," *Harvard Business Review*, 61(3), 30–50.

Clark, Bruce H. & David B. Montgomery (1996). "Perceiving Competitive Reactions: The Value of Accuracy (and Paranoia)," *Marketing Letters*, 7(2), 115–129.

Clarke, Thomas (1998). "The Stakeholder Corporation: A Business Philosophy for the Information Age," *Long Range Planning*, 31(2), 171–180.

Clarkson, Max B. E. (1995). "A Stakeholder Framework for Analyzing and Evaluating Corporate Social Performance," *Academy of Management Review*, 20(1), 92–117.

Coase, R. H. (1937). "The Nature of the Firm," *Economica, New Series*, 4(16), 386–405.

Coase, R. H. (1988a). "The Nature of the Firm: Origin," *Journal of Law and Economics*, 43(1), 3–17.

Coase, R. H. (1988b). "The Nature of the Firm: Meaning," *Journal of Law and Economics*, 43(1), 19–32.

Coase, R. H. (1988c). "The Nature of the Firm: Influence," *Journal of Law and Economics*, 43(1), 33–47.

Coase, R. H. (2000). "The Acquisition of Fisher Body by General Motors," *Journal of Law and Economics*, 43(1), 15–31.

Coff, Russel W. (1999). "How Buyers Cope with Uncertainty when Acquiring Firms in Knowledge-Incentive Industries: Caveat Emptor," *Organization Science*, 10(2), 144–161.

Coff, Russel W. (2002). "Human Capital, Shared Expertise, and the Likelihood of Impasse in Corporate Acquisitions," *Journal of Management*, 28(1), 107–128.

Coff, Russel W. (2003). "Bidding Wars over R&D-Intensive Firms: Knowledge, Opportunism, and the Market for Corporate Control," *Academy of Management Journal*, 46(1), 74–85.

Coles, Jerilyn, Victoria B. McWilliams, & Nilanjan Sen (2001). "An Examination of the Relationship of Governance Mechanisms to Performance," *Journal of Management*, 27(1), 23–50.

Collis, David J. (1995). "The Walt Disney Company (A): Corporate Strategy. Harvard Business School," *Teaching Note* 5-795-152.

Collis, David J. & Cynthia A. Montgomery (1998). "Creating Corporate Advantage," *Harvard Business Review*, 76(3), 70–84.

Collis, David J. & Cynthia A. Montgomery (2005). *Corporate Strategy: A Resource-Based Approach*. Second edition. Boston, MA: McGraw-Hill/Irwin.

Collis, David, David Young, & Michael Goold (2007). "The Size, Structure, and Performance of Corporate Headquarters," *Strategic Management Journal*, 28(4), 383–405.

Comment, Robert and Gregg A. Jarrell (1995). "Corporate Focus and Stock Returns," *Journal of Financial Economics*, 37(1), 67–87.

Copland, Tom & Peter Tufano (2004). "A Real-World Way to Manage Real Options," *Harvard Business Review*, 82(3), 90–99.

Cordeiro, James J., & Rajaram Veliyath (2003). "Beyond Pay for Performance: A Panel Study of the Determinant of CEO Compensation," *American Business Review*, 21(1), 56–66.

Cording, Margaret, Petra Christmann, & L. J. Bourgeois III (2002). "A Focus on Resources in M&A Success: A Literature Review and Research Agenda to Resolve Two Paradoxes," Paper presented at the Academy of Management Meeting, August 12.

Cording, Margaret, Petra Christmann, & David R. King (2008). "Reducing Causal Ambiguity in

Acquisition Integration: Intermediate Goals as Mediators of Integration Decisions and Acquisition Performance," *Academy of Management Journal*, 51(4), 744–767.

Cornett, Marci M., Gayane Hovakimian, Darius Palla, & Hassan Tehrarian (2003). "The Impact of the Manager-Shareholder Conflict on Acquiring Bank Returns," *Journal of Banking & Finance*, 27(1), 103–131.

Croyle, Randy & Patrick Kager (2002). "Giving Mergers a Head Start," *Harvard Business Review*, 80(10), 20–21.

Cyriac, Joseph, Tim Koller, & Jannick Thomsen (2012). "Testing the Limits of Diversification," *McKinsey Quarterly*, February, 2–5.

Daft, Richard L. & Robert H. Lengel (1986). "Organizational Information Requirements, Media Richness and Structural Design," *Management Science*, 32(5), 554–571.

Daily, Catherine M., Dan R. Dalton, & Albert A. Cannella (2003). "Corporate Governance: Decades of Dialogue and Data," *Academy of Management Review*, 28(3), 371–382.

Darragh, John & Andrew Campbell (2001). "Why Corporate Initiatives Get Stuck?" *Long Range Planning*, 34(1), 33–52.

Das, T. K, & Bing-Sheng Teng (2000). "Instabilities of Strategic Alliances: An Internal Tension Perspective," *Organization Science*, 11(1), 77–102.

Dastidar, Protiti (2009). "International Corporate Diversification and Performance: Does Firm Self-Selection Matter?" *Journal of International Business Studies*, 40(1), 71–85.

Datta Deepak K. (1991). "Organizational Fit and Acquisition Performance: Effects of Postacquisition Integration," *Strategic Management Journal*, 12(4), 281–297.

Datta-Chaudhuri, Mrinal (1990). "Market Failure and Government Failure," *The Journal of Economic Perspectives*, 4(3), 25–39.

D'Aveni, Richard A. (1994). *Hypercompetition*. Free Press: New York.

D'Aveni, Richard A. (2002). "Competitive Pressure Systems: Mapping and Managing Multimarket Contact," *MIT Sloan Management Review*, 44(1), 39–49.

D'Aveni, Richard A. (2004). "Corporate Spheres of Influence," *MIT Sloan Management Review*, 44(4), 38–46.

David, Parthiban, Jonathan P. O'Brien, Toru Yoshikawa, & Andrew Delios (2010). "Do Shareholders or Stakeholders Appropriate the Rents from Corporate Diversification? The Influence of Ownership Structure," *Academy of Management Journal*, 53(3), 636–654.

David, Robert J. & Shin-Kap Han (2004). "A Systematic Assessment of the Empirical Support for Transaction Cost Economics," *Strategic Management Journal*, 25(1), 39–58.

Davidow, W. H. & M. S. Malone (1992). *The Virtual Corporation*. New York: HaperCollins.

Davis, James H., F. David Schoorman, & Lex Donaldson (1997). "Toward a Stewardship Theory of Management," *Academy of Management Review*, 22(1), 20–47.

Davis, Rachel & Irine M. Duhaime (1992). "Diversification, Industry Analysis and Vertical Integration: New Perspective and Measurement," *Strategic Management Journal*, 13(7), 511–524.

Davis, Gerald F., Kristina A. Diekman, & Catherine F. Tinsley (1994). "The Decline and Fall of the Conglomerate Firm in the 1980s: A Study in the De-Institutionalization of an Organizational Form," *American Sociological Review*, 59(4), 547–570.

Day, George S., Allan D. Shocker, & Rajendra K. Srivastava (1979). "Customer-Oriented Approaches to Identifying Product Markets," *Journal of Marketing*, 43(4), 8–19.

DeAngelo, Harry & Linda DeAngelo (2000). "Controlling Stockholders and the Disciplinary Role of Corporate Payout Policy: A Study of the Times Mirror Company," *Journal of Financial Economics*, 56(2), 153–207.

Decker, Carolin & Thomas Mellewigt (2007). "Thirty Years After Michael E. Porter: What De We Know About Business Exit?" *Academy of Management Perspectives*, 21(2), 41–55.

Delong, Gayle L. (2001). "Stockholder Gains from Focusing versus Diversifying Bank Mergers," *Journal of Financial Economics*, 59(2), 221–252.

Demsetz, Harold (1983). "The Structure of Ownership and the Theory of the Firm," *Journal of Law and Economics*, 26(2), 375–390.

Denis, David J., Diane. K. Denis, & Atulya Sarin (1997). "Agency Problems, Equity Ownership, and Corporate Diversification," *Journal of Finance*, 52(1), 135–160.

Denis, David J., Diane. K. Denis, & Atulya Sarin (1999). "Agency Theory and the Reference of Equity Ownership Structure on Corporate Diversification Strategies," *Strategic Management Journal*, 20(11), 1071–1076.

Denis, David J., Diane K. Denis, & Keven Yost (2002). "Global Diversification, Industrial Diversification, and Firm Value," *Journal of Finance*, 57(5), 1951–1979.

Dess, Gregory G., Anil Gupta, Jean–François Hennart, & Charles W. L. Hill (1995). "Conducting and Integrating Strategy Research at the International, Corporate, and Business Levels: Issues and Directions," *Journal of Management*, 21(3), 357–393.

Dess, Gregory G., G. Tom Lumpkin, & Alan B. Eisner (2008). *Strategic Management: Text & Cases*. Fifth edition. Boston, MA: McGraw-Hill Irwin.

De Vries, Jan, and Ad van der Woude (1997). *The First Modern Economy: Success, Failure, and Perseverance of the Dutch Economy, 1500–1815*. Cambridge: Cambridge University Press.

De Waal, André (2007). *Strategic Performance Management: A Managerial and Behavioural Approach*. New York: Palgrave Macmillan.

Dewenter, Kathryn, Walter Novaes, & Richard H. Pettway (2001). "Visibility versus Complexity in Business Groups: Evidence from Japanese Keiretsus," *Journal of Business*, 74(1), 79–100.

De Wit, Bob & Ron Meyer (2010). *Strategy Process, Content, Context: An International Perspective*. Fourth Edition. London: Thomson Learning.

Devinney, Timothy M., David F. Midgley, & Sunil Venaik (2000). "The Optimal Performance of the Global Firm: Formalizing and Extending the Integration-Responsiveness Framework," *Organization Science*, 11(6), 674–695.

Dicken, Peter (2007). *Global Shift: Mapping the Changing Contours of the World Economy*. London: Sage.

Dierickx, Ingemar, & Karel Cool (1989). "Asset Stock Accumulation and Sustainability of Competitive Advantage," *Management Science*, 35(12), 1504–1514.

DiMaggio, Paul J. & Walter W. Powell (1983). "The Iron Cage Revisited: Institutional Isomorphism and Collective Rationality in Organizational Fields," *American Sociological Review*, 48(2), 147–160.

Ding, John Y. & Julie A. Caswell (1995). "Changes in Diversification Among Very Large Food Manufacturing Firms in the 1980s," *Agribusiness*, 11(6), 553–564.

Dixit, Avinash K. & Robert S. Pindyck (1994). *Investment Under Uncertainty*. Princeton, NJ: Princeton University Press.

Dodd, Peter (1980). "Merger Proposals, Managerial Discretion and Stockholder Wealth," *Journal of Financial Economics*, 8(2), 105–137.

Donaldson, Gordon & Jay W. Lorsch (1983). *Decision Making at the Top*. New York: Basic Books.

Donaldson, Lex (2001). *The Contingency Theory of Organisations*. London: Sage.

Donaldson, Lex & James H. Davis (1991). "Stewardship Theory or Agency Theory: CEO Governance and Shareholder Returns," *Australian Journal of Management*, 16(1), 49–65.

Douglas, Susan P. & C. Samuel Craig (1989). "Evolution of Global Marketing Strategy: Scale, Scope and Synergy," *Columbia Journal of World Business*, 24(3), 47–59.

Doukas, John. A. & L. H. P. Lang, (2003). "Foreign Direct Investment, Diversification and Firm Performance," *Journal of International Business Studies*, 34(2), 153–172.

Doukas, John & Nickolaos G. Travlos (1988). "The Effect of Corporate Multinationalism on Shareholders' Wealth: Evidence from International Acquisitions," *Journal of Finance*, 43(5), 1161–1175.

Doz, Yves & C. K. Prahalad (1991). "Managing MNCs: A Search for a New Paradigm," *Strategic Management Journal*, 12(SSI), 145–164.

Dranikoff, Lee, Tim Koller, & Antoon Schneider (2002). "Divestiture: Strategy's Missing Link," *Harvard Business Review*, 80(5), 74–83.

Dunlap, Riley E., George H. Gallup, Jr., & Alec M. Gallup (1993). "Of Global Concern: Results of the Health of the Planet Survey," *Environment*, 35(9): 6–14, 33–40.

Dunning, John H. (1977). "Trade, Location of Economic Activity and the MNE: A Search for an Eclectic

Approach," in Ohlin, Bertil Gotthard, Per-Ove Hesselborn & Per Magnus Wijkman (eds) *The International Allocation of Economic Activity: Proceedings of a Nobel Symposium Held at Stockholm*, pp. 394–418. London: Holmes and Meier.

Dunning, John H. (1981). *International Production and the Multinational Enterprise*. Winchester, MA: Allen & Unwin.

Dyer, Jeffrey H. (1996a). "Specialized Supplier Networks as a Source of Competitive Advantage: Evidence from the Auto Industry," *Strategic Management Journal*, 17(4), 271–292.

Dyer, Jeffrey H. (1996b). "How Chrysler Created an American Keiretsu," *Harvard Business Review*, 74(4) 42–56.

Dyer, Jeffrey H. (1997). Effective Interfirm Collaboration: How Firms Minimize Transaction Costs and Maximize Transaction Value," *Strategic Management Journal*, 18(7), 535–556.

Dyer, Jeffrey H. & Kentaro Nobeoka (2000). "Creating and Managing a High-Performance Knowledge-Sharing Network: The Toyota Case," *Strategic Management Journal*, 21(3), 345–368.

Dyer, Jeffrey H., Prashant Kale, & Harbir Singh (2001). "How to Make Strategic Alliances Work," *Sloan Management Journal*, 42(4), 37–43.

Economist (2001). "Spoilt for Choice," July 5 [www.economist.com/business/displayStory.cfm?Story_ID=684525].

Economist (2006). "Microsoft on Trial," April 28 [http://globaltechforum.eiu.com/index.asp?categoryid=&channelid=&doc_id=8487&layout=rich_story&search=Brussels].

Edwards, Corbin D. (1953). "Vertical Integration and the Monopoly Problem," *Journal of Marketing*, 17(4), 404–410.

Edwards, Corbin D. (1955). "Conglomerate Bigness as a Source of Power," in National Bureau of Economic Research, Inc (Ed.) *Business Concentration and Public Policy*, pp. 331–352. Princeton, NJ: Princeton University Press.

Egelhoff, William G., Joachim Wolf, & Mihael Adzic (2013). "Designing Matrix Structures to Fit MNC Strategy," *Global Strategy Journal*, 3(3), 205–226.

Eger, Carrol E. (1983). "An Empirical Test of the Redistribution Effect of Mergers," *Journal of Financial and Quantitative Analysis*, 18(4), 547–572.

Eisenhardt, Kathleen M. (1985). "Control: Organizational and Economic Approaches," *Management Science*, 31(2), 134–149

Eisenhardt, Kathleen M. (1989). "Agency Theory: An Assessment and Review," *Academy of Management Review*, 14(1), 57–74.

Eisenhardt, Kathleen M. & D. Charles Galunic (2000). "Coevolving: At Last, a Way to Make Synergies Work," *Harvard Business Review*, 37(1), 91–101.

Eisenhardt, Kathleen M. & Jeffrey A. Martin (2000). "Dynamic Capabilities: What are they?" *Strategic Management Journal*, 21(10/11), 1105–1121.

Eun, Cheol S., Richard Kolodny & Carl Scherega (1996). "Cross-border Acquisitions and Shareholder Wealth: Tests of the Synergy and Internalization Hypotheses," *Journal of Banking and Finance*, 20(9), 1559–1582.

Fama, Eugene F. (1980). "Agency Problems and the Theory of the Firm," *Journal of Political Economy*, 88(2), 288–307.

Fama, Eugene F. & Michael C. Jensen (1983). "Separation of Ownership and Control," *Journal of Law & Economics*, 26(2), 301–325.

Fan, Joseph P. H. & Larry H. P. Lang (2000). "The Measurement of Relatedness: An Application to Corporate Diversification," *Journal of Business*, 73(4), 629–660.

Farjoun, Moshe (1994). "Beyond Industry Boundaries: Human Expertise, Diversification, and Resource-Related Industry Groups," *Organization Science*, 5(2), 185–199.

Farjoun, Moshe (1998). "The Independent and Joint Effects of the Skill and Physical Bases of Relatedness in Diversification," *Strategic Management Journal*, 19(7), 611–630.

Farjoun, Moshe & Linda Lai (1997). "Similarity Judgments in Strategy Formulation: Role, Process and Implications," *Strategic Management Journal*, 19(7), 611–630.

Fauver, Larry, Joel Houston, & Andy Naranjo (2003). "Capital Market Development, International

Integration, Legal Systems, and the Value of Corporate Diversification: A Cross-Country Analysis," *Journal of Financial and Quantitative Analysis*, 38(1), 135–157.

Feinberg, Robert M. (1985). "Sales-at-Risk: A Test of the Mutual Forbearance Theory of Conglomerate Behavior," *Journal of Business*, 58(2), 225–241.

Ferris, Stephen P., Kenneth A. Kim, & Pattanaporn Kitsabunnarat (2003). "The Costs (and Benefits?) of Diversified Business Groups: The Case of Korean Chaebols," *Journal of Banking & Finance*, 27(1), 251–273.

Fichman, Robert G. (2004). "Real Options and IT Platform Adoption: Implications for Theory and Practice," *Information Systems Research*, 15(2), 132–154.

Fichman, Robert G., Mark Keil, & Amrit Tiwana (2005), "Beyond Valuation: Options Thinking in IT Project Management," *California Management Review*, 47(2), 74–96.

Filatotchev, Igor & Steve Toms (2006). "Corporate Governance and Financial Constraints on Strategic Turnarounds," *Journal of Management Studies*, 43(3), 407–433.

Finkelstein, Sydney & Donald C. Hambrick (1989). "Chief Executive Compensation: A Study of the Intersection of Markets and Political Processes," *Strategic Management Journal*, 10(2), 121–134.

Financial Times (2003). "Wanadoo Fined € 10m for Predatory Pricing," July 17.

Financial Times (2008a). "Vertical Reintegration," *Financial Times*, May 22, [www.ft.com/cms/s/3/908563cc-279a-11dd-b7cb-000077b07658.html].

Financial Times (2008b). "BASF Follows Trend of Integration," *Financial Times*, September 15, [www.ft.com/cms/s/0/daeeb746-8349-11dd-907e-000077b07658.html].

Financial Times (2008c). "Matsushita to Build LCD Factory," *Financial Times*, February 18, [www.ft.com/cms/s/0/056e90cc-ddc3-11dc-ad7e-0000779fd2ac.html].

Financial Times (2009). "Reaggregating the Supply Chain," *Financial Times*, July 15, [www.ft.com/cms/s/3/883ad91c-7119-11de-877c-00144feabdc0.html].

Fisher, Susan Reynolds & Margaret A. White (2000). "Downsizing in a Learning Organization: Are there Hidden Costs?" *Academy of Management Review*, 25(1), 244–251.

Fligstein, Neil (1985). "The Spread of the Multidivisional Form among Large Firms, 1919–1979," *American Sociological Review*, 50(3), 377–391.

Fligstein, Neil (2001). *The Architecture of Markets: An Economic Sociology of Twenty-First Century Capitalist Societies*. Princeton (NJ): Princeton University Press.

Fligstein, Neil & Peter Brantley (1992). "Bank Control, Owner Control or Organizational Dynamics", *American Journal of Sociology*, 98(2), 280-307. Fligstein, Neil & Peter Brantley (1992). "Bank Control, Owner Control or Organizational Dynamics," *American Journal of Sociology*, 98(2), 280–307.

Fligstein, Neil, & Taekjin Shin (2007). "Shareholder Value and the Transformation of the U.S. Economy, 1984–2000," *Sociological Forum*, 22(4), 399–424.

Folta, Timothy B. (1998). "Governance and Uncertainty: The Trade-Off between Administrative Control and Commitment," *Strategic Management Journal*, 19(11), 1007–1028.

Folta, Timothy B., Douglas R. Johnson, & Jonathan O'Brien (2006), "Uncertainty, Irreversibility, and the Likelihood of Entry: An Empirical Assessment of the Option to Defer," *Journal of Economic Behavior & Organization*, 61(2), 432–452.

Foss, Nicolai J. (1997). "On the Rationales of Corporate Headquarters," *Industrial and Corporate Change*, 6(2), 313–338.

Fouraker, Lawrence E. & John M. Stopford (1968). "Organizational Structure and the Multinational Strategy," *Administrative Science Quarterly*, 13(1), 47–64.

Fox, Isaac, Shaker Srinivasan & Paul Vaaler (1997). "A Descriptive Alternative to Cluster Analysis: Understanding Strategic Group Performance with Simulated Annealing," in Michel Ghertman, Jacques Obadia, Jean-Luc Arregle (Ed.), *Statistical Models for Strategic Management*, pp. 81–110. London: Springer.

Franko, Lawrence G. (1974). "The Move toward a Multi-Divisional Structure in European Organizations," *Administrative Science Quarterly*, 19(4), 493–506.

Franko, Lawrence G. (2004). "The death of Diversification? The Focusing of the World's Industrial Firms, 1980–2000," *Business Horizons*, 47(4), 41–50.

Freeland, Robert F. (2000). "Creating Holdup through Vertical Integration: Fisher Body Revisited," *Journal of Law and Economics*, 43(1), 33–66.

Freeman, R. Edward (1984). *Strategic Management: A Stakeholder Approach*. Boston: Pitman.

Freeman, R. Edward & John McVea (2001). "A Stakeholder Approach to Strategic Management," in Michael A. Hitt, R. Edward Freeman, & Jeffrey S. Harrison (eds) *Handbook Strategic Management*, pp. 189–207. Oxford, UK: Blackwell.

Freeman, R. Edward, Andrew C. Wicks, & Bidhan Parmar (2004). "Stakeholder Theory and 'The Corporate Objective Revisited'," *Organizational Science*, 15(3), 364–369.

Friedman, Milton (1970). "The Social Responsibility of Business is to Increase its Profits," *New York Times*, September 13: 122–126.

Froot, Kenneth A., David S. Scharfstein, & Jeremy C. Stein (1994). "A Framework for Risk Management," *Harvard Business Review*, 72(6), 91–102.

Fuentelsaz, Lucio & Jaime Gómez (2006). "Multipoint Competition, Strategic Similarity and Entry into Geographic Markets. *Strategic Management Journal*, 27(5), 477–499.

Furrer, Olivier (2008). *Nestlé: Divesting Perrier?* Radboud University Nijmegen Case Study. The Case Center 306–063–1.

Furrer, Olivier (2010). "A Customer Relationship Typology of Product Services Strategies," in Faïz Gallouj & Faridah Djellal (eds) *Handbook of Innovation and Services: A Multi-disciplinary Perspective*, pp. 701–721. Cheltenham: Edward Elgar.

Furrer, Olivier (2013). "Integrity and Corporate Governance: Controlling Managers and Meeting Corporate social Responsibilities," in Wolfgang Amann & Agata Stachowicz–Stamusch (eds) *Integrity in Organizations: Building the Foundations for Humanistic Management*, pp. 480–497. Basingstoke: Palgrave Macmillan.

Furrer, Olivier & Howard Thomas (2000). "The Rivalry Matrix: Understanding Rivalry and Competitive Dynamics," *European Management Journal*, 18(6), 619–637.

Furrer, Olivier, D. Sudharshan, & Howard Thomas (2001). "Organizational Structure in a Global Context: The Structure-Intangible Asset Portfolio Link," in Farok J. Contractor (Ed.) *Valuation of Intangible Assets in Global Operations*, pp. 334–353. Westport, CT: Quorum Books.

Furrer, Olivier, Jeffrey A. Krug, D. Sudharshan, & Howard Thomas (2004). "The Resource–Based Theory and its Link to the Global Strategy, Structure, and Performance Relationship: An Integrative Framework," *International Journal of Management and Decision Making*, 5(2–3), 99–116.

Furrer, Olivier, J. Rajendran Pandian, & Howard Thomas (2007a). "Corporate Strategy and Shareholder Value During Decline and Turnaround," *Management Decision*, 45(3), 372–392.

Furrer, Olivier, Howard Thomas & Anna Goussevskaia (2007b). "The Structure and Evolution of the Strategic Management Field: A Content Analysis of 26 Years of Strategic Management Research," *International Journal of Management Reviews*, 10(2), 1–23.

Furrer, Olivier, Carolyn P. Egri, David A. Ralston, Wade Danis, Emmanuelle Reynaud, Irina Naoumova, Mario Molteni, Arunas Starkus, Fidel León Darder, Marina Dabic, & Amandine Furrer-Perrinjaquet (2010). "Attitudes toward Corporate Responsibilities in Western Europe and in Central and East Europe," *Management International Review*, 50(3), 379–398.

Galbraith, Jay R. (1977). *Organization Design*. Reading, MA: Addison-Wesley.

Galbraith, Jay R. (1995). *Designing Organizations*. San Francisco, CA: Jossey-Bass.

Galbraith, Jay R. & Robert Kazanjian (1986). *Strategy Implementation: Structure, Systems and Process*. Second edition. St Paul, MN: West.

Galbraith, John S. (1957). *The Hudson's Bay Company as an Imperial Factor 1821–1869*. Berkeley: University of California Press.

Garrod, Neil & Williams Rees (1998). "International Diversification and Firm Value," *Journal of Business Finance and Accounting*, 25(9–10), 1255–1281.

Gatignon, Hubert & Erin Anderson (1988). "The Multinational Corporation's Degree of Control over Foreign Subsidiaries: An Empirical Test of a Transaction Cost Explanation," *Journal of Law, Economics, and Organization*, 4(2), 305–336.

Gaughan, Patrick A. (2002). *Mergers, Acquisitions, and Corporate Restructurings*. Third edition. New York: Wiley.

Gaughan, Patrick A. (2011). *Mergers, Acquisitions, and Corporate Restructurings*. Fifth edition. New York: Wiley.

Geletkanycz, Marta A., Brian K. Boyd, & Sydney Finkelstein (2003). "The Strategic Value of CEO External Directorate Networks: Implications for CEO Compensation," *Strategic Management Journal*, 22(9), 889–898.

Geroski, P. A. (1995). "What Do We Know about Entry?" *International Journal of Industrial Organization*, 13(4), 421–440.

Gertner, Robert H., David S. Scharfstein, & Jeremy C. Stein (1994). "Internal versus External Capital Markets," *Quarterly Journal of Economics*, 109(4), 1211–1230.

Geyskens, Inge, Jan-Benedict E. M. Steenkamp, & Nirmalya Kumar (2006). "Make, Buy, or Ally: A Transaction Cost Theory Meta-Analysis," *Academy of Management Journal*, 49(3), 519–543.

Ghemawat, Pankaj (1985), "Building Strategy on the Experience Curve," *Harvard Business Review*, 63(2), 143–149.

Ghemawat, Pankaj & Joan E. Ricart i Costa (1993). "The Organizational Tension between Static and Dynamic Efficiency," *Strategic Management Journal*, 14(WSI), 59–73.

Ghoshal, Sumantra (1987). "Global Strategy: An Organizing Framework," *Strategic Management Journal*, 8(5), 425–440.

Ghoshal, Sumantra (2006). "Bad Management Theories Are Destroying Good Management Practices," *Academy of Management Learning & Education*, 4(1), 75–91.

Ghoshal, Sumantra & Christopher A. Bartlett (1990). "The Multinational Corporation as an Interorganizational Network," *Academy of Management Review*, 15(4), 603–625.

Gibbs, Philip A. (1993). "Determinant of Corporate Restructuring: The Relative Importance of Corporate Governance, Takeover Threats, and Free Cash Flow," *Strategic Management Journal*, 14(SSI), 51–68.

Gimeno, Javier (1994). "Multipoint Competition, Market Rivalry, and Firm Performance: A Mutual Forbearance Hypothesis in the U.S. Airline Industry, 1984–1988," doctoral dissertation, Krannert Graduate School of Management.

Gimeno, Javier (1999). "Reciprocal Threats in Multimarket Rivalry: Staking Out 'Spheres of Influence' in the U.S. Airline Industry," *Strategic Management Journal*, 20(2), 101–128.

Gimeno, Javier & Eui Jeong (2001). "Multimarket Contact: Meaning and Measurement at Multiple Levels of Analysis," in Joel A. C. Baum & Henry R. Greve (eds) *Multiunit Organization and Multimarket Strategy: Advances in Strategic Management*, Vol. 18, pp. 357–408. Oxford, UK: JAI Press.

Gimeno, Javier & Carolyn Y. Woo (1996). "Hypercompetition in a Multimarket Environment: The Role of Strategic Similarity and Multimarket Contact on Competitive De-Escalation," *Organization Science*, 7(3), 322–341.

Gimeno, Javier & Carolyn Y. Woo (1999), "Multimarket Contact, Economies of Scope, and Firm Performance," *Academy of Management Journal*, 43(3), 239–259.

Gimeno, Javier, Pedro L. Marin, & Carolyn Y. Woo (1998). "How Do Market Structures Influence Multimarket Competition? An Empirical Test of Bernheim and Whinston's Hypothesis," Working Paper, Department of Management, Texas A&M University.

Ginsberg, Ari (1990). "Connecting Diversification to Performance: A Sociocognitive Approach," *Academy of Management Review*, 15(3), 514–535.

Golden, Brian R. & Hao Ma (2003). "Mutual Forbearance: The Role of Intrafirm Integration and Rewards," *Academy of Management Review*, 28(3), 479–493.

Gomes, Lenn & Kannan Ramaswamy (1999). "An Empirical Examination of the Form of Relationship between Multinationality and Performance," *Journal of International Business Studies*, 30(1) 173–188.

Gomez-Mejia, Luis R., Manuel Nunez-Nickel, & Isabel Guitirez (2001). "The Role of Family Ties in Agency Contracts," *Academy of Management Journal*, 44(1), 81–95.

Gomez–Mejia, Luis R. & Robert M. Wiseman (1997). "Reframing Executive Compensation: An Assessment and Outlook," *Journal of Management*, 23(3), 291–374.

Goold, Michael C. & Andrew Campbell (1987). *Strategy and Style: The Role of the Centre in Managing Diverse Corporations*. Oxford, UK: Basil Blackwell.

Goold, Michael C. & Andrew Campbell (1998). "Desperately Seeking Synergy," *Harvard Business Review*, 76(5), 131–143.

Goold, Michael C. & Kathleen Luchs (1993). "Why Diversify? Four Decades of Management Thinking," *Academy of Management Executive*, 7(3), 7–25.

Goold, Michael C. & John J. Quinn (1990). "The Paradox of Strategic Controls," *Strategic Management Journal*, 11(1), 43–57.

Goold, Michael, Andrew Campbell, & Marcus Alexander (1994). *Corporate-Level Strategy: Creating Value in the Multibusiness Company*. John Wiley & Sons: New York.

Goold, Michael C., David Pettifer, & David Young (2001). "Redesigning the Corporate Centre," *European Management Journal*, 19(1), 83–91.

Gort, Michael (1962). *Diversification and Integration in American Industry*. Princeton, NJ: Princeton University Press.

Govindarajan, Vijay & Joseph Fisher (1990). "Strategy, Control Systems, and Resource Sharing: Effects on Business-Unit Performance," *Academy of Management Journal*, 33(2), 259–285.

Graebner, Melissa E., Katheleen M. Eisenhardt, & Philip T. Roundy (2010). "Success and Failure in Technology Acquisitions: Lessons for Buyers and Sellers. *Academy of Management Perspectives*, 24(3), 73–92.

Grant, Robert M. (1987). "Multinationality and Performance Among British Manufacturing Companies," *Journal of International Business Studies*, 18(3), 79–89.

Grant, Robert M. (1988). "On 'Dominant Logic', Relatedness and the Link between Diversity and Performance," *Strategic Management Journal*, 9(6), 639–642.

Grant, Robert M. (2002). "Corporate Strategy: Managing Scope and Strategy Content," in Andrew Pettigrew, Howard Thomas, and Richard Whittington (eds) *Handbook of Strategy and Management*, pp. 72–97. London: Sage.

Grant, Robert M. (2008). *Contemporary Strategy Analysis*. Sixth edition. Oxford: Blackwell Publishing.

Grant, Robert M. (2013). *Contemporary Strategy Analysis*. Eighth edition. Chichester, UK: Wiley.

Grant, Robert M. & Azar P. Jammine (1988). "Performance Differences between the Wrigley/Rumelt Strategic Categories," *Strategic Management Journal*, 9(4), 333–346.

Grant, Robert M., Azar P. Jammine, & Howard Thomas (1988). "Diversity, Diversification and Profitability among British Manufacturing Companies: 1972–1984," *Academy of Management Journal*, 31(4), 771–801.

Gray, Samuel R. & Albert A. Cannella, Jr. (1997). "The Role of Risk in Executive Compensation," *Journal of Management*, 23(4), 517–540.

Greiner, Larry E. (1972). "Evolution and Revolution as Organization Grow," *Harvard Business Review*, 50(4), 37–46.

Griffin, Ricky W. & Michael W. Pustay (2010). *International Business*. Sixth edition. Boston: Pearson.

Grosse, Robert & Len J. Trevino (1996). "Foreign Direct Investment in the United States: An Analysis by Country of Origin," *Journal of International Business Studies*, 27(1), 139–155.

Grossman, Sanford J. & Oliver D. Hart (1986). "The Costs and Benefits of Ownership: A Theory of Vertical and Lateral Integration," *Journal of Political Economy*, 94(4), 691–719.

Grover, Ronald (2006). "Disney-Pixar: It's a Wrap," *Business Week*, January 24, [www.businessweek.com/print/technology/content/jan2006/tc20060124_959402.htm].

Gulati, Ranjay & Harbir Singh (1998). "The Architecture of Cooperation: Managing Coordination Costs and Appropriation Concerns in Strategic Alliances," *Administrative Science Quarterly*, 43(4), 781–814.

Gupta, Anil K. & Vijay Govindarajan (1986). "Resource Sharing among SBUs: Strategic Antecedents and Administrative Implications," *Academy of Management Journal*, 29(4), 695–714.

Gupta, Diwakar & Yigal Gerchak (2002). "Quantifying Operational Synergies in a Merger/Acquisition," *Management Science*, 48(4), 517–533.

Haberberg, Adrian & Alison Rieple (2001). *The Strategic Management of Organizations*. Harlow (UK): Financial Times – Prentice Hall.

Hagiu, Andrei (2007). "Microsoft Xbox: Changing the Game?" *Harvard Business School Case Study*, 9–707–501.

Hall, Ernst H., Jr. & Caron St John (1994). "A Methodological Note on Diversity Measurement," *Strategic Management Review*, 15(2), 153–168.

Hall, Peter A. & David Soskice (2001). *Varieties of Capitalism: The Institutional Foundations of Comparative Advantage*. Oxford: Oxford University Press.

Hamel, Gary (1991). "Competition for Competence in Inter-Partner Learning within International Strategic Alliances," *Strategic Management Journal*, 12(SSI), 83–103.

Hamel, Gary & C. K. Prahalad (1985). "Do You Really Have a Global Strategy?" *Harvard Business Review*, 63(4), 139–149.

Hamel, Gary & C. K. Prahalad (1990). "The Core Competence of the Corporation," *Harvard Business Review*, 68(3), 79–91.

Hamel, Gary & C. K. Prahalad (1993). "Strategy as Stretch and Leverage," *Harvard Business Review*, 71(2), 75–84.

Hamel, Gary & C. K. Prahalad (1994). *Competing for the Future*. Cambridge, MA: Harvard Business School Press.

Hannah, Leslie (1976). *The Rise of the Corporate Economy*. London: Methuen.

Hannah, Leslie (1991). "Scale and Scope: Towards a European Visible Hand?" *Business History*, 33(2), 297–309.

Hannan, Michael T. & John Freeman (1977). "The Population Ecology of Organizations," *American Journal of Sociology*, 82(5), 929–964.

Hannan, Michael T. & John Freeman (1984). "Structural Inertia and Organizational Change," *American Sociological Review*, 49(2), 149–164.

Harper, Neil W. C. & S. Patrick Viguerie (2002). "Are You too Focused?" *The McKinsey Quarterly*, Mid-Summer, 29–38.

Harrigan, Kathryn Rudie (1981). "Deterrents to Divestiture," *Academy of Management Journal*, 24(2), 306–323.

Harrigan, Kathryn Rudie (1984). "Formulating Vertical Integration Strategies," *Academy of Management Review*, 9(4), 638–652.

Harrigan, Kathryn Rudie (1985a). "Vertical Integration and Corporate Strategy," *Academy of Management Journal*, 28(2), 397–425.

Harrigan, Kathryn Rudie (1985b). "Exit Barriers and Vertical Integration," *Academy of Management Journal*, 28(3), 686–697.

Harrigan, Kathryn Rudie (1985c). *Strategic Flexibility*. Lexington, MA: Lexington Books.

Harrigan, Kathryn Rudie (1986). "Matching Vertical Integration Strategies to Competitive Conditions," *Strategic Management Journal*, 7(6), 535–555.

Harrison, Jeffrey S., Ernest H. Hall, Jr., & Rajendra Nargundkar (1993). "Resource Allocation as an Outcropping of Strategic Consistency: Performance Implications," *Academy of Management Journal*, 36(5), 1026–1051.

Harrison, Jeffrey S., Michael A.Hitt, Robert E. Hoskisson, & R. Duane Ireland (2001). "Resource Complementarity in Business Combinations: Extending the Logic to Organizational Alliances. *Journal of Management*, 27(6), 679–690.

Haspeslagh, Philippe C. (1982). "Portfolio Planning: Uses and Limits," *Harvard Business Review*, 60(1), 58–73.

Haspeslagh, Philippe C. (1983). "Portfolio Planning Approaches and the Strategic Management Process in Diversified Industrial Corporations." DBA dissertation, Harvard Business School.

Haspeslagh, Philippe C. & David B. Jemison (1991). *Managing Acquisitions*. New York: Free Press.

Hatfield, Donald E., Julia P. Liebskind, & Tim C. Opler (1996). "The Effects of Corporate Restructuring on Aggregate Industry Specialization," *Strategic Management Journal*, 17(1), 55–72.

Haveman, Heather A., & Lynn Nonnemaker (2000). "Competition in Multiple Geographic Markets: The Impact on Growth and Market Entry," *Administrative Science Quarterly*, 45(2), 232–267.

Hayes, Robert H. & William J. Abernathy (1980). "Managing our Way to Economic Decline," *Harvard Business Review*, 58(4), 67–77.

Hayward, Mathew L. A., Donald C. Hambrick (1997). "Explaining the Premium Paid for Large

Acquisitions: Evidence of CEO Hubris," *Administrative Science Quarterly*, 42(1), 103–127.

Hedlund, Gunnar (1994). "A Model of Knowledge Management and the N-Form Corporation," *Strategic Management Journal*, 15(SI), 73–90.

Heide, Jan B. (1994). "Interorganizational Governance in Marketing Channels," *Journal of Marketing*, 58(1), 71–85.

Heide, Jan B. & George John (1990). "Alliances in Industrial Purchasing: The Determinants of Joint Action in Buyer–Supplier Relationships," *Journal of Marketing Research*, 27(1), 24–36.

Heide, Jan B. & Anne S. Miner (1992). "The Shadow of the Future: Effects of Anticipated Interactions and Frequency of Contact on Buyer–Seller Cooperation," *Academy of Management Journal*, 35(2), 265–291.

Helfat, Constance E. & Kathleen M. Eisenhardt (2004). "Inter-Temporal Economies of Scope, Organizational Modularity, and the Dynamics of Diversification," *Strategic Management Journal*, 25(13), 1217–1232.

Helman, Christopher (2015) "How Cheap Oil Has Delta Air Lines Jet Fooled," *Forbes*, January 21. [www.forbes.com/sites/christopherhelman/2015/01/21/how-cheap-oil-has-delta-air-lines-jet-fooled/].

Hennart, Jean-François (1982a). *A Theory of the Multinational Enterprise*. Ann Arbor: University of Michigan.

Hennart, Jean-François (1982b). "Upstream Vertical Integration in the Aluminum and Tin Industries: A Comparative Study of the Choice between Market and Intrafirm Coordination," *Journal of Economic Behavior and Organization*, 9(3), 281–299.

Hennart, Jean-François (1988). "A Transaction Costs Theory of Equity Joint Ventures," *Strategic Management Journal*, 9(4), 361–374.

Hennart, Jean-François & Sabine Reddy (1997). "The Choice between Mergers/Acquisitions and Joint Ventures: The Case of Japanese Investors in the United States," *Strategic Management Journal*, 18(1), 1–12.

Heriot, Kirk C. & Subodh P. Kulkarni (2001). "The Use of Intermediate Sourcing Strategies," *Journal of Supply Chain Management*, 37(1), 18–26.

Higgins, Robert C. & Lawrence D. Schall (1975). "Corporate Bankruptcy and Conglomerate Merger," *Journal of Finance*, 30(1), 93–113.

Hill, Charles W. L. (1988). "Internal Capital Market Controls and Financial Performance in Multidivisional Firms," *Journal of Industrial Economics*, 37(1), 67–83.

Hill, Charles W. L. (1994). "Diversification and Economic Performance: Bringing Structure and Corporate Management Back into the Picture," in Richard P. Rumelt, Dan E. Schendel, and David J. Teece (eds) *Fundamental Issues in Strategy: A Research Agenda*, pp. 297–321. Boston, MA: Harvard Business School Press.

Hill, Charles W. L. (1995). "National Institutional Structures, Transaction Cost Economizing and Competitive Advantage: The Case of Japan," *Organization Science*, 6(1), 119–131.

Hill, Charles W. L. (2010). *International Business: Competing in the Global Marketplace*. Eighth edition. New York: McGraw-Hill.

Hill, Charles W. L., Gary S. Hansen (1991). "A Longitudinal Study of the Cause and Consequence of Changes in Diversification in the U.S. Pharmaceutical Industry, 1977–1986," *Strategic Management Journal*, 12(3), 187–199.

Hill, Charles W. L. & Robert E. Hoskisson (1987). "Strategy and Structure in the Multiproduct Firm," *Academy of Management Review*, 12(2), 331–341.

Hill, Charles W. L. & Gareth R. Jones (2001). *Strategic Management: An Integrated Approach*. Fifth edition. Boston, MA: Houghton Mifflin.

Hill, Charles W. L. & Gareth R. Jones (2004). *Strategic Management: An Integrated Approach*. Sixth edition. Boston, MA: Houghton Mifflin.

Hill, Charles W. L. & J. F. Pickering (1986). "Divisionalization, Decentralization and Performance of Large United-Kingdom Companies," *Journal of Management Studies*, 23(1), 26–50.

Hill, Charles W. L. & Scott A. Snell (1989). "Effect of Ownership Structure on Control and Corporate

Productivity," *Academy of Management Journal*, 32(1), 25–46.

Hill, Charles W. L., Michael A. Hitt, & Robert E. Hoskisson (1988). "Declining U.S. Competitiveness: Reflections on a Crisis," *Academy of Management Executive*, 2(1), 51–60.

Hill, Charles W. L., Peter Hwang, & W. Chan Kim (1990). "An Eclectic Theory of the Choice of International Entry Mode," *Strategic Management Journal*, 11(2), 117–128.

Hill, Charles W. L., Michael A. Hitt, & Robert E. Hoskisson (1992). "Cooperative versus Competitive Structures in Related and Unrelated Diversified Firms," *Organization Science*, 3(4), 501–521.

Hillman, Amy J., Gerald D. Keim, & Rebecca A. Luce (2001). "Board Composition and Stakeholder Performance: Do Stakeholder Directors Make a Difference?" *Business and Society*, 40(3), 295–314.

Hite, Gailen L., James E. Owers, & Ronald C. Rogers (1987). "The Market for Interfirm Asset Sales: Partial Sell-offs and Total Liquidations," *Journal of Financial Economics*, 18(2), 229–252.

Hitt, Michael A., Robert E. Hoskisson & R. Duane Ireland (1990). "Mergers and Acquisitions and Managerial Commitment to Innovation in M-Form Firms," *Strategic Management Journal*, 11(SI), 29–47.

Hitt, Michael A., Robert E. Hoskisson & R. Duane Ireland (1994). "A Midrange Theory of the Interactive Effects of International and Product Diversification on Innovation and Performance," *Journal of Management*, 20(2), 297–326.

Hitt, Michael A., Robert E. Hoskisson, Richard A. Johnson, & Donald D. Moesel (1996). "The Market for Corporate Control and Firm Innovation," *Academy of Management Journal*, 39(5), 1084–1119.

Hitt, Michael A., Robert E. Hoskisson & Hicheon Kim (1997). "International Diversification: Effects on Innovation and Firm Performance in Product–Diversified Firms," *Academy of Management Journal*, 40(4), 767–798.

Hitt, Michael A., Leonard Biermant, Katsuhiko Shimizu & Rahul Kochhar (2001a). "Direct and Moderating Effects of Human Capital on Strategy and Performance in Professional Service Firms: A Resource-based Perspective," *Academy of Management Journal*, 44(1), 13–28.

Hitt, Michael A., Jeffrey S. Harrison, & R. Duane Ireland (2001b). *Mergers and Acquisitions: A Guide to Creating Value to Shareholders*. New York: Oxford University Press.

Hitt, Michael A., Richard A. Johnson, Daphne Yiu, & William P. Wan (2001c). "Restructuring Strategies and Diversified Business Groups: Differences Associated with Country Institutional Environments," in Michael A. Hitt, Robert E. Freeman, & Jeffrey S. Harrison (eds) *Handbook Strategic Management*, pp. 433–463. Oxford, UK: Blackwell.

Hitt, Michael A., R. Duane Ireland & Robert E. Hoskisson (2004). *Strategic Management: Competitiveness and Globalization*. Sixth edition. Mason, OH: South-Western.

Hitt, Michael A., Laszlo Tihanyi, Toyah Miller, & Brian Connelly (2006). "International Diversification: Antecedents, Outcomes, and Moderators," *Journal of Management*, 32(6), 831–867.

Hofer, Charles W. (1980). "Turnaround Strategies," *Journal of Business Strategy*, 1(1), 19–31.

Hofer, Charles W. & Dan Schendel (1978). *Strategic Formulation: Analytical Concepts*, St. Paul: West Publishing Company.

Hoffman, Richard C. (1984). "Strategies for Corporate Turnarounds: What Do We Know About Them?" *Journal of General Management*, 14(3), 46–66.

Hofstede, Geert (2001). *Culture's Consequences: Comparing Values, Behaviors, Institutions, and Organizations Across Nations*. Second edition. Thousand Oaks, CA: Sage.

Hofstede, Geert & Gert Jan Hofstede (2004). *Cultures and Organizations: Software of the Mind*. Second edition. London: McGraw-Hill.

Hoskisson, Robert E. (1987). "Multidivisional Structure and Performance: The Contingency of Diversification Strategy," *Academy of Management Journal*, 30(4), 625–644.

Hoskisson, Robert E. & Michael A. Hitt (1988). "Strategic Control Systems and Relative R&D Investment in Large Multiproduct Firms," *Strategic Management Journal*, 9(6), 605–621.

Hoskisson, Robert E. & Michael A. Hitt (1990). "The Antecedents and Performance Outcomes of Diversification: Review and Critique of Theoretical Perspectives," *Journal of Management*, 16(2), 461–509.

Hoskisson, Robert E. & Michael A. Hitt (1994). *Downscoping: How to Tame the Diversified Firm*. Oxford:

Oxford University Press.

Hoskisson, Robert E. & Richard A. Johnson (1992). "Corporate Restructuring and Strategic Change: The Effect on Diversification Strategy and R&D Intensity," *Strategic Management Journal*, 13(8), 625–634.

Hoskisson, Robert E. & Thomas A. Turk (1990). "Corporate Restructuring: Governance and Control Limits of the Internal Market," *Academy of Management Review*, 15(3), 459–477.

Hoskisson, Robert E., Charles W. L. Hill, & Hicheon Kim (1993a). "The Multidivisional Structure: Organizational Fossil or Source of Value?" *Journal of Management* 19(2) 269–298.

Hoskisson, Robert E., Michael A. Hitt, & Charles W. L. Hill (1993b). "Managerial Incentives and Investment in R&D in Large Multiproduct Firms," *Organizational Science*, 4(2), 325–341.

Hoskisson, Robert E., Michael A. Hitt, Richard A. Johnson, & Douglas D. Moesel (1993c). "Construct Validity of an Objective (Entropy) Categorical Measure of Diversification Strategy," *Strategic Management Journal*, 14(3), 215–235.

Hoskisson, Robert E., Richard A. Johnson, & Douglas D. Moesel (1994). "Corporate Divestiture Intensity in Restructuring Firms: Effects of Governance, Strategy and Performance," *Academy of Management Journal*, 37(5), 1207–1251.

Hoskisson, Robert E., Michael A. Hitt, Richard A. Johnson, & Wayne Grossman (2002). "Conflicting Voices: The Effects of Ownership Heterogeneity and Internal Governance on Corporate Strategy," *Academy of Management Journal*, 45(4), 697–716.

Hout, Thomas, Michael E. Porter, & Eileen Rudden (1982). "How Global Companies Win Out," *Harvard Business Review*, 60(5), 98–109.

Hovakimian, Gayané & Sheridan Titman (2006). "Corporate Investment with Financial Constraints: Sensitivity of Investment to Funds from Voluntary Asset Sales," *Journal of Money, Credit, and Banking*, 38(2), 257–274.

Hunt, John W. (1990). "Changing Pattern of Acquisition Behaviour in Takeovers and the Consequences for Acquisition Processes," *Strategic Management Journal*, 11(1), 69–77.

Ilinitch, Anne Y. & Carl P. Zeithaml (1995). "Operationalizing and Testing Gabraith's Center of Gravity Theory," *Strategic Management Journal*, 16(5), 401–410.

Inagaki, Kana (2015). "Technology: Sony rewired," *Financial Times*, September 3 [www.ft.com/intl/cms/s/0/f44a8ad8–521a–11e5–b029–b9d50a74fd14.html#axzz3m0AgIOnA].

Itami, Hiroyuki, Tadao Kagano, Hideki Yoshihara, & Akimitu Sakuma (1982). "Diversification Strategies and Economic Performance," *Japanese Economic Studies*, 11(1), 78–110.

Jacquemin, Alexis P. & Charles H. Berry (1979). "Entropy Measure of Diversification and Corporate Growth," *Journal of Industrial Economics*, 27(4), 359–369.

Jamali, Dima & Ramez Mirshak (2007). "Corporate Social Responsibility (CSR): Theory and Practice in a Developing Country Context," *Journal of Business Ethics*, 72(3), 243–262.

Jammine, Azar P. (1984). "Product Diversification, international expansion and performance: A study of strategic risk management in UK manufacturing," Ph.D. thesis, University of London.

Jandik, Thomas & Anil K. Makhija (2005). "Can Diversification Create Value? Evidence from the Electric Utility Industry," *Financial Management*, 34(1), 61–93.

Janney, Jay J. (2002). "Eat or Get Eaten? How Equity Ownership and Diversification Shape CEO Risk–Taking," *Academy of Management Executive*, 14(ç), 157–158.

Jarrell, Gregg A., James A. Brickley, & Jeffry M. Netter (1988). "The Market for Corporate Control: The Empirical Evidence since 1980," *Journal of Economic Perspectives*, 2(1), 49–68.

Jayachandran, Satish, Javier Gimeno, & P. Rajan Varadarajan (1999). "Theory of Multimarket Competition: A Synthesis and Implications for Marketing Strategy," *Journal of Marketing*, 63(3), 49–66.

Jensen, Michael C. (1968). "The Performance of Mutual Funds in the Period 1945–64," *Journal of Finance*, 23(2), 389–416.

Jensen, Michael C. (1986). "Agency Costs of Free Cash Flow, Corporate Financing and Takeovers," *American Economic Review*, 76(2), 323–329.

Jensen, Michael C. (1988). "Takeovers: Their Causes and Consequences," *Journal of Economic*

Perspectives, 1(2), 21–48.

Jensen, Michael C. (1989). "Eclipse of the Public Corporation," *Harvard Business Review*, 67(5), 61–74.

Jensen, Michael C. & William H. Meckling (1976). "Theory of the Firm: Managerial Behavior, Agency Costs and Ownership Structure," *Journal of Financial Economics*, 3(4), 305–360.

Jensen, Michael C. & Kevin J. Murphy (1990). "Performance Pay and Top-Management Incentives," *Journal of Political Economy*, 98(2), 225–264.

Jensen, Michael C. & Richard S. Ruback (1983). "The Market for Corporate Control: The Scientific Evidence," *Journal of Financial Economics*, 11(1), 5–50.

John, Kose, & Eli Ofek (1995). "Asset Sales and Increase in Focus," *Journal of Financial Economics*, 37(1), 105–126.

Johnson, Gerry & Howard Thomas (1987). "The Industry Context of Strategy, Structure and Performance: The U.K. Brewing Industry," *Strategic Management Journal*, 8(4), 343–361.

Johnson, Jo & Martine Orange (2004). *The Man Who Tried to Buy the World*. London: Penguin Books.

Johnson, Julius H., Jr. (1995). "An Empirical Analysis of the Integration-Responsiveness Framework: U.S. Construction Equipment Industry Firms in Global Competition," *Journal of International Business Studies*, 26(3), 621–635.

Johnson, Richard A. (1996). "Antecedents and Outcomes of Corporate Refocusing," *Journal of Management*, 22(3), 437–481.

Johnson, Richard A., Robert E. Hoskisson, & Michael A. Hitt (1993). "Board of Director Involvement in Restructuring: The Effects of Board Versus Managerial, Controls and Characteristics," *Strategic Management Journal*, 14(SSI), 33–50

Jones, Gareth R. & Charles W. L. Hill (1988). "Transaction Cost-Analysis of Strategy-Structure Choice," *Strategic Management Journal*, 9(2), 159–172.

Joskow, Paul L. (1985). "Vertical Integration and Long-Term Contracts: The Case of Coal-Burning Electric Generating Plants," *Journal of Law, Economics, & Organization*, 1(1), 33–80.

Joskow, Paul L. & Alvin K. Klevorick (1979). "A Framework for Analyzing Predatory Pricing Policy," *Yale Law Journal*, 89(2), 213–270.

Kahan, Marcel & Edward B. Rock (2002). "How I Learned to Stop Worrying and Love the Pill: Adaptive Responses to Takeover Law," *University of Chicago Law Review*, 69(3), 871–915.

Kanter, Rosabeth M. (1989). *When Giants Learn to Dance*. New York: Simon & Schuster.

Kaplan, Steven N. & Michael N. Weisbach (1992). "The Success of Acquisitions: Evidence from Divestures," *Journal of Finance*, 47(1), 107–138.

Karim, Samina & Will Mitchell (2000). "Path-dependent and Path-breaking Change: Reconfiguring Business Resources Following Acquisitions in the U.S. Medical Sector, 1978–1995," *Strategic Management Journal*, 21(10–11), 1061–1081.

Karnani, Aneel & Birger Wernerfelt (1985). "Multiple Point Competition," *Strategic Management Journal*, 6(1), 87–96.

Kay, Neil M. & Adamantios Diamantopoulos (1987). "Uncertainty and Synergy: Towards a Formal Model of Corporate Strategy," *Managerial and Decision Economics*, 8(2), 121–130.

Keats, Barbara V. (1990). "Diversification and Business Economic Performance Revisited: Issues of Measurement and Causality," *Journal of Management*, 16(1), 61–72.

Keats, Barbara V. & Hugh M. O'Neill (2001). "Organizational Structure: Looking through a Strategy Lens," in Michael A. Hitt, R. Edward Freeman, & Jeffrey S. Harrison (eds) *The Blackwell Handbook of Strategic Management*, pp. 520–542. Oxford, UK: Blackwell Business.

Keeton, A. (2003). "Class-Action is Approved Against DaimlerChrysler," *Wall Street Journal*, June 13, B2.

Keister, Lisa A. (2000). *Chinese Business Groups: The Structure and Impact of Inter-Firm Relations During Economic Development*. New York: Oxford University Press.

Kerr, Jeffrey L. (1985). "Diversification Strategies and Managerial Rewards: An Empirical Study," *Academy of Management Journal*, 28(1), 155–179.

Kester, W. Carl (1984). "Today's Options for Tomorrow's Growth," *Harvard Business Review*, 62(2), 153–160.

Ketchen, David J., Charles C. Snow, & Vera L. Hoover (2004). "Research on Competitive Dynamics: Recent Accomplishments and Future Challenges," *Journal of Management*, 30(6), 779–804.

Khanna, Tarun & Krishna Palepu (1997a). "Why Focused Strategies May Be Wrong for Emerging Markets," *Harvard Business Review*, 75(4), 41–50.

Khanna, Tarun & Krishna Palepu (1997b). "Policy Shocks, Market Intermediaries, and Corporate Strategy: The Evolution of Business Groups in Chile and India," *Journal of Economics & Management Strategy*, 8(2), 271–310.

Khanna, Tarun & Krishna Palepu (2000a). "Is Group Affiliation Profitable in Emerging Markets? An Analysis of Diversified Indian Business Groups," *Journal of Finance*, 55(2), 867–892.

Khanna, Tarun & Krishna Palepu (2000b). "The Future of Business Groups in Emerging Markets: Long-run Evidence from Chile," *Academy of Management Journal*, 43(2), 268–285.

Khanna, Tarun & Jan W. Rivkin (2001). "Estimating the Performance Effects of Business Groups in Emerging Markets," *Strategic Management Journal*, 22(1), 45–74.

Kim, Hicheon, Robert E. Hoskisson, Laszlo Tihanyi & Jaebum Hong (2004). "The Evolution and Restructuring of Diversified Business Group in Emerging Markets: The Lessons from Chaebols in Korea," *Asia Pacific Journal of Management*, 21(1–2), 25–48.

Kim, Jongwook & Joseph T. Mahoney (2005). "Property Rights Theory, Transaction Costs Theory, and Agency Theory: An Organizational Economics Approach to Strategic Management," *Managerial and Decision Economics*, 26(4), 223–242.

Kim, W. Chan, Peter Hwang, & Willem P. Burgers (1993). "Multinationals' Diversification and the Risk-Return Trade-Off," *Strategic Management Journal,* 14(4), 275–286.

Klein, Benjamin (1988). "Vertical Integration as Organizational Ownership: The Fisher Body-General Motors Relationship Revisited," *Journal of Law, Economics, & Organization*, 4(1), 199–213.

Klein, Benjamin (2000). "Fisher-General Motors and the Nature of the Firm," *Journal of Law and Economics*, 43(1), 105–141.

Klein, Benjamin, Robert G. Crawford, & Armen A. Alchian (1978). "Vertical Integration, Appropriable Rents, and the Competitive Contracting Process," *Journal of Law and Economics*, 21(2), 297–326.

Klein, Saul (1989). "A Transaction Cost Explanation of Vertical Control in International Markets," *Journal of the Academy of Marketing Science*, 17(3), 253–260.

Knowledge@Wharton (2012). "Vertical Integration Works for Apple — But It Won't for Everyone," March 14. [http://knowledge.wharton.upenn.edu/article/vertical–integration–works–for–apple–but–it–wont–for–everyone/].

Kobrin, Stephen J. (1991). "An Empirical Analysis of the Determinants of Global Integration," *Strategic Management Journal*, 12(SSI), 17–32.

Kobrin, Stephen J. (1994). "Is there a Relationship Between a Geocentric Mind-Set and Multinational Strategy?" *Journal of International Business Studies*, 25(3), 493–511.

Kochhar, Rahul (1996). "Explaining firm Capital Structure: The Role of Agency Theory vs. Transaction Cost Economics," *Strategic Management Journal*, 17(9), 713–728.

Kochhar, Rahul and Michael A. Hitt (1998). "Linking Corporate Strategy to Capital Structure," *Strategic Management Journal*, 19(6), 601–610.

Kock, Carl J., & Mauro F. Guillén (2001). "Strategy and Structure in Developing Countries: Business Groups as an Evolutionary Response to Opportunities for Unrelated Diversification," *Industrial and Corporate Change*, 10(1), 77–113.

Koen, Carla I. (2005). *Comparative International Management*. London: McGraw–Hill.

Kogut, Bruce (1985). "Designing Global Strategies: Comparative and Competitive Value Added Chains," *Sloan Management Review*, 26(4), 15–28.

Kogut, Bruce (1989). "A Note on Global Strategies," *Strategic Management Journal*, 10(4), 383–389.

Kogut, Bruce (1991). "Joint Ventures and the Option to Expand and Acquire," *Management Science*, 37(1), 19–33.

Kogut, Bruce & Nalin Kulatilaka (1994). "Operating Flexibility, Global Manufacturing, and the Option Value of a Multinational Network," *Management Science*, 40(1), 123–139.

Kogut, Bruce & Harbir Singh (1988). "The Effects of National Culture on the Choice of Entry Mode,"

Journal of International Business Studies, 19(3), 411–432.

Kogut, Bruce & Udo Zander (1992). "Knowledge of the Firm, Combinative Capabilities, and the Replication of Technology," *Organization science*, 3(3), 383–397.

Kogut, Bruce, Gordon Walker, & Jaideep Anand (2002). "Agency and Institutions: National Divergences in Diversification Behavior," *Organization Science*, 13(2), 162–178.

Kono, Toyohiro (1984). *Strategy and Structure of Japanese Enterprises*. London: Macmillan.

Kono, Toyohiro (1999). "A Strong Head Office Makes a Strong Company," *Long Range Planning*, 32(3), 225–236.

Korean Times (2004). "Samsung, LG Speed Up Vertical Integration," May 16.

Kotabe, Masaaki, Xavier Martin, & Hiroshi Domoto (2003). "Gaining from Vertical Partnerships: Knowledge Transfer, Relationship Duration, and Supplier Performance Improvement in the U.S. and Japanese Automotive Industries," *Strategic Management Journal*, 24(4), 293–316.

Kotler, Philip (1975) *Marketing Management: Analysis, Planning, and Control*. Englewood Cliffs, NJ: Prentice Hall.

Kotter, John P. (1979). "Managing External Dependence," *Academy of Management Review*, 4(1), 87–92.

Kownatzki, Maximilian, Jorge Walter, Steven W. Floyd, & Christoph Lechner (2013). "Corporate Control and the Speed of Strategic Business Unit Decision Making," *Academy of Management Journal*, 56(5), 1295–1324.

Kwak, Mary (2001). "Spinoffs Lead to Better Financing Decisions," *MIT Sloan Management Review*, 42(4), 10–13.

Lajili, Kaouthar & Joseph T. Mahoney (2006). "Revisiting Agency and Transaction Costs Theory Predictions on Vertical Financial Ownership and Contracting: Electronic Integration as an Organizational Form Choice," *Managerial and Decision Economics*, 27(7), 573–586.

Lamont, Owen A. & Christopher Polk (2001). "The Diversification Discount: Cash Flows versus Returns," *Journal of Finance*, 56(5), 1693–1721.

Lamont, Owen A. & Christopher Polk (2002). "Does Diversification Destroy Value? Evidence from Industry Shocks," *Journal of Financial Economics*, 63(2), 51–77.

Landau, Christian & Carolin Bock (2013). "Value Creation through Vertical Intervention of Corporate Centres in Single Business Units of Unrelated Diversified Portfolios: The Case of Private Equity Firms," *Long Range Planning*, 46(1), 97–124.

Lang, Larry H. P. & René M. Stulz (1994). "Tobin's q, Corporate Diversification, and Firm Performance," *Journal of Political Economy*, 102(6), 1248–1280.

Lang, Larry H. P., Annette Poulsen, & René M. Stulz (1995). "Asset Sales, Firm Performance, and the Agency Costs of Managerial Discretion," *Journal of Financial Economics*, 37(1), 3–37.

La Porta, Rafael, Florencio Lopez-de-Silanes, Andrei Shleifer, & Robert W. Vishny (1998). "Law and Finance," *Journal of Political Economy*, 106(6), 1113–1155.

Lawrence, Paul R. & Jay W. Lorsch (1967). *Organization and Environment*. Cambridge, MA: Harvard University Press.

Learned, Edmund P., C. Rolland Christensen, & Kenneth P. Andrews (1971). *Business Policy: Text and Cases*. Butt Ridge, IL: Dow Jones-Irwin.

Lecraw, Donald J. (1984). "Diversification Strategy and Performance," *Journal of Industrial Economics*, 33(2), 179–197.

Lee, Donghun "Don" & Ravi Madhavan (2010). "Divestiture and Firm Performance: A Meta-Analysis," *Journal of Management*, 36(6), 1345–1371.

Lee, Gwendolyn K. & Marvin B. Lieberman (2010). "Acquisition vs. Internal Development as Modes of Market Entry," *Strategic Management Journal*, 31(2), 140–158.

Lee, Ji-Hwan & Jin-Young Sirh (1999). "Institutional Context, Structural Adjustment, and Diversification of the Korean Chaebol," Paper presented at the Academy of International Business, Michigan State University.

Lemelin, André (1982). "Relatedness in the Patterns of Interindustry Diversification," *Review of Economics and Statistics*, 64(4), 646–657.

Leonard-Barton, Dorothy (1992). "Core Capabilities and Core Rigidities: A Paradox in Managing New

Product Development," *Strategic Management Journal*, 13(SSI), 111–125.

Levitt, Theodore (1960). "Marketing Myopia," *Harvard Business Review*, 38(4), 45–56.

Levitt, Theodore (1983). "The Globalization of Markets," *Harvard Business Review*, 61(3), 92–102.

Levy, Haim & Marshall Sarnat (1970). "Diversification, Portfolio Analysis and the Uneasy Case for Conglomerate Mergers," *Journal of Finance*, 25(4), 795–802.

Lewellen, Wilbur G. (1971). "A Pure Financial Rationale for the Conglomerate Merger," *Journal of Finance*, 26(2), 521–537.

Li, Jiatao & Stephen Guisinger (1992). "The Globalization of Service Multinationals in the 'Triad' Regions: Japan, Western Europe and North America," *Journal of International Business Studies*, 23(4), 675–696.

Li, Mingfang & Roy L. Simerly (1998). "The Moderating Effect of Environmental Dynamism on the Ownership and Performance Relationship," *Strategic Management Journal*, 19(2), 169–179.

Li, Yong, Barclay E. James, Ravi Madhavan, & Joseph T. Mahoney (2007). "Real Options: Taking Stock and Looking Ahead," *Advances in Strategic Management*, 24, 31–66.

Lieberman, Marvin (1984). "The Learning Curve and Pricing in the Chemical Processing Industries," *RAND Journal of Economics*, 15(2), 213–228.

Lien, Lasse B. & Peter G. Klein (2009). "Using Competition to Measure Relatedness," *Journal of Management*, 35(4), 1078–1107.

Lins, Karl V. & Henri Servaes (2002). "Is Corporate Diversification Beneficial in Emerging Markets?" *Financial Management*, 31(2), 5–31.

Lintner, John (1965). "Security Prices, Risk, and Maximal Gains from Diversification," *Journal of Finance*, 20(4), 587–615.

Lippman, Steven A. & Richard P. Rumelt (1982). "Uncertain Imitability: An Analysis of Interfirm Differences in Efficiency under Competition," *Bell Journal of Economics*, 13(2), 418–438.

Livesay, Harold C. (1999) *Andrew Carnegie and the Rise of Big Business*. Second edition. Boston: Little, Brown.

Lorsch, Jay W. & Stephen A. Allen (1973). *Managing Diversity and Interdependence: An Organizational Study of Multidivisional Firms*. Graduate School of Business Administration, Harvard University, Boston, MA.

Lorsch, Jay W., Andargachew S. Zelleke, & Katharina Pick (2001). "Unbalanced Boards," *Harvard Business Review*, 79(2), 28–30.

Lubatkin, Michael (1987). "Merger Strategies and Stockholder Value," *Strategic Management Journal*, 8(1), 1987, 39–53.

Lubatkin, Michael & Sayan Chatterjee (1994). "Extending Modern Portfolio Theory into the Domain of Corporate Strategy: Does it Apply?" *Academy of Management Journal*, 37(1), 109–136.

Lubatkin, Michael & Hugh M. O'Neill (1987). "Merger Strategies and Capital Market Risk," *Academy of Management Journal*, 30(4), 665–684.

Lubatkin, Michael, Hemant Merchant, & Narasimhan Srinivasan (1993). "Construct Validity of Some Unweighted Product-Count Diversification Measures," *Strategic Management Journal*, 14(6), 433–449.

Lubatkin, Michael, Narasimhan Srinivasan, & Hemant Merchant (1997). "Merger Strategies and Shareholder Value During Times of Relaxed Antitrust Enforcement: The Case of Large Mergers During the 1980s," *Journal of Management*, 23(1), 61–81.

Lubatkin, Michael, Peter J. Lane, Sven Collin, & Philippe Very (2007). "An Embeddedness Framing of Governance and Opportunism: Towards a Cross-Nationally Accommodating Theory of Agency," *Journal of Organizational Behaviour*, 28(1), 43–58.

Luehrman, Timothy A. (1998). "Strategy as a Portfolio of Real Options," *Harvard Business Review*, 76(5), 89–99.

Luffman, G. A. & R. Reed (1982). "Diversification in British Industry in the 1970s," *Strategic Management Journal*, 3(4), 303–314.

Luo, Yadong (2001). "Determinants of Local Responsiveness: Perspective form Foreign Subsidiaries in an Emerging Market," *Journal of Management*, 27(4), 451–477.

Ma, Hao (1999). "Determinants of Strategic Options in Multinational Market Competition," *Journal of International Management*, 5(2), 93–113.

MacMillan, Ian C. and Robin George (1985). "Corporate Venturing: Challenges for Senior Managers," *Journal of Business Strategy*, 5(3), 34–43.

MacMillan, Ian C., Alexander B. van Putten, & Rita Gunther McGrath (2003). "Global Gamesmanship," *Harvard Business Review*, 81(5), 62–71.

Madden, Sean (2013). "Design as a New Vertical Forcing Function," *HBR Blog*, October 21. [https://hbr.org/2013/10/design-as-a-new-vertical-forcing-function/].

Maddigan, Ruth J. (1979). "The Impact of Vertical Integration on Business Performance." Unpublished Doctoral Dissertation, Indiana University at Bloomington.

Mahnke, Volker & Torben Pedersen (2004). *Knowledge Flows, Governance and the MNC.* Houndsmills: Palgrave Macmillan.

Mahoney, Joseph T. (1992a). "Organizational Economics within the Conversation of Strategic Management," *Advances in Strategic Management*, 8, 103–155.

Mahoney, Joseph T. (1992b). "The Choice of Organizational Form: Vertical Financial Ownership versus Other Methods of Vertical Integration," *Strategic Management Journal*, 13(8), 559–584.

Mahoney, Joseph T. (2005). *Economic Foundations of Strategy.* Thousand Oaks: Sage Publications.

Mahoney, Joseph T. & J. Rajendran Pandian (1992). "The Resource-Based View within the Conversation of Strategic Management," *Strategic Management Journal*, 13(5), 363–380.

Mahoney, Joseph T. & Lihong Qian (2013). "Market Frictions as Building Blocks of an Organizational Economics Approach to Strategic Management," *Strategic Management Journal*, 34(9), 1019–1041.

Maignan, Isabelle & O. C. Ferrell (2003). "Nature of Corporate Responsibilities: Perspectives from American, French, and German Consumers," *Journal of Business Research*, 56(1), 55–67.

Maignan, Isabelle, O. C. Ferrell, & G. Thomas M. Hult (1999). "Corporate Citizenship: Cultural Antecedents and Business Benefits," *Journal of the Academy of Marketing Science*, 27(4), 455–469.

Makadok, Richard (2001). "Toward a Synthesis of the Resource-Based and Dynamic-Capability Views of Rent Creation," *Strategic Management Journal*, 22(5), 387–401.

Maksimovic, Vojislav, & Gordon Phillips (2002). "Do Conglomerate Firms Allocate Resources Inefficiently across Industries? Theory and Evidence," *Journal of Finance*, 57(2), 721–767.

Malatesta, Paul (1983). "The Wealth Effect of Merger Activity and the Objective Functions of Merging Firms," *Journal of Financial Economics*, 11(1–4), 155–181.

Manikutty, Sankaran (2000). "Family Business Groups in India: A Resource-Based View of the Emerging Trends," *Family Business Review*, 13(4), 279–292.

Markides, Constantinos (1992). "Consequences of Corporate Refocusing: Ex Ante Evidence," *Academy of Management Journal*, 35(2), 398–412.

Markides, Constantinos (1993). "Corporate Refocusing," *Business Strategy Review*, 4(1), 1–15.

Markides, Constantinos (1995). *Diversification, Refocusing and Economic Performance.* Cambridge, MA: MIT Press.

Markides, Constantinos (2002). "Corporate Strategy: The Role of the Centre," in Andrew Pettigrew, Howard Thomas, & Richard Whittington (eds) *Handbook of Strategy and Management*, pp. 98–112. London: Sage.

Markides, Constantinos & Harbir Singh (1997). "Corporate Restructuring: A Symptom of Poor Governance or a Solution to Past Managerial Mistakes," *European Management Journal*, 15(3), 213–219.

Markides, Constantinos & Peter J. Williamson (1994). "Related Diversification, Core Competences and Corporate Performance," *Strategic Management Journal*, 15(SSI), 149–165.

Markides, Constantinos & Peter J. Williamson (1996). "Corporate Diversification and Organizational Structure: A Resource-Based View," *Academy of Management Journal*, 39(2), 340–367.

Markham, Jesse W. (1973). *Conglomerate Enterprise and Economic Performance.* Cambridge, MA: Harvard University Press.

Marks, Mitchell L. & Philip H. Mirvis (2000). "Managing Mergers, Acquisitions, and Alliances: Creating and Effective Transition Structure," *Organizational Dynamics*, 28(3), 35–47.

Marris, Robin (1964). *The Economic Theory of Managerial Capitalism*. London: Macmillan.

Marsh, Peter (2008). "Electrolux sheds 3000 jobs," *Financial Times*, December, 15. [www.iht.com/articles/2008/12/15/business/15electro.php].

Martin, John D. & Akin Sayrak (2003). "Corporate Diversification and Shareholder Value: A Survey of Recent Literature," *Journal of Corporate Finance*, 9(1), 37–57.

Masten, Scott E., James W. Meehan, & Edward A. Snyder (1989). "Vertical Integration in the U.S. Auto Industry: A Note on the Influence of Transaction Specific Assets," *Journal of Economic Behavior & Organization*, 12(2), 265–273.

Mathur, Ike, Manohar Singh, & Kimberly C. Gleason (2004). "Multinational Diversification and Corporate Performance: Evidence from European Firms," *European Financial Management*, 10(3), 439–464.

Matsusaka, John G. (1993). "Takeover Motives During the Conglomerate Merger Wave," *RAND Journal of Economics*, 24(3), 357–379.

Matsusaka, John G. (2001). "Corporate Diversification, Value Maximization, and Organizational Capabilities," *Journal of Business*, 74(3), 409–432.

Mayer, Michael & Richard Whittington (2003). "Diversification in Context: A Cross-National and Cross-Temporal Extension," *Strategic Management Journal*, 24(8), 773–781.

McCutcheon, Barbara J. (1991). "What Caused Conglomerate Formation? An Examination of Managerial Behavior and Internal Capital Markets in the 1960s Conglomerates." Doctoral dissertation, University of Chicago.

McGahan Anita M. & Michael E. Porter (1997). "How Much Does Industry Matter Really," *Strategic Management Journal*, 18(SSI), 15–30.

McGuire, Jean & Elie Matta (2003). "CEO Stock Options: The Silent Dimension of Ownership," *Academy of Management Journal*, 46(2), 255–265.

McGrath, Rita Gunther, Ming-Jer Chen, & Ian C. Macmillan (1998). "Multimarket Maneuvering in Uncertain Spheres of Influence: Resource Diversion Strategies," *Academy of Management Review*, 23(4), 724–740.

McKinsey (2008). "Enduring Ideas: The GE–McKinsey Nine–Box Matrix," [www.mckinsey.com/insights/strategy/enduring_ideas_the_ge_and_mckinsey_nine–box_matrix].

McWilliams, Abagail & Donald Siegel (2001). "Corporate Social Responsibility: A Theory of the Firm Perspective," *Academy of Management Review*, 26(1), 117–127.

Mehra, Ajay (1996). "Resource and Market Based Determinants of Performance in the U.S. Banking Industry," *Strategic Management Journal*, 17(4), 307–322.

Mellahi, Kamel & Adrian J. Wilkinson (2004). "Organisational Failure: A Critique of Recent Research and a Proposed Integrative Framework," *International Journal of Management Reviews*, 5–6(1), 21–41.

Merchant, Hemant & Dan Schendel (2000). "How Do International Joint Ventures Create Shareholder Value?" *Strategic Management Journal*, 21(7), 723–737.

Mester, Loretta J. (1987). "Multiple Market Contact between Savings and Loans: Note," *Journal of Money, Credit, and Banking*, 19(4), 538–549.

Meyer, Margaret, Paul Milgrom, & John Roberts (1992). "Organizational Prospects, Influence Costs, and Ownership Changes," *Journal of Economics and Management Strategy*, 1(1), 9–35.

Michael, Bryane (2003). "Corporate Social Responsibility in International Development: An Overview and Critique," *Corporate Social-Responsibility and Environmental Management*, 10(3), 115–128.

Michel, Allen & Israel Shaked (1984). "Does Business Diversification Affect Performance," *Financial Management*, 13(4), 18–24.

Milgrom, Paul & John Roberts (1990). "The Economics of Modern Manufacturing: Technology, Strategy, and Organization," *The American Economic Review*, 80(3), 511–528.

Miller, Danny, Russel Eisenstat, & Nathaniel Foote (2002). "Strategy from the Inside Out: Building Capability-Creating Organizations," *California Management Review*, 44(3), 37–54.

Miller, Douglas J. (2004). "Firms' Technological Resources and the Performance Effects of Diversification: A Longitudinal Study," *Strategic Management Journal*, 25(11), 1097–1119.

Miller, Douglas J. (2006). "Technological Diversity, Related Diversification, and Firm Performance," *Strategic Management Journal*, 27(7), 601–619.

Miller, Janice S., Robert M. Wiseman, & Luis M. Gomez-Mejia (2002). "The Fit Between CEO Compensation Design and Firm Risk," *Academy of Management Journal*, 45(4), 745–756.

Miller, Kent D. & Timothy B. Folta (2002). "Option Value and Entry Timing," *Strategic Management Journal*, 23, 655–665.

Mintzberg, Henry (1983). *Structure in Fives: Designing Effective Organizations*. Englewood Cliffs, NJ: Prentice Hall.

Mishra, Chandra & David H. Gobeli (1998). "Managerial Incentives, Internalization, and Market Valuation of Multinational Firms," *Journal of International Business Studies*, 29(3), 583–598.

Mitchell, Ronald K., Bradley R. Agle, & Donna J. Wood (1997). "Toward a Theory of Stakeholder Identification and Salience: Defining the Principle of Who and What Really Counts," *Academy of Management Review*, 22(4), 853–886.

Mitchell, Will & Kulwant Singh (1992). "Incumbents' Use of Pre-Entry Alliances before Expansion into New Technical Subfields of an Industry," *Journal of Economic Behavior and Organization*, 18(3), 347–372.

Moir, Lance (2001). "What Do We Mean by Corporate Social Responsibility?" *Corporate Governance*, 1(2), 16–23.

Monteverde, Kirk (1995). "Technical Dialog as an Incentive for Vertical Integration in the Semiconductor Industry," *Management Science*, 41(10) 1624–1638.

Monteverde, Kirk & David J. Teece (1982). "Supplier Switching Costs and Vertical Integration in the Auto Industry," *Bell Journal of Economics*, 13(1) 206–231.

Montgomery, Cynthia A. (1982). "The Measurement of Firm Diversification: Some New Empirical Evidence," *Academy of Management Journal*, 25(2), 299–307.

Montgomery, Cynthia A. (1985). "Product-Market Diversification and Market Power," *Academy of Management Journal*, 28(4), 789–798.

Montgomery, Cynthia A. (1992). "Resources: The Essence of Corporate Advantage," Harvard Business School, *Teaching Note* 9-792-064.

Montgomery, Cynthia A. (1994). "Corporate Diversification," *Journal of Economic Perspectives*, 8(3), 163–178.

Montgomery, Cynthia A. & S. Hariharan (1991). "Diversified Expansion by Large Established Firms," *Journal of Economic Behavior and Organization*, 15(1), 71–89.

Montgomery, Cynthia A. & Michael E. Porter (eds) (1991). *Strategy: Seeking and Securing Competitive Advantage*. Boston, MA: Harvard Business Review Book.

Montgomery, Cynthia A. & Birger Wernerfelt (1988). "Diversification, Ricardian Rents, and Tobin's *q*," *Rand Journal of Economics*, 19(4), 623–632.

Montgomery, Cynthia A. & Birger Wernerfelt (1992). "Risk Reduction and Umbrella Branding," *Journal of Business*, 65(1), 31–50.

Morck, Randall & Bernard Yeung (1991). "Why Investors Value Multinationality," *Journal of Business*, 64(2), 165–187.

Moschieri, Caterina & Johanna Mair (2008). "Research on Corporate Divestures: A Synthesis," *Journal of Management & Organization*, 14(4), 399–422.

Mulherin, J. Harold & Audra L. Boone (2000). "Comparing Acquisitions and Divestitures," *Journal of Corporate Finance*, 6(2), 117–139.

Muralidharan, Raman (1997). "Strategic Control for Fast-Moving Markets: Updating the Strategy and Monitoring Performance," *Long Range Planning*, 30(1), 64–73.

Myers, Stewart C. (1977), "Determinants of Corporate Borrowing," *Journal of Financial Economics*, 5(2), 147–175.

Myers, Stewart C. (1984). "Finance Theory and Financial Strategy," *Interfaces*, 14(1), 126–137.

Nayyar, Praveen R. (1992). "On the Measurement of Corporate Diversification Strategy: Evidence from Large U.S. Service Firms," *Strategic Management Journal*, 13(3), 219–235.

Nell, Philip C. & Björn Ambos (2013). "Parenting Advantage in the MNC: An Embeddedness Perspective on the Value Added by Headquarters," *Strategic Management Journal*, 34(9), 1086–1103.

Nelson, Richard R. & Sidney G. Winter (1982). *An Evolutionary Theory of Economic Change*. Cambridge,

MA: Belknap Press of Harvard University Press.

Ng, Wilson & Christian de Cock (2002). "Battle in the Boardroom: A Discursive Perspective," *Journal of Management Studies*, 39(1), 23–49.

Nightengale, John (1978). "On the Definition of Industry and Market," *Journal of Industrial Economics*, 27(1), 31–40.

Nippa, Michael, Ulrich Pidun, & Harald Rubner (2011). "Corporate Portfolio Management: Appraising Four Decades of Academic Research," *Academy of Management Perspectives*, 25(4), 50–66.

Nöldeke, Georg & Klaus M. Schmidt (1998). "Sequential Investments and Options to Own," *The RAND Journal of Economics*, 29(4), 633–653.

North, Douglas (1990). *Institutions, Institutional Change, and Economic Performance*. New York: Norton.

O'Reilly, Charles A., & Michael L. Tushman (2004). "The Ambidextrous Organization," *Harvard Business Review*, 82(4), 74–81.

O'Reilly, Charles A., & Michael L. Tushman (2008). "Ambidexterity as a Dynamic Capability: Resolving the Innovator's Dilemma," *Research in Organizational Behavior*, 28, 185–206.

Orlitzky, Mark, Frank L. Schmidt, & Sara L. Rynes (2003). "Corporate Social and Financial Performance: A Meta-Analysis," *Organization studies*, 24(3), 403–441.

Ouchi, William G. (1979). "Conceptual Framework for the Design of Organizational Control Mechanisms," *Management Science*, 25(9), 833–848.

Ouchi, William G. (1980). "Markets, Bureaucracies, and Clans," *Administrative Science Quarterly*, 25(1), 129–141.

Palepu, Krishna (1985). "Diversification Strategy, Profit Performance, and the Entropy Measures," *Strategic Management Journal*, 6(3), 239–255.

Palich, Leslie E., Laura B. Cardinal, & C. Chet Miller (2000). "Curvilinearity in the Diversification–Performance Linkage: An Examination of over Three Decades of Research," *Strategic Management Journal*, 21(2), 155–174.

Panzar, John C. & Robert D. Willig (1981). "Economies of Scope," *American Economic Review*, 71(2), 268–272.

Park, Choelsoon (2002). "The Effects of Prior Performance on the Choice between Related and Unrelated Acquisitions: Implications for the Performance Consequences of Diversification Strategy," *Journal of Management Journal*, 39(7), 1003–1019.

Park, Choelsoon (2003). "Prior Performance Characteristics of Related and Unrelated Acquires," *Strategic Management Journal*, 24(5), 471–480.

Parker, Philip M. & Lars H. Röller (1997), "Collusive Conduct in Duopolies: Multimarket Contact and Cross–Ownership in the Mobile Telephone Industry," *The RAND Journal of Economics*, 28(2), 304–322.

Parkhe, Arvind (1993). "Strategic Alliance Structuring: A Game Theoretic and Transaction Cost Examination of Interfirm Cooperation," *Academy of Management Journal*, 36(4), 794–829.

Pavan, Robert J. (1972). "The Strategy and Structure of Italian Enterprise." DBA dissertation, Harvard Business School.

Pearce, John A. (1982). "The Company Mission as a Strategic Tool," *Sloan Management Review*, 23(3), 15–24.

Pearce, John A. II & Richard B Robinson Jr. (2007). *Strategic Management: Formulation Implementation, and Control*. Tenth Edition. New York: McGraw Hill International.

Pedersen, Torben, Bent Petersen, & Gabriel R. G. Benito (2002). "Change of Foreign Operation Method: Impetus and Switching Costs. *International Business Review*, 11(3), 325–345.

Pedersen, Torben & Steen Thomsen (1997). "European Patterns of Corporate Ownership," *Journal of International Business Studies*, 28(4), 759–778.

Pehrsson, Anders (2006a). "Business Relatedness and Performance: A Study of Managerial Perceptions," *Strategic Management Journal*, 27(3), 265–282.

Pehrsson, Anders (2006b). "Business Relatedness Measurement: State-of-the-Art and a Proposal," *European Business Review*, 18(5), 350–363.

Peng, Mike W. (2001). "The Resource-Based View and International Business," *Journal of Management*,

27(6), 803–829.

Peng, Mike W. (2003). "Institutional Transition and Strategic Choices," *Academy of Management*, 28(2), 275–296.

Peng, Mike W. (2006). *Global Strategy*. Mason, OH: Thomason South-Western.

Peng, Mike W. & Andrew Delios (2006). "What Determine the Scope of the Firm over Time and around the World? An Asia Pacific Perspective," *Asia Pacific Journal of Management*, 23(4), 385–405.

Peng, Mike W., Seung-Hyun Lee, & Denis Y. L. Wang (2005). "What Determines the Scope of the Firm over Time? A Focus on Institutional Relatedness," *Academy of Management Review*, 30(3), 622–633.

Pennings, Johannes, Harry Barkema, & Sytse Douma (1994). "Organizational Learning and Diversification," *Academy of Management Journal*, 37(3), 608–641.

Penrose, E Edith T. (1955). "Limits to the Growth and Size of Firms," *The American Economic Review*, 45(2), 531–543.

Penrose, Edith T. (1959). *The Theory of the Growth of the Firm*. London: Basil Blackwell.

Perlmutter, Howard (1969). "The Tortuous Evolution of the Multinational Corporation," *Columbia Journal of World Business*, 4(1), 9–18.

Perrow, Charles (1970). "Departmental Power and Perspectives in Industrial Firms," in Zald Mayer (ed.) *Power in Organizations*, pp. 59–89. Nashville, TN: Vanderbilt University Press.

Perrow, Charles (1981). "Markets, Hierarchies, and Hegemony," in Andrew Van de Ven & William Joyce (eds) *Perspectives on Organization Design and Behavior*, pp. 371–186. New York: Wiley.

Peteraf, Margaret A. (1993). "The Cornerstones of Competitive Advantage: A Resource-Based View," *Strategic Management Journal*, 14(3), 179–191.

Pfeffer, J. (1981). *Power in Organizations*. Marshfield, MA: Pitman Publishing.

Pfeffer, Jeffrey & Gerald R. Salancik (1978). *The External Control of Organizations: A Resource Dependence Perspective*. New York: Harper & Row.

Philippe, Henri (2005). "Corporate Governance: A New Limit to Real Options Valuations?" *Journal of Management and Governance*, 9(2), 129–149.

Pidun, Ulrich, Harald Rubner, Matthias Krühler, Robert Untiedt, & Michael Nippa (2011). "Corporate Portfolio Management: Theory and Practice," *Journal of Applied Corporate Finance*, 23(1), 63–76.

Pinkston, Tammie S. & Archie B. Carroll (1994). "Corporate Citizenship Perspectives and Foreign Direct Investments in the U.S.," *Journal of Business Ethics*, 13(3), 157–169.

Pinkston, Tammie S. & Archie B. Carroll (1996). "A Retrospective Examination of CSR Orientations: Have They Changed?" *Journal of Business Ethics*, 15(2), 199–206.

Pisano, Gary (1990). "The R&D Boundaries of the Firm: An Empirical Analysis," *Administrative Science Quarterly*, 35(1), 153–176.

Piscitello, Lucia (2000). "Relatedness and Coherence in Technological and Product Diversification of the World's Largest Firms," *Structural Change and Economic Dynamics*, 11(3), 295–315.

Pitts, Robert A. (1974). "Incentive Compensation and Organization Design," *Personnel Journal*, 53(5), 338–344.

Pitts, Robert A. (1977), "Strategies and Structures for Diversification," *Academy of Management Journal*, 20(2), 197–208.

Pitts, Robert A. & H. Donald Hopkins (1982). "Firm Diversity: Conceptualization and Measurement," *Academy of Management Review*, 7(4), 620–629.

Poitevin, Michel (1989). "Financial Signaling and the 'Deep-Pocket' Argument," *The RAND Journal of Economics*, 20(1), 26–40.

Polyani, Michael (1962). *Personal Knowledge*. New York: Harper Torchbooks.

Poppo, Laura & Todd Zenger (2002). "Do Formal Contract and Relational Governance Function as Substitutes or Complements?" *Strategic Management Journal*, 23(8), 707–725.

Porac, Joseph F. & Jose Antonio Rosa (1996). "Rivalry, Industry Models, and the Cognitive Embeddedness of the Comparable Firm," *Advances in Strategic Management*, 13, 363–388.

Porac, Joseph F. & Howard Thomas (1990). "Taxonomic Mental Models of Competitor Definition," *Academy of Management Review*, 15(2), 224–240.

Porac, Joseph F., Howard Thomas, & Charles Baden-Fuller (1989). "Competitive Groups as Cognitive Communities: The Case of Scottish Knitwear Manufacturers," *Journal of Management Studies*, 26(4), 397–416.

Porter, Michael E. (1980). *Competitive Strategy: Techniques for Analyzing Industries and Competitors*. New York: Free Press.

Porter, Michael E. (1985). *Competitive Advantage: Creating and Sustaining Superior Performance*. New York: Free Press.

Porter, Michael E. (1986). *Competition in Global Industries*. Boston, MA: Harvard Business School Press.

Porter, Michael E. (1987). "From Competitive Advantage to Corporate Strategy," *Harvard Business Review*, 65(3), 42–59.

Porter, Michael E. (1990). *The Competitive Advantage of Nations*. New York: The Free Press.

Powell, Walter W. (1990). "Neither Market nor Hierarchy: Network Forms of Organization," in Larry L. Cunnings and Barry M. Staw (eds) *Research in Organizational Behavior*, pp. 295–336. Greenwich (CT): JAI.

Prahalad, C. K. (2004). "The Blinders of Dominant Logic," *Long Range Planning*, 37(2), 171–179.

Prahalad, C. K. & Richard A. Bettis (1986). "The Dominant Logic: A New Linkage Between Diversity and Performance," *Strategic Management Journal*, 7(6), 485–501.

Prahalad, C. K. & Yves Doz (1987). *The Multinational Mission*. New York: The Free Press.

Prahalad, C. K. & Gary Hamel (1989). "Strategic Intent," *Harvard Business Review*, 67(3), 63–77.

Prahalad, C. K. & Gary Hamel, (1990). "The Core Competence of the Corporation," *Harvard Business Review*, 68(3), 79–91.

Priem, Richard L. (2007). "A Consumer Perspective on Value Creation," *Academy of Management Review*, 32(1), 219–235.

Qiu, Jane X. & Lex Donaldson (2012). "Stopford and Wells were Right! MNC Matrix Structures *do* fit a 'High-High' Strategy," *Management International Review*, 52(5), 671–689.

Rajan, Raghuram, Henri Servaes, & Luigi Zingales (2000). "The Cost of Diversify: The Diversification Discount and Inefficient Investment," *Journal of Finance*, 55(1), 35–79.

Rajand, Mahendra & Michael Forsyth (2002). "Hostile Bidders, Long-Term Performance, and Restructuring Methods: Evidence from the UK," *American Business Review*, 20(1), 71–81.

Ramanujam, Vasudevan & P. Varadarajan (1989). "Research on Corporate Diversification: A Synthesis," *Strategic Management Journal*, 10(6), 523–551.

Ramaswamy, Kannan (1997). "The Performance Impact of Strategic Similarity in Horizontal Mergers," *Academy of Management Journal*, 40(3), 697–717.

Ramaswamy, Kannan, Mingfang Li, Rajaram Veliath (2002). "Variations in Ownership Behavior and Propensity to Diversify: A Study of the Indian Corporate Context," *Strategic Management Journal*, 23(4), 345–358.

Ranft, Annette L. & Michael D. Lord (2000). "Acquiring new Knowledge: The Role of Retaining Human Capital in Acquisitions of High-Tech Firms," *Journal of High Technology Management Research*, 11(2), 295–319.

Rao, Vithala R. & Joel H. Steckel (1998). *Analysis for Strategic Marketing*. New York: Addison Wesley.

Rappaport, Alfred & Mark L. Sirower (1999). "Stock or Cash?" *Harvard Business Review*, 77(6), 147–148.

Ravenscraft, David J. & Frederic M. Scherer (1987). *Mergers, Selloffs, and Economic Efficiency*. Washington, DC: Brookings Institution.

Ravenscraft, David J. & Frederic M. Scherer (1991). "Divisional Sell-Off: A Hazard Function Analysis," *Managerial and Decision Economics*, 12(6), 429–438.

Rawls, John (1999). *A Theory of Justice*. Revised edition. Cambridge, MA: The Belknap Press of Harvard University Press.

Raynor, Michael E. (2002). "Diversification as Real Options and the Implications of Firm-Specific Risk and Performance," *Engineering Economist*, 47(4), 371–389.

Raynor, Michael E. & Joseph L. Bower (2001). "Lead from the Center: How to Manage Divisions Dynamically," *Harvard Business Review*, 79(5), 92–100.

Rebeiz, Karim S. (2001). "Corporate Governance Effectiveness in American Corporations: A Survey,"

International Management Journal, 18(1), 74–80.

Reed, Richard & Robert J. DeFillippi (1990). "Causal Ambiguity, Barriers to Imitation, and Sustainable Competitive Advantage," *Academy of Management Review*, 15(1), 88–102.

Reimann, Bernard C. & Allan Reichert (1996), "Portfolio Planning Methods for Strategic Capital Allocation: A Survey of Fortune 500 Firms," *International Journal of Management*, 13(1), 84–93.

Reuters (2007). "Toyota taps Japan for exports to small markets," July 18, [www.reuters.com/articlePrint?articleId=USSP767042007071].

Rhoades, Stephen A. (1973). "The Effect of Diversification on Industry Profit Performance in 241 Manufacturing Industries: 1963," *Review of Economics and Statistics*, 55(2), 146–155.

Rhoades, Stephen A. & Arnold A. Heggestad (1985). "Multimarket Interdependence and Performance in Banking: Two Tests," *The Antitrust Bulletin*, 30, 975–995.

Robbins, D. Keith & John A. Pearce II (1992). "Turnaround: Retrenchment and Recovery," *Strategic Management Journal*, 13(4), 287–309.

Robins, James A. & Margarethe F. Wiersema (1995). "A Resource-Based Approach to the Multibusiness Firm: Empirical Analysis of Portfolio Interrelationships and Corporate Financial Performance', *Strategic Management Journal*, 16(4), 277–299.

Robins, James A. & Margarethe F. Wiersema (2003). "The Measurement of Corporate Portfolio Strategy: Analysis of the Content Validity of Related Diversification Indexes," *Strategic Management Journal*, 24(1), 39–59.

Robinson, Joan T. (1956). "The Industry and the Market," *Economic Journal*, 66(262), 360–361.

Roll, Richard (1986). "The Hubris Hypothesis of Corporate Takeovers," *Journal of Business*, 59(2), 197–216.

Roquebert Jaime A., Robert L. Philips, & Peter A. Westfall (1996). "Markets vs. Management: What Drives Profitability," *Strategic Management Journal*, 17(8), 653–664.

Roth, Kendall & Allan J. Morrison (1990). "An Empirical Analysis of the Integration-Responsiveness Framework in Global Industries," *Journal of International Business Studies*, 21(4), 541–564.

Roth, Kendall, David M. Schweiger & Allan J. Morrison (1991). "Global Strategy Implementation at the Business Unit Level: Operational Capabilities and Administrative Mechanisms," *Journal of International Business Studies*, 22(3), 369–402.

Rothaermel, Frank T., Michael A. Hitt, & Lloyd A. Jobe (2006). "Balancing Vertical Integration and Strategic Outsourcing: Effects on Product Portfolio, Product Success, and Firm Performance," *Strategic Management Journal*, 27(11), 1033–1056.

Rugman, Allan M. (1979). *International Diversification and the Multinational Enterprise*. Lexington, MA: Lexington Books.

Rumelt, Richard P. (1974). *Strategy, Structure and Economic Performance*. Cambridge, MA: Harvard University Press.

Rumelt, Richard P. (1982). "Diversification Strategy and Profitability," *Strategic Management Journal*, 3(4), 359–370.

Rumelt, Richard P. (1991). "How Much Does Industry Matter?" *Strategic Management Journal*, 12(3), 167–185.

Saloner, Gareth (1987). "Predation, Mergers, and Incomplete Information," *RAND Journal of Economics*, 18(2), 165–186.

Salter, Malcolm S. (1973). "Tailor Incentive Compensation to Strategy," *Harvard Business Review*, 51(2), 94–102.

Sanders, W. M. Gerard & Mason A. Carpenter (1998). "Internationalization and Firm Governance: The Roles of CEO Compensation, Top Team Composition and Board Structure," *Academy of Management Journal*, 41(2), 158–178.

Sandvig, J. Christopher & Lori Coakley (1998). "Best Practice in Small Firm Diversification," *Business Horizons*, 43(3), 33–40.

Saudagaran, Shahrokh M. (2002). "A Review of the Literature on the Market Valuation of Multinational Firms," *Managerial Finance*, 28(3), 5–19.

Schelling, Thomas C. (1960). *The Strategy of Conflict*. Cambridge, MA: Harvard University Press.

Schendel, Dan & G. Richard Patton (1976). "Corporate Stagnation and Turnaround," *Journal of*

Economics and Business, 28(3), 236–241.

Schendel, Dan, G. Richard Patton, & James Riggs (1976). "Corporate Turnaround Strategies: A Study of Profit Decline and Recovery," *Journal of General Management*, 3(3), 3–11.

Scherer, Frederic M. & David Ross (1990). *Industrial Market Structure and Economic Performance*. Boston: Houghton Mifflin.

Schmalensee, Richard (1985). "Do Markets Differ Much?" *American Economic Review*, 75(3), 167–185.

Schmidt, Jens & Thomas Keil (2013). "What Makes a Resource Valuable? Identifying the Drivers of Firm-Idiosyncratic Resource Value," *Academy of Management Review*, 38(2), 206–228.

Schnaiberg, Allan & Kenneth Gould (1994). *Environment and Society: The Enduring Conflict*. New York: St. Martin's Press.

Schoar, Antoinette (2002). "Effects of Corporate Diversification on Productivity," *Journal of Finance*, 57(6), 2379–2403.

Schroeder, Roger R., Kimberly A. Bates & Mikko A. Junttila (2002). "A Resource-Based View of Manufacturing Strategy and the Relationship to Manufacturing Performance," *Strategic Management Journal*, 23(2), 105–117.

Scott, James H. (1977). "On the Theory of Conglomerate Mergers," *Journal of Finance*, 32(4), 1235–1250.

Scott, W. Richard (1995). *Institutions and Organizations*. Thousand Oaks, CA: Sage.

Servaes, Henri (1996). "The Value of Diversification During the Conglomerate Merger Wave," *Journal of Finance*, 51(4), 1201–1225.

Seth, Anju (1990). "Value Creation in Acquisitions: A Re-examination of Performance Issues." *Strategic Management Journal*, 11(2), 99–116.

Seth, Anju & Sung Min Kim (2001). "Valuation of International Joint Ventures: A Real Options Approach," in Farok J. Contractor (Ed.) *Valuation of Intangible Assets in Global Operations*, pp. 147–169. Westpot, CT: Quorum Book.

Seward, James K. & James P. Walsh (1996). "The Governance and Control of Voluntary Corporate Spin Offs," *Strategic Management Journal*, 17(1), 25–39.

Sharma, Anurag (1998). "Mode of Entry and Ex-Post Performance," *Strategic Management Journal*, 19(9), 879–900.

Sharpe, William F. (1964). "Capital Asset Prices: A Theory of Market Equilibrium Under Conditions of Risk," *Journal of Finance*, 19(3), 425–442.

Shelanski, Howard A. & Peter G. Klein (1995). "Empirical Research in Transaction Cost Economics: A Review and Assessment," *Journal of Law, Economics, and Organization*, 11(2), 335–361.

Shepherd, William G. (1970). *Market Power and Economic Welfare*. New York: Random House.

Sheppard, J. & S. Chowdhury (2005). "Riding the Wrong Wave: Organisational Failure as a Failed Turnaround," *Long Range Planning*, 38(3), 239–261.

Shleifer, Andrei & Robert W. Vishny (1990). "The Takeover Wave of the 1980s," *Journal of Applied Corporate Finance*, 4(3), 49–56.

Shleifer, Andrei & Robert W. Vishny (1991). "Takeovers in the 60s and 80s: Evidence and Implications," *Strategic Management Journal*, 12(WSI), 51–60.

Shleifer, Andrei & Robert W. Vishny (1997). "A Survey of Corporate Governance," *Journal of Finance*, 52(2), 737–783.

Shrivastava, Paul (1996). *Greening Business: Profiting the Corporation and the Environment*. Cincinnati: Thompson Executive Press.

Simerly, Roy L. & Mingfang Li (1999). "Environmental Dynamism, Capital Structure and Performance: A Theoretical Integration and an Empirical Test," *Strategic Management Journal*, 21(1), 31–49.

Simmel, Georg (1950). "Superordination and Subordination and Degrees of Domination and Freedom," in Kurt H. Wolff (Ed.) *The Sociology of Georg Simmel*, pp. 268–303. New York: The Free Press.

Simmonds, Paul G. (1990). "The Combined Diversification Breadth and Mode Dimensions and the Performance of Large Diversified Firms," *Strategic Management Journal*, 11(5), 399–410.

Simon, Herbert A. (1961). *Administrative Behavior*. Second edition. New York: The Macmillan Company.

Simonian, Haig & Louise Lucas (2010). "Nestlé to Take on Pharmaceutical Sector," *Financial Times*,

September 27 [www.ft.com/intl/cms/s/0/dfa59814-ca04-11df-87b8-00144feab49a.html#axzz3sPUv7rgc].

Singh, Deeksha A., Ajai S. Gaur, & Florian P. Schmid (2010). "Corporate Diversification, TMT Experience, and Performance," *Management International Review*, 50(1), 35–56.

Sirower, Mark L. (1997). *The Synergy Trap: How Companies Lose the Acquisition Game*. New York: Free Press.

Sloan, Afred P., Jr. (1963). *My Years with General Motors*. New York: MacFadden-Bartell.

Slovin, Myron B., Marie E. Sushka, & Steven R. Ferraro (1995). "A Comparison of the Information Conveyed by Equity Carve-Outs, Spin-Offs, and Asset Sell-Offs," *Journal of Financial Economics*, 37(1), 89–104.

Smith, Clayton G. & Arnold C. Cooper (1988). "Established Companies Diversifying into Young Industries: A Comparison of Firms with Different Levels of Performance," *Strategic Management Journal*, 9(2), 111–121.

Smith, Faye L. & Rick L. Wilson (1995). "The Predictive Validity of the Karnani and Wernerfelt Model of Multipoint Competition," *Strategic Management Journal*, 16(2) 143–160.

Sobel, Robert (1984). *The Rise and Fall of the Conglomerate Kings*. New York: Stein and Day.

Spencer, Jennifer W. (2003). "Firms' Knowledge-Sharing Strategies in the Global Innovation System: Empirical Evidence from the Flat panel Display Industry," *Strategic Management Journal*, 24(3), 217–233.

Stapleton, R. C. (1982). "Mergers, Debt Capacity, and the Valuation of Corporate Loans," in M. Keenan & L. J. White (eds) *Mergers and Acquisitions*, pp. 9–28. Lexington, MA: D. C. Heath.

Stephan, John, Johann Peter Murmann, Warren Boeker, & Jerry Goodstein (2003). "Bringing Manager into Theories of Multimarket Competition: CEOs and the Determinants of Market Entry," *Organization Science*, 14(4), 403–421.

Stiles, Philip (2001). "The Impact of Board on Strategy: An Empirical Examination," *Journal of Management Studies*, 38(5), 627–650.

Stimpert, J. L. & Irene M. Duhaime (1997). "In the Eye of the Beholder: Conceptualizations of Relatedness Held by the Managers of Large Diversified Firms," *Strategic Management Journal*, 18(2), 111–125.

St John, Caron H. & Jeffrey S. Harrison (1999). "Manufacturing-Based Relatedness, Synergy, and Coordination," *Strategic Management Journal*, 20(2), 129–145.

Stopford, John M. & Louis T. Wells (1972). *Managing the Multinational Enterprise*. New York: Basic Books.

Stulz, René (1990). "Managerial Discretion and Optimal Financing Policies," *Journal of Financial Economics*, 26(1), 3–27.

Subramani, Mani R. & N. Venkatraman (2003). "Safeguarding Investments in Asymmetric Interorganizational Relationships: Theory and Evidence," *Academy of Management Journal*, 46(1), 46–62.

Suzuki, Y. (1980). "The Strategy and Structure of Top Japanese Industrial Enterprises 1950–1970," *Strategic Management Journal*, 1(3), 265–291.

Szeless, Georg, Margarethe Wiersema, & Günter Müller-Stewens (2003). "Portfolio Interrelationships and Financial Performance in the Context of European Firms," *European Management Journal*, 21(2), 146–163.

Tanriverdi, Hüseyin & Chi-Hyon Lee (2008). "Within-Industry Diversification and Firm Performance in the Presence of Network Externalities: Evidence from the Software Industry," *Academy of Management Journal*, 51(2), 381–397.

Tanriverdi, Hüseyin & N. Venkatraman (2005). "Knowledge Relatedness and the Performance of Multibusiness Firms," *Strategic Management Journal*, 26(2), 97–119.

Taylor, Peter & Julian Lowe (1995). "A Note on Corporate Strategy and Capital Structure," *Strategic Management Journal*, 16(5), 411–414.

Teece, David J. (1980). "Economies of Scope and the Scope of the Enterprise," *Journal of Economic Behavior and Organization*, 1(3), 223–245.

Teece, David J. (1981a). "Internal Organization and Economic Performance," *Journal of Industrial*

Economics, 30(2), 173–199.

Teece, David J. (1981b). "Multinational Enterprise: Market-Failure and Market-Power Considerations," *Sloan Management Review*, 22(3), 3–17.

Teece, David J. (1982). "Toward an Economic Theory of the Multiproduct Firm," *Journal of Economic Behavior and Organization*, 3(1), 39–63.

Teece, David J. (1986). "Transactions Cost Economics and the Multinational Enterprise," *Journal of Economic Behaviour and Organisation*, 7(1), 21–45.

Teece, David J., Gary Pisano, & Amy Shuen (1997). "Dynamic Capabilities and Strategic Management," *Strategic Management Journal*, 18(7), 509–534.

Telser, Lester G. (1966). "Cutthroat Competition and the Long Purse," *Journal of Law and Economics*, 9, 259–277.

Thanheiser, Heinz (1973). "Strategy and structure of German firms," Unpublished doctoral dissertation, Harvard University.

Tihanyi, Laszlo, David A. Griffith, & Craig J. Russell (2005). "The Effect of Cultural Distance on Entry Mode Choice, International Diversification, and MNE Performance: A Meta-Analysis," *Journal of International Business Studies*, 36(3), 270–283.

Trigeorgis, Lenos (1993). "The Nature of Option Interactions and the Valuation of Investments with Multiple Real Options," *Journal of Financial and Quantitative Analysis*, 28(1), 1–20.

Tsai, Wenspin (2000). "Social Capital, Strategic Relatedness and the Formation of Interorganizational Linkages," *Strategic Management Journal*, 21(9), 925–939.

Tsai, Wenspin (2001). "Knowledge Transfer in Intraorganizational Networks: Effects of Network Position and Absorptive Capacity on Business Unit Innovation and Performance," *Academy of Management Journal*, 44(5), 996–1004.

Tucker, Irvin & Ronald P. Wilder (1977). "Trends in Vertical Integration in the U.S. Manufacturing Sector," *Journal of Industrial Economics*, 26(1), 81–94.

Upson, John W. & Annette L. Ranft (2010). "When Strategies Collide: Divergent Multipoint Strategies within Competitive Triads. *Business Horizons*, 53(1), 49–57.

Usunier, Jean–Claude, Olivier Furrer & Amandine Furrer-Perrinjaquet (2011). "The Perceived Trade-Off between Corporate Social and Economic Responsibility: A Cross-National Study," *International Journal of Cross Cultural Management*, 11(3), 279–302.

Utton, Michael A. (1979). *Diversification and Competition*. Cambridge, UK: Cambridge University Press.

Van den Bossche, Anne-Marie, Jacques Derenne, Paul Nihoul, Christophe Verdure (2015). *Sourcebook on EU Competition Law 2015–2016*. Bruxelles: Larcier.

van Oijen, Aswin & Sytse Douma (2000). "Diversification Strategy and the Roles of the Centre," *Long Range Planning*, 33(4), 560–578.

van Witteloostuijn, Arjen (1998). "Bridging Behavioral and Economic Theories of Decline: Organizational Inertia, Strategic Competition, and Chronic Failure," *Management Science*, 44(4), 501–519.

Vancil, Richard F. (1978). *Decentralization: Managerial Ambiguity by Design*. Homewood Il: Dow Jones-Irwin.

Varadarajan, P. "Rajan" & Vasudevan Ramanujam (1987). "Diversification and Performance: A Reexamination Using a New Two–Dimensional Conceptualization of Diversity in Firms," *Academy of Management Journal*, 30(2), 380–393.

Varaiya, Nikhil P. (1988). "Winners Curse Hypothesis and Corporate Takeovers," *Managerial and Decision Economics*, 9(3), 209–219.

Veld, Chris & Yulia V. Yulia. (2004). "Do Spin-Offs Really Create Value? The European Case," *Journal of Banking & Finance*, 28(5), 1111–1135.

Venkatraman, N. (1989). "The Concept of Fit in Strategy Research: Toward Verbal and Statistical Correspondence," *Academy of Management Review*, 14(3), 423–444.

Vernon, Raymond (1966). "International Investment and International Trade in the Product Life Cycle," *Quarterly Journal of Economics*, 80(2), 190–207.

Vernon, Raymond (1971). *Sovereignty at Bay*. New York: Basic Books.

Vernon, Raymond (1980). "Gone Are the Cash Cows of Yesteryear," *Harvard Business Review*, 58(6), 150–155.

Villalonga, Belen (2004a). "Diversification Discount or Premium? New Evidence from the Business Information Tracking Series," *Journal of Finance*, 59(2), 479–506.

Villalonga, Belen (2004b). "Does Diversification Cause the Diversification Discount?" *Financial Management*, 33(2), 5–27.

Walker, Gordon, & David Weber (1984). "A Transaction Cost Approach to Make-or-Buy Decisions," *Administrative Science Quarterly*, 29(3), 373–391.

Walker, Gordon, & David Weber (1987). "Supplier Competition, Uncertainty and Make-or-Buy Decisions," *Academy of Management Journal*, 30(3), 589–596.

Walker, Orville C. Jr. & Robert W. Ruekert (1987), "Marketing's Role in the Implementation of Business Strategies: A Critical Review and Conceptual Framework," *Journal of Marketing*, 51(3), 15–33.

Walsh, James P. (1988). "Top Management Turnover Following Mergers and Acquisitions," *Strategic Management Journal*, 9(2), 173–183.

Walsh, James P. & Rita D. Kosnik (1993). "Corporate Raiders and their Disciplinary Role in the Market for Corporate Control," *Academy of Management Journal*, 36(4), 671–700.

Walsh, James P. & James K. Seward (1990). "On the Efficiency of Internal and External Corporate Control Mechanisms," *Academy of Management Review*, 15(3), 421–458.

Wan, William P. & Robert E. Hoskisson (2003). "Home Country Environments, Corporate Diversification Strategies and Firm Performance," *Academy of Management Journal*, 46(1), 27–45.

Wan, William P., Robert E. Hoskisson, Jeremy C. Short, & Daphne W. Yiu (2011). "Resource-based Theory and Corporate Diversification: Accomplishments and Opportunities," *Journal of Management*, 37(5), 1335–1368.

Wang, Heli C. Jay B. & Barney (2006). "Employee Incentives to Make Firm-Specific Investments: Implications for Resource-based Theories of Corporate Diversification," *Academy of Management Review*, 31(2), 466–476.

Wang, Heli C., Jinyu He & Joseph T. Mahoney (2009). "Firm-Specific Knowledge Resources and Competitive Advantage: The Roles of Economic- and Relationship-based Employee Governance Mechanisms," *Strategic Management Journal*, 30(12), 1265–1285.

Weber Roberto A. & Colin F. Camerer (2003). "Cultural Conflict and Merger Failure: An Experimental Approach," *Management Science*, 49(4), 400–415.

Weisbach, Micahel S. (1988). "Outside Directors and CEO Turnover," *Journal of Financial Economics*, 20(January–March), 431–460.

Wernerfelt, Birger (1984). "A Resource-Based View of the Firm," *Strategic Management Journal*, 5(2), 171–180.

Wernerfelt, Birger & Cynthia A. Montgomery (1988). "Tobin's q and the Importance of Focus in Firm Performance," *American Economic Review*, 78(1), 246–250.

Weston, J. Fred, Kwang S. Chung, & Juan A. Siu (1998). *Takeovers, Restructuring, and Corporate Governance*. Upper Saddle River (NJ): Prentice Hall.

Westphal, James D. (1998). "Board Games: How CEOs Adapt to Increases in Structural Board Independence from Management," *Administrative Science Quarterly*, 43(3), 511–537.

Westphal, James D. & Laurie P. Milton (2000). "How Experience and Network Ties Affect the Influence of Demographic Minorities on Corporate Boards," *Administrative Science Quarterly*, 45(2), 366–399.

Whittington, Richard, Andrew Pettigrew, Simon Peck, Evelyn Fenton & Martin Conyon (1999). "Change and Complementarities in the New Competitive Landscape: A European Panel Study, 1992–1996," *Organization Science*, 10(5), 583–600.

Wiersema, Margarethe (2002). "Holes at the Top: Why CEO Firings Backfire," *Harvard Business Review*, 80(12), 70–77.

Wiersema, Margarethe F. & Karen A. Bantel (1992). "Top Management Team Demography and Corporate Strategic Change," *Academy of Management Journal*, 35(1), 91–121.

Wiersema, Margarethe F. & Julia Porter Lebeskind (1995). "The Effect of Leveraged Buyouts on Corporate Growth and Diversification in Large Firms," *Strategic Management Journal*, 16(6), 447–460.

Williams, Jeffrey R., Betty L. Paez, & Leonard Sanders (1988). "Conglomerates Revisited," *Strategic Management Journal*, 9(5), 403–414.

Williamson, Oliver E. (1970). *Corporate Control and Business Behavior. An Inquiry into the Effect of Organization Form on Enterprise Behavior.* Englewood Cliffs, NJ: Prentice Hall.

Williamson, Oliver E. (1975). *Markets and Hierarchies: Analysis and Antitrust Implication.* New York: The Free Press.

Williamson, Oliver E. (1979). "Transaction-Cost Economics: The Governance of Contractual Relations," *Journal of Law and Economics*, 22(2), 233–261.

Williamson, Oliver E. (1981). "The Modern Corporation: Origins, Evolution, Attributes," *Journal of Economic Literature*, 19(4), 1537–1568.

Williamson, Oliver E. (1985). *The Economic Institutions of Capitalism.* New York: The Free Press.

Williamson, Oliver E. (1986). *Economic Organization: Firms, Markets and Policy Control.* New York: New York University Press.

Williamson, Oliver E. (1991). "Comparative Economic Organization: The Analysis of Discrete Structural Alternatives," *Administrative Science Quarterly*, 36(2), 269–296.

Williamson, Oliver E. (1996). "Economics and Organization: A Primer," *California Management Review*, 38(2), 131–146.

Winter, S. G. (1987). "Knowledge and Competence as Strategic Assets," in David J. Teece (Ed.) *The Competitive Challenge: Strategies for Industrial Innovation and Renewal*, pp. 159–184. Cambridge, MA: Ballinger Publishing Company.

Wood, Adrian (1971). "Diversification, Merger and Research Expenditures: A Review of Empirical Studies," in Robin Morris & Adrian Wood (eds) *The Corporate Economy: Growth, Competition and Innovation Potential*, pp. 428–453. Cambridge, MA: Harvard University Press.

Wood, Donna J. (1991). "Corporate Social Performance Revisited," *Academy of Management Review*, 16(4), 691–718.

Wright, Peter, Mark Kroll, & Detelin Elenkov (2002). "Acquisition Returns, Increase in Firm Size and Chief Executive Officer Compensation: The Moderating Role of Monitoring," *Academy of Management Journal*, 45(3), 599–608.

Wrigley, Leonard (1970). "Divisional Autonomy and Diversification," Unpublished doctoral dissertation, Harvard Business School.

Yan, An (2006). "Value of Conglomerates and Capital Market Conditions," *Financial Management*, 35(4), 5–30.

Ye, Guangliang, Richard L. Priem, & Abdullah A. Alshwer (2012). "Achieving Demand-side Synergy from Strategic Diversification: How Combining Mundane Assets can Leverage Consumer Utilities," *Organization Science*, 23(1), 207–224.

Yip, George S. (1982). "Diversification Entry: Internal Development versus Acquisition," *Strategic Management Journal*, 3(4), 331–345.

Young, Greg, Ken G. Smith, Curtis M. Grimm, & Daniel Simon (2000). "Multimarket Contact and Resource Dissimilarity: A Competitive Dynamics Perspective," *Journal of Management*, 26(6), 1217–1236.

Zalewski, David A. (2001). "Corporate Takeovers, Fairness, and Public Policy," *Journal of Economic Issues*, 35(2), 431–437.

Zeithaml, Carl P. & Valarie A. Zeithaml (1984). "Environmental Management: Revisiting the Marketing Perspective," *Journal of Marketing*, 48(2), 46–53.

Zhang, Hao (1995). "Wealth Effects of U.S. Bank Takeover," *Applied Financial Economics*, 5(5), 329–336.

Zhao, Hongxin, Yadong Luo, & Taewon Suh (2004). "Transaction Cost Determinants and Ownership-Based Entry Mode Choice: A Meta-Analytical Review," *Journal of International Business Studies*, 35(6), 524–544.

INDEX

Abell, Derek F. 45, 46, 49, 51–59, 83, 198, 225
Abernathy, William J. 101
Achrol, Ravi S. 130, 141
Ackoff, Russell L. 46
acquisitions: adverse selection 166, 173, 224; economic profits related to 62, 163–164; failure 160, 164, 166, 173; firm's growth xiii, 13–14, 30, 67, 70, 109, 127, 154, 163–166; firm scope 58, 91, 127; legal constraints 19, 30; postacquisition integration process 164–166; restructuring 31, 68, 73, 119, 158, 170–171, 181–182; synergies 78 see M&A
Adamy, J. 181
added value 70, 72, 143
administrative hierarchy; see hierarchy, governance
advantage; see competitive advantage; corporate advantage
adverse selection 155, 224
Afuah, Allan 149
Agarwal, Rajshree 31
agency costs 101, 107, 114, 140, 172, 218
agency problems, governance failure 25–26, 45, 48–49, 99, 104, 133–134, 180, 183, 213, 215, 224, 230
agency theory xiii, 17, 24–27, 29, 35, 38–39, 42, 61, 100, 109, 159, 202, 204, 212–217, 222
Agle, Bradley R. 213, 220, 221
Aguilera, Ruth V. 212, 222
Ahuja, Gautam 163
Akerlof, George A. 146, 155. 224
Alchian, Armen A. 22, 27, 135, 145, 155
Alexander, Donald L. 192
Alexander, Marcus 9, 11–14, 17, 45, 60–63, 67, 81, 96 106, 107, 110, 112–116, 121, 123, 162, 181, 205, 224, 229
alignment: corporate strategy 35, 38, 172, 175; internal 53, 171, 175
Allen, Stephen A. 39, 103, 111, 115, 134–136, 140
Allen, Steve G. 134
Alliances: governance structure 11, 15, 42, 54, 59, 60, 130, 147, 150, 151, 155, 167–168, 178,

227, 229, 231; growth strategy xiii, 10, 18, 28, 70, 91, 109, 123, 154, 156–161, 162, 167–168; vertical 147, 148, 150, 178
allocation: of decision authority 9, 49, 131, 133, 232; resources 12, 36, 38, 42, 45, 47, 68, 70, 71, 74, 77, 93, 99, 109, 111, 113, 127, 128, 133, 138, 196, 226, 228, 230
Ambos, Björn 106–107, 115, 203, 205
Ambrosini, Véronique 1
Amburgey, Terry L. 125, 178
Amihud, Yakov 25, 26, 61, 174, 212, 229
Amit, Raphael 60, 71, 85
Amram, Martha 33, 147, 231
analysis, industry; see industry and industry analysis
Anand, Bharat N. 167
Anand, Jaideep 29, 43
Anderson, Erin 145, 156, 158, 159, 161
Anderson, Ronald C. 27
Andrews, Kenneth R. 1, 12, 29, 45, 154
Angwin, Duncan 216
Ansoff, H. Igor 12, 46–48, 51, 55, 64, 154, 198
anticompetitive: economies of scope 62–63, 74–76, 81, 96, 135; market power 19, 22
antitrust enforcement 17, 19–20, 22, 29–30, 173, 177
Aoki, Masahiko 212
AOL 20, 30, 43–44, 184, 196
Apple 142, 176
Argyres, Nicholas 146, 147
Armour, Henry O. 104
Armstrong, Craig E. 67, 106
Arnould, Richard J. 74
Arrow, Kenneth J. 144, 146
Asquith, Paul 160
assets: complementary 31, 76, 168; financial 33, 106, 171; intangible 22, 24, 64, 67, 72, 91, 162, 199, 210, 226; sell-off 171, 181, 226; specificity 22, 24, 34, 61, 84, 145, 150, 155, 158; stock of 8, 14, 27, 42, 64, 68, 72, 86, 91, 101, 147, 161, 168, 171, 174, 178, 180, 181, 200, 202, 204, 207, 213, 216, 226; tangible 24,

28 33, 39, 155; transaction-specific 155, 158; value-based strategy 30, 92, 94
Attiyeh, Robert S. 14
attractiveness of industries 31, 37, 59, 62, 70, 72, 116–121, 229
audit(s) 101, 106, 137, 216, 231
Aupperle, Kenneth E. 213, 220, 221
authority 9, 107, 122, 125, 127, 129, 132, 158, 224, 226, 232, 233
autonomous business units 26, 37, 43, 47, 68, 70, 109, 110, 112, 113, 122, 123, 135, 137, 164, 165, 175, 207

backward vertical integration 75, 141–142, 144, 146, 148, 233
Bain, Joe S. 18, 36, 154, 156, 157
Baker, George P. 228
Balakrishnan, Srinivasan 149, 155
bargaining power 2, 18, 24, 36–37, 61–63, 74, 77, 94, 146
Barkema, Harry G. 85, 125, 155, 161, 171
Barnard, Chester I. 25, 212, 230
Barnett, William P. 178
Barney, Jay B. 8, 17, 27, 28, 60, 61, 62, 63, 73, 76, 77, 96, 98, 131, 143, 146, 147, 151, 152, 163, 184, 196
barriers to entry *see* entry barriers
Bartlett, Christopher A. 68, 127, 128, 130, 198–201, 203–210, 230, 231
Bates, Kimberly A. 64
Bates, Thomas W. 27
Bator, Francis M. 229
Baum, Joel A. C. 125 185, 186, 187, 189, 190, 193, 194
Bausch, Andreas 98
Bayer 53–55, 70, 106
Baysinger, Barry 101, 215
Bazerman, Max H. 164, 166
BCG matrix 116–121
Beamish, Paul W. 68, 127, 130, 167, 198, 230
Becht, Marco 214
Berg, Norman A. 135
Berger, Philip G. 20, 22, 25, 26, 27, 73, 97, 99, 100, 174, 212
Bergh, Donald D. 3, 30, 32, 67, 85, 180, 228
Berle, Adolf A. 24, 25, 174, 212, 230
Bernardo, Antonio E. 32, 42
Bernheim, Douglas 185, 186, 189, 190, 192
Berry, Charles H. 74, 83, 84, 85, 87, 88, 227
Besanko, David 156, 157, 228
Best, Ronald W. 99
Bethel, Jennifer E. 170, 174, 231
Bettis, Richard A. 8, 28, 42, 43, 45, 47, 64, 70, 81, 85, 92, 93, 95, 100, 134, 205, 226
Bhide, Amar V. 71, 96
bidding 32, 150, 151, 166, 178
Biggadike, Ralph E. 162, 163

Birkinshaw, Julian 134, 138
Bizjak, John M. 27
Black, Fisher 32
Blocher, James 85
Block, Zenas 162, 163
board; *see* corporate boards
Boeker, Warren 186, 187 194
Boone, Audra L. 181, 226
Boston Consulting Group (BCG) 12, 116, 117; *see also* BCG matrix
bounded rationality 49, 94, 97, 100, 128, 131, 224
Bourgeois III, L. J. 165
Bower, Joseph H. 38, 133, 134
Bower, Joseph L. 33, 47, 71
Bowman, Cliff 1
Bowman, Edward H. 6, 7, 72, 170, 171, 172, 178, 180, 181, 182
Bradley, Michael 160
Bradley, Sarah 216
Brammer, Stephen J. 222
brand 14, 39, 44, 46, 53, 54, 58, 64, 66, 77, 78, 79, 82, 83, 91, 94, 102, 108, 118, 122, 142, 152, 156, 164, 170, 176, 177, 181, 185, 200, 201, 202
Brantley, Peter 104
Brauer, Matthias 171, 181, 183, 226
Brenner, Steffen 25, 213
Breschi, Stefano 85
Bromiley, Philip 6, 106
Brouthers, Keith D. 154, 161
Brouthers, Lance E. 161
Brown, James R. 154, 159
Brush, Thomas H. 6, 25, 67, 81, 85, 106, 164
Bryce, David J. 85, 91
Bruton, Garry D. 85
BTR 43
Buckley, Peter J. 199, 229
Bühner, Rolf 106
bureaucracy 15, 129, 175
Burgelman, Robert A. 9, 106, 162
Burgers, Willem P. 161
Burrough, Bryan 97, 170
business: business-level strategy 1, 2, 36, 42, 88, 109, 110, 133–138, 185, 187, 197, 212, 225; business portfolio 5–6, 8, 10, 12, 35, 38, 81, 82, 84, 90–91, 102, 107, 109, 113, 115, 116, 127, 171–172, 174–175, 181, 185–186, 224, 226; core business 4–6, 13–14, 15, 31, 38, 61, 67, 73, 170, 173, 176–177, 180, 181, 183, 227, 232; corporate strategy triangle 7–10, 76–77, 107, 172, 179; definition xiii, 45–59, 86, 225, 232; diversification choices 3, 4–6, 12–14, 29, 30, 36, 37–38, 67, 68, 71, 86, 95, 111; single business firm xiii, 3, 6, 17, 20, 25, 29, 42, 60, 68, 74, 86, 97–98 *see also* corporate, industry and industry analysis

Index

business unit 2, 11, 36, 39, 60, 64, 66, 67, 68, 70, 81, 84, 97, 100, 101–103, 106–110, 112–115, 116–123, 130, 138, 147, 175, 181–182, 191, 202, 225
Buzzell, Robert D. 12

Calori, Roland 8
Camerer, Colin F. 164
Campa, Jose M. 71
Campbell, Andrew 9, 11, 12, 13, 14, 17, 42, 43, 45, 60, 61, 62, 63, 64, 67, 78, 81, 96, 97, 106, 107, 110, 111, 112, 113, 114, 115, 116, 120, 121, 122, 123, 134, 162, 175, 181, 205, 224, 229
Cannella, Albert A. 25, 164, 212
capability, capabilities 15, 17, 24, 28, 29, 40, 42, 47, 49, 51, 59, 64, 65, 68, 73, 84, 90–93, 97, 100, 101, 103, 107, 109, 118, 121, 131, 145, 146, 147, 149, 150, 151, 152, 155, 159, 162, 163, 165, 166, 168, 186, 190, 192, 199, 201, 203, 204, 205, 210, 224, 225, 226, 232
capacity 28, 29, 39, 43, 46, 64, 68, 73, 75, 76, 77, 91, 97, 99, 101, 136, 144, 157, 162, 164, 168, 177, 208, 224, 225, 226, 227
capital allocation 68, 71, 77
capital markets 8, 10, 16, 18, 37–38, 40, 47, 63, 68, 70, 71–72, 76, 77, 81, 96, 98–99, 100, 103, 107, 108, 113, 115, 116, 133, 135, 137, 138, 166, 177, 210, 228
Capron, Laurence 39, 64, 67, 68, 85, 87, 171, 178
Cardinal, Laura B. 20, 21, 71, 85, 95, 96–99, 104
Carnegie Steel Company 141
Carpenter, Mason A. 215
Carroll, Archie B. 212, 213, 220–222
Carroll, Glenn R. 6
Casadesus-Masanell, Ramon 22
Cascio, Wayne F. 72, 179
cash cows, BCG matrix 117–121
cash flow 20, 28, 30, 32, 33, 35, 38, 42, 60, 73, 77, 116–118, 120, 121, 136–138, 180, 207, 210, 214, 231: excess, free 10, 11, 25, 30, 36, 38, 39, 100, 180, 228; future 17, 29, 32, 42
Cassing, James 166
Casson, Mark 199, 229
Caswell, Julie A. 85, 87, 89
Cavanagh, Edward D. 21
Caves, Richard E. 20, 24, 29, 36, 85, 87, 89, 164, 198, 199, 200
centralization 107, 108, 111, 112, 114–115, 121, 122, 134, 135, 139, 207, 208, 209, 210
CEMEX 46, 198
CEOs (chief executive officers) 8, 15, 23, 44, 66, 73, 79–80, 118, 122, 127, 128, 132, 148, 152, 160, 174, 180, 189, 192, 212, 216, 217, 221, 225 see also corporate governance; corporate transformation; compensation

chaebols 16, 150, 225
Chakrabarti, Abhirup 15, 103
Chairman of the board 118, 225
Champlin, Dell P. 29
Chandler, Alfred D., Jr. 11, 12, 13, 17, 24, 28, 101, 107, 113, 115, 125, 127, 128, 132–133, 136, 145, 174, 176, 178, 200, 212, 226, 227, 230, 232
Chang, Sea Jin 6, 72, 103, 128, 154, 158, 159, 160, 161, 164
Chang, Yegmin 60
Channon, Derek F. 128
Charoen Pokphand 16
Chatterjee, Sayan 14, 29, 30, 39, 40, 67, 68, 74, 76, 85, 96, 97, 143, 146, 154, 156, 160, 161
Chen, Ming-Jer 185, 186, 187, 190
Chen, Sheng-Syan 214
Chenall, Robert H. 128
Chief executive officers; see CEOs (chief executive officers)
Child, John 135
Chiron Corporation 57, 73
Choi, Unghwan 128
Chowdhry, Bhagwan C. 32, 42
Chowdhury, S. 172
Christensen, C. Rolland 12, 45
Christensen, H. K. 95
Christmann, Petra 165
Chrysler 13, 43, 163
Chung, Chi-nien 103
Chung, Kwang S. 110
Chung, Lai Hong 181
Churchill, Neil C. 132, 176
Clark, Bruce H. 186
Clarke, Thomas 219
Clarkson, Max B. E. 220
Coakley, Lori 32, 263
Coase, R. H. 22, 99, 121
Coca-Cola 102, 106, 200
Coff, Russel W. 32, 72, 84, 91, 215, 229
Coherence xiii, 58, 109, 123
Coles, Jerilyn 214
Collis, David J. xii, 1, 2, 5, 6, 7, 8, 9, 11, 15, 16, 59, 62, 63, 64, 84, 93, 96, 106, 107, 109, 110, 111, 115, 121, 122, 123, 145, 154, 162, 168, 175, 191, 225, 226, 231, 232
collusion: explicit 19, 186, 225, 227; tacit 76, 177, 186, 187, 191, 192, 197, 226, 232
Comment, Robert 71, 96, 97
commitment 57, 146, 150, 154, 158, 161, 162, 168, 171, 183, 196, 217, 225, 231
committees, corporate board 127
compensation: CEO 17, 25, 26, 27, 116, 160, 212–213, 214, 216, 227, 228, 229; executive management control systems and 70, 179, 202, 204, 215, 216
competition 18, 37, 43, 47, 74, 77, 91, 145, 146,

150, 152, 155, 167, 172, 173, 176, 182, 203, 220, 232: internal 38, 39, 102, 113, 135, 137, 138, 139, 140, 179; law 17, 19–20, 21, 22, 29–30, 75, 173, 177, 225; multipoint, multimarket ii, xiii, 2, 63, 74, 76, 77, 81, 125, 172, 183, 184–197, 225, 230
competitive advantage 1, 2, 8, 36, 37, 39, 40, 47, 54, 58, 61, 62, 67, 71, 72, 84, 92, 99, 119, 123, 127, 130, 143, 145, 147, 151, 156, 163, 178, 190, 197, 200, 201, 206, 207, 224, 225
competitive bidding 150, 151, 178
competitive disadvantage 19, 36, 103
competitive environment 36, 103, 129, 147, 186, 190
competitive superiority 45, 55
competitive strategy 1, 2, 9, 46, 78, 81, 103, 107, 109, 111, 112, 114, 122, 196, 201
competitors 17, 18, 20, 21, 26, 31, 33, 36, 37, 38, 46, 47, 49, 51, 55, 59, 61, 62, 64, 67, 71, 74, 75, 76, 82, 94, 106, 119, 129, 138, 145, 147, 149, 157, 159, 164, 168, 171, 172, 176, 177, 178, 179, 184–197, 201, 219, 220, 229
complementary: acquisition 14; assets, resources, skills 10, 31, 161, 168, 226; business 57; functions 55, 90
complexity, complexity costs 25, 65, 66, 96, 97, 101, 127, 132, 135, 145, 146, 152, 194, 212
compromise costs 66
concentration: industry, market 19–20, 29, 89, 159, 171, 183, 192, 228; ownership 214, 231; seller, supply 171, 189, 191–192
configuration xii, 2, 10, 16, 17, 33, 68, 107, 139, 171, 181, 210, 225, 226
conflict 25, 49, 61, 66, 100, 114, 129, 130, 131, 133, 151, 155, 168, 196, 212, 213, 220
conglomerate 1, 4, 10–11, 13–14, 15, 16, 30, 43, 78, 96, 98, 103, 104, 136, 137, 138, 142, 181, 225: discount 14, 71, 96, 225; merger 29–30, 75, 225
consistency 50, 58, 86, 107
constrained diversification *see* diversified expansion
contracts 19, 21, 22, 23, 24, 25, 71, 92, 113, 144, 146, 148–149, 151, 153, 154, 155, 158, 159, 167, 182, 215, 227, 228, 229, 231, 232
control: agency problems 25–26, 45, 48–49, 99, 104, 133–134, 180–183, 213, 215, 224, 230; corporate 27, 38, 62, 104, 109, 111, 175, 179, 214–215, 229; managerial behavior control 100, 110–111, 115, 179, 213, 216–218; market for corporate 38, 62, 214–215, 229; mechanisms 36, 66, 111, 134, 174, 179, 217, 229; of key resources 156; organization structure 131–134, 215–216; outcome controls 110–111; ownership separation 13, 24, 212, 230
Cool, Karel 28, 61, 162

Cooper, Arnold C. 32
cooperative organizational structures 135–139, 150
coordination: of activities; 29, 144, 191, 228; costs of; 66, 97; vertical integration ii, xiii, 3–4, 15, 17, 27, 29, 58, 63, 74, 76, 87, 96, 140–153, 155, 177–178, 183–184, 198, 200, 225, 230–231, 233
Copland, Tom 42
Cordeiro, James J. 25, 212
Cording, Margaret 165
core competencies 11, 40–41, 46, 56, 63, 64, 67, 68, 76, 77, 78, 91, 107, 120, 121, 123, 175, 176, 178, 179, 181, 198, 210, 225, 226, 232
core rigidities 41, 226
Cornett, Marci M. 62
corporate advantage i, xii, 7–10, 70, 82, 98, 107, 149, 163, 172, 199, 202–204, 208–210
corporate boards 15
corporate culture 164, 209
corporate governance xiii, 17, 42, 104, 109, 179, 183, 212–214, 220, 222–223
corporate headquarters, role of 1–2, 7, 9, 11–12, 14, 16, 36–38, 49, 60–61, 65, 67, 70, 72, 97, 100, 102, 106–117, 121–124, 127, 133–139, 158, 162–163, 175, 203, 210, 225–226, 228
corporate hierarchy; *see* hierarchy, governance
corporate planning 107, 220
corporate social responsibility ii, 212–213, 220–222
corporate strategy triangle 7–8, 10, 34–35, 172, 179, 205
corporation i, 11–15, 21, 24, 33, 48, 57, 62, 73, 92, 95–96, 106, 115, 121, 123, 127, 130, 134, 143, 151, 159, 181, 197–198, 212, 214, 225–226, 228, 230, 232
costs: bureaucratic; 76, 100–101, 145, 148–150, 225; drivers 64–65; entry 62, 70, 72, 116, 154, 160–161, 227; exit 158; opportunity costs 78, 123, 148; production 19, 23, 129; transaction xiii, 17, 22, 24, 27–29, 34–35, 37–38, 40, 76, 95, 100, 121–122, 128, 140–141, 144–146, 151–153, 155–156, 158, 161, 167, 183, 199, 200, 225, 229, 231–232
Craig, C. Samuel 200–201, 208
Crawford, Robert G. 22, 145, 155
cross-subsidization 20–22, 35, 74, 99, 201, 226
Croyle, Randy 30
culture 110, 130, 135, 161–162, 164–166, 168, 209, 217
Cyriac, Joseph 11

D&S 75
Dacin, Tina 125
Daewoo 16, 150
Daft, Richard L. 136
Daily, Catherine M. 213

Daimler 43, 163
Dalton, Dan R. 213
D&S 75
Darragh, John 121–122
Das, T. K. 168
Dastidar, Protiti 198, 202
Datta Deepak K. 164
Datta-Chaudhuri, Mrinal. 229
D'Aveni, Richard A. 185, 189
David, Parthiban 96, 99
David, Robert J. 155
Davidow, W. H. 15, 143, 151
Davis, Gerald F. 13, 15
Davis, James H. 213, 216–218
Davis, Rachel 87–88
Day, George S. 51
DeAngelo, Harry 25
DeAngelo, Linda 25
debt: capacity 68, 73, 77, 97; financing 15
decentralization 112–113, 122, 134
decision making 131, 133, 158, 162
Decker, Carolin 170
De Cock, Christian 72
deep pockets 20, 226
Dell 179, 193, 205
Delong, Gayle L. 67
Delta Air Line 148
Demsetz, Harold 24, 27, 100, 135, 212
Denis, David J. 25–26, 71, 99, 198, 212–213
Denis, Diane K. 25–26, 71, 99, 198, 212–213
Deregulation 16, 30, 176
Desai, Anand 160
design, of organizational structure 1
Dess, Gregory G. 63, 72, 74, 76, 96, 154
deterrence 186–189, 191–192
Deutsche Telekom 21
Dev, C. S. 154, 159
Devinney, Timothy M. 205
De Vries, Jan 11
De Waal, André 112–113
Dewenter, Kathryn 103
De Wit, Bob 2, 36, 45
Diamantopoulos, Adamantios 43
Dicken, Peter 203
Diekman, Kristina A. 13, 15
Dierickx, Ingemar 28, 61, 162
differentiation 44, 47, 51–53, 55–56, 64–65,
    67–68, 83, 90, 92, 94, 144, 156, 198–199,
    203–206
diffusion 16, 98
DiMaggio, Paul J. 128–129
Ding, John Y. 85, 87, 89
diseconomies of scale 29
diseconomies of scope 95
Disney; see Walt Disney Company
distinctive capabilities 147
distribution channels 32, 39, 81, 146, 156

diversification; see diversified expansion
diversification discount 97, 202
diversified expansion: 28, 91: agency problems
    25–26, 45, 48, 49, 99, 104, 133–134, 180, 183,
    213, 215, 224, 230; antitrust enforcement 30
divestitures 14–15, 30, 158, 170–171, 173, 178,
    180–183, 226–227
divisions 12–13, 45, 53–54, 57–58, 68, 71, 76, 92,
    100–102, 105, 107, 109, 114, 126–128,
    130–131, 133–140, 179–180, 215, 225–226,
    228, 230, 233
Dixit, Avinash, K. 33
Dodd, Peter 160
dogs, BCG matrix 117–121
dominant business firms 3–4, 97, 226
dominant logic xiii, 7–8, 10, 42–47, 62, 81,
    92–93, 98, 172, 179, 205, 226
Domoto, Hiroshi 68
Donaldson, Gordon 42
Donaldson, Lex 115, 127, 130, 213, 216–216
Douglas, Richard W. 166
Douglas, Susan P. 200–201, 208
Doukas, John 64, 199
Douma, Sytse 67, 107–108
downscoping 171, 227
downsizing 15, 171–172, 178–181, 227
Doz, Yves 199, 205–206, 209
Dranikoff, Lee 174, 182
Dranove, David 156, 157, 228
due diligence 109, 166, 227
Duhaime, Irene M. 44, 47, 51, 81, 84–85, 87–88,
    91, 94
Dunlap, Riley E. 222
Dunning, John H. 198–200
DuPont de Nemours 12, 127–129
Dussauge, Pierre 68
Dutch East India Company 11
Dyer, Jeffrey H. 150, 167

earnings 13, 30, 96, 171, 179, 183, 201, 231
eBay 63, 79–80
economic deterrence 186–189, 191–192
economic organization; see organizational
    economics
economic value added (EVA) 141, 143
economies of scale 10–11, 26, 28, 34, 64,
    75–76, 82, 99, 114–115, 120, 122, 138, 141,
    156, 164, 175, 198–201, 203–204, 206, 208,
    210, 227
economies of scope 5, 15, 17, 26, 28–29, 32,
    34, 37–39, 47, 60, 62–64, 67–68, 73–74,
    76–77, 81, 83–84, 90, 92–94, 96–99, 102,
    107–108, 110, 112, 114, 121–122, 130,
    134–136, 138–140, 182–183, 189, 191,
    198–201, 203, 206, 208, 227
Edwards, Corbin D. 76, 146, 185–187, 189
Efelhoff, William G. 127, 130

Eger, Carrol E. 160
Egri, Carolyn P. 63, 213
Eisenhardt, Kathleen M. 31, 104, 109, 110
Eisenstat, Russel 42, 71, 215
Eisner, Alan B. 63, 72, 154
Electrolux 201
Elenkov, Detelin, 25, 212–213
emerging countries 16
emerging industry 50
employment risk 25–26, 61, 213, 229
entrenchment 25, 229
entropy index 87–89, 227, 232
entry barriers: 120, 146, 152, 154, 156–157, 160, 164, 227: capital requirements as 156; control of key resources as 156; economies of scale as 156; government policy as 157; marketing advantages from differentiation as 156; switching costs as 156–157
environmental changes 32, 175, 178
equity 20, 26, 73, 150, 159, 161, 167, 170–171, 180–181, 213, 226, 227, 228
equity alliances 167, 227
equity holders 227
ethical values 73, 213, 220–221
Eun, Cheol S. 199, 202
European Commission (EC) 19–21, 177
European Union (EU) 19, 74
EVA *see* economic value added
exit barriers 66, 154, 158–159
excess capacity 28–29, 39, 144, 208, 227
executive compensation *see* managerial compensation
expansion 20, 28, 29, 69, 87, 91, 99, 118, 128, 157, 162, 191, 225, 230: expansion mode 154–169; overexpansion 174, 231, *see also* diversified expansion
experience 26, 30, 40, 48, 54, 68, 74, 77, 83, 94, 121, 132, 134, 142, 160, 162, 163, 164, 168, 192, 194, 200: curve 118, 162, 163, 200, 227, 229 *see also* learning curve
export 208–209, 230
externality 34, 63, 162
ExxonMobil 141

failure 26, 32, 43, 134, 154, 160, 162–164, 166, 168, 170, 172, 174,178, 181: of corporate governance 49, 130, 175, 191, 192, 215; market 22, 24, 29, 34, 35, 37–38, 122, 154, 155, 158, 228–230
Falabella 75
Fama, Eugene F. 24, 26–27, 100, 174, 212–213, 230
Fan, Joseph P. H. 78, 85, 90
Farjoun, Moshe 28–29, 81, 84–85, 90–91
Fauver, Larry 103
Feinberg, Robert M. 192, 221
Ferrell, O. C. 221

Ferris, Stephen P. 103
Fichman, Robert G. 41
Filatotchev, Igor 172
financial control 11, 93, 110, 112–113, 116, 139, 164, 172–173, 175, 205
Finkelstein, Sydney 25, 212–213
firm-specific investments 158
first-mover advantages 195
Fisher Body 22, 24, 155
Fisher, Joseph 135–136
fit 7, 9–10, 29, 36, 70, 83, 93, 103, 106–109, 123, 140, 172, 175, 179, 200
five forces framework 62
fixed costs 66, 158
flexibility 20, 32–33, 36, 41, 76, 110, 138, 145, 147, 151–152, 155, 158, 161–162, 204, 207–210, 230–231
Fligstein, Neil xii, 12, 15, 104, 127–129, 212–213, 228, 230, 232
Folta, Timothy B. 41–42, 71, 168, 215
Foote, Nathaniel 42, 71, 215
forbearance, mutual 17, 21, 37, 76–77, 120, 185–187, 190–194, 196–197, 225
Ford 141, 176
Foss, Nicolai J. 107, 115
Fouraker, Lawrence E. 198
Fox, Isaac 7
fragmented industries 146
franchising 11, 167
Franko, Lawrence G. 11, 78, 128
free cash flow 10–11, 25, 30, 39, 100, 180, 228
Freeland, Robert F. 22
Freeman, R. Edward 128, 172, 175, 178, 212–213, 219–222
free riding 39, 100, 103
Friedman, Milton 213, 220
Froot, Kenneth A. 20
Fuentelsaz, Lucio 186, 190
function 9, 15, 45–46, 49–56, 58–59, 64, 67–68, 79, 83, 92, 100, 106–107, 109, 113116, 121, 127, 129–130, 133, 135, 137–138, 142, 151, 156, 159, 167, 210, 225–226
Furrer, Olivier i-iv, xii, 29, 61, 63, 67–68, 172, 175, 177, 186, 194, 201, 212–214, 222–223
Furrer-Perrinjaquet, Amandine 63, 212–213, 222

Galbraith, Jay R. 85, 132, 135, 176
Galbraith, John S. 11
Gale, Bradley T. 12
game theory 187
gap ii, 172, 221
Garrod, Neil 199
Gatignon, Hubert 156, 158–159, 161
Gaughan, Patrick A. 27, 29, 174, 180
Gaur, Ajai S. 96, 99
Geletkanycz, Marta A. 25, 212
General Electric (GE) 67, 116, 174, 206

Index | 275

general equilibrium theory xiii, 17, 34, 104, 191, 195
General Motors (GM) 12, 46, 127–129, 155
generic strategies 7, 67, 198, 206, 210
geographical scope 12
geographical structure 228, 232
George, Robin 163
Geroski, P.A. 22
Gertner, Robert H. 20
Geyskens, Inge 155, 232
Ghemawat, Pankaj 6, 200
Ghoshal, Sumantra 27, 68, 127–128, 130, 198–201, 203–210, 213, 230–231
Gibbs, Philip A. 174
Gimeno, Javier 81, 185–193
Ginsberg, Ari 42
global strategy 122, 199, 202, 204, 206, 208
goals 1, 8–10, 16, 20, 39, 45–46, 49, 53–54, 70, 83, 92–93, 100–101, 106–107, 110, 111, 131, 133–134, 198, 202, 204, 210, 213–214, 219–220, 222, 230, 232
Gobeli, David H. 199, 201–202
Golden, Brian R. 190
golden parachute 27, 228
Goldstar 16
Gomes, Lenn 199
Gomez-Mejia, Luis M. 25, 215
Goodstein, Jerry 186–187, 189, 192–194
Goodyear 184, 186
Goold, Michael xii, 8–9, 11–14, 17, 42–43, 45, 60–64, 67, 78, 81, 96, 106–107, 110–116, 120–121, 123, 162, 175, 181, 205, 224, 229
Gort, Michael 74, 95–96, 143
Govindarajan, Vijay 39, 103, 110, 135–136, 140
Gould, Kenneth 222
governance; see corporate governance
Graebner, Melissa E. 31, 163
Grant, Robert M. 11, 13, 15, 20–22, 36, 38, 42, 64, 71, 78, 81, 85–86, 92–93, 95–96, 98–99, 104, 107, 112, 116, 118–119, 121, 127, 141, 151, 158, 163, 168, 170, 175, 199, 233
Gray, Samuel R. 25, 212
Greiner, Larry E. 132, 176, 178
Griffin, Ricky W. 203
Griffith, David A. 161
Grimm, Curtis M. 190
Grosse, Robert 161
Grossman, Wayne 215
Grover, Ronald 23
growth matrix, Ansoff 48
growth-share matrix, BCG 116
Guisinger, Stephen 161
Gulati, Ranjay 93
Gupta, Anil K. 39, 102, 110, 135–136, 140, 225

Haberberg, Adrian, 116, 118, 120–121
Hagiu, Andrei 194

Hall, Peter A. 214
Hall, William K. 70, 95, 100
Hall, Ernst H., Jr. 85
Hambrick, Donald C. 25, 160, 164, 192, 213
Hamel, Gary 8, 40–41, 46, 67, 84, 120, 162, 168, 199, 232
Hammond, John S. 45, 51, 225
Haniel 70
Hannah, Leslie 12, 128
Hannan, Michael T. 128, 172, 175, 178
Hansen, Gary S. 60
Hanson Trust 43
Hariharan, S. 39, 85, 87, 89, 162, 226
Harper, Neil W. C. 32
Harrigan, Kathryn R. 141, 143, 144–146, 148–150, 158, 233
Harrison, Jeffrey S. 11, 30, 68, 81, 84–85, 90, 94
Haspeslagh, Philippe C. 5, 12, 47, 100, 116, 120, 155, 164–166
Hatfield, Donald E. 170
Hatfield, John D. 213, 220–221
Haveman, Heather A. 187, 193–194
Hayes, Robert H. 101
Hayward, Mathew L. A. 160, 164, 192
headquarters i, xiii, 1–2, 7, 9–12, 14, 16–18, 35–38, 49, 60–61, 65, 67, 69–70, 72, 79, 97, 100, 102, 106–117, 121–124, 127, 129, 133–139, 158, 162–163, 172, 175, 198, 203, 205, 207–208, 210, 221, 225–226, 228
Hedlund, Gunnar 130, 231–232
Heggestad, Arnold A. 187
Heide, Jan B. 155
Heineken 122
Helfat, Constance E. 6–7, 31, 232
Helman, Christopher 148
Helyar, John 97, 170
Hendrickx, Margaretha 25, 106
Hennart, Jean-François 144, 154, 161, 199, 225
Heriot, Kirk C. 149
Hewlett-Packard 179, 193
hierarchy: corporate hierarchy xii, 2, 9, 122, 225, 232; cost of hierarchy 100, 225; industry hierarchy 89; market vs. hierarchy 155, 167
Higgins, Robert C. 95
Hill, Charles W. L. 8, 16–17, 39, 60, 86, 89, 97, 100–101, 110–111, 115–116, 120, 125, 128–130, 133–140, 144–146, 149, 154–156, 158, 162, 175, 178–179, 191, 194, 225, 228
Hite, Gailen L. 181
Hitt, Michael A. 3, 11, 15, 17–18, 25–26, 29–30, 32, 38–40, 63–64, 66, 72, 76–77, 85–87, 89, 96, 100–101, 110–111, 115, 125, 130, 133, 135–140, 144–145, 150, 157, 163, 166, 171–172, 175, 179, 181, 191, 198–199, 212, 214–215, 224–225, 227, 229, 231, 233
Hofer, Charles W. xii, 1, 29, 45, 141
Hoffman, Richard C. 172, 174, 176

Hofstede, Geert 204
Hogler, Raymond L. 215
Honda 40
Hong, Jaebum 103, 201
Holbein, Gordon F. 180
holding company 11–12, 70, 127, 228, 232
holdup 23–24, 145, 228
Hoover, Vera L. 185, 193, 197
Hopkins, H. Donald 85
horizontal diversification xiii, 96, 140, 143, 177, 198
horizontal merger 30
Hoskisson, Robert E. 3, 6, 11, 15, 17–18, 25–30, 32, 38–39, 63, 66, 85–87, 89, 96, 100–101, 103, 110–111, 115, 125, 130, 133–136, 137–140, 144–145, 157, 149, 163, 171–172, 174–175, 178–179, 181, 191, 201, 212, 214–216, 224–229, 231, 233
hostile takeover 15, 160, 173–174, 181, 224, 226, 228
Houston, Joel, 103
Hout, Thomas 200
Hovakimian, Gayané 62, 181
hubris 159–160, 166, 192, 199, 228
Hudson's Bay Company 11
Hulland, John 39
Hult, G. Thomas M. 221
Hunt, John W. 164
Hwang, Peter 154–156, 158, 161
Hyundai 16, 150, 225

Ilinitch, Anne Y. 85, 90
imperfect information 34, 51
implementation xii-xiii, 2, 14, 18, 45, 69, 81, 125, 128, 132, 205, 222, 225
Inagaki, Kana 176
incentives 10, 17–18, 28–31, 35–36, 38–39, 47, 66, 71, 100–103, 108, 110, 133, 136–140, 144–145, 149–151, 156, 171–171, 174, 178–179, 186, 191, 194, 212, 214–216, 225, 227–230
incremental 58–59, 162–163, 168
individual business 6, 9, 36, 107, 109, 118, 233
industry attractiveness 119–120
inertia 41, 128, 138, 172–173, 175, 226
inflexibility costs 66
influence costs 99–101, 228
initial public offering (IPO) 80, 228
innovation 12–14, 23, 41, 46, 53–55, 65–66, 82, 108, 118, 122, 127, 146, 150–152, 172–173, 176, 177, 207–210
institutional change 172–173, 176–177
institutional investors 15, 214, 231
institutional power 217
institutional theory xiii, 17, 29, 129
integration: acquisitions, post-merger integration (or PMI) ii, xiii, 10, 13–14, 19–20, 23–24, 30–31, 58–59, 62, 67–68, 70, 73, 78–79, 91, 97, 109, 116, 119, 127, 148, 154, 157–158–161, 163–166, 168, 170–171, 173, 177, 180–182, 188, 224–225, 227–228; horizontal integration 29, 135; vertical integration ii, xiii, 3–4, 15, 17, 27, 29, 58, 63, 74, 76, 87, 96, 140–153, 155, 177–178, 183–184, 198, 200, 225, 230–231, 233
integration-responsiveness (IR) framework Intel 206
Interdependencies 1, 47, 86, 100, 135, 138, 183
internal alignment 34, 38, 53, 171, 172, 175
internal capital market 8, 37–38, 47, 63, 68, 70–72, 76–77, 96, 98–100, 107–108, 113, 115–116, 133, 135, 137–138, 177, 210, 228
internal consistency 50, 58
internal development 10, 18, 24, 28, 60, 68, 109, 115, 154–164, 167–169, 207
internal governance 18, 27, 100, 136, 140, 183, 214
internal environment 16–17, 29
internal incentives 17–18, 28, 100
internal markets 71, 96
internal politics 100, 225
international strategy 206–207
internationalization 16, 175, 183, 199–201, 206, 210
internalization 16, 24, 141, 228
Ireland, R. Duane 3, 11, 15, 17–18, 25–26, 29–30, 32, 38, 63, 130, 133, 135, 137–139, 157, 163, 171–172, 179, 181, 212, 214, 224, 227, 229, 231, 233
Itami, Hiroyuki 95, 99

Jackson, Gregory 212, 222
Jacquemin, Alexis P. 85, 87–88, 227
Jamali, Dima 220
Jammine, Azar P. 15, 86, 104
Jandik, Thomas 99
Janney, Jay J. 27
Japan 11, 16, 50, 69, 80, 103, 106, 127–128, 152, 202, 208–209, 211, 214, 221
Jarrell, Gregg A. 71, 96–97
Jayachandran, Satish 186–189, 191
Jemison, David B. 155, 164–166
Jensen, Michael C. 13–14, 17, 24–27, 30, 60, 62, 100, 107, 109, 134, 159, 164, 174, 180, 183, 202, 204, 212–213, 228, 230
Jobe, Lloyd A. 150
John, George 31, 71, 96, 155
John, Kose 97, 181
Johnson, Douglas R. 42
Johnson, Gerry 8, 29
Johnson, Julius H., Jr. 205
Johnson, Richard A. 15, 38, 72, 85, 87, 89, 170, 181, 215, 229, 231
joint venture 11, 19, 41–42, 61, 81, 147, 154,

158–159, 161–162, 167–168, 229
Jones, Gareth R. 100, 111, 116, 120, 135, 140, 144–146, 149, 154, 162, 194
Joskow, Paul L. 24, 231

Kager, Patrick 30
Kahan, Marcel 27
Kale, Prashant 167
Kanter, Rosabeth M. 94
Kaplan, Steven N. 172–173
Karim, Samina 31, 215
Karnani, Aneel 184, 186, 194–196
Katila, Riitta 163
Kay, Neil M. 32
Kazanjian, Robert 85, 132, 176
Keats, Barbara V. 85, 93, 125
Kedia, Simi 71
Keeton, A. 163
Keil, Mark 41
Keil, Thomas 28
keiretsu 16, 150
Keister, Lisa A. 103
Kelly, Dawn 178
Keppel Group 16
Kerr, Jeffrey L. 39, 103, 136, 140
Kester, W. Carl 32
Ketchen, David J. 185, 193, 197
key success factors 93
Khanna, Tarun xii, 15–16, 71, 103–104, 167, 177
Kim, E. Han 160
Kim, Kenneth A. 103
Kim, Hicheon 6, 96, 130, 134–135, 139, 201
Kim, Sung Min 41, 168
Kim, W. Chan 154–156, 158, 161
Kitsabunnarat, Pattanaporn 103
KKR & Co. *see* Kohlberg Kravis Roberts
Klein, Benjamin 22, 145, 155
Klein, Peter G. 85, 91, 155
Klein, Saul 155
Klevorick, Alvin K. 231
Kobrin, Stephen J. 203, 205, 209
Kochhar, Rahul 39–41, 64
Kock, Carl J. 15
Koen, Carla I. 37
Kogut, Bruce 29, 32–33, 41, 147, 155, 161–163, 168, 175, 199–201, 204, 230
Kohlberg Kravis Roberts 97, 106, 170
Kolodny, Richard 199, 202
Kono, Toyohiro 67, 128
Kosnik, Rita D. 215, 229
Kotabe, Masaaki 68
Kotler, Philip 55, 141
Kotter, John P 29
Kownatzki, Maximilian 106, 110–111
Knoedler, Janet T. 29
know-how 28, 37, 40, 64, 67, 91, 121, 162, 168, 209, 231

knowledge: accumulated 40, 68; assets 72; distinctive 53; industry-specific 12–13; sharing 64, 115, 132; tacit 162, 229, 232; transfer 39, 102, 206–207, 210; technological 68, 189
Korn, Helaine J. 185–187, 189–190, 193–194
KPN 33
Kroll, Mark 25, 212–213
Krug, Jeffrey A. 201
Kulatilaka, Nalin 33, 147
Kwak, Mary 71

labor market 26, 72, 177
Lajili, Kaouthar 153
Lamont, Owen A. 22, 71
Landau, Christian 114
Lang, Larry H. P. 20, 64, 78, 85, 90, 95, 97, 99, 181
La Porta, Rafael 214
Lawless, Michael W. 32
Lawrence, Paul R. 135
LBO; *see* Leveraged buyout (LBO)
leadership xii, 12–13, 57, 79–81, 107, 109, 112, 114, 118
Learned, Edmund P. 12, 45
learning 147, 156–157, 162, 168, 181, 186, 191, 199–201, 203–204, 208, 210, 229
learning curve 147, 156, 200, 229
Lecraw, Donald J. 95
Lee, Ji-Hwan 16
Lee, Donghun "Don" 172
Lee, Gwendolyn K. 85, 91, 160
Lemelin, André 39, 84–85, 90
Lemmon, Michael L. 27
Lengel, Robert H. 136
Leonard-Barton, Dorothy 33, 41, 67, 175, 226
Lev, Baruch 25–26, 61, 174, 212, 229
leverage: financial 30, 73, 181; core competencies/resources 31 39, 67, 82, 97, 118, 121, 123, 162, 198, 202, 207, 208
leveraged buyout (LBO) 10, 97, 170–171, 173, 180, 226, 229
Levitt, Theodore 46, 199, 208
Levy, Haim 95
Lewellen, Wilbur G. 73, 95
Lewis, Virginia L. 132, 176, 178
LG 150, 225
Li, Jiatao 161
Li, Mingfang 32, 104
licensing 157–158, 161, 167
Lieberman, Marvin 85, 91, 160, 200, 229
Liebeskind, Julia P. 174
Lien, Lasse B 85, 91
life cycle 71, 116
linked diversification 4, 86, 104
Lippo 16
Lins, Karl V. 103

Lintner, John 14
Lippman, Steven A. 29
Livesay, Harold C. 141
Livnat, Joshua 60, 71, 85
local responsiveness 198, 204, 207, 210, 229
location specificity 24
Lorsch, Jay W. 27, 39, 42, 103, 111, 115, 134–136, 140
Lowe, Julian 71, 96
Lubatkin, Michael 14, 29, 30, 67, 81, 85, 87, 96–98, 154, 156, 160–161, 177, 212, 225, 230
Luehrman, Timothy A. 32–33
Luffman, G. A. 28, 96
Lumpkin, Tom 63, 72, 154
Luo, Yadong 155, 161, 203–204, 228–229, 231

Ma, Hao 185, 189–190
Macmillan, Ian C. 162–163, 185, 189, 196, 201
McCutcheon, Barbara J. 20, 22
McGahan, Anita M. 6, 106
McGrath, Rita G. 185, 189, 196, 201
McGuire, Jean 215
McKinsey 116, 119, 121
McVea, John 219–220
McWilliams, Abagail 213
McWilliams, Victoria B. 214
Madden, Sean 142
Maddigan, Ruth J. 143
Mahmood, Ishtiaq 15, 103
Mahnke, Volker 203, 205
Mahoney, Joseph T. 22, 27–28, 34, 39, 61, 153
Maignan, Isabelle 221
Makadok, Richard 62, 154, 163
Maksimovic, Vojislav 99
Malatesta, Paul 160
Malone, M. S. 15, 143, 151
management buyout (MBO) 171, 180–181
managerial compensation 17, 25, 213
Mangoosta 21
Manikutty, Sankaran 103
Mannix, Elizabeth A. 125
market: attractiveness 229; boundaries xii, 2, 12, 33, 211; business 4, 51; capital 8, 10, 16, 18, 37–38, 40, 47, 63, 68, 70–72, 76–77, 81, 96, 98–100, 103, 107–108, 113, 115–116, 133, 135, 137–138, 166, 177, 210, 228; entry 154, 158, 162, 190, 193–194; failures 22, 24, 29, 34–35, 37, 122, 154–155, 158, 228–229; for corporate control 27, 38, 62, 214–215, 229; for information 38, 51, 62, 67, 71, 77, 79, 96, 201, 224; for managerial talent 18, 27, 38; geographic 133, 185, 198, 230; governance 122, 155; multimarket ii, xii, 2–3, 8–10, 17, 184, 225–226, 230; power 17–19, 22, 29, 35–37, 74–77, 96, 99, 144, 146, 151–152, 177, 183–185, 197, 199, 201, 230; structure 12, 75, 159

market share 19, 21, 42–43, 47, 75, 117–120, 136, 156, 163–164, 175, 177, 185, 189, 191, 195, 202, 228
Markides, Constantinos 14, 17, 28, 40, 63, 71–72, 78, 81, 84–85, 91–92, 94–99, 107, 115–116, 121, 125, 135, 140, 172, 174, 177, 180–181, 231
Markham, Jesse W. 95
Marks, Mitchell L. 67
Marris, Robin 13
Marsh, Peter 201
Martin, Jeffrey A. 104
Martin, John D. 85, 87
Martin, Xavier 68
Masten, Scott E. 24
Mathur, Ike 99
matrix: BCG 116–121; GE/McKinsey 116, 119, 121; growth 12, 47–48, 116; organization structure 127, 129–130, 132–135
Matsusaka, John G. 31, 71, 96
Matsushita 128, 152, 159, 208
Matta, Elie 215
mature industry 25, 117
Mayer, Michael 103–104
MCA 159
McCutcheon, Barbara J. 20, 22
McGahan Anita M. 6, 106
McGuire, Jean 215
McGrath 185, 189, 196, 201
McKinsey 121
McWilliams, Abagail 213, 220
Means, Gardiner C. 24–25, 174, 212, 230
Meckling, William H. 17, 25–27, 60, 100, 107, 109, 134, 159, 174, 180, 212–213, 230
Mehra, Ajay 68
Mellahi, Kamel 172
Merchant, Hemant 29–30, 81, 85, 87, 177, 225, 230
merger and acquisition (or M&A) 10–12, 15, 18–19, 28, 30, 60, 78, 81, 109, 123, 154–159, 161–164, 167–169, 171, 178, 182, 202, 207
Mester, Loretta J. 187
Meyer, Margaret 20
Meyer, Ron 2, 36, 45
Michael, Bryane 220
Michel, Allen 96
Michelin 184, 186
Microsoft 19, 21, 72, 142, 171, 176, 180, 194
Midgley, David F. 205
Milgrom, Paul 20, 100–101, 225, 228
Miller C. Chet 20–21, 71, 85, 95–96, 98, 99, 104
Miller, Danny 71, 186
Miller, Douglas J. 28
Miller, Janice S. 215
Miller, Kent D. 42
Milton, Laurie P. 215
mimetic behavior 129

Miner, Anne S. 187
Mintzberg, Henry 134–135, 137, 140
Mirshak, Ramez 220
Mirvis, Philip H. 67
Mishra, Chandra 199, 201–202
mission, corporate 8, 45, 58
mission statements 53, 70
Mitchell, Ronald K. 213, 220–221
Mitchell, Will 31, 68, 154, 171, 178
Mitsubishi 131
mobility barriers 144
mode of diversified expansion 35, 154–169
Moesel, Donald D. 85, 87, 89, 174, 214–216, 229
Moir, Lance 220
monitoring 27, 38, 42, 93, 100–101, 110, 113,
   127, 137, 144, 163, 202, 212, 214–215
monopolistic competition 75
Monteverde, Kirk 149
Montgomery, Cynthia A. xii, 1–2, 5–9, 11, 15–16,
   18, 20–21, 25, 28, 36, 39, 59, 62–64, 84–87,
   89, 90, 93, 95–96, 99, 106–107, 109–110, 121,
   123, 145, 154, 162, 168, 175, 186, 191, 212,
   225–226, 231–232
moral hazard 25, 229–230
Morck, Randall 199, 201
Morrison, Allan J. 205–206, 209
Moschieri, Caterina 226
Mulherin, J. Harold 181, 226
Müller-Stewens, Günter 85, 89
multidivisional structure (or M-Form) xiii, 12,
   125–131, 133–140, 215, 226, 228, 230
multimarket competition, see multipoint
   competition
multinational corporation (MNC) 33, 96, 127,
   130, 141, 198, 205
multinational strategy 199, 206–208
multipoint competition xiii, 2, 63, 74, 76–77, 81,
   125, 172, 183–197, 225
Muralidharan, Raman 110
Murmann, Johann P. 186–187, 189, 192–194
Murphy, Kevin J. 25–26, 174, 212, 228
mutual forbearance 17, 21, 37, 76–77, 120,
   185–187, 190–194, 196–197, 225
Myers, Stewart C. 32–33

Nabisco 97, 170, 174
Naranjo, Andy 103
narrow spectrum diversification 87, 225, 230
Nayyar, Praveen R. 66, 81, 85, 91, 93, 95, 98
Nell, Philip C. 106–107, 115
Nelson, Richard R. 29, 64
Nestlé 46, 64–66, 74, 114, 122, 127, 170–171,
   175, 177, 181, 207
net present value (or NPV) 25, 32–33, 202, 228
network structure (N-Form) 126, 130, 132–133,
   231
Ng, Wilson 72

niche markets 202
Nightengale, John 51
Nike Nöldeke, Georg 41, 168
Nippa, Michael 12, 70, 95, 98–99, 116
Nöldeke, Georg 41, 168
nonequity alliances 167
Nonnemaker, Lynn 187, 193–194
North, Douglas 198
Novaes, Walter 103
Novartis 56–58, 73, 170

objective ii, xiii, 1, 8, 16, 45, 51, 58, 68, 74–75,
   81, 85, 91, 95, 101, 107, 110, 112, 118, 120,
   129, 136–138, 142, 154, 160, 165, 167, 172,
   178–179, 186, 200, 216–219, 224
O'Brien, Jonathan 42, 96, 99
Ofek, Eli 20, 22, 25–27, 73, 97, 99–100, 174, 181,
   212
O'Neill, Hugh M. 98, 125, 132
Opler, Tim C. 170
opportunism 22, 34–35, 38–39, 98, 100–101,
   103, 105, 122, 128, 145–147, 150–152, 154,
   159, 161, 172–174, 180, 200, 212–216,
   222–223, 228, 231
opportunity costs 78, 123, 148
option see real option
O'Reilly, Charles A. 31, 224
organizational capability 15, 162
organizational change 128
organizational culture 110
organizational inertia 172–173, 175
organizational structure xiii, 1, 5, 9–10, 16, 45,
   47, 93, 95, 105, 107, 113, 124–130, 132–140,
   162, 164, 170–172, 174, 176, 178, 189–190,
   228, 231–233
Orlitzky, Mark 222
Ouchi, William G. 27, 110, 136
outsourcing 15, 148, 150–151, 153, 178, 231
overhead cost 14, 107, 112, 156
overdiversification 174, 231
overexpansion 174, 231
overpayment, for acquisitions 166
Owers, James E. 181
ownership; see also shareholders:

P&G 46, 82, 118
Paez, Betty L. 30, 174
Palepu, Krishna xii, 15–16, 20, 71, 85, 87–88,
   103, 177, 227
Palich, Leslie E. 20–21, 71, 85, 95–96, 98–99,
   104
Panasonic 152
Pandian, J. Rajendran 28, 39, 172
Panzar, John C. 28, 37, 64, 200, 227
parenting 67, 81, 99, 107, 109, 111–113, 116,
   123, 205
Park, Choelsoon 31, 67

Parker, Philip M. 187
Parkhe, Arvind 187
Parmar, Bidhan 220
patent 28, 57–58, 156, 167, 197, 201–202, 231
Patton, G. Richard 172, 176
Pavan, Robert J. 128
Pearce, John A. II 46, 172, 216
Pedersen, Torben xii, 154, 205
Pehrsson, Anders 44, 81, 83–87, 90–91
Peng, Mike W. 198–199
Pennings, Johannes M. 85, 155
Penrose, Edith T. 28, 37, 39, 42, 48, 94, 99, 162, 201
pension funds 214, 228 *see also* institutional owners
Perlmutter, Howard 201
Perrier 66, 175, 177
Perrinjaquet, Amandine 63, 212–213, 222
Perrow, Charles 128
Peteraf, Margaret A. 28, 201
Pettway, Richard H. 103
Pfeffer, J. 29, 128, 141, 146
Pfizer 202, 206
Philippe, Henri 42
Philips (company) 46, 71, 107–108, 127, 151, 207
Pick, Katharina 27
Pickering, J. F. 128, 134–135
Pidun, Ulrich 12, 70, 95, 98–99, 116
Pindyck, Robert S. 33
Pinkston, Tammie S. 221
Pisano, Gary 149, 186, 190, 226
Piscitello, Lucia 85
Pistre, Nathalie 67
Pitts, Robert A. 39, 85, 103, 135–136, 140
Pixar 22–24
planning; portfolio planning, *see also* BCG matrix
Poitevin, Michel 226
Polk, Christopher 22, 71
Polyani, Michael 232
Poppo, Laura 155
population ecology 128
Porac, Joseph F. 46, 51, 186, 190
Porter, Michael E. 1, 6, 9, 11, 12, 17, 18, 36, 47, 56, 59, 62, 64–68, 70, 72, 74, 84, 93–94, 96–97, 106, 113, 115, 120–121, 123, 135, 137, 145–146, 149, 154, 156, 158, 162, 172, 184–186, 198–201, 207–208, 210, 224, 229, 233
portfolio ii, ix, xi, 4–14, 17, 20, 23, 25–26, 35, 38, 42, 46, 53–54, 56–57, 60, 62–3, 68, 70–73, 77, 80–84, 89–91, 93–94, 97–98, 100, 102, 107, 109, 112–123, 127, 138–139, 163, 169–172, 174–175, 177–179, 181–183, 185–186, 202, 207, 210, 212–213, 224, 226–228, 230, 232
postacquisition integration process (or PMI) 164
Poulsen, Annette 20, 181

Powell, Walter W. 128–130, 231
power, market 74
Prahalad, C. K. 8, 28, 40, 42–43, 45–47, 64, 67, 81, 84–85, 92–93, 120–121, 162, 199, 205–206, 209, 226, 232
predatory pricing 19–20, 22, 74, 231
Priem, Richard L. 60, 63
principal 1, 26, 100, 128, 164, 218–219
prisoners' dilemma x, 218
profits 21, 23, 39, 44, 62, 68, 73–77, 92, 101, 104, 106, 118, 120, 133, 147, 154, 157, 164, 167–168, 177, 185, 202, 204, 216, 229
property rights x, 22, 27, 34, 232
Pustay, Michael W. 203

Qiu, Jane X. 127, 130
question marks 117–121; BCG matrix ix, xi, 116–121

Rajan, Raghuram 71, 99, 263
Ralston, David A. 247
Ramanujam, Vasudevan 28, 87, 115, 225, 230
Ramaswamy, Kannan 81, 85, 104, 199, 248
Ranft, Annette L. 163, 193
Rao, Vithala R. 51, 264
Rappaport, Alfred 166, 264
Ravenscraft, David J. 30, 71, 96, 158, 164
Rawls, John 222
Raynor, Michael E. 32–33, 41, 71
RBV; *see* resource-based view (RBV) 28–29, 34–35, 39, 41, 61, 84, 90, 99, 121, 146, 151
R&D; *see* research and development (R&D) 31, 47, 55, 59, 64–66, 73, 94, 101, 107, 113, 115, 122, 126–127, 129, 132–133, 135–136, 147, 149, 167, 175, 180–181, 200–202, 208–210, 228
Rebeiz, Karim S. 215
reciprocal buying and selling 21, 36
Reddy, Sabine 161
Reed, R. 28, 96, 178
Rees, Williams 199
refocusing 11, 15–16, 78, 97
regulations 17–19, 30, 71, 74, 156, 200, 204, 206–207
Reichert, Allan 116
Reimann, Bernard C. 116
related diversification 4, 10, 28–29, 32, 39, 71, 77–78, 83–84, 88–89, 92, 95–98, 107, 110, 112, 114, 130, 136–138, 140, 174, 178–179, 198–199, 203, 227
relatedness vii, x, xi, xiii, 4–5, 15, 32, 35, 43–45, 47, 49, 51, 71, 77–96, 111, 115, 120, 122, 140, 160, 183, 207, 210–211, 226–227
reputation 25, 27, 31, 58, 64, 83, 153, 156, 164, 229
research and development (R&D) 30–31, 53
resource i, xi, xiii, 1–3, 6–10, 12–13, 16–18, 20,

23, 25,27–29, 31, 35–43, 47, 55, 59, 63–65,
67–72, 76–78, 80–81, 84–85, 90, 92–99, 107,
109, 111, 113–119, 121–123, 126, 128, 133,
135, 137, 145–147, 151, 156, 160–163,
167–168, 172, 175–176, 178, 181, 184–185,
190, 196, 198–199, 201, 203, 207, 209,
225–232: corporate resources 67, 98, 137,
168; excess resources 28–29, 37–38, 41, 145,
160, 199, 201; leverage 10, 30–31, 39, 67, 73,
82, 97, 118, 121, 123, 162, 170–171, 173,
180–181, 198, 202, 207–208, 226, 229;
resource allocation 12, 36, 42, 45, 47, 70–72,
93, 109, 111, 113, 127, 133, 138, 196, 226,
230; resource similarity 189, 190; sharing ix,
1, 8, 10, 32, 47, 63–68, 76–78, 81, 93, 97–98,
107–115, 121, 132, 135, 140, 150, 158,
164–165, 191, 207–208, 210
resource-based view (RBV) 28, 29, 34–35, 39,
41, 61, 84, 90, 99, 121, 146, 151
responsiveness viii, x, 35–36, 103, 198–199,
203–207, 210, 229
restructuring ii, vii, ix, x, xiii, 8, 10–11, 14, 30, 63,
68, 72–73, 76–77, 109, 115, 123, 137, 165,
170–183, 210, 226, 229, 231–232
Reuters 208
Reynolds Tobacco 170
Rhoades, Stephen A. 20, 187, 264
Rieple, Alison 116, 118, 120, 121
Riggs, James 265
rigidities 41, 67, 134, 175, 226: core ix, 4–6,
10–11, 13–16, 31, 37–38, 40–41, 46–47, 54,
56–57, 61, 63–64, 67–68, 70, 73, 76–78, 80,
83, 86–87, 91, 95, 107, 114, 118, 120–123,
131, 151, 159, 161, 170, 173, 175–181, 183,
198, 210, 225–227, 230, 232
risk x, 10, 14, 17, 25, 26, 27, 29, 32–33, 35, 38,
48, 59–61, 64, 67, 72, 76, 93, 97, 99, 103, 105,
110, 116, 118, 120, 143–147, 150–151,
154–159, 161–163, 165, 167–168, 170, 174,
179, 181, 198–200, 204–205, 207–208, 210,
212–213, 215, 217, 219, 222, 229–230:
employment risk 25, 26, 61, 229; or reduce
risk 26, 60, 162, 217; risk level ix; risk of
opportunism 146, 150–151, 212, 222; spread
x, xi, 10, 14–15, 29, 35, 57, 60, 61, 69, 128,
129, 147, 199, 209
rivalry ix, 26, 39, 63, 74, 102, 125, 146, 164, 176,
185–191, 194, 196–197, 230
Rivkin, Jan W. 71, 103–104
Robbins, D. Keith 172
Roberts, John 97, 100, 106, 170, 225, 228
Robins, James A. 28, 84–85, 87–88, 90–92
Robinson, Joan T. 51
Robinson Jr., Richard B. 216
Rock, Edward B. 27
Röell, Ailsa 214
Rogers, Ronald C. 181

role of corporate office 8, 9, 16, 37–38, 67, 105,
107
Roll, Richard 159–160, 164, 166, 228
Röller, Lars H. 187
Roquebert Jaime A. 6
Rosa, Jose Antonio 186
Ross, David 20–21, 30, 36, 38, 49, 141, 146
Roth, Kendall 205, 209
Rothaermel, Frank T. 150
Royal Dutch Shell 127, 141
Ruback, Richard S. 164
Rudden, Eileen 200
Rugman, Allan M. 199, 264
Rumelt, Richard P. ix, x, 3–4, 6–7, 9, 12–13,
28–29, 31, 59, 64, 71, 81, 83–86, 88, 90,
95–96, 99, 106, 128, 136, 151, 226, 232
Rynes, Sara L. 222

Sadtler, David 97
St John, Caron H. 68, 81, 84, 85, 90, 94
Salancik, Gerald R. 29, 141, 146
Saloner, Gareth 20, 21, 226
Salter, Malcolm S. 39, 103, 136, 140
Samuelson, William F. 164, 166
Samsung 16, 142, 150, 152, 225
Sanders, Leonard 30, 174
Sanders, W. M. Gerard 215
Sandvig, J. Christopher 32
Sara Lee 181
Sarbanes-Oxley Act xi, 216, 231
Sarin, Atulya 25, 26, 71, 212, 213
Sarnat, Marshall 95, 257
Saudagaran, Shahrokh M. 199, 202
SBU (strategic business unit) ix, 45, 70, 138–140,
225, 232
scale xi, 10–13, 15, 26, 28–29, 34, 41, 47, 50, 64,
75–76, 82, 89–90, 99, 114, 120, 122, 138, 141,
144–145, 156, 159, 163–164, 175, 198–204,
206–208, 210, 220, 227, 229–230; economies
of see economies of scale
scarcity 27, 94, 128, 210
Schaefer, Scott 156, 157, 228
Schall, Lawrence D. 95
Scharfstein, David S. 20, 100
Schelling, Thomas C. 187
Schendel, Dan E. xii, 1, 29, 45, 81, 85, 87, 141,
172, 176
Scherer, Frederic M. 20, 21, 30, 36, 38, 49, 71,
96, 141, 146, 158, 164
Schijven, Mario 171
Schmalensee, Richard 6–7, 9, 59, 99
Schmid, Florian P. 96, 99
Schmidt, Frank L. 222
Schmidt, Jens 28
Schmidt, Klaus M. 41, 168
Schnaiberg, Allan 222
Schoar, Antoinette 99

Scholes, Myron 32
Schoorman, F. David 213, 216–218
Schroeder, Roger R 64
Schwalbach, Joachim 25, 213
Scott, James H. 73
Scott, W. Richard 198
Sears Roebuck 127
self-interest 22, 25, 27, 97, 109, 174–175, 212–213, 216, 222, 231
Servaes, Henri 38, 71, 97, 99, 103
Seth, Anju 41, 81, 168
Seward, James K. 27, 215
Shaked, Israel 96
Shanley, Mark 156, 157, 228
shareholder xiii, 15, 16, 17, 25, 26, 29, 30, 48, 49, 60, 61, 71, 100, 106, 109, 118, 134, 137, 174, 179, 202, 205, 212–218, 219–220, 222–223, 224, 227, 228, 229, 230, 231: activism 15, 228; value xii, 11, 14, 15, 25, 26, 30, 62, 67, 78, 97, 134, 160, 171, 174, 202, 204, 212–214, 219–220, 222–223, 229, 230
Sharma, Anurag 81, 85
Sharpe, William F. 14, 183
Shelanski, Howard A. 155
Shepherd, William G. 18, 20, 230
Sheppard, J. 172
Shimizu, Katsuhiko 64, 67, 106
Shleifer, Andrei 30, 38, 97, 104, 172, 174, 214, 229
Shocker, Allan D. 51
Shrivastava, Paul 213, 221
Shuen, Amy 186, 190, 226
SIC *see* Standard Industry Classification
Siegel, Donald 213, 220
signaling 65
Simerly, Roy L. 32, 104
Simmel, Georg 185
Simmonds, Paul G. 85
Simon, Daniel 190
Simon, Herbert A. 94, 100, 131, 224
Simonian, Haig 114
Singh, Deeksha A. 96, 99
Singh, Harbir 6, 29, 72, 93, 154, 155, 158, 159, 160, 161, 162, 164, 170, 171, 178, 180
Singh, Jagdip 74
Singh, Kulwant 15, 103, 154
Singh, Manohar 99
Sirh, Jin-Young 16
Sirower, Mark L. 62, 166
Siu, Juan A. 181
skill 1, 24, 25, 40, 42, 44, 47, 50, 51, 53–54, 61, 72, 75, 81, 83, 84, 86, 91, 93, 120, 135, 147, 165 168, 207, 210, 226: transfer of skills 8, 9, 10, 39, 63, 67–69, 76, 77, 102, 107, 108, 113, 114, 115, 121, 122, 164, 207, 210
Skype xi, 79–80
Sloan, Afred P., Jr. 12, 127

Smith, Clayton G. 32
Smith, Faye L. 195, 196
Smith, Ken G. 190
Snell, Scott A. 175
Snow, Charles C. 185, 193, 197
Sobel, Robert 20, 21
Sony 142, 152, 176, 194
Soskice, David 214
specialization: 4, 15, 86, 95, 130, 132, 147, 189, 210, 231: functional 1, 12, 28, 47, 50, 54, 84, 91, 112–114, 126–127, 132–133, 192, 208, 225, 228, 232; horizontal xiii, 29, 30, 96, 135, 140, 143, 151–152, 177, 184, 197–198, 206, 225; vertical ii, vii, ix, x, xi, xii, xiii, 2–4, 15, 17, 22, 27, 29, 58, 63, 74, 76–77, 86–87, 90, 96, 114, 127, 140–155, 177, 183–184, 197–198, 200, 206, 225, 230–233
specificity, asset 22, 24, 34, 155
Spencer, Jennifer W. 67
spin-off 108, 226–227, 231
Spulber, Daniel F. 22
Srinivasan, Narasimhan 7, 29, 30, 81, 85, 87, 177, 225, 230
Srivastava, Rajendra K. 51
stakeholder x, 16, 60–61, 108–109, 198, 212–214, 216–217, 219–223
Standard Industry Classification (SIC) 49–51, 84–91, 94, 225–227, 230–231,
Standard Oil 127, 146
Standardization 112, 122, 127, 134
Stapleton, R. C. 73
Stars, BCG matrix ix, xi, 116–121
start-up 162, 236
Stein, Jeremy C. 20
Stephan, John 187, 188, 192, 193
Stern, Philip 216
steward, stewardship 27, 213, 214, 216–219, 222–223
Stimpert, J. L. 44, 47, 51, 78, 81, 84, 85, 91, 94
St John, Caron H. 68, 81, 84–85, 90, 94
stock options 179
Stopford, John M. 127, 130, 198
strategic alliance vii, ix, xiii, 10, 11, 15, 28, 59, 60, 91, 109, 123, 130, 147, 148, 150, 151, 154–157, 159, 161, 162, 167–169, 178, 229, 231
strategic business unit *see* SBU
strategic intent 232
strengths, weaknesses, opportunities, threats *see* SWOT
structure–conduct–performance (S–C–P) paradigm 18
Stulz, René M. 20, 95, 97, 99, 100, 181
Subramani, Mani R. 146
Sudharshan, D. 29, 61, 67, 68, 201
sunk costs 34, 61, 147, 232
Suzuki, Y. 128

Index **283**

SWOT (strengths, weaknesses, opportunities, threats) 12
symbiosis 165
synergy 1, 4, 11, 14, 17, 32, 41, 44, 47, 48, 66, 78, 81, 84, 94, 115, 120, 159, 207, 232
systems xii, 7–11, 14, 16, 21, 35–36, 38, 39, 42, 43, 46, 47, 55, 57, 64, 66, 70, 72, 93, 101–103, 106, 107, 109, 110, 112, 120, 123, 133–135, 137, 140, 142, 148, 171, 174, 178, 179, 194, 200, 204, 206, 212–214, 222, 223, 226, 228, 232; *see* structure
Szeless, Georg 85, 89

tacit collusion 76, 177, 186, 187, 191, 232, 192, 197, 225, 232; *see* collusion
tacit knowledge 162, 229, 232
takeover xi, 15, 19, 20, 22, 27, 30, 43, 97, 160, 163, 166, 173, 174, 181, 215, 224, 226, 228
Tanriverdi, Hüseyin 28, 63, 85
Tata 46, 176
tax advantages 30, 63, 68, 73, 76
Taylor, Peter 71, 96
Teece, David J. 17, 27, 28, 29, 34, 37, 39, 60, 64, 85, 94, 99, 104, 107, 149, 186, 190, 199–201, 226
Telser, Lester G. 226
Teng, Bing-Sheng 168
Textron x, 13, 14
Thanheiser, Heinz 128,
Thomas, Howard xii, 29, 46, 51, 60, 186, 190, 194
Tihanyi, Laszlo 161, 198, 199, 201
Time Warner x, xi, 30, 43–44, 184, 196
Tinsley, Catherine F. 13, 15
Titman, Sheridan 181
Tiwana, Amrit 41
Toms, Steve 172
top management 1, 13, 26, 28, 42, 49, 71–73, 92, 98, 100, 122, 127, 134, 163, 166, 215
Touchstone 6
Toyota xi, 69, 208
trade-off 72, 151, 154, 155, 179
transactions, xiii, 12, 16, 17, 19, 22, 23, 24, 27–29, 34, 37, 38, 40, 60, 73: cost of 9, 22, 33, 37, 39, 62, 64, 65–68, 70, 72, 97, 101, 116, 148, 154, 156, 160, 166, 168, 207, 227–229
transaction-specific assets 61, 155, 158, 181, 228, 232
transfer of skills and resources *see* skill, resource
transnational strategy 199, 206, 209, 210
Trevino, Len J. 161
Triangle, Corporate Strategy ix, x, 7–10, 34–35, 77, 107, 172, 179, 205
Trigeorgis, Lenos 33, 41
Tsai, Wenspin 67, 81, 84, 85
Tucker, Irvin 143
Tufano, Peter 42

Turk, Thomas A. 26, 27, 174, 215, 226, 228–229

uncertainty 22, 24, 29, 32, 33, 34, 72, 145–147, 149, 152, 155, 156, 161–163, 183, 198, 229
Unilever 127, 207
United Nations (UN) 50
unrelated diversification; 3, 4, 29, 32, 35, 39, 71, 72, 76–78, 83, 84, 88, 89, 95–97, 107, 109, 110, 112, 114, 136–140, 174, 178, 179, 198, 199, 203, 210, 227 *see* diversified expansion
unitary structure (U-Form) 132, 230, 233
Upson, John W. 193
Usunier, Jean-Claude 212, 222
Utton, Michael A. 74

Van den Bossche, Anne-Marie 20
Van der Woude, Ad, 11
Van Oijen, Aswin 67, 107, 108
Van Witteloosstuijn, Arjen 172
Vancil, Richard F. 111, 134, 135, 137, 140
value chain 65, 67, 83, 84, 85, 140–148, 175, 200, 233
Varadarajan, P. Rajan 28, 87, 115, 186, 187, 188, 191, 225, 230
Varaiya, Nikhil P. 160, 164, 166
Veld, Chris 231
Venaik, Sunil 205
Venkatraman, N. 28, 29, 85, 146
Veliath, Rajaram 104
Veliyath, Rajaram 25, 212
Vereenigde Oost-Indische Compagnie (VOC); *see* Dutch East India Company
Vermeulen, Freek 161
Vernon, Raymond 201, 206
vertical integration ii, vii, ix, x, xi, xiii, 3, 4, 15, 17, 27, 29, 58, 63, 74, 76, 87, 96, 140–153, 177, 183, 184, 198, 200, 225, 230, 231
Villalonga, Belen xii, 97, 99
Viguerie, S. Patrick 32
Virgin xi, 64, 77, 83, 180
virtual corporation 15, 134, 143, 151
Vishny, Robert W. 25, 30, 38, 97, 104, 172, 174, 214, 229
vision xi, xiii, 8, 14, 16, 23, 58, 69, 79, 107

Walker, Gordon 29, 155
Walker, Orville C. Jr 47
Walker, Slater 14
Walsh, James P. 27, 164, 182, 215, 229
Walt Disney Company 5, 23, 196
Wan, William P. 28, 29, 103
Wanadoo 20, 21
Wang, Heli C. 61
Weber, David 155
Weber, Roberto A. 164
Weisbach, Michael S. 25, 172, 173, 229
Wells, Louis T. 127, 130

Index

Wernerfelt, Birger 6, 8, 9, 28, 29, 39, 40, 42, 59, 64, 68, 85, 87, 89, 99, 149, 154, 155, 184, 186, 194, 195, 196, 226
Westfall, Peter A. 6
Weston, J. Fred 181
Westphal, James D. 215
Whinston, Michael D. 185, 186, 189, 190, 192
Whittington, Richard 72, 103, 104
Wicks, Andrew C. 220
Wiersema, Margarethe F. 8, 27, 28, 84, 85, 87, 88, 90, 91, 92
Wilder, Ronald P. 143
Wilkinson, Adrian J. 172
Williams, Jeffrey R. 30, 174
Williamson, Oliver E. 20, 21, 22, 24, 28, 29, 37, 38, 39, 47, 49, 60, 70, 71, 76, 96, 100, 101, 102, 116, 122, 128, 131, 134, 137, 138, 141, 143, 144, 145, 146, 149, 150, 153, 154–156, 158, 167, 213, 215, 225, 228, 229, 230–232
Williamson, Peter J. 28, 40, 84, 85, 91, 92, 94, 95, 121, 125, 135, 140, 231
Willig, Robert D. 28, 37, 64, 200, 227
Wilson, Rick L. 195, 196
Winter, Sidney G. 29, 64, 85, 91
Wiseman, Robert M. 215

Wood, Adrian 85, 87, 225, 230
Wood, Donna J. 213, 220, 221
World Trade Organization (WTO) 22, 203
Wright, Peter 25, 212, 213
Wrigley, Leonard 13, 83, 85, 86, 128

Yan, An 99
Ye, Guangliang 60, 63
Yermack, David L. 25, 26, 27, 174, 212
Yeung, Bernard 199, 201
Yip, George S. 154, 159, 160
Yiu, Daphne 28, 29, 72
Yost, Keven 99, 198
Young, Greg 9, 12, 190
Yulia, Yulia V. 231

Zalewski, David A., 30
Zeithaml, Carl P. 29, 85, 90
Zeithaml, Valarie A. 29
Zelleke, Andargachew S. 27
Zenger, Todd, 155
Zhang, Hao, 67
Zhao, Hongxin 155, 161
Zhou, Z., 154, 159
Zingales, Luigi, 71, 99